PHILO'S *FLACCUS*

Philo of Alexandria
Commentary Series

General Editor
Gregory E. Sterling
Associate Editor
David T. Runia

Editorial Board
Harold W. Attridge
Ellen Birnbaum
John Dillon
David Hay
Annewies van den Hoek
Alan Mendelson
Thomas Tobin, S.J.
David Winston

Number 2

PHILO'S *FLACCUS*
THE FIRST POGROM

Pieter Willem van der Horst

PHILO'S *FLACCUS*
THE FIRST POGROM

Translation and
Commentary by
Pieter Willem van der Horst

SBL
Society of Biblical Literature
Atlanta

PHILO'S *FLACCUS*

Copyright © 2003 by Koninklijke Brill NV, Leiden,
The Netherlands

This edition published under license from Koninklijke Brill NV,
Leiden, The Netherlands by the Society of Biblical Literature.

All rights reserved. No part of this work may be reproduced or
transmitted in any form or by any means, electronic or mechanical,
including photocopying and recording, or by any means of any
information storage or retrieval system, except as may be expressly
permitted by the 1976 Copyright Act or in writing from the Publisher. Requests for permission should be addressed in writing to the
Rights and Permissions Department, Koninklijke Brill NV, Leiden,
The Netherlands.

Library of Congress Cataloging-in-Publication Data

Horst, Pieter Willem van der.
  Philo's Flaccus : the first pogrom / translation and commentary
by Pieter W. van der Horst.
    p. cm. — (Philo of Alexandria commentary series, ISSN 1570-095X; v. 2)
  Includes bibliographical references and index.
  ISBN-13: 978-1-58983-188-9 (paper binding : alk. paper)
  ISBN-10: 1-58983-188-8 (paper binding : alk. paper)
  1. Avillius Flaccus, Governor of Egypt, d. 38 or 39. 2. Jews—
Persecutions—Egypt—Alexandria. 3. Alexandria—Egypt—
History. 4. Philo, of Alexandria. In Flaccum. I. Philo, of Alexandria. In Flaccum. English. II. Title. III. Series: Philo of Alexandria commentary series (Society of Biblical Literature) ; v. 2.
  DS135.E42A4337 2005
  932'.022092—dc22
                                                         2005024455

Printed in the United States of America
on acid-free paper

For those I love

CONTENTS

Preface	ix
Abbreviations	xi
Introduction	1
1. The place of the treatise in the Philonic corpus	1
2. The contents and structure of the treatise (with an excursus on the sequel)	6
3. The genre of the treatise	11
4. Main themes of the treatise	16
5. The historical background (with an excursus on Flaccus)	18
6. Previous scholarship	38
7. The text of the treatise	49
8. The present commentary (with a note on *Nachleben*)	51
Translation	54
Commentary	88
I. Flaccus' persecution of the Jews (§§1-96)	89
§§ 1-7: Flaccus' promising start	89
§§ 8-20: Flaccus' degeneration	99
§§ 21-24: Flaccus begins to injure the Jews	112
§§ 25-35: King Agrippa	114
§§ 36-40: Karabas	128
§§ 41-44: The overtures to the pogrom	132
§§ 45-52: The Jewish point of view	138
§§ 53-96: The pogrom at its height	152
II. Punishment and death of Flaccus (§§97-191)	187
§§ 97-103: The declaration of loyalty	187
§§ 104-118: Flaccus' arrest	191
§§ 119-124: Gratitude for Flaccus' arrest	199
§§ 125-145: Lampo and Isidorus	207
§§ 146-161: Flaccus on trial	219
§§ 162-180a: Flaccus at Andros	230
§§ 180b-190: Caligula has Flaccus killed	240
§ 191: Epilogue	244

Bibliography 246

Indices 262
   1. Index of passages from ancient authors 262
         Philonic texts... 262
         Biblical passages 266
         Jewish documents 268
         Christian documents... 269
         Pagan documents.. 270

   2. Index of subjects and names (including Greek terms) 274

PREFACE

Writing a commentary to Philo's *In Flaccum* is a daunting task that I could not have brought to completion without the help of many others. In a more or less random order I would like to mention the people who, one way or another, have helped me over the past two years.

Firstly, I want to thank the editors of the series *Philo of Alexandria Commentary Series*, Gregory Sterling and David Runia, for inviting me to write the present volume. In particular, my friend David Runia has always freely placed at my disposal his vast erudition in matters Philonic. I owe him and Greg Sterling many thanks for the numerous useful suggestions they gave me, saving me from making many an error. I am also grateful to Gé de Vries, the author of the most recent Dutch translation of *In Flaccum*, for reading the whole manuscript and sharing his valuable insights with me. The same applies to Jan Bremmer, always a rich source of bibliographical and other knowledge. As usual, Klaas Worp was of great assistance in papyrological matters as was Johan Strubbe in solving epigraphical problems. Fik Meijer advised me on nautical issues, as did J.E. Spruit in matters of Roman law. I am also very grateful to Erich Gruen, Walter Ameling, Anders Runesson, and Gideon Bohak for sending me copies of their books or articles, both published and not yet published, from which I profited greatly. Allen Kerkeslager did me the great service of reading the entire manuscript and pointing out several mistakes. I owe thanks to Mark Geller for inviting me to give a lecture on the topic of this book at University College in London and to Tom Tobin for inviting me to present some of my findings at a meeting of the SBL Philo Seminar in Toronto (2002). The critical comments offered at that meeting by John Barclay, Ellen Birnbaum, and Sarah Pearce were most helpful. Thanks are also due to the Faculty of Theology at Utrecht University for allowing me to spend a sabbatical year at the Netherlands Institute for Advanced Study in the Humanities and Social Sciences (NIAS) in the year 2001-2002, and to the Netherlands Organization for Research (NWO) for the grant which made the stay at NIAS possible. I owe many thanks to the superb staff at NIAS, of which I single out Petry Tyson and Anne Simpson, who corrected the English of this book, and the library staff who provided me with, literally, every publication I needed.

The manuscript of this book was completed in the summer of 2002.

ABBREVIATIONS

ABD	*Anchor Bible Dictionary*, ed. D.N. Freedman, 6 vols., New York: Doubleday, 1992
AIPHOS	*Annuaire de l'Institut de Philologie et d'Histoire Orientales et Slaves*
ANRW	*Aufstieg und Niedergang der Römischen Welt*
ARW	*Archiv für Religionswissenschaft*
BDAG	W. Bauer, *Greek-English Lexicon of the New Testament and Other Early Christian Literature*, rev. ed. by F.W. Danker (based on previous editions by W.F. Arndt & F.W. Gingrich), Chicago-London: Chicago University Press, 2000
CHJ	*Cambridge History of Judaism*
CIG	*Corpus Inscriptionum Graecarum*, ed. A. Boeckh et al., Berlin, 1828-1877
CIJ	*Corpus Inscriptionum Judaicarum*, 2 vols., ed. J.-B. Frey, Rome: Pontificio Istituto di Archeologia Cristiana, 1936-1952
CJZC	G. Lüderitz, *Corpus jüdischer Zeugnisse aus der Cyrenaika*, Wiesbaden: Reichert, 1983
CPJ	*Corpus Papyrorum Judaicarum*, 3 vols., edd. V.A. Tcherikover & A. Fuks, Cambridge MA: Harvard University Press, 1957-1964
DBS	*Supplément au Dictionnaire de la Bible*
DDD	K. van der Toorn, B. Becking & P.W. van der Horst (eds.), *Dictionary of Deities and Demons in the Bible*, 2nd ed., Leiden-Grand Rapids: Brill-Eerdmans, 1999
DNTB	C.A. Evans & S.E. Porter (eds.), *Dictionary of New Testament Background*, Downers Grove: Intervarsity Press, 2000
ER	*The Encyclopedia of Religion*, ed. M. Eliade, 16 vols., New York: Macmillan – London: Collier Macmillan, 1987
IGRR	*Inscriptiones Graecae ad Res Romanas Pertinentes*, 3 vols, edd. R. Cagnat et al., Paris: Gabalda, 1906-1927
GLAJJ	*Greek and Latin Authors on Jews and Judaism*, ed. M. Stern, 3 vols., Jerusalem: The Israel Academy of Sciences and Humanities, 1974-1984
JBL	*Journal of Biblical Literature*
JIGRE	W. Horbury & D. Noy, *Jewish Inscriptions of Graeco-Roman Egypt*, Cambridge: Cambridge University Press, 1992
JIWE	D. Noy, *Jewish Inscriptions of Western Europe*, 2 vols., Cambridge: Cambridge University Press, 1993-1995
JJS	*Journal of Jewish Studies*
JRS	*Journal of Roman Studies*
JSJ	*Journal for the Study of Judaism*
JTS	*Journal of Theological Studies*
LCL	Loeb Classical Library
LSJ	H.G. Liddell, R. Scott & H.S. Jones, *Greek-English Lexicon*, Oxford: Clarendon Press, 1940

NP	*Der Neue Pauly*, Enzyklopädie der Antike hrsg. von H. Cancik & H. Schneider, Stuttgart – Weimar: J.B. Metzler, 1996 – ...
NT	*Novum Testamentum*
NTS	*New Testament Studies*
OCD	S. Hornblower & A. Spawforth (eds.), *The Oxford Classical Dictionary*, 3rd ed., Oxford-New York: Oxford University Press, 1996
OGIS	*Orientis Graeci Inscriptiones Selectae*, ed. W. Dittenberger, 2 vols., Leipzig: Hirzel, 1903-1905
OLD	P.G.W. Glare (ed.), *Oxford Latin Dictionary*, Oxford: Clarendon Press, 1982
PW (RE)	*Pauly-Wissowas Realencyclopädie der classischen Altertumswissenschaft*
R-R	R. Radice & D.T. Runia, *Philo of Alexandria. An Annotated Bibliography 1937-1986*, Leiden: Brill, 1988
RAC	*Reallexikon für Antike und Christentum*
RE	see PW
RBLG	P. Boned Colera *e.a.* (eds.), *Repertorio bibliográfico de la lexicografía griega*, Madrid: Consejo Superior de Investigaciones Científicas, 1998
RGG	*Die Religion in Geschichte und Gegenwart*, 4. Aufl., eds. H.D. Betz et alii, Tübingen: Mohr Siebeck, 1999-...
SB	*Sammelbuch griechischer Urkunden aus Ägypten*, ed. F. Preisigke, F. Bilabel, E. Kiessling & H.A. Rupprecht, Berlin: W. de Gruyter – Wiesbaden: Harassowitz, 22 vols., 1913 – 2001
SBLSP	*Society of Biblical Literature Seminar Papers*
SCI	*Scripta Classica Israelica*
SPhA	*Studia Philonica Annual*
SVF	*Stoicorum veterum fragmenta*
TAPA	*Transactions of the American Philological Association*
ZPE	*Zeitschrift für Papyrologie und Epigraphik*

INTRODUCTION[1]

1. *The place of the treatise in the Philonic corpus*

Together with the *Legatio ad Gaium*, the work called *In Flaccum* has an exceptional place in the corpus of Philonic writings. Most of Philo's œuvre is of a philosophical and exegetical nature (for Philo philosophy and exegesis coincide) but this cannot be said of the two treatises that are commonly dubbed his 'historical' treatises. The word 'historical' is often put between quotation marks, and rightly so. Philo does intend to write history but he does so not for reasons of historical interest. His real concern in the two historical treatises is not primarily of a historiographical, but rather of a theological, or pastoral, nature. There is no better way of illustrating this than quoting the final line of *In Flaccum* where he says about the main protagonist of his story, Flaccus: "Thus he became an indubitable proof that the Jewish people had not been deprived of the help of God" (§191). He takes up the same theme again in the sequel to *Flacc.*, in the opening paragraphs of *Legat.*, where he says: "Some people have come to disbelieve that God exercises providence for humanity, and particularly for the nation of suppliants (i.e. Israel)" (§3). In other words, what Philo is attempting to do in his treatise *In Flaccum* (and also in the *Legatio*), is to convince those of his co-religionists who have begun to doubt that God can and will intervene on their behalf, that he did intervene and that therefore there is no reason for doubt or disbelief. His pastoral concern is apparent also from the fact that the whole of *In Flaccum* has been structured as a kind of diptych: the first half about the sufferings of the Jews is mirrored exactly in the second half,[2] not only because both halves are of equal length (§§1-96 ~ §§97-191), but also because, as Philo

---

[1] *Terminological note.* In the present work the term 'pogrom' is used not in the original sense it had in Russian, namely 'destruction' in general, but in the more specialized sense the word had acquired by the time it was taken up in other European languages, namely "organized and officially tolerated massacre and looting of Jews." The terms 'anti-Semitism' and 'anti-Semitic' are avoided not only because of their anachronistic nature but also since they are inadequate and misleading. They have been substituted by 'Jew-hatred' and 'anti-Jewish.'
[2] Alston 1997:166.

has Flaccus himself confess, "all the mad acts that I have committed against the Jews I have now suffered myself" (§170; in this very same paragraph Flaccus says that it is true what the Jews say about God's providence for his people!). So, Philo's work is first and foremost a plea for belief in divine justice, a theodicy, and as such also, as a German translator of the work has rightly called it, a *Trostschrift*, a piece of consolation literature.[3] It is, however, more than that because Philo here had a twofold audience in mind, but we defer treatment of that aspect to the end of section 3.

This brings us to the question of its genre, but before that will be dealt with (in section 3), we first have to raise the question of *why* Philo wrote these exceptional treatises, which deviate so much from the usual pattern in his exegetical writings, in which the biblical text of the Pentateuch is always his point of departure. The reason for this deviation must be sought in the historical circumstances of the Jewish community in Alexandria in the years 38-41 CE. In 38 tensions between Jews and Greeks in the city had mounted to the highest pitch. Never before had the relationships between Jews and Greeks deteriorated to such a degree of overt hostility, and, consequently, violence broke out. Afterwards both parties sent embassies to Rome in order to plead their cause before the emperor. The Greeks chose their most powerful and prestigious personalities (persons such as the gymnasiarch Isidorus and the scholar Apion) to lead their embassy (of five persons). The Jews did the same by asking Philo to be the head of their deputation (five persons as well). There can be little doubt that Philo is referring to these events when he writes the following in the opening passage of *Spec.* 3.1-6, a typically Philonic passage that deserves to be quoted in full:

> There was a time when I had leisure for philosophy and for the contemplation of the universe and its contents, when I made its spirit my own in all its beauty and loveliness and true blessedness, when my constant companions were divine themes and verities, wherein I rejoiced with a joy that never cloyed or sated. I had no base or abject thoughts nor grovelled in search of reputation or of wealth or bodily comforts, but seemed always to be borne aloft into the heights with a soul possessed by some God-sent inspiration, a fellow traveller with the sun and moon and the whole heaven and universe. (2) Ah then I gazed down from the upper air, and straining the mind's eye beheld, as from some commanding peak, the multitudinous worldwide spectacles of earthly things, and blessed my lot in that I had escaped by

---

[3] Gerschmann 1964:124.

main force from the plagues of mortal life. (3) But, as it proved, my steps were dogged by the deadliest of mischiefs, the hater of the good, envy, which suddenly set upon me and did not cease to pull me down with violence till it had plunged me in the ocean of civil cares, in which I am swept away, unable even to raise my head above the water. (4) Yet amid the groans I hold my own, for planted in my soul from my earliest days I keep the yearning for culture which ever has pity and compassion for me, lifts me up and relieves my pain. To this I owe it that sometimes I raise my head and with the soul's eyes — dimly indeed because the mist of extraneous affairs has clouded their clear vision — I yet make shift to look around me in my desire to inhale a breath of life pure and unmixed with evil. (5) And if unexpectedly I obtain a spell of fine weather and a calm from civic turmoils, I take wings and ride the waves and almost tread the lower air, wafted by the breezes of knowledge which often urges me to come to spend my days with her, a truant as it were from merciless masters in the shape not only of men but of affairs, which pour in upon me like a torrent from different sides. (6) Yet it is well for me to give thanks to God even for this, that though submerged I am not sucked down into the depths, but can also open the soul's eyes, which in my despair of comforting hope I thought had now lost their sight, and am irradiated by the light of wisdom, and am not given over to lifelong darkness. So behold me daring, not only to read the sacred messages of Moses, but also in my love of knowledge to peer into each of them and unfold and reveal what is not known to the multitude (transl. Colson, LCL).

Even though Philo does not make explicitly clear what he is referring to when speaking about his being drawn down from his lofty meditations and speculations into the hard reality of politics, and even though the idealization of leisure that permits philosophical life is sometimes a literary topos,[4] there still can be little doubt that it is the dramatic events of the years 38-41 CE that he has in mind here.[5] He mentions 'envy' (φθόνος) as the main cause of the disturbances to which he had, willy-nilly, to expose himself (§3), and it is the same motif that he mentions in *Flacc.* 29 and 30 as the driving force behind the riots that broke out in 38: The Greeks were bursting from envy when the Jewish king Agrippa arrived in Alexandria because they were vexed by the idea that a Jew had become a king, and that to such a degree as if each of them had been deprived of an ancestral kingdom. Flaccus was provoked by his companions into the same state of envy as their own (cf. also *Legat.* 48 where this motif recurs).

---

[4] Allen Kerkeslager drew my attention to Pliny, *Ep.* 1.9; 2.8; 2.17; 5.6 etc.
[5] I realize that there is a possibility that Philo refers here to events other than the riots in 38 CE, but I am not convinced by these alternative suggestions (see next note).

It was this envy, says Philo, that finally led to the eruption of violence in the summer of 38 CE. Even though, then, we cannot reach absolute certainty about which events he refers to in *Spec.* 3.1-6, he is most likely hinting at the riots of 38.[6]

That is to say that Philo had to embark upon political affairs, but much against his will, as this passage makes abundantly clear.[7] No other conclusion can be drawn than that such a strong appeal was made to Philo to throw his weight into the scales on behalf of the Jewish community that he could not decline (was it because his brother Alexander, who held a leading position in the administration of the city, had in the meantime been imprisoned [Josephus, *Ant.* 19.276]?). This must have been extremely hard for our philosopher, who so much loved to be left alone in his study. Even so, he says that, in spite of the fact that it was very difficult for him to keep his head above the water, he had to thank God for the fact that he did not drown. Writing the historical treatises under consideration was part of an enterprise that was very unusual to Philo, and for that reason the treatises are unusual within the Philonic corpus as a whole.

We cannot be sure about the exact date of composition and publication of *In Flaccum*. Of course, the *terminus post quem* is 38 CE, but exactly how long after the pogrom Philo penned down his report of the events of that year is unknown. It stands to reason, however, that the work stood in the service of his task as leader of the Jewish embassy to Gaius in 39-40 CE. That is to say, Philo almost certainly collected data and evidence he could use in his plea for the Jewish cause before the emperor, and he undoubtedly made notes which were later used in the composition of his book. But how much later he composed *In Flaccum*, we do not know, although it is reasonable to assume that it was not long after his lengthy visit to Italy where he got into contact with Gaius. The fact that in *Flacc.* 180 Philo speaks about this emperor with such undisguised hostility may suggest that he published the work only after Caligula's death in January 41, but we cannot be sure whether Philo may not have been courageous enough to use such strong language even when the emperor was still alive. Be that as it may, 40 or 41 was most probably the period in which Philo published *In Flaccum*.

---

[6] For a different view see Goodenough 1926.
[7] Williamson 1989:7-18.

INTRODUCTION 5

This brings us to the final point of this chapter. In his *Historia Ecclesiastica*, published about 325 CE, the church historian Eusebius writes the following: "Philo has reported in five books what happened to the Jews during the reign of Gaius: the insanity of the emperor, how he proclaimed himself a god and committed innumerable insolent deeds, the misery of the Jews in his time, his own mission to Rome on behalf of his compatriots in Alexandria, and how he received nothing but laughter and ridicule from Gaius in defending their ancestral laws and narrowly escaped with his life" (*Hist. Eccl.* 2.5.1). Which are the five books Eusebius has in mind? There has been much speculation about this passage, but no consensus has been reached.[8] It is not necessary to repeat the wide variety of interpretations of what Eusebius was referring to in his mention of the five books. Let me rather state succinctly what I think is the most reasonable explanation.

Both the opening and the closing paragraphs of *In Flaccum* make it clear that Philo wrote a separate book on Sejanus' persecution of the Jews as well (see the commentary *ad* §§1 and 191), a work that preceded *In Flaccum*. Most scholars agree that this work must have been one of the five mentioned by Eusebius, even though the latter refers only to events during Caligula's reign (Sejanus died before Caligula's rise to power), since only a few lines later Eusebius corrects himself and speaks about Philo's description of the fate of the Jews under Tiberius and Sejanus (2.5.7). Since the *Legatio* closes with the words, "Thus I have set forth quite briefly the reason for Gaius' hatred for the whole Jewish nation, but I must now proceed to the *palinode*" (373),[9] it is also evident that a further book will have followed. So we have already four books. Since Eusebius says in his *Chronicle* that the work on Sejanus was the second in the row of five,[10] the lacking fifth one must be the number one in the series. In *Hist. Eccl.* 2.5.7, Eusebius says that Philo wrote not only about Sejanus' attempts to eradicate the whole Jewish nation, but also about how "in Judaea, Pilate (...) made an attempt on the temple in Jerusalem, contrary to the privileges accorded the Jews, and harrassed them severely." Now this

---

[8] For a survey see Box 1939:xxxiii-xxxvii; Smallwood 1961:36-43; Pelletier 1967:14-16; Morris in Schürer 1973-1987: III.859-864.
[9] Smallwood 1961:325 interprets the 'palinode' here as a story of the fall of Gaius, "represented as divine retribution for his attack on the Jews, and the change for the better which Jewish fortunes underwent after Claudius' succession." In view of Philo's procedure in *Flacc.*, Smallwood is certainly right.
[10] See the text(s) quoted in full by Morris 1987:860 note 198.

can hardly refer to the occasional remarks about Pilate in the extant books.[11] So we have to postulate a separate work on Pilate. Then most probably the five works referred to by Eusebius, of which three have been lost, were: (1) the work on Pilate; (2) the work on Sejanus; (3) *In Flaccum*; (4) *Legatio ad Gaium*; (5) the *palinodia*. Another possibility (proposed by Morris 1987:861) is: (1) general introduction to the theme of persecution and providence; (2) a work on persecutions in the time of Tiberius by Sejanus and Pilate; (3) *In Flaccum*; (4) *Legatio*; (5) the palinode about the downfall of Gaius. No certainty can be reached in this matter, however, and the above sketched solutions are no more than guesses, but very reasonable ones.[12]

2. *The contents and structure of the treatise (with an excursus on the sequel)*

As has already been remarked, the work is divided like a diptych into two parts of equal length which mirror each other: §§1-96 deal with Flaccus' persecution of the Jews; §§ 97-191 treat the divine punishment and death of Flaccus. We will now summarize the contents according to the following structure:

I. Flaccus' persecution of the Jews (§§1-96)
   §§ 1-7: Flaccus' promising start
   §§ 8-20: Flaccus' degeneration
   §§ 21-24: Flaccus begins to injure the Jews
   §§ 25-35: King Agrippa
   §§ 36-40: Karabas
   §§ 41-44: The overtures to the pogrom
   §§ 45-52: The Jewish point of view
   §§ 53-96: The pogrom at its height
II. Punishment and death of Flaccus (§§97-191)
   §§ 97-103: The declaration of loyalty
   §§ 104-118: Flaccus' arrest
   §§ 119-124: Gratitude for Flaccus' arrest
   §§ 125-145: Lampo and Isidorus
   §§ 146-161: Flaccus on trial
   §§ 162-180a: Flaccus at Andros
   §§ 180b-190: Caligula has Flaccus killed
   §§ 191: Epilogue

---

[11] So rightly Morris 1987:860.
[12] The problem of the title of *In Flaccum* will be discussed at the beginning of the commentary.

INTRODUCTION 7

(1-7) Flaccus was appointed Roman governor of Egypt and Alexandria by the emperor Tiberius. In the first five years he demonstrated his great and exemplary ability in handling his responsibilities.

(8-20) That began to change, however, when Tiberius was succeeded on the throne by Caligula in 37. This event marked the onset of Flaccus' degeneration. He first became depressed and anxious because he had supported the rival candidate for this succession and he had also played an active role in the prosecution of Caligula's mother, Agrippina.

(21-24) At this juncture the leaders of the anti-Jewish party (or parties) in Alexandria advised him to win back the emperor's favor by giving them his support in their planned actions against the Jews in the city. Bit by bit Flaccus began to hurt the Jews, first by demonstrating partiality as a judge in lawsuits, later by other, more drastic measures.

(25-35) The climax came when Herod Agrippa, the grandson of Herod the Great, visited Alexandria on his way from Rome to his new kingdom in Palestine that he had just received from his friend Caligula. He was enthusiastically welcomed by the Jews.

(36-40) The enemies, however, reacted furiously and staged a mock ceremony, bringing a local lunatic into the gymnasium, greeting him with royal honors and hailing him 'our Lord.' Instead of punishing the instigators of this insult to a friend of the emperor, Flaccus turned a blind eye.

(41-44) This encouraged the enemies to go on and erect statues of the emperor in Jewish synagogues: an act of utter desecration.

(45-53) Now there existed a real danger that the riots would spread to other parts of the Empire, since Jews live everywhere. Even though Jerusalem always remains their mother-city, the countries where they live are their fatherland.

(54-96) The desecration of synagogues was followed by the issuing of a decree by Flaccus to the effect that Jews were from now on to be regarded as foreigners and aliens in the city. This opened the floodgates to massive plundering of Jewish houses and shops and rounding up the Jews in one quarter of the city, where already a great number of Jews lived, so that an overcrowded ghetto was created where the Jews had to live under terrible circumstances. Synagogues and houses were sacked and set on fire. Then followed a long series of events of unchecked savagery by the Alexandrians, when they caught Jews who strayed outside the ghetto in search for help. Jews were set upon by mobs, who patrolled the edge of the ghetto in search of their victims. They beat them up, or burned them to death, or bound them together and dragged them through the market square, kicking them and trampling on them until their bodies were mutilated beyond recognition. At the end of August, on Caligula's birthday, a large group of Jews was arrested, marched through the streets to the theatre where they were beaten and forced to eat pork. If they refused, they were finished off by way of birthday celebration for the emperor. Many also died of diseases that broke out because of the atrocious conditions in the ghetto.

(97-103) But the tide began to turn. On Gaius' accession to the throne the Jewish community of Alexandria had delivered to Flaccus a declaration of loyalty to the new emperor with the request to pass it on to Gaius, which he said he would do but did not. Fortunately, when Agrippa heard of the matter, he intervened to rectify it.

(104-118) Some weeks later a detachment of troops suddenly arrived from Rome, sent by Caligula, to arrest Flaccus. He was arrested during the feast of Sukkoth.

(119-124) In prayers and hymns the Jews offered thanks to God for his sudden intervention.

(125-145) The men who were mentioned earlier as leaders of the anti-Jewish faction, which had urged him to secure his position by persecuting the Jews, now appeared as his accusers, namely the archcriminals Isidorus and Lampo.

(146-161) Flaccus stood trial and was condemned; his property was confiscated and he himself sentenced for deportation to the miserable island of Andros in the Aegean Sea. His journey to Andros was a great humiliation because the people who had seen him on his way to assume the office of governor of Egypt now saw him back as a deportee.

(162-180a) His plight after his arrival at Andros is great. He holds dramatic soliloquies and even says prayers in which he acknowledges that his punishment by the God of Israel is just.

(180b-190) In Rome, Caligula comes to the conclusion that the fate of his many deportees is too mild a punishment and he orders them to be executed; Flaccus is at the top of the list. Soldiers land on Andros and chase Flaccus who immediately realizes what is going to happen to him. He fights back with the only result that "his body received the same number of wounds as that of the Jews who had been unlawfully murdered by him." Then he is murdered.

(191) Thus "he became an indubitable proof that the Jewish people had not been deprived of the help of God."

Excursus: The sequel

Philo describes the sequel to the events of the summer/autumn of 38 CE in his *Legatio ad Gaium*. What I shall present here, however, is not just a summary of this treatise but a tentative historical reconstruction based on both *Legat.* and the famous Epistle of Claudius to the Alexandrians and some other circumstantial evidence, mainly from Josephus. Since a detailed treatment of this matter is the subject of the commentary on *Legat.*, this excursus will be kept very brief (and without references to sources); it serves only to wet the appetite of those readers who would like to know how things in Alexandria developed after Flaccus' death.

Probably rather soon after Flaccus' arrest a certain degree of order was restored in Alexandria by the new governor, Vitrasius Pollio. In the spring of 39 CE, an embassy of (probably) five Jews, headed by Philo, and another of five Greeks, headed by Apion or Isidorus, left for Rome in order to get a decision about the matters at stake from the emperor Gaius. He had them wait for months on end, however, before granting them an audience. The primary claim of the Jews was the restoration of their freedom to live according to their own laws. Whether the issue of their citizenship was also raised is a moot point, although it cannot be excluded. The Greeks tried to prejudice Gaius by reminding him that it was only the Jews who refused to sacrifice to him. When the Jews reacted by saying that they had offered hecatombs on his behalf, the emperor acutely remarked that offering sacrifices *for* him was not the same as sacrificing *to* him. Then he got a report that Jews in Palestine had pulled down an altar dedicated to him as a god. In a furious reaction he sent orders to the governor of Syria to set up his statue in the temple of Jerusalem. The dismay of the Jews in Palestine was so great that Agrippa I tried to intervene, succesfully — it would seem — for the emperor withdrew his order. When later Gaius reinstated the order, the governor protracted the matter by masterful inactivity. Gaius came to learn of this and ordered his suicide, but before the letter with the order to commit suicide reached the governor, Gaius himself had been murdered (in January 41 CE). Upon hearing this news, the Jews of Alexandria took up their arms and attacked their former opponents. The new prefect informed the new emperor, Claudius, who quickly sent an edict to the Alexandrians in which he confirmed the Jews in all the rights they had enjoyed before Gaius' principate and warned both sides against a repetition of the riots. In another edict he conceded to all the Jews in the empire the same rights as those enjoyed by the Alexandrian Jews, but he also warns the Jews not to set at naught the religious beliefs of the non-Jewish peoples. Again rival embassies hastened to Rome — the Jews even sent two (or another apart from Philo's, a problem I have to leave aside here)[13] — each of them blaming their opponents for the renewed troubles. Claudius then sent his famous letter of November 41 (which was spectacularly rediscovered on a papyrus in the early twenties of the last century: *P. Lond.* 1912 = *CPJ* 153). It is a considered an acid reply in which he distances himself from the policy of Gaius and urges the Alexandrian Greeks "to behave gently and kindly towards the Jews who have inhabited the same city for many years, and not to dishonor any of their customs in their worship of their god, as they did in the time of the god Augustus and as I too, having heard both sides, have confirmed." But in the same breath the emperor also sternly warns the Jews "not to aim at more than they have previously had (...) and not to intrude themselves into the games presided over by the gymnasiarchs and the cosmetes [*i.e.*, to strive for citizenship], since they enjoy what is their own and in a city *which is not their own* they possess an abundance of all good things."

If we are to believe the largely novellistic *Acts of the Alexandrian Martyrs* (= *CPJ* 154-156), shortly afterwards the same emperor had Isidorus and Lampo, who were the driving forces behind the pogrom according to Philo because they inspired Flaccus to his anti-Jewish actions, brought to court. They insulted him with extremely rude anti-Jewish remarks, also aimed at his friend Herod Agrippa, and Claudius condemned them to death.

Literature: Tcherikover-Fuks 1957/64: I.69-74; Smallwood 1976:242-255; Schürer 1973/87: I.391-398; Mélèze-Modrzejewski 1995:173-183; Schäfer 1997:145-156; Smallwood 1999:183-187.

---

[13] See Gruen 2002:290 note 186 for discussion and literature.

3. The genre of the treatise

As was already said in the first chapter of the Introduction, Philo's *In Flaccum* is not just a piece of historiography, it is more than that. Philo's book is, however, not exceptional in so far as there is no historical document from antiquity that strives for completely detached or disinterested objectivity. It was part and parcel of the art of the historian in ancient times to convey a message, either moral or philosophical or religious or anti-religious, and the 'events' narrated were used for this purpose. In this connection, one speaks of 'rhetorical' historiography or of 'dramatic' or 'tragic' or 'empathic' historiography, but there is no generally accepted designation for the genre. The difference with non-rhetorical or non-dramatic historiography is that, for instance, instead of "Two million Armenians died during World War I," one writes, "Millions of completely innocent Armenian men, women and children, became the victims of a brutal massacre by the ruthless and criminal Turkish regime!" The information in the second formulation is not false, but its phraseology is full of pathos and is intended to evoke emotions. And it is this intention that often has exaggeration follow in its wake. That is not to say that ancient historical texts should be thrown out into the bin as having little value for the historian. After all, they were written by the same historians who were developing criteria for writing reliable historiographical works: trustworthy sources, eyewitness accounts, personal observation etc. But at the same time it is clear that their use of rhetorical and dramatic techniques must make us pause and see with how many grains of salt or even downright skepticism we should take their statements. And this is what makes so much of ancient historical writing such a striking mixture of fact and fiction, of legend and history.

It is clear that Philo could not have had any knowledge at all of the thoughts of Flaccus when he was in exile. So when he writes about Flaccus's inner monologues, his utterances of despair, yes even quotes the prayers he said, all of that is pure invention by our author. It seems Philo has been inspired by Greek novels here. There, too, one finds jeremiadic monologues by the protagonists, in which they lament their fate, their loneliness, their horrible plight, their despair, their fear of death.[14] This means that a great part of what Philo relates in the second half of *In Flaccum* is simply unhistorical; only the

---

[14] Gerschmann 1964:126.

bare framework, that is, Flaccus' arrest, condemnation, exile and death at Andros are historical facts.

But what about the first half, which deals with the events in Alexandria in the summer of 38 CE? Here he writes about things that every one of his readers in the city could easily check. Many of them had been eyewitnesses and, moreover, when he published the work, the events were still fresh in their memory (Philo published his work not later than 41 CE). Philo would have made a fool of himself if he had distorted the facts too drastically. He may have exaggerated (he was probably even expected to do so by his fellow Jews); he may have left out important information that was not conducive to his goal (which he probably did); but he could never have got away with a complete invention of 'events' that everyone knew, and could prove, had never taken place. What Philo presents in *In Flaccum* is dramatic or rhetorical historiography: it aims at evoking emotions, indignation and anger, pity and sadness, piety and awe for the deity. That is exactly what he wants to do, as did so many of his contemporary fellow historians. But, as should be clear by now, in spite of this, we can, with due caution, use the first half of the work *In Flaccum* as a source for the history of a Jewish community in the Diaspora at the beginning of our era.

Philo's work is a mixture of historiography, pastoral theology, apologetics and theodicy, "it draws on various genres but belongs to none, a mélange that represents primarily the inventiveness of its creator."[15] He describes events but does so in such a way that his Jewish readers are called upon not to doubt God's providence. While trying to demonstrate to his Roman audience that no people under the sun is more faithful to the Roman imperial family and stands closer to the values of the Roman elite of their time, at the same time Philo tries to console his co-religionists for the calamity that has befallen them by arguing that there has been no moment that God had abandoned them. So Philo tries to do several things at the same time, and this raises the issue of his intended audience that we will deal with in a moment. First, however, we have to cast a glance at a striking parallel in early Christian literature.

Almost at the end of his *De mortibus persecutorum*, written in the second decade of the 4th century CE, Lactantius says: "In this way God vanquished all the persecutors of His Name, so that no stem or

---

[15] Gruen 2002:191, there said, however, of the *Testament of Abraham*.

root of theirs remained" (50.1; ed. Creed 1984:75). This is the conclusion of a work in which the author describes the miserable fate of all those who tried to annihilate the adherents of the Christian faith and were consequently punished very severely by God. Here Lactantius stands in a long tradition: The theme of the violent death of those who fight against or resisted the or a deity (or its worshippers), called θεομάχοι since Euripides, reaches back till far in the pre-Christian period,[16] and there can be little doubt that Philo was acquainted with it. The motif of θεομαχεῖν is as old as Homer, but we meet it in connection with historical persons not before Herodotus. That historian tells us that the Persian king Cambyses purposefully humiliated the Egyptian god Apis, whose sacred bull was wounded by him, with the result that Cambyses was later fatally wounded in the same part of his body where he himself had once smitten Apis (3.64; a motif that we encounter also, *mutatis mutandis*, in *Flacc.* 189). Cambyses is only the first in a long row of sinners who were punished for their impiety, quite often by being eaten by worms (σκωληκόβρωτος, cf. Acts 12:23), according to tradition; shipwreck is the favorite kind of punishment for atheists (e.g., Diagoras and Protagoras); further we come across insanity, being struck by lightning, being torn apart by wild animals or humans, being burnt etc.[17]

From Jewish tradition we have, e.g., the biblical story about the punishment of the Egyptian Pharaoh in the book of Exodus, of the Sodomites in Genesis 18, and of Haman in the book of Esther (ch. 7); further the apocryphal stories about the horrible fate of Holophernes in the book of Judith (ch. 13), Antiochus IV in 2 Maccabees (ch. 9), Heliodorus in 2 Macc. (ch. 3); but all of these are of a legendary nature (Antiochus' being eaten by worms shows special indebtedness to the Greek tradition). The arch-Jew-hater Apion, who had ridiculed circumcision, died from a tumor on his genitals, says Josephus (*C. Ap.* 2.143), but the historical value of this tradition is debatable as well, as is the case with the rabbinic stories about Titus' death (b. *Gittin* 56b, *Bereshith Rabba* 10.7, *Vayikra Rabba* 22.3, *Pirqe de Rabbi Eliezer* 49).[18]

The motif is taken up also in early Christianity. The New Testament stories about the death of Judas (albeit suicide, see Matt. 27:5

---

[16] Nestle 1936; Speyer 1981; Creed 1984.
[17] See Speyer 1981:1017-1020.
[18] For more examples see, besides Nestle 1936 and Speyer 1981, also Van der Horst 1983.

and Acts 1:18) and that of Herod Agrippa (Acts 12:20-23) are the earliest examples. In the second and third centuries CE stories are circulating about similar fates of Pilate (the source of Eusebius, *Hist.Eccl.* 2.7) and of the persecutor Claudius Lucius Herminianus (Tertullian, *Scap.* 3).[19] There can be little doubt that the author of *De mortibus persecutorum* stood in this Graeco-Jewish-Christian tradition of what Nestle has called "Legenden vom Tod der Gottesverächter" (Nestle 1936). In most of the stories by Lactantius, punishment by God has the form of the persecutor's being violently murdered by his enemies, exactly as in Philo's *In Flaccum*. Philo himself stood at the crossroads of Greek and biblical traditions in this respect, and he himself may have served as the springwell for Lactantius and his sources.[20] If it is the declared purpose of Lactantius' *De mortibus persecutorum* "to testify to all men as to God's revelation of His greatness in the punishment and destruction of the enemies of his name,"[21] almost the same could be said of the purpose of *In Flaccum*. The most recent editor of *De mortibus persecutorum* remarks that this writing "can almost be seen as a piece of epideictic oratory devoted not to *encomium* but to *vituperatio*, designed to hold up to execration the characters of the persecuting emperors; but (...) its true antecedents lie in the Jewish background to Christian literature; the second book of Maccabees (...) has almost precisely the same combination of detailed historical record and praise of divine judgment."[22] He could have added a reference to Philo's *In Flaccum*.[23] He also points to an embarassing element in Lactantius' work, namely the "uncharitable delight it seems to take in the sufferings of the discomfited persecutors" (Creed 1984:xxxix), again a feature one comes across frequently in the second part of *In Flaccum*. All this is not to say that Lactantius used Philo as one of his sources (even though that cannot be excluded), my point is rather that Philo's work stands in a long tradition that begins in classical Greece and finds its apogee in that fourth-century Christian author.[24] There is no doubt that *De mortibus persecutorum* was primarily addressed to the author's fellow-Christians who could join in rejoicing at the discomfiture of their persecutors, but there is also an element of warning in it, a warning not improbably

---

[19] Other examples, also later than Lactantius, in Speyer 1981:1027-1041.
[20] Runia 1993 does not discuss this question.
[21] Creed 1984:xxxv.
[22] Creed 1984:xxxviii.
[23] Nestle 1936:263 does mention it in this connection.
[24] Cf. Morris 1987:861.

addressed to Roman rulers not to relapse in the old errors. And this brings us back again to the problem of what kind of audience was envisaged by Philo for *In Flaccum*.

In the scholarly literature one often finds either-or positions as far as the target audience of *In Flaccum* is concerned: either Jewish or Roman. Those who emphasize the theme of divine providence as the purple thread throughout the treatise plead for an exclusively Jewish audience, whereas those who emphasize the striking length of the description of Flaccus' ruination and death (half of the work!) plead for a Roman audience, more specifically for an audience in terms of Flaccus' successor, who should be warned in this way not to make the same fatal mistakes as his predecessor. In my opinion, neither position is compelling and neither can be proved to be wrong. This points the way to a more balanced solution. There can be no doubt that Philo had indeed a Jewish audience in mind because, as was already said, he indicates in the final sentence of the work (§191 quoted above) that he hopes to have made clear that God never abandons his own people. But at the same time the work gives several indications that Philo had also a non-Jewish audience in mind. He explains Jewish customs in a way that was unnecessary for Jewish readers and only makes sense in terms of a pagan audience. For instance, when speaking about the fact that the Jews were in great distress during the festival of Sukkoth, Philo writes: "It was the national Jewish festival of the autumn equinox, in which it is the custom of the Jews to live in tents" (§116). This kind of information can only have been meant for non-Jewish readers. In §25 he tells us that the Jewish king Agrippa was the grandson of king Herod and that he received from the emperor the former tetrarchy of Philip as his kingdom, again the kind of information that presupposes a non-Jewish audience. Another example is Philo's remark to the effect that Alexandria had five districts, named after the first letters of the alphabet. "Two of them are called the Jewish quarters because the majority of the inhabitants are Jews. In the other quarters there also live quite a number of Jews, although scattered about" (§55). And in §37 he informs the reader that papyrus was 'native' to Egypt. All this is definitely not the kind of information that an Alexandrian Jewish audience needed to have. And more instances could be given which make it very probable that Philo envisaged also a Roman audience. There is certainly more than one grain of truth in Goodenough's statement, "He wrote this document (...) to give it to the new prefect. He does not, still, dare to give direct instructions to the prefect, but he has so obviously schematized the events of the past few years and the reasons for the fall of Flaccus that the new prefect must perfectly have understood that he was faced with a people whom one offended at one's peril."[25] Or, as Ellen Birnbaum put it, by his emphasis on divine providence "Philo may, on the one hand, wish to bolster the spirits of his fellow Jews during a time of suffering; on the other hand, he may also wish to sound a warning to Gentiles to stop their maltreatment of his people."[26] So it would seem safe to assume that he had a dual readership in mind.[27] This is in itself not a very surprising or unexpected conclusion. The conflict described in *Flacc.* was one between Jews and non-Jews. Philo himself, although a Jew, stood with one leg in the world of the non-Jews; he stood on the threshhold between these two worlds. No wonder that he wanted to address audiences on both sides of that threshhold. After all, he had a message for both parties involved in the conflict, a message that had to be delivered clearly and loudly.[28]

4. *Main themes of the treatise*

(a) Providence and Justice

After what has been said in the previous chapters, it need hardly be repeated that the motif of providence looms large in *Flacc.*, even though the word πρόνοια is used only three times in the whole treatise (§§125, 126, 170; the word occurs 80 times in Philo's œuvre as a whole). But Philo implicitly refers to this concept in §§102, 104, 107, 115, 121, 146, 191 as well. When providence is spoken of or implied by Philo, it is always an activity of God on behalf of his people or those who live in accordance with his will. But there is another side to that coin, and that is justice (δίκη), or rather Justice (Δίκη),

---

[25] Goodenough 1962:59.
[26] Birnbaum 1996:21.
[27] Here I disagree with Niehoff 2001:39-44. Hay 1991:50-52 even suggests that Philo may have had in mind future generations as readers when he wrote his works.
[28] According to Cheon 1997 the *Wisdom of Solomon* was also written in reaction to the pogrom in 38. He argues that the function of the Exodus story in *Wisdom* was "to provide the self-understanding of the Alexandrian Jewish community just after the riot against Jews in 38 CE. It not only intended to provide hope and consolation for his community, but also to counteract the anti-Semitic prejudice of the Gentiles" (149). For a similar position see Winston 1979.

since Philo often personifies the concept (see, e.g., *Flacc.* 104, 107, 115, 146, 189). Justice becomes manifest in God's action against his opponents or the enemies of his people; it is *justitia retributiva,* punitive justice or *nemesis.* Philo uses δίκη no less than ten times in *Flacc.* (145 times in his whole œuvre). The motif of the punishment and death of the enemy of God and his people plays as prominent a role in *Flacc.* as God's providence. God's beneficient providence and his punitive justice belong hand in glove to the same central idea that governs the whole treatise (and *Legat.* as well). As has already been stressed, the concepts of divine providence and justice are no sheer theoretical issues in *Flacc.*, they play such a prominent role precisely because of the practical problems of the Alexandrian Jews: it is the horrible persecution that has undermined their faith in God's providence and justice. Philo has set himself the task of restoring this faith.

(b) Loyalty to Rome and the Baseness of the Egyptians

Less important than the motifs of providence and justice but still important enough to be singled out in this short section are the themes of Jewish loyalty to Rome and the base character of the Egyptians. These two themes, too, hang closely together. As Maren Niehoff has demonstrated at length in her valuable recent monograph (2001), Philo marshals all his eloquence in his attempts to prove that the Jews are more congenial to the Romans than others, especially more than the unruly Egyptians, and they share with the Romans their scorn for the Egyptians. Egyptian violence against the Jews is an inevitable consequence of their character, which is always inclined to *stasis* and given to jealousy and what Philo calls "an old and innate hatred" (*Flacc.* 29). For that reason a strong Roman government is needed to keep the Egyptians in check and limit the baneful effects of their inherent weaknesses. The Jews, on the other hand, are the ideal subjects of the Roman Empire. Their loyalty to the emperors is unrivalled. Philo stresses that "their synagogues clearly form the basis for their piety towards the imperial family" (*Flacc.* 49), and that "they were the only people under the sun who by being deprived of their synagogues would at the same time be deprived of their means of showing their piety towards their benefactors [the emperors], which is something they would have regarded as worth dying for many thousands of deaths" (*Flacc.* 48). The attitude of the Egyptians is the opposite of that of the Jews. For that reason, for

Philo the boundary between humanity and subhumans is identical to the boundary between Jews and Egyptians. The xenophobic overtones in his statements find their closest parallels in Roman literature of Philo's time (especially in the Augustan propaganda). By having the Jews emerge as a nation sharing Rome's 'barbarian Other,' Philo integrates the Jews into the contemporary Roman discourse, and in this way he suggests "a profound Roman-Jewish congeniality."[29] It is for that reason that throughout this treatise Philo tries to create as close a connection as possible between the opponents of the Jews and the Egyptians. There is no doubt that Philo regarded the Jew-haters and their leaders as essentially Egyptians, even if they were Greeks or of mixed Graeco-Egyptian descent. Of course, the opponents of the Jews considered themselves to be Greeks: hence both Apion (*GLAJJ* no. 164 §8) and the *Acts of the Alexandrian Martyrs* (4C25) suggest that the Jews were in fact the opposite of Greeks: they were Egyptians! As Goudriaan puts it (although somewhat overstating his case), "Philo on the one hand and the Jew-haters on the other mapped the ethnic composition of the society they were obliged to share in different and even incompatible ways. Both parties tried to associate themselves as much as possible with the Hellenic ethnic entity and claimed to be real Alexandrians, with the exclusion of the other; both parties kept the Egyptians at the largest possible distance and tried to push down the adversaries to that level. (...) Both sides rivalled with each other in their contempt for the Egyptians."[30] Apparently, the only thing that counted in this cultural and political struggle was the way ethnic labels were applied. So in a sense one might say that ethnic labelling is another major element in *Flacc.*

5. *The historical background (with an excursus on Flaccus)*

One of the greatest problems to be dealt with is that Philo does spell out in detail *what* happened in the clash between the Jews and the non-Jews (mainly Greeks but very probably also Egyptians) of Alexandria but does not spend even one word on the burning question of *why* all this happened. Why did the non-Jews of that city hate the Jews so much? In one paragraph Philo mentions in passing that the Alexandrians had "an ancient and in a sense innate enmity towards the Jews" (§29), but he fails to explain the source of this enmity. In

---

[29] Niehoff 2001:60.
[30] Goudriaan 1992:88.

his next written work, on the embassy to Caligula, Philo does explain why the emperor treated the Jewish delegation so badly: Among all the nations in the Roman Empire it was only the Jews who refused to acknowledge the divinity of Caligula. That they did not want to regard him as a god made him furious. But in *In Flaccum* we are denied every sort of explanation. And here comparisons with later pogroms are misleading rather than helpful. In the pogroms of the 17th-20th century the driving forces behind the persecutions were always the anti-Jewish preaching by the Christian church or theories on the racial inferiority of the Jews, or a mixture of both. These factors played no role at all, however, in first century Alexandria for the simple reason that neither Christianity nor racist theories were in existence there at that time. So even though the similarity between what happened in first century Alexandria and in 17th-20th century Europe is striking, the background must be completely different. But what is that background? It is *a priori* implausible that there was only one cause or one reason for this outburst of anti-Jewish violence. It stands to reason that it must have been more complex. Since outbursts of such a scale took place nowhere else in the ancient world of the first half of the first century, it must probably have to do with something specifically Alexandrian. It is to this problem that we will now devote extra attention.

I will first deal briefly with the possible political factors and thereafter with elements that are related to Jewish religious beliefs and non-Jewish reactions to them.

To begin with the political factors, it should be borne in mind that the Jewish presence in Egypt in the first century was not something new. In spite of the biblical stories about the liberation of the Israelites from the oppressive Egyptians in the time of Moses (the 13th cent. BCE), Jews had already settled again in Egypt in biblical times. In the book of Jeremiah (ch. 43) we read that many Israelites took refuge in Egypt in the face of the Babylonian armies that overran Judea and Jerusalem at the beginning of the sixth century BCE. And the find of a rich trove of Aramaic letters from Elephantine, an island in the Nile near Aswan, proves that a Jewish military settlement existed there from the sixth to the fourth centuries BCE as a kind of border police in the service of the Persians.[31] It is interesting to see that after a period of peaceful co-existence these Jewish soldiers and

---

[31] For details see Porten 1992, 1996.

their families came into a serious conflict with their Egyptian neighbours in the final decades of the fifth century. The Jews had their own temple at Elephantine, and so did the Egyptians who had a shrine for Khnum, the ram-god who was creator and also the 'Lord of the Nile.' In the eyes of the priests of Khnum, the Jews who sacrificed rams (Khnum's sacred animal) on the altar of their temple committed deicide (killing their god). Finally, in 410 BCE, a band of Egyptians vented their anger on the Jews by destroying the sanctuary of Yahweh at Elephantine, which was followed by the pillage of Jewish houses.

Less than a century later, Alexander the Great founded the great city in northern Egypt which he named Alexandria after himself.[32] The Jews were there almost from the beginning as one of the groups of non-Egyptians who had been brought there by the Greek overlords, the Ptolemies.[33] This was the beginning of a long history, which was by and large peaceful for almost three centuries.[34] The Jewish community grew and flourished there. After one generation they had already become so acculturated that the Hebrew Bible had to be translated into Greek (the Septuagint); and thereafter an impressive Jewish literature in Greek came into being on a scale that one could see nowhere else.[35] Alexandria was the place *par excellence* of the Judaeo-Greek cultural synthesis. Around the turn of the era probably some 100,000 Jews lived in the city, many of whom were highly educated. "Integration in the social, economic, and cultural life of Alexandria was open to them, and they took advantage of that opening. Jews served in the armies, obtained administrative posts, took part in commerce, shipping, finance, farming, and every form of occupation, reached posts of prestige and importance, and played a role in the world of the Hellenic intelligentsia."[36]

This peaceful situation began to change, however, when the Romans took power over Egypt.[37] Pompey's envoy Gabinius was

---

[32] See Fraser 1972: I.3-7.
[33] According to Josephus even by Alexander himself: *C. Ap.* 2.35; but see Pucci Ben Zeev 1998:299.
[34] There are only a very few indications that there might have been violent clashes between Jews and non-Jews before 38 CE. *CPJ* 141 (first half of the first cent. BCE) may be a case in point, but it is ambiguous. For a survey of other evidence (none of it conclusive) see Ameling ms. 2003:25-29.
[35] Schürer 1973/87: III.470-704; Collins 2000; see also the helpful chart in Sterling 2001:288-290.
[36] Gruen 2002:69.
[37] Tcherikover 1963.

helped by the Jews on his march into Egypt in 57 BCE after having been advised to do so by Antipater, Herod the Great's father.[38] When later, in 48/47 BCE, Julius Caesar intervened in Alexandria on behalf of Cleopatra, he received military aid from the Jews who lived there.[39] In 30 BCE Egypt came under Roman rule and it became a province of the Roman empire, subject to Roman officials, taxation, and law. Shortly afterwards it was grouped with the so-called 'imperial' provinces whose governors were appointed by the emperor.[40] The first Roman emperor, Augustus, confirmed all existing Jewish privileges which he had engraved on a marble slab and set up in the city. He thanked the Alexandrian Jews for their services against Cleopatra.[41] The Roman confirmation of the privileges of religious freedom and ethnic identity thus won by the Jews from the latter two rulers probably embittered their relations with the other peoples of Alexandria, their Greek and Egyptian neighbours, who were notoriously anti-Roman and felt betrayed by the Jews. In the eyes of the Greeks, the Jews had furthered the decline of their city from a royal residence and head of a sovereign state to a mere provincial capital. Alexandria's glory was gone, and the Greeks felt humiliated by the Jews, a sentiment that was probably shared by the Egyptians of the city. After that, attacking the Jews became an indirect, and therefore relatively safe, way to attack the authority of Rome.

Augustus, who otherwise favored the Jews, also introduced a much-hated poll tax (called *laographia*) from which only Greek Alexandrians with full citizenship were exempted.[42] So the vast majority of the Jews had to pay this burdensome tax as well. Since the payment of this tax implied not only a heavy financial burden, causing impoverishment of the population, but also personal human degradation, it made the question of citizenship acute and that created much tension between the 'haves' and 'have-nots' of this privilege. Among the evidence for this tension is one of the papyri with fragments of the so-called *Acts of the Alexandrian Martyrs*, where the protagonist of the anti-Jewish cause, the gymnasiarch Isidorus, says to the emperor

---

[38] Details in Fuchs 1924:17.
[39] Josephus, *Ant.* 14.127-136; *Bell.* 1.187-192; *C.Ap.* 2.61; Barraclough 1984:423 note 27; Huzar 1988:635-6.
[40] See Bowman & Rathbone 1992 and Montevecchi 1988.
[41] Josephus, *Ant.* 14.188; *C.Ap.* 2.60. Josephus, however, mistakenly ascribes this declaration to Julius Caesar; see Tcherikover 1963:3 note 1. Maybe the detail about the engraving of the marble slab should be taken *cum grano salis*.
[42] For details see *CPJ* 1.60, with lit. in note 26.

Claudius: "They [the Jews] are not of the same nature as the Alexandrians [=Greeks], but are rather like Egyptians. Are they not on a level with those who pay the poll-tax?" (*CPJ* 156c25-27). Jewish evidence may perhaps be found in 3 Macc. 2:28-30.[43]

The various Jewish sources which deal with or mention this subject, especially Josephus, seem to be unanimous in asserting Jewish citizenship in Alexandria from the very beginning, but non-Jewish sources give a rather different impression. Since the acquisition of citizenship became a burning question at the beginning of the Roman period and created enmity between Jews and Greeks, it is not surprising that the sources "do not excel in neutrality and tend to exaggerate — sometimes even to falsify — the state of affairs in regard to it."[44] The legal status of the Alexandrian Jews is a very complicated issue that has been hotly debated not only in antiquity but also in modern scholarly literature, and much still remains very uncertain. I will summarize only some important data here, and that as briefly as possible because not all details are necessary for a better understanding of Philo's book.[45]

The Jews enjoyed a certain degree of self-government in Alexandria probably right from the beginning, although their political rights were distinct from the citizenship of Alexandrian Greeks. Their internal autonomy "was not political but religious and social only."[46] It included a kind of governing body (in Roman times this was a council of elders or *gerousia*), the right to build synagogues and to educate the youth in the traditions of the Jewish people, and the establishment of their own law courts. In this way the Greek and Roman overlords enabled the Jews to live in accordance with their own ancestral customs (πάτρια ἔθη). The first-century BCE geographer Strabo informs us that in his time the head of the Jewish community in Alexandria, the ethnarch, "ruled the people, judged its cases, and supervised the implementation of contracts and orders, like the ruler of an independent state" (quoted in Josephus, *Ant.* 14.117). So, the Jews were privileged residents, not just foreigners with temporary domicile, and set well above the ordinary Egyptians,

---

[43] But see Anderson 1985:511 and Gruen 2002:76-77.
[44] Tcherikover 1959:309.
[45] For a survey and bibliography see Tcherikover 1959:309-332; Kasher 1985 *passim*; Mélèze-Modrzejewski 1995:161-183; Barclay 1996:60-71; Schäfer 1997:136-160; Honigman 1997; Sly 2000:249-265; Gruen 2002:73-83; for detailed documentation the reader is referred to these works.
[46] Tcherikover 1959:301.

although still below the fully enfranchised Greeks (their civic rights did not entail citizenship). It was these privileges that Flaccus suddenly dissolved in 38 CE. It would seem that he had been instigated to do so by the Greek nationalists who were of the opinion that Jews did not deserve a higher status than the Egyptians. One of the reasons for this instigation may have been that "at the peak of the Jewish social pyramid were a minority of families (...) who had attained citizen status"[47] and therefore equal rights with the Greeks. No doubt Philo's own family was one of these, for his brother, Alexander, was one of the highest officials in the government of the city and his nephew, Tiberius Julius Alexander, even became Roman governor of Egypt. The status of full citizen was usually acquired by inheritance but this privilege could also be granted to select individuals by kings, emperors, or the citizen body. Since we know of several Jews with leading positions in the administration of the city or the country, it is certain that some individual Jews did acquire the status of an Alexandrian citizen.[48] The Greeks, however, felt that in their city only they and not the Jews were entitled to this desired status. And there is reason to believe that the Greek delegation that went to Caligula after the events of 38 "challenged the privileges of Alexandrian Jewish citizens, in line with the long-standing uneasiness in Alexandria about the 'infiltration' of unworthy individuals into the citizen body."[49] In a telling papyrus from about 20 BCE an Alexandrian official expresses the wish of his Greek fellow citizens "to take care that the *pure* citizen body of Alexandria is not corrupted by men who are uncultured and uneducated" (*CPJ* 150.5-6), i.e. by non-Greeks. Jews are not mentioned explicitly here, but there can be little doubt that they were in the mind of the writer. The document makes clear that non-Greeks tried to be enrolled as citizens because this was the only way to avoid the heavy poll-tax that the Romans levied. As we almost never hear of Egyptians trying to do this, it is most probably the Jews that the Greeks tried to keep outside their prestigious body politic.[50]

The leader of the Greek-Alexandrian delegation complains to Caligula, "Why is it that, if they are citizens, they do not worship the same gods as the Alexandrians?" (Josephus, *C.Ap.* 2.65). This makes

---

[47] Barclay 1996:67.
[48] See Tcherikover 1959:515-516 note 90. Bowman & Rathbone 1992:114 argue that there may have been a sort of *numerus clausus* of citizens.
[49] Barclay 1996:69.
[50] *Pace* Gruen 2002:75-76.

clear that (1) there were Jews with full citizenship in Alexandria, (2) these had not abandoned their traditional Jewish faith, and (3) for that very reason they were hated by the Greeks, because citizenship normally involved participation in religious activities, in civic cults, and this was forbidden to the Jews as being idolatrous. "Whatever exemptions or compromises were worked out here were clearly resented by Alexandrians who denied that one could uphold Judaean ethnic customs while also enjoying the status of Alexandrian citizenship."[51] So the crisis of 38 "concerned *both* the immediate and general loss of their [the Jews'] communal privileges in Alexandria *and* the long-standing dispute about Jews entering the citizen class."[52]

In the year 41 Caligula's successor, the emperor Claudius, writes a long letter to the Alexandrians (*CPJ* 153) in order to settle the matter. He urges the Alexandrians to show more tolerance towards the Jews, and he upholds the social and ancestral rights of the Jewish community. His language is firm: "Unless you stop this destructive and obstinate mutual enmity, I shall be forced to show what a benevolent ruler can be when he is turned to righteous indignation" (79-81). But at the same time he states that Jews cannot claim citizenship in Alexandria, "a city which is not their own" (95). So, the right to live in accordance with Jewish ancestral customs and probably also their limited autonomy were restored to them, but "the door to citizenship was slammed firmly in the faces of the few who had achieved, or aspired to, this status."[53] Or, to put it in the words of Tcherikover, "From the events of the years 38-41 Alexandrian Jewry emerged victorious in the sphere of national-religious autonomy, but as regards civic rights the year 41 marked a definite defeat in the struggle for emancipation."[54]

Why were the Greeks so adamantly opposed to 'contamination' of their body politic by the Jews? From where did this hatred come in Alexandria where anti-Jewish slander, as Philo says, was nurtured and taught to everyone right from the cradle (*Legat.* 170)? It is this aspect to which we now turn.

Although it is undeniable that in Greek and Roman sources from the 3rd century BCE to the 1st century CE we encounter a remarkable

---

[51] Barclay 1996:70.
[52] *Ibid.*
[53] Barclay 1996:71.
[54] Tcherikover 1963:20.

degree of sympathy for Judaism on the part of several pagan writers, it is also undeniable that in the same period other pagan writers demonstrate a strong animosity towards the Jews. For lack of a better term I will call it Jew-hatred.[55]

Let me begin by giving a striking example of this phenomenon. Some 70 years after the pogrom, in the first decade of the 2nd century CE, the famous Roman historian Tacitus, who has the reputation of being well-informed, writes the following about the Jewish people (*Hist.* 5.3-5 = *GLAJJ* no. 281):

> Most writers agree that once a disease, which horribly disfigured the body, broke out over Egypt. King Bocchoris, seeking a remedy, consulted the oracle of Hammon, and was bidden to cleanse his realm, and to convey into some foreign land this people [the Jews] that was detested by the gods. The people, who had been collected after diligent search, found themselves left in a desert and sat for the most part in a stupor of grief, till one of the exiles, Moses by name, warned them not to look for any relief from God or man, forsaken as they were of both, but to trust to themselves, taking for their heaven-sent leader that man who should first help them to be relieved of their present misery. They agreed, and in utter ignorance began to advance at random. Nothing, however, distressed them so much as the scarcity of water, and they had sunk ready to perish in all directions over the plain, when a herd of wild asses was seen to retire from their pasture to a rock shaded by trees. Moses followed them, and, guided by the appearance of a grassy spot, discovered an abundant spring of water. This furnished relief. After a continuous journey for six days, on the seventh they possessed themselves of a country, from which they expelled the inhabitants, and in which they founded a city and a temple.
>
> Moses, wishing to secure for the future his authority over the nation, gave them a novel form of worship, opposed to all that is practised by other men. Things sacred with us have no sanctity with them, while they allow what is forbidden with us. In their holy place they have consecrated an image of the animal by whose guidance they found deliverance from their long and thirsty wanderings. They slay the ram, seemingly in derision of Hammon, and they sacrifice the ox, because the Egyptians worship it as Apis. They abstain from swine's flesh, in consideration of what they suffered when they were infected by the leprosy to which this animal is liable. (...) We are told that the rest of the seventh day was adopted, because this day brought with it a termination of their toils; after a while the charm of indolence beguiled them into giving up the seventh year also to inaction. (...) All their other customs, which are at once perverse and disgusting,

---

[55] For the anachronistic nature of the term 'anti-Semitism' see, e.g., Yavetz 1997:19-21; others would prefer 'Judaeophobia' (Schäfer 1997), but that is not yet a current term.

owe their strength to their very badness. The most degraded out of other nations, scorning their national beliefs, brought to them their contributions and presents. This augmented the wealth of the Jews, as also did the fact, that among themselves they are inflexibly honest and ever ready to show compassion, though they regard the rest of mankind with all the hatred of enemies. They sit apart at meals, they sleep apart, and though, as a nation, they are singularly prone to lust, they abstain from intercourse with foreign women; among themselves nothing is unlawful. Circumcision was adopted by them as a mark of difference from other men. Those who come over to their religion adopt that practice, and have this lesson first instilled into them: to despise all gods, to disown their country, and set at naught parents, children, and brethren.[56]

What we see in this spiteful caricature is a culmination of 400 years of anti-Jewish propaganda, which we find in many written sources from the preceding centuries. What is so striking about this literature is that not only are the first instances known to us of Alexandrian provenance, but that also many of the other instances derive from this city.[57] Let us pass some of them briefly in review.

The first Egyptian intellectual to write in Greek was the Alexandrian priest Manetho, who lived in the early 3rd century BCE. In his great work on Egyptian history (*GLAJJ* nos. 19-21),[58] he tells about pharaoh Amenophis' wish to see the gods — a wish, so he was told, that could be fulfilled only if he purified the whole land of lepers and other polluted persons. He collected some 80.000 of such people and sent them to the quarries. Then the polluted people joined forces with the lepers, convened in the city of Avaris, and revolted under the leadership of a priest called Osarsiph whom at the end Manetho says to be identical with Moses. This priest made it a law that they should neither worship the gods nor refrain from killing any of the animals regarded as sacred in Egypt but that they should sacrifice and consume all alike, and that they should have contact with nobody except those of their own confederacy. He decreed a great number of laws that were fully opposed to Egyptian custom and then asked the inhabitants of Jerusalem, old enemies of the Egyptians, to join them in an attack on Egypt. Not only did they set villages and towns on fire, pillaging the temples and mutilating images of the gods

---

[56] On this passage see now esp. Bloch 2002.
[57] See Aziza 1987; on the Egyptian origin of anti-Jewish attitudes see Mélèze-Modrzejewski 1981 and Schäfer 1997.
[58] Actually there are two versions of the exodus in Manetho, but for our purposes that is irrelevant; see Stern *ad locum* in *GLAJJ*.

without restraint, but they also used the sanctuaries as kitchens to roast the sacred animals that the Egyptians worshipped. They even compelled the Egyptian religious officials to sacrifice their own sacred animals and afterwards cast them naked out of the temple. So this brutal regime was characterized by *misanthrôpia* and by hatred of the indigenous Egyptian religion. But fortunately, after some time, this regime of terror was expelled and the criminals settled in Syria (Palestine). Such, says this Alexandrian priest, were the origins of the Jewish people.

Although there can be no doubt that older Egyptian stories dealing originally with the reigns of terror by Semitic peoples like the Hyksos have been applied here by Manetho only secondarily to the Jews,[59] it is clear that what we have here is an anti-Jewish version of the biblical story of the exodus from Egypt. Here is no story of liberation from Egyptian oppression by God; on the contrary, it was the gods who commanded that these not only polluted but also oppressive persons of extreme impiety be expelled from their territory. This is a motif that will recur from this time on in all sorts of variations, as we have already seen in Tacitus.

It was probably in the 2nd, or perhaps in the 1st century BCE, that the Graeco-Egyptian author Lysimachus wrote his work, *Aegyptiaka*. The work is now lost but Josephus quotes him as saying (*GLAJJ* no. 158) that pharaoh Bokchoris ordered that Egypt be purged of lepers as well as of impure and impious people; the former should be killed by drowning, the latter should be driven into the desert. These gathered around a certain Moses who instructed them to show goodwill to nobody, to offer not the best but always the worst advice, and to overthrow any temples and altars of the gods which they found. Thereupon these impure and impious people maltreated the population of Egypt and plundered and set fire to the temples wherever they came until they reached the country now called Judaea, where they settled and built Jerusalem. Different than Manetho, "Lysimachus is unambiguous as to who the impure people are. We learn that they are Jews not only at the end of the story when they reach Judea; rather, we are told from the very outset that the Jewish people were afflicted with leprosy, scurvy, and other maladies."[60] Lysimachus remodels the motifs of impiety and misanthropy in a very negative

---

[59] Schäfer 1997:163-167.
[60] Schäfer 1997:28.

way: the Jews deliberately destroy all the temples of other peoples and they are hostile to all humankind, intentionally offering everyone the worst advice.

Another version, probably Alexandrian as well, of the story of the Egyptian origin of the Jews is also related by the historian Diodorus of Sicily in the first century BCE. He tells us (*GLAJJ* no. 63) that when in 135 BCE king Antiochus VII tried to capture Jerusalem, his advisers said to him that he should take the city by storm and wipe out the nation of the Jews completely, since they alone of all nations avoided dealings with any other people. They also pointed out that the ancestors of the Jews had been driven out of Egypt as people who were impious and detested by the gods. For by way of purging the country, all persons who had white and leprous marks on their bodies had been assembled and driven across the border as being under a curse. The refugees had occupied the territory around Jerusalem and had organized the nation of the Jews. They had made hatred of humankind into a tradition and on this account had introduced utterly outlandish laws: neither to break bread with any other people nor to show them any goodwill at all. The most striking feature in this account is that the Jews had adopted hatred of humankind and atheism as a permanent tradition. Impiety and misanthropy have now become stock elements in anti-Jewish propaganda of Alexandria.

We see that again in the first century CE when Apion, a philologist of Egyptian origin,[61] publishes his work on the history of Egypt. His attacks on the Jewish people are so vehement and influential that several decades after his death the Jewish historian Josephus still finds it necessary to devote a whole work to the refutation of the slanders of this arch-Jew-hater, his *Contra Apionem*. Apart from the elements that have become familiar by now he adds the following new detail that the Jews after leaving Egypt marched for six days and then "developed tumours in the groin, and that was why, after safely reaching the country now called Judaea, they rested on the seventh day, and called that day *sabbaton*, preserving the Egyptian terminology; for disease of the groin is called *sabbatosis* in Egyptian" (*GLAJJ* no. 165). But this etymological speculation, which was a specialty of Apion, is innocent as compared to what he adds later, namely that the Seleucid king Antiochus IV entered the Jerusalem temple and

---

[61] See van der Horst 2002:207-221.

he found there a couch on which a man was reclining, with a table before him laden with a banquet of fish of the sea, beasts of the earth, and birds of the air, at which the poor man was gazing in stupefaction. The king's entry was instantly hailed by him with adoration, as about to procure him profound relief. Falling at the king's knees, he stretched out his right hand and implored him to set him free. The king reassured him and asked him to tell him who he was, why he was living there, what was the meaning of his abundant fare. Thereupon, with sighs and tears, the man told in a pitiful tone the tale of his distress. He said that he was a Greek and that while travelling around in this province in order to make his living, he was suddenly kidnapped by foreigners and brought to this temple, and shut up there. He was seen by nobody, but was fattened on feasts of the most lavish description. At first such unexpected advantages seemed to him a pleasure, but after a while they made him suspicious, and finally astonished. At last he inquired of the servants that came to him and was informed by them that it was in order to fulfill a law of the Jews, which they were forbidden to tell him, that he was being fattened. They did the same at a fixed time every year: they used to catch a Greek foreigner, fatten him up for a year, and then lead him to a certain wood, kill him, sacrifice his body with their customary ritual, and partake of his flesh. While immolating the Greek, they swore an oath of hostility to the Greeks (*GLAJJ* no. 171).

We should keep in mind that it was this man, Apion, who during the reign of Caligula was not only honored by the city of Alexandria with a grant of citizenship — Josephus tells that Apion congratulated the city on that occasion for having so great a man as he as a citizen (*C. Ap.* 2.135) — but that the city also asked him to act as leader of the Alexandrian delegation to Rome in the conflict between Greeks and Jews that divided the city in 38 CE.[62] If this man was so prestigious that the Greeks of Alexandria decided to confer full citizenship upon him, it should surprise no one that his incredible accusation of Jewish cannibalism (eating a Greek at that!) was taken seriously and believed by these Greeks. One can imagine that his ideas were eagerly exploited and divulged by hatemongers such as Isidorus and Lampo in their Alexandrian clubs and in the gymnasia of the city. They will certainly have sown a lot of hatred there.

Apion's ridiculing remark about the sabbath (which he derived from an Egyptian word for groin disease) brings us to the following element: the accusations of Jewish laziness. Here again we encounter

---

[62] Significantly enough, another notorious Alexandrian Jew-hater, the priest Chaeremon (first cent. CE), who wrote an anti-Jewish work in the same period as Apion, probably also was a member of the Greek delegation to Gaius (see Van der Horst 1984:47).

a malevolent interpretation of a Jewish custom. The sabbath is interpreted as a sign of Jewish idleness and indolence by several ancient authors. To mention only one instance, the famous Roman philosopher Seneca, a contemporary of Philo, says that the Jewish observance of the sabbath is very inexpedient since by introducing one day of rest in every seven they lose in idleness a seventh of their life (*GLAJJ* no. 186). This is echoed by Tacitus, as we have seen, when he remarks that the pleasures of indolence on the sabbath induced the Jews to giving up the seventh year as well to inaction, a clear reference to the so-called sabbatical year (*Hist.* 5.4). His contemporary, the Greek philosopher Plutarch, lists keeping of the sabbath among the stupid forms of barbarian superstition that have been adopted even by some Greeks (*GLAJJ* no. 255). Passages such as *Spec.* 2.60 and *Hyp.* 7.14 show that Philo was acquainted with this kind of ridicule.

Circumcision is a Jewish custom that forms an easy target for ridicule. To the Jews it was the most important external sign of the covenant between God and Israel, but to the Greeks and Romans it was just discreditable mutilation. They regarded a circumcised penis as obscene and ugly, and as a sign of lewdness. Although several ancient authors still show some awareness of the fact that circumcision is of Egyptian origin, many others regard it as a typically Jewish custom, and their perception of it "varies from neutrality to irony to derision and outspoken hostility."[63] We have already seen how Tacitus makes a connection between circumcision and Jewish separatism, which he interprets as misanthropy. They chose it deliberately, he says, to distinguish themselves from other people and to express their hate and enmity against others (*Hist.* 5.5.1). Other authors speak about circumcision with all kinds of sexual innuendo, the implication often being that Jewish men are well-endowed and sexually extremely active and very potent. The association of circumcision with lechery is not uncommon, but I will refrain from quoting texts here[64] (that Philo was familiar with this kind of ridicule is apparent from *Spec.* 1.1-2 and *QG* 3.47-48). Another target of pagan criticism is the Jewish abstinence from pork, one of the most prominent dietary laws in the Bible. But since it is ridiculed mainly by Roman satirical authors, not by Greeks, I will not deal with it in the present context.

Let me finally add some remarks on what Graeco-Roman authors say about the Jewish belief in one god. What struck them more than

---

[63] Schäfer 1997:96.
[64] See Schäfer 1997:99-102.

anything else is that the Jewish God is an iconic, which is contrary to all the customs of the Greeks and Romans. And since this deity without image is invisible, the conclusion that is often drawn is that the Jews do not recognize any god at all and are atheists. Since the Jews differ from all other peoples in this respect, it is said that this contributes to their xenophobic life-style. More than one ancient author, therefore, condemns the Jews as both atheists and misanthropes. "In the eyes of the Greeks there could hardly be a verdict more devastating than this one."[65] Others comment upon the arrogance that goes hand in hand with the exclusiveness of Jewish monotheism (e.g., Celsus in Origen, *CC* 5.2.41 = *GLAJJ* no. 375). The separatism that this entails is clearly worded by the third century CE historian Cassius Dio, when he says that the Jews are distinguished from the rest of humanity in practically every detail of life, but especially by the fact that they do not honor any of the usual gods, but show extreme reverence for only one particular divinity (*Hist. Rom.* 37.17.1 = *GLAJJ* no. 406). Others, however, assert that the Jews worship an ass, a motif that had its origin in Alexandria, where stories about a statue of a pack-ass in the Jerusalem temple circulated (see Mnaseas in *GLAJJ* no. 28). Here one should bear in mind that this animal was associated with the malicious Egyptian deity Seth (in Greek Typhon), an evil power who embodies the foreign rulers who have to be expelled from Egypt. In certain Egyptian circles one tried "to connect the origin of the Jews with Seth-Typhon, feared and despised in both Greek and Egyptian mythology."[66] It is no coincidence that Manetho, the earliest Alexandrian anti-Jewish author we know of, writes that the expelled unclean and leprous persons joined forces in the city of Avaris, and adds that "according to religious tradition this city was from earliest times dedicated to Typhon" (*C. Ap.* 1.237 = *GLAJJ* no. 21). And his later fellow countryman, Apion, states that in the innermost sanctuary of the Jerusalem temple the Jews kept an ass's head which they worshipped with the greatest reverence, thus characterizing them as followers of this power of evil (*C.Ap.* 2.80 = *GLAJJ* no. 170). How dangerous such a crude anti-Jewish statement could be can be gauged from the fact that Josephus found it necessary to write a lengthy refutation (*C.Ap.* 2.81-88).

---

[65] Schäfer 1997:36.
[66] Schäfer 1997:57.

Now it must immediately be added, that I have shown here only one side of the coin. It would have been equally possible to present a completely opposite picture. We have an abundance of material in which Graeco-Roman authors (but not from Alexandria!) express a widely very different view of the Jews. Moses is depicted by these authors as a wise lawgiver and his followers as a people of philosophers, who have one of the most exalted forms of spiritual worship.[67] Some authors say the Jews set an example that should be followed by other nations. And from other sources we know that Judaism exerted a great fascination on many gentiles in the ancient world.[68] We do not know of many proselytes, but we do hear of large numbers of gentiles who sympathized with Judaism and gathered on the fringes of many a synagogue in the Jewish Diaspora.[69] They came to the services on shabbat, studied the Torah, and kept some of the biblical commandments, although they did not usually become members of the community. These sympathizers, often dubbed 'godfearers' in the ancient sources, sometimes made substantial contributions to the Jewish communities, for instance by financing buildings such as synagogues. So, the negative picture sketched above is not the whole picture. But for our present purpose it is important to notice that the dark side was there and that it had from the very beginning a strongly Alexandrian stamp.

What happened in Alexandria in the, roughly, three centuries preceding the pogrom was a complex process. It would be unwise to speak in the simplifying terms of a monocausal model. Brief though my sketch has been, I hope that, at least, I have highlighted clearly some aspects that can contribute to a better understanding of the events of 38 CE. First, there was the long-standing tradition of Alexandrian Jew-hatred. We do not know whether the Graeco-Alexandrians were incited to produce their anti-Jewish versions of the exodus story because they read the first Greek translation of the Jewish Bible and reacted to the anti-Egyptian version of the story it contained, or rather reacted to hearsay.[70] Whatever the case, the

---

[67] Tcherikover 1959:359-360; Mélèze-Modrzejewski 1981:419; Gager 1983:35-112.
[68] See Feldman 1993:177-297 for a plethora of evidence.
[69] See Wander 1998. In this connection it is interesting to see that Philo himself claims that each year Jews and non-Jews alike gathered on the peninsula of Pharos to celebrate the translation of the Hebrew Bible into Greek (*Mos.* 2.41).
[70] See Tcherikover 1959:363.

bitter antagonism that these anti-Jewish versions bespeak from the very beginning lingers on from the start of the Hellenistic period till far into the Roman period (even a quick glance at *GLAJJ* makes that abundantly clear). On top of that come the many stories of Jewish separatism, hatred of Egyptian civilization, inevitably widened to hatred of humanity in general, until it reached its bizarre final stage with the accusation of an annual cannibalistic ritual in which a Greek was sacrificed and eaten in Jerusalem (of course with the implication that it is the Jewish God who demands the sacrifice of foreigners). This unabated anti-Jewish propaganda cannot have failed to have a dramatic effect.[71] As we ourselves can witness even today, in the continual and unabashed stream of anti-Jewish propaganda — however full of obvious lies and horrible slander it may be (including the notorious nonsense from the so-called *Protocols of the Elders of Zion*) — hatred is very easily sown. But it needs a trigger to set it off. And triggers were not lacking in Alexandria.

The explosive mixture of verbal Jew-hatred and political reality came into being with the Roman conquest of the Near East in the first century BCE. The first factor was that the Alexandrian Jews sided with the Romans, sensing that they would gain privileges by that, which was true, but the price was high. The semi-autonomous status they received in Alexandria from the Romans gave rise to an enormous resentment among the Greeks and Egyptians, who felt that their city had lost its status whereas the Jewish community had won prestige. This exacerbated the antagonism. The second trigger, which actually put the spark to the tinder, was the visit of the Jewish puppet-king Agrippa to Alexandria with a flashing show of his bodyguards. This was too much for the frustrated Greeks and Egyptians. In their midst was a people whom they regarded as foreigners, yes even as barbarians; these were people who had no regard for the traditional gods of the civilized world whatsoever, for they practised a arrogant exclusivist religion. These unbearable separatists were not only full of hatred of humankind in general; what was even worse was that every year they fattened up a human person, a Greek at that, to be slaughtered in a cruel cannibalistic ritual. When this scum of the world had the affront to hail a king of their own, while the others had not even

---

[71] Bludau 1906:79 ominously speaks in this connection of "eine natürliche Reaktion des hellenistischen Volksgefühls gegen ein fremdes Element, das in seinem Leben einen allzu breiten Raum eingenommen hatte" (!).

a modicum of self-rule,[72] this was the bloody limit. Their fury could no longer be contained; and when they realized that the Roman governor, who was supposed to keep them in check, was himself in deep trouble because of the ascension of Caligula, they grabbed their chance. They could now vent their anger by attacking the Jews because they could blackmail their governor, Flaccus, into connivance.[73]

Excursus: Aulus Avillius Flaccus

We do not know much about Flaccus with certainty. Philo's *Flacc.* and *Legat.*, our main sources, are heavily biased, and there is little else that is informative. Flaccus was born in Rome, probably around 15 BCE (so he was approximately of the same age as Philo), since in *Flacc.* 158 Philo has him say: "I was the schoolmate and companion of the grandchildren of Augustus" (συμφοιτητὴς δὲ καὶ συμβιωτὴς γενόμενος τῶν θυγατριδῶν τοῦ Σεβαστοῦ), by which he means the children of Augustus' daughter(s), *i.c.* of Julia from her marriage with M. Vipsanius Agrippa: C. Caesar (20 BCE-4CE), L. Caesar (17 BCE-2CE), and Agrippa Postumus (12 BCE-14CE). If this information is correct, Flaccus grew up and was educated together with three members of the imperial family who were born in the second decade before the Common Era, *i.e.*, approximately 15 BCE. It also implies that he came from a high-ranking family that had close ties with the court. This is confirmed by the information Philo gives in *Flacc.* 2 to the effect that "he was reckoned among the friends of the emperor Tiberius," which is a somewhat formal title for an informal circle of courtiers who were the emperor's main advisors. His close friendship with Macro (mentioned in *Flacc.* 11), who had the most predominant

---

[72] On the abolition of the Alexandrian Senate (*boulê*) and the Greeks' requests for permission to restore one see Bowman & Rathbone 1992:118-119.
[73] Although Philo speaks only about the persecution of the Jews of Alexandria, not of the Samaritans in the city, it cannot be excluded that Samaritans belonged to the victims of the pogrom as well. Two things have to be borne in mind here: firstly, it is certain that there had been a sizeable Samaritan community in Alexandria from the third century BCE onwards; and, secondly, outsiders very often could not make any distinction between Jews and Samaritans, even though the two parties were opposed to each other. So even although Philo's emphasis on Jerusalem as the "mother city" of the persecuted Jews rules out that he envisaged Samaritans as victims, in practice this group may well have undergone the same violence as the Jews. See for Samaritans in Alexandria van der Horst 1990:138-147; and for the indistinguishability of Jews and Samaritans van der Horst 2002:257-258.

position in politics after the emperor, namely that of commander of Tiberius' praetorian guard (*praefectus praetorio*), fits in with this picture, as does his friendship with Aemilius Lepidus, the husband of Gaius' sister Drusilla (see *Flacc.* 151).

We know next to nothing about Flaccus' career before the year 32, when he was appointed governor of Egypt by Tiberius. He must have been in his middle forties by that time. It is in this period, but probably already before 32 as well, that he seems to have played an active role in the prosecution of Agrippina: "He had belonged to those who conspired against Gaius' mother," says Philo (§9). The process ended with her banishment by Tiberius in 29 CE (she died in 33 CE), and it was probably one of the reasons why Flaccus became nervous when Gaius acceded to the throne in 37 CE, although we do not know any details of his role in this affair. Also in this period, but later than the process against Agrippina, he tried to promote Gemellus, Tiberius' grandson, as the most suitable successor to his grandfather, instead of the son of Tiberius' nephew, Gaius; as Philo says, "he had sided with the party of the real rather than the adopted children" (§9). So he had bet on the wrong horse, which was another reason for some anxiety in 37.[74]

From the six years he was *praefectus Aegypti* (32-38 CE), two inscriptions have been preserved in which he is mentioned, as well as two papyri, all of them of Egyptian provenance. In the inscriptions, *OGIS* 661 (=*CIG* 4716, *IGRR* I.1164, *SB* V.8329) and *OGIS* 669 (=*CIG* 4957, *IGRR* I.1263, *SB* V.8444), hardly more than his name is mentioned. The first one is a dedicatory inscription from a temple for Aphrodite in Dendera dating to the middle of the thirties of the first century CE, in which the dedication is said to have been done ἐπὶ Αὔλου Αὐιλλίου Φλάκκου ἡγεμόνος. The second one is a very long edict by Tiberius Julius Alexander from 68 CE, found in the oasis of Khargeh, in which this prefect of Egypt reminds the readers of the fact that one

---

[74] Sherwin-White 1972 finds this "a strange story" (820), and he adds, "it is difficult to see what part Flaccus can have played in advocating the claims of Gemellus during the last five years of Tiberius' principate. The whole notion is rendered improbable by his connection with Macro, who was then busy protecting the interests of Gaius against those of Gemellus" (821). It is, however, even more difficult to see why Philo would have made up this whole point when it could easily be falsified and other, more feasible explanations were available. Sherwin-White's own speculative explanation is "that Flaccus, after five years tenure of the prefecture, one of the longest in the history of the office, expected to be replaced in due course, and prepared to conciliate the most dangerous of his local enemies in order to forestall a malicious prosecution for maladministration" (825).

of his predecessors, namely Flaccus, seems to have been rather lenient as far as the levying of certain taxes was concerned (see line 26). The striking aspect of this decree is not so much the contents of the communication as the fact that here Philo's own nephew (Tiberius Julius Alexander was the son of his brother) mentions the arch-enemy of his uncle without even the slightest hint of criticism. But we should bear in mind here that Philo's nephew was an apostate from Judaism.[75]

As to the papyri, in *Pap. Boissier* 1[76] we find the text of an edict issued in 34 CE by Flaccus that prohibits the carrying of arms and limits the use of them to strictly circumscribed persons and groups in the Egyptian *chôra*. It was probably during a visit to Thebes that he discovered that large numbers of civilians possessed weaponry, and fearing revolt he took instant measures: a search for weapons was done and those that were found were brought by river and by land to Alexandria (the episode is referred to by Philo in *Flacc.* 92). In *P.Oxy* 1089 (= *CPJ* 154), one of the manuscripts of the so-called *Acts of the Alexandrian Martyrs*, Flaccus is presented as having a secret meeting in the Sarapieion with Isidorus and Dionysius, two of the leaders of the Alexandrian Jew-haters also mentioned by Philo (*Flacc.* 20 *et aliter*). However, not only is the papyrus full of lacunae and the text obscure, but also the story as far as it has been preserved is more of a novel than a historical document, as is the case with the other papyri containing fragments of the *Acts of the Alexandrian Martyrs*.[77] Finally there is an ostracon from 34 CE, a purchase-deed found in Thebes, in which Flaccus is only mentioned in passing as being present as the governor of that year.[78] So this non-literary material does not yield much useful information.

For the rest all we have to go by is Philo's *In Flaccum*, which informs us mainly about the final year of Flaccus' life (38-39 CE). If we leave aside most of what can reasonably be considered to be Philo's invention or interpretation or at least exaggeration, we are left with the following outline. Flaccus made a promising start as governor since he demonstrated that he had great ability in handling his responsibilities. In order to prevent political unrest he closed the

---

[75] See Burr 1955. For a recent edition of the two inscriptions with translation and commentary see Bernand 1992:I.126-136; II.141-153.
[76] Mitteis-Wilcken 1912: no. 13.
[77] See Musurillo 1954.
[78] Wilcken 1899:II no. 1372 = Mitteis-Wilcken 1912: no. 414.

clubs and associations and forbade the unlicensed possession of weapons. The situation began to change, however, after Caligula succeeded Tiberius in 37 CE. He became extremely nervous since he had supported Gemellus for this succession and also played a role in the prosecution of Caligula's mother. Moreover, the emperor had forced Flaccus' influential friend Macro, from whom he expected protection, to commit suicide. In this situation he was strongly advised by the leaders of the anti-Jewish Greeks in Alexandria to regain the emperor's favor by backing them in their actions against the Alexandrian Jews. Under this pressure Flaccus began to damage the interests the Jews, first by withholding their congratulatory letter to Gaius on the occasion of his succession, later by other means. Things got out of hand when, in the summer of 38, a friend of the emperor, Agrippa (I), who was the grandson of Herod the Great, visited Alexandria on his way to his new kingdom in Palestine that he had just received from Caligula. The Jews welcomed him warmly and asked him to pass on their letter of congratulation to Gaius that Flaccus had neglected to forward to him. But the enemies of the Jews staged a mock ceremony in which Agrippa was ridiculed. Instead of punishing the instigators of this insult to a friend of the emperor, Flaccus turned a blind eye. He then issued a decree to the effect that Jews were from now on to be regarded as foreigners without rights in the city. This marked the beginning of violence against the Jews, and Flaccus refrained from taking official cognisance of the disturbances. In the weeks or months that followed many Jews were maltreated, tortured or killed in the violence that was tolerated by Flaccus, who apparently thought it was in his personal interest. Some time later, however, in the autumn of 38, suddenly a small detachment of undercover troops arrived from Rome, sent by Caligula, to arrest Flaccus. He was brought to Rome where he stood trial — we do not know the charges (see the notes *ad* §147) — and the men who were his accusers turned out to be the leaders of the faction which had urged him to secure his position by letting them persecute the Jews. Flaccus was sentenced for deportation to the island of Andros and his property was confiscated. He was brought to the island by Roman soldiers. Somewhat later, Caligula decided that this fate was too mild a punishment and he ordered Flaccus (and other deportees as well) to be executed. This execution took place on the island of Andros in the spring of 39 CE.

Literature: Rohden 1896; Nicole 1898; Stein 1903; Mitteis-Wilcken 1913:22-24; Groag-Stein 1933:290; Balsdon 1934:129-134; Stein 1950: 26-28; Reinmuth 1956:528; Pelletier 1967:21-23; Kraus 1967:39-40 note 25; Sherwin-White 1972; Hennig 1974; Barraclough 1984:461-468; Bureth 1988:477; Kienast 1997 (Parker 2000 deals only with the meaning of the name Flaccus: 'lop-eared')

6. Previous scholarship

Major studies of *Flacc.* are few and far between. Apart from text editions (on which see below, §7), the most important works from the last century dealing with our treatise are the commentaries or annotated translations by Lewy 1935, Box 1939, Colson 1941, Gerschmann 1964, Pelletier 1967, Kraus 1967, and De Vries 1999.[79]

The only work from the period preceding the 20th century that deserves to be mentioned here is Delaunay 1867 (2nd ed. 1870). It is the most elaborate study of *Flacc.* and *Legat.* before 1900. The book consists of two parts: an almost 200-page introduction to the two historical treatises, and an almost 200 page annotated translation of them. In the lengthy introduction Delaunay deals first with Philo's life and works in general. Thereafter he turns to the historical writings more specifically and describes their contents and literary merits. The bulk of the introduction, however, is taken up by a description of the vicissitudinous fate of the Jews during the first 100 years of Roman rule, from Pompey till Caligula. Most of the introduction is completely outdated now. The translation of the two treatises and the explanatory notes do not contain surprises. The tone of the annotations is sometimes moralizing and condescending. Even though he regards Philo as a trustworthy historian, he ends the final note on *Flacc.* with the remark that "c'est un document précieux et inédit d'histoire où se révèle, en traits éloquents, le caractère vindicatif de la race juive" (270). The book has mainly antiquarian value.

Lewy 1935 is a small booklet (85 pages) which consists mainly of a German translation (and sometimes paraphrase) of a selection of passages from *Flacc.* and *Legat.*, preceded by a very brief introduction of 4 pages; it is meant for a non-scholarly readership. The title, "Von

---

[79] I have not been able to obtain or read the translations into modern Hebrew by Stein 1937 and Kasher in Daniel-Nataf 1986 and the recent Japanese translation by Hata 2000.

den Machterweisen Gottes," makes clear how Lewy understood the secondary title of *Legat.* in several manuscripts, περὶ ἀρετῶν. He emphasizes that Philo's message in his historical work (including the lost parts) is: "Alle vier Urheber der Verfolgungen: Sejan, Pilatus, Flaccus, Caligula, hatten nebst ihren Helfern im Laufe weniger Jahre ein schreckliches Ende gefunden" (7). Philo's treatises are a "großartige Demonstration eines Judentums, das seinen Platz in der Welt kannte und wahrte, und dessen innere Kraft ausreichte, um die schwerste Probe zu bestehen" (8). Someone who writes and publishes sentences like these in Berlin in 1935, surrounded by Nazis, is a man whose courage should not be underestimated (neither should that of his publisher, Schocken Verlag). One can only surmise that Lewy's motives for translating Philo's treatises in Germany in the Hitler period were more or less the same as Philo's own for writing them (cf. p. 10, "...die zeitlose Wirkung des Werkes, dessen Eindruck sich gerade geschichtsnahe Perioden wie die unsrige nicht entziehen können"). It is, therefore, *honoris causa* that I mention this book here.

Box 1939 was the first major commentary on *Flacc.* and after almost 65 years it still remains a fundamental work. Box prints Reiter's text (see §7) with his own translation on facing pages. It is preceded by a 50-page introduction and followed by a selective 65-page commentary on the Greek text. In the Introduction, Box deals in 8 chapters with all the major problems of Philo's treatise. In "Alexandria and Rome" (xiii-xviii), he sketches the strained relationship between the city and Rome since the fall of Cleopatra and Anthony in 30 BCE. Octavianus' victory "inaugurated an era of national humiliation" (xvi). The negative image of Alexandria in the Roman and Greek literature of the Empire is related to that tension. But "[i]f the Alexandrines were unstable, flippant, frivolous, superficial, it was because there was nothing for them on which to exercise their brains, except trade. Theirs was the tragedy of futility" (xvi). The anti-Roman sentiments come clearest to expression in the so-called *Acts of the Alexandrian Martyrs.* In "The Alexandrine Dispersion" (xviii-xxx), Box discusses at length the position of the Jews in the city. He describes the mostly harmonious relations with the Ptolemies, evidenced — inter alia — by the fact that often the highest military commands in the Ptolemaic armies were in Jewish hands. Rome's entry into Egyptian politics changed the situation drastically, however, because several times in the first century BCE the Jews supported the Romans against the Ptolemaic rulers. "The Jews fell away from the Ptolemies as soon as they realized that the fortunes of the dynasty were on the wane (...) and the deeply humiliated Alexandrines saw the Jews of the city favored by the Roman tyrants" (xix-xx). Small wonder that they were inclined to vent their anger upon the Jews with greater intensity because they could not direct it towards the Romans themselves. Box emphasizes that, after the publication of Claudius' rediscovered letter to the Alexandrians and Jews of that city (= *CPJ* 153), it is no longer possible to maintain that the Jews had Alexandrian citizenship. Some individual Jews may have had it, the majority did not, however, and that had been the situation since the first Ptolemies till early Imperial times. They formed a *politeuma* (see *Ep. Arist.* 310), a semi-autonomous corporation with its own constitution and officials (although Box doubts whether all Jews were indeed members of this *politeuma*, rightly so; see Lüderitz 1994, who argues that the *politeuma* was only the governing body of the community). The advent of Rome induced the Jews to strive for a formally higher status in the city, that of fully enfranchised citizens. This angered the Greek Alexandrians who were adamantly opposed to it, and Claudius' letter makes clear that the whole attempt on the part of the Jews was futile: the Jews live in a city "not their own," even though he guaranteed them all the rights for which he found evidence in the past. Box' next chapter, "Philo" (xxxi-xxxii), presents the meagre information we have about the author's life, and he also points out that "by a curious irony of history the renegade nephew of the author of *In Flaccum* (...) became prefect of Egypt (67-70) and in that capacity quelled with ruthless but statesmanlike severity a rising of the Alexandrian Jews against their Greek neighbours" (xxxii; see Josephus, *Bell.* 2.492-498).

In "In Flaccum" (xxxiii-xxxvii), Box deals with the relation between *Flacc.* and *Legat*: the complicated problem of the meaning of the very first word of *Flacc.*, δεύτερος (see the note *ad* §1 'Sejanus'), the confusing reports of Eusebius, John of Damascus, and Photius about the works (how many, five or more?) Philo wrote about the events in the years 38-41 CE, the variety of titles of our treatise in the manuscript tradition, and related problems are dealt with concisely but yet in remarkable detail. In the extremely short paragraph "Character of *In Flaccum*" (xxxviii), Box only states that he follows Reiter in that probably the overall title of Philo's five-volume work (of which *Flacc.* was the upbeat) was ἀρεταί, meaning "manifestations of God's power in saving His chosen people."He says that this word "gives us the key to Philo's conception of history."

In the chapter "The Conflict" (xxxviii-xlviii) Box argues that the real cause of the conflict was the Jewish attempt to obtain recognition of a claim to Alexandrian citizenship. Philo is unwilling to mention this cause since it ended in a debacle with Claudius' rebuff. Philo's own explanation is that the Greek leaders of the city, who had always hated the Jews, took advantage of the anxiety felt by Flaccus on the accession of Gaius whom he had very good reasons to fear, but Philo makes it hard for us to believe him fully since he does not explain the hatred of the Greeks. In "Sequel" (xlviii-liv) Box briefly summarizes the events of the period 38-41 CE, mainly on the basis of *Legat.* and Claudius' letter (*CPJ* 153), partly also on what can be trusted to reflect historical circumstances in the *Acts of the Alexandrian Martyrs*. Since this summary hardly deviates from our own (see above, the excursus at the end of §3), we will not summarize it here. In the final paragraph, "Summing Up" (liv-lvi), Box states that "the bloody conflict that broke out in Alexandria in the summer of 38 A.D. was traceable in the last analysis to the sinister repercussion on the imperial administration of the politics of the Roman court" (liv). But he now also states that Jewish monotheism, with its claim to be the chosen people of the one true God, could not go hand in hand with a claim to Alexandrian citizenship. "It was a selfish claim, an unneighbourly coveting of another's vineyard, an intrusion into a realm the spiritual structure of which they affected to abhor" (lv). But the eviction of the Jews who lived outside the original Jewish quarter (a natural result of three centuries of growth of the Jewish community) "was as unneighbourly as the Jewish claim to Alexandrian citizenship" (lvi).

Box's commentary is characterized by its special attention for papyrological and epigraphic evidence that sheds light upon historical problems raised by Philo's text. In this respect it remains unsurpassed and of lasting value, even though it is based upon a state of knowledge that is now outdated. The only real flaw of the book is that the commentary is rather uneven: some paragraphs of Philo's work receive detailed attention, whereas others are simply skipped, even when there is ample reason for comment. The reader of the present commentary will notice that Box is the scholar most often referred to, which is to be taken as a testimony to the great achievement of this commentator.

Colson's Loeb Classical Library edition plus translation with notes was published very shortly after Box's edition (in 1941). The text printed is that of Reiter in the Cohn-Wendland edition with only a handful of variant readings. In a short introduction (7 pages) Colson mainly summarizes the contents of the treatise. It is only on the final page that he gives his personal opinion on Philo's treatise, which deserves to be quoted in full: "It is a powerful embodiment of that profound conviction that the nation is under the special Providence of God which has been the life and soul of Judaism throughout the centuries. This conviction naturally entails a belief that the enemies of Judaism are the enemies of God and their punishment a divine visitation. But this belief has its evil side, which seems to me to be very strongly exhibited in this treatise. In § 117 the Jews are represented as saying, 'We do not rejoice at the punishment of an enemy because we have been taught by the Holy Laws to have human sympathy.' This is easily said but not so easily done, and if Philo believed that he himself had learnt this lesson I think he deceived himself. He gloats over the misery of Flaccus in his fall, exile, and death, with a vindictiveness which I feel to be repulsive. (...) This is the only [treatise] which those who admire the beauty and spirituality so often shown both in the Commentary and Exposition might well wish to have been left unwritten" (301).

Colson's explanatory notes are very succinct as compared to those of Box and they mainly concern text-critical, grammatical and semantic matters, but he deals with some of the more important issues in the Appendix (531-538). There we find information about major figures such as Sejanus, Agrippa, Drusilla, Isidorus; but some of the major philological problems are dealt with as well, especially where Colson disagrees with Box. In his preface, Colson states that Box's commentary "is on a scale which I could not attempt to rival" (ix), and he says that many of his own notes are largely founded on Box's work.

Pelletier (1967) too prints Reiter's text, with a French translation on facing pages. There are 30 pages of introduction in which Pelletier deals with the nature of the treatise ("C'est une arétalogie," 17), which he sees as patterned on the book of Esther and 2 Maccabees (Flaccus being the new Haman, Antiochus Epiphanes, and Nicanor); the historical value of the book, which he regards to be high ("il faut seulement tenir compte des inévitables déformations de l'éloquence chez les historiens de l'époque," 19); the main actors in the story (Flaccus, Gaius, Agrippa, Macro, Isidorus, Lampo); and finally the political situation of the Jews in Alexandria. Here, as well as in his notes, Pelletier heavily leans upon Box; sometimes he simply translates Box's notes (which he fairly indicates by an asterisk). But maybe Mary Smallwood's judgement is too harsh when she says, "On the whole this is a disappointing book, but Pelletier's task was a very difficult one when most of his thunder had been stolen thirty years ago [sc., by Box]" (Smallwood 1968:259), for at many places Pelletier adds new explanatory notes, and in general his interpretative remarks are much more elaborate than Colson's. He, too, has an appendix with 16 'notes complémentaires' and 4 excurses on a wide variety of topics, all of them very valuable. Reference will be duly made to most of them in my own commentary.

In the same year as Pelletier's commentary, the Italian scholar Clara Kraus (-Reggiani) published a major monograph on both *Flacc.* and *Legat.* (Kraus 1967). It is basically a translation of both treatises into Italian with a substantial introduction of some 160 pages instead of explanatory notes. Her study has a special background in that she was inspired to write this book by her own experiences during the Second World War. In her Introduction she states: "Ogni particolare del testo filoniano trova un parallelo perfettamente adeguato nei documenti storici e nelle trasposizioni drammatiche che testimoniano della persecuzione nazionalsocialistica" (10). It makes her critical of suggestions that Philo has exaggerated the degree of atrocity. After a brief sketch of the life and thoughtworld of Philo, Kraus presents a 20-page analysis of *Flacc.*, the most important part of which is her investigation of and emphasis on the central role of *dikê* and *pronoia* in *Flacc.*: *dikê* (*justitia punitiva*) in God's confronting the persecutor and *pronoia* (*providentia*) in God's care for the persecuted. After a similar analysis of *Legat.*, there is a chapter on the composition and structure of both historical treatises. Here Kraus deals with the problem of the relationship between *Flacc.* and *Legat.* and the question of whether there were more (now lost) writings by Philo, dealing with Sejanus and the death of Gaius, and with the problem of the title(s). No new solutions are proposed, but the evidence is presented and there is a useful criticul discussion of the confused and confusing evidence in Eusebius (both in his *Chronicon* and in the *Historia Ecclesiastica*). Kraus does, however, offer a new interpretation of the *palinôdia* in *Legat.* 373: in Philo's view a *palinôdia* is always the result of *metanoia* (repentance, conversion); so the lost book (or chapters) with the *palinôdia* must have contained a story of Gaius' repentance about the injustice and evil he had inflicted upon the Jews, thus creating a perfect parallellism with *In Flaccum* where Flaccus, too, utters a *palinôdia* in §§170-175 recognizing the righteousness of God's punishment for his misdeeds. This seems a very probable suggestion indeed. In a chapter called 'Interpretations' (111-140), Kraus deals with a variety of topics, among which the following receive the most attention: the dating of the embassy to Gaius, comparison of data from Philo with those in the *Acts of the Alexandrian Martyrs*, the independence of *Flacc.* vis-à-vis *Legat.* and vice versa, and the relationship between Philo's philosophical and politico-historical writings. Finally she discusses the well-known problem of whether or not the Jews had full Alexandrian citizenship (most of them did not, only a happy few did). Thereafter follows the (non-annotated) Italian translation of both treatises. Even though this book does not offer striking new insights, it is a thorough study of the major issues in both Philonic treatises.

The most recent annotated translation is that by a Dutch historian of antiquity, De Vries (1999; it also contains the *Legatio*). In a 30 page introduction De Vries presents a brief sketch of the historical circumstances in Alexandria during the years 38-41 CE, with special attention to the position of the Jews in the city. He also briefly discusses the phenomenon of ancient Jew-hatred. The main protagonists of the drama (Flaccus, Caligula, Agrippa) are dealt with as well. Under the title "Pogrom in Alexandrië" a rather free but eminently readable Dutch translation is offered, followed by 15 pages of short explanatory notes, mainly of a historical nature. What gives the book a special value is the large appendix (70 pages) in which De Vries presents (in Dutch translation) a wide selection of ancient texts that are relevant to the understanding of both *Flacc.* and *Legat.* Papyri, inscriptions, biblical passages, Strabo's description of Alexandria, many chapters from Josephus, Cassius Dio, Tacitus, Suetonius, but also from the Talmud and midrashic works are presented here in translation, with annotations added.

Finally we will briefly pass in review only a selection of the most important short studies in the form of articles or chapters in books, all of them published in the past 15 years.

Bergmann-Hoffmann 1987 deal with *Flacc.* as a source for the study of the political dimensions of the conflict in 38 CE, which they argue are the most important ones. They view the situation as one of a conflict of interests and as a situation of political competition between Greeks and Jews. The whole conflict was a matter of power struggle and of purposeful political action. For that reason the Alexandrian clubs or associations that formed the political centre of the Greek *polis* played a crucial role in the riots. Anti-Semitism was not the cause but the result of this conflict of interest. Philo's view that "innate hatred" on the part of the non-Jews played a major role is a distortion of the factual situation. The Greeks simply were adamantly opposed to the Jewish wish for greater political rights and power. Religion played hardly a role in the conflict.

Severe criticism of this interpretation of the events came from Schäfer 1997:136-160 (esp. 156-160). He argues that this approach is very problematic and accuses the authors of downplaying evidence that points in the direction of 'Judaeophobia' among the population of Alexandria at large. Schäfer opines that when Philo speaks of Alexandrians he means first and foremost the native Egyptians, only in the second instance the Greeks. The Jews became their victims when Caligula's accession disturbed the balance of power in Alexandria. Not that the Jews were only passive players, for the events around Agrippa's visit prove that they tried to turn this into a political advantage. Flaccus' edict seems to have pertained to "the most essential elements of the social and political life of the Jews in Alexandria" (144). Whatever the civic status of the Jews before 38 may have been, "it becomes clear that the Alexandrians succeeded in changing radically the delicate and complicated balance between the different ethnic factions in Alexandria; Flaccus' decree is taken as a charter for anti-Jewish riots and paves the way for horrible massacres" (144). Philo's message is that more than the Greeks it is the Egyptians "who represent the hotbed of anti-Jewish resentment" (145). This is to be explained against the background of centuries of hate-mongering by Alexandrian writers who published ever more glaring anti-Jewish stories in which the Jews were painted as criminals and the archenemies of not only the Egyptians but of humankind as a whole. So even though the conflict between Jews, Greeks, and Egyptians was first and foremost a political conflict, it is naive to separate this from the cultural-religious aspects of the conflict. "Cultural-religious and political aspects were inextricably interwoven in the conflict in Alexandria, and it is precisely this amalgam of political goals and (mainly) Egyptian hatred of the Jews which makes it unique and may allow us to speak of Alexandrian anti-Semitism" (160).

Kraus 1994 (not the same person as Kraus 1967) argues that it is improbable that an author who spent most of his time in interpreting the Bible from a philosophical point of view would suddenly cease to be a philosopher when he wrote about historical events and, therefore, "the classification of *In Flaccum* as an historical work obscures reasons for a philosophical reading of Philo's narrative" (478). Philo's emphasis on God's providence and his assumption that character and politics are intertwined illustrate this. Moreover, "the relationship between God and the ideal character of government indicates that Philo's philosophy informs his politics" (479). Philo's philosophical world-view governs his interpretation of current historical events, and that is why he constructed an exact symmetry between the suffering of the Jews and the punishment of Flaccus. It is especially in his rendering of Flaccus' inner monologues and his prayers (which Philo could not have known) that the Jewish thinker reveals his philosophy of divine juistice and retribution.

Alston 1997 observes that, according to *Flacc.*, during the persecutions the Jews were excluded from public space but that exactly the same happened to Flaccus after his deportation. This symmetry demonstrates that God's justice was at work. A detailed list of parallels demonstrates that in Philo's 'diptych' the parallellism has the function to underscore the operation of justice. So the best and only defence of the Jews was to rely on God.

Meiser 1999 classifies *Flacc.* as a work of 'mimetic historiography,' a genre the purpose of which is to present the events in such a way as to influence the readers and to encourage them to act accordingly. The target audience, therefore, was not Jewish but pagan readers (426-9). Flaccus' speeches at Andros make these readers aware of the punishing providence of the God of the Jews. So they better change their ways of treating the Jews.

In a recent contribution, Peder Borgen (2000) regards this treatise as not just a historical work but as 'interpreted history.' After summarizing the positions of Kraus, Meiser, and Alston, he presents a list of similarities between *Flacc.* and other writings of Philo. For instance the motif of leaders and nations going beyond human limits by exalting themselves above men and nature and consequently being thrown down by God occurs in several writings by Philo, as it does in *Flacc.*, so too sharp a distinction between *Flacc.* and his other writings should not be drawn. Other similarities as well "support the view that Philo has applied Pentateuchal principles, as understood and formulated by him, to his interpretation of historical events in *Against Flaccus*" (49). Borgen claims that in *Flacc.*, too, Philo interprets the Mosaic laws as the community laws of the Jews; see for instance the violation of the customs relative to the synagogue when Flaccus permitted the installation of statues of the emperor in them (§§41-53), or the scene with the forcible eating of pork by Jewish women (§96). The events themselves "needed somehow to be interpreted within the context of Jewish laws which were a manifestation of God's cosmic law" (52). The implication is that Philo had a dual audience in mind, both Jews and non-Jews. Borgen then compares the way Antiochus IV is described in 2 Macc. with Philo's picture of Flaccus (suggested already by Pelletier 1967:16-19). Both were punished for their persecution of the Jews and repented, but in vain; their divine death sentences were carried out even so (Antiochus' letter to the Jews in 2 Macc. 9 is the parallel to Flaccus' prayer in §§170-174). By examining similarities and differences between *Flacc.* and other Jewish writings, Philo's treatise can be understood within a broader context.

In the most recent contribution to the study of *Flacc.*, Gruen (2002:54-83) argues in a detailed exposition that Philo is unconvincing when he tries to portray Flaccus as the arch villain. "Philo's narrative itself undermines his own portrait, one guided more by dramatic needs (a story culminating in Flaccus' fall and repentance) than by history. Flaccus' insecurities after the loss of his patrons in Rome, his anxieties about alienating constituencies in Alexandria, and the need to fend off pressures from militant Alexandrians and lobbying by Jewish leaders, while maintaining a semblance of order in the city lest he be denounced to the authorities at home, created a bundle of tensions that the prefect never successfully negotiated. (...) His tenure collapsed through ineptitude rather than malice" (60). The real culprits were the Greek leaders (Isidorus c.s.) whom Flaccus had made into his enemies by his measures against their associations or clubs (*Flacc.* 4). "The[se] prodders endeavored to create disturbances that could demonstrate the incompetence of the prefect" (61). Flaccus, who was nervous after Gaius' accession and in need of influential support, went along with the anti-Jewish attacks but events spiraled out of his control and "the hapless governor had to take the blame" (61). Isidorus *cum suis* now bribed demonstrators to hurl public abuse at Flaccus, and as a countermeasure the governor set up a tribunal which resulted in the flight of the instigators of the riots (*Flacc.* 137-145). But it was already too late. In the meantime information about the riots had reached Gaius, who had Flaccus arrested and brought back to Rome where his erstwhile "friends" now seized the opportunity to denounce him, which finally led to his condemnation.

Gruen makes the suggestion that Isidorus c.s. "may well have been behind the initial denunciations that led to Flaccus' removal to Rome" (61). But all this, says Gruen, does not yet account sufficiently for the scale and the viciousness of the attacks on the Jews. There is more to it. Gruen argues that so far research has been focussing too much on the Greeks as the antagonists of the Jews in Alexandria. It is much more probable that it was the unprivileged underclass of the Egyptians in the city that seized this opportunity to vent their frustrations on the privileged Jews. It is exactly for that reason that Philo speaks of the deep-rooted hostility of rank and file Egyptians (*Flacc.* 29). So it is wrong when scholars explain Philo's censuring the Egyptians as the culprits as nothing but a deliberate insult to the Alexandrian Greeks by lumping them with Egyptians, because that fails to account for the fact that Philo sometimes sharply distinguishes between Alexandrians and Egyptians (280-1 note 74). Josephus, too, singles out the Egyptians as the principal antagonists of the Jews, and so did the authors of *Or. Sib.* 3, *Sap. Sal.*, *Jos. et As.*, and *3 Macc.* "Certain Greek malcontents may have set matters in motion, prodding Flaccus into actions that would discredit him and providing the outlet for pent-up passions among the populace to explode on the scene; but the pent-up passions belonged primarily to Egyptians rather than to the Greeks" (65). Also the sequel of the story, the ways in which Gaius and Claudius dealt with the conflict, does not give proof of anti-Jewish animosity on the part of these rulers, only irritation. Like the Greeks, the Romans were amused or surprised about or indifferent towards the Jews, not hostile. For whatever reasons, it was the Egyptians who evinced hatred of the Jews. In a very detailed argument that cannot be summarized here Gruen also argues that the much-debated matter of whether or not the Jews had or strove after citizenship in Alexandria is a non-issue: They did not have it, they did not try to get it, it was totally irrelevant to them, and it had nothing to do with the outburst of violence in 38. The pogrom of that year was an exceptional event. On the whole one could say that the Jewish community of Alexandria flourished for nearly four full centuries (from the founding of the city at the beginning of the Ptolemaic era to the outburst of the great war of in 66 CE). "The dreadful pogrom of 38 in no way defines or exemplifies the history of Jews in Alexandria" (83).[80]

---

[80] Since Gruen's work was published only when the manuscript of the present book was practically completed, the debate with Gruen's interpretation in my

Looking back, we can say without exaggeration that Box's commentary of 1939 is the most fundamental work that has been published on *Flacc.* in the 20th century. It is, however, inevitably out of date in several respects since it reflects the state of research of 65 years ago. A new commentary that incorporates knowledge and insights won in those years is, therefore, a *desideratum*.

7. The text of the treatise

The manuscript tradition of the Greek text of *Flacc.* has been described in admirable detail by Reiter in the Prolegomena (in Latin) to vol. 6 of the standard edition by Cohn-Wendland (Reiter 1915; but see also Cohn 1896). The reader is referred to that publication for full information. It is also Reiter's text edition in the same volume that forms the basis of our translation. All later editions of *Flacc.* are based on Reiter's excellent edition (with minor deviations) and no new textual evidence has come to light in the meantime. Where I depart from his text, on the basis of data from his own *apparatus criticus*, will be noted in footnotes to the translation and in the commentary. Since there is no need to repeat what every interested student can read in Reiter's 40-page textual study, I will present the reader only with a brief summary of the textual evidence.

There are only five manuscripts that contain the text of *Flacc.*: M, A, G, H, and L (on which see below). In some of the other codices containing works of Philo one sometimes finds short excerpts or citations from *Flacc.*, but these hardly yield materials important for the constitution of the text. In the 11 excerpts from *Flacc.* in the *Sacra Parallella* of John of Damascus, the majority of the variant readings are inferior, only occasionally do they offer a text that is superior to that in the manuscripts (see, for instance, the note on 'documents' in §131). Sometimes they support the only manuscript or a minority of manuscripts with the correct reading over against the others. (The same applies to the quotations in medieval gnomologies which are mainly based upon the *Sacra Parallella*.) There is one place, however, where John of Damascus quotes a passage ἐκ τῶν κατὰ Φλάκκον [sic] that is not to be found in any of the extant manuscripts:

οὐκ ἔστι παρὰ θεῷ οὔτε πονηρὸν ὄντα ἀπολέσαι τὸν ἀγαθὸν μισθὸν περὶ ἑνὸς ἀγαθοῦ μετὰ πλειόνων κακῶν πεπραγμένου οὔτε πάλιν ἀγαθὸν

commentary could only be very limited.

ὄντα ἀπολέσαι τὴν κόλασιν καὶ μὴ λαβεῖν αὐτὴν εἰ μετὰ πλειόνων ἀγαθῶν ἕν τι γένηται πονηρόν· ἀνάγκη γὰρ ζυγῷ καὶ σταθμῷ πάντα ἀποδιδόναι τὸν θεόν (with God it is neither possible that a bad person does not receive his good recompense for the one good thing he did amidst of a majority of bad things nor that a good person would escape and not receive punishment if among the majority of his good acts there is one bad act; for it is of necessity the case that in all instances God pays recompense in balance and fairness).

It is very hard to say where in *Flacc.* this passage could have belonged. If, however, John of Damascus is right that these sentences are from *Flacc.* — and we have no way of knowing it for sure — we have to assume that the treatise as it has come down to us is incomplete. And according to some scholars there are other reasons to assume this as well.

One of these reasons is the abrupt and strange transition between §§ 28 and 29 which has been taken by some scholars to imply that there is a gap in the text here. That is, however, not compelling (see my note *ad locum*). Others have interpreted the way Philo begins the book as presented in the manuscripts as implying that something now lost preceded it. The words Δεύτερος μετὰ Σηιανὸν Φλάκκος κτλ. seem to suggest that the story about Flaccus' persecution of the Jews was only the sequel to a similar story about Sejanus. And the same seems to be implied at the end of the book, where Philo says "Such were the sufferings of Flaccus, too (τοιαῦτα καὶ Φλάκκος ἔπαθε)," another reference to a lost story about Sejanus. But this need not imply the loss of text of passages in *Flacc.* It more probably implies loss of a separate book, or a part of a book, in which Philo described Sejanus' activities.[81] Finally, in §76 Philo says that the enormous scale of Flaccus' aggression has been fully proved "by other evidence" but this translation of δι' ἑτέρων is uncertain (see my note *ad locum*) and, even if the translation proves correct, it does not necessarily imply that someplace else in the text there are lacunae (*pace* Box 1939: xxxiii note 1). So the only weighty reason to assume that the text of *Flacc.* has not been preserved integrally is the quote from John of Damascus. But John may simply be mistaken. It is impossible to solve this problem.

Now back to the manuscripts themselves. Reiter reckons M and G to the category of superior codices, judges A to take a middle position, and relegates H and L to the inferior category. Although M

---

[81] See above (pp. 5-6) and Morris 1973/87:859-860.

and G are the best witnesses, G is not complete for it has a large lacuna halfway. Ms. M, from Florence, which is our best complete witness (see Reiter 1915:liv-lv), dates to the beginning of the 13th century; ms. G, from the Vatican, is from the 14th century; ms. A, from München, dates from the 13th century; ms. H, from Venice, is from the 14th century; and ms. L, from Paris, dates to the first half of the 16th century. So all major mss. were produced in the period between 1200 and 1550. However reliable the mss. M and G may be regarded to be, the reader should realize that there is a time gap of at least some 11 or 12 centuries between Philo's autograph and the copies we use to reconstruct this autograph; and unfortunately we don't have any early papyri of *Flacc.* that enable us to check modern reconstructions against evidence more ancient than our oldest manuscripts. Even so there is no reason to despair about the reconstruction of a relatively reliable text of Philo. In the case of many other authors from antiquity the textual tradition is often considerably less favorable. The meticulous analysis of the manuscript tradition by Cohn and Reiter can still be relied upon.

8. *The present commentary*

In the new translation offered here I heavily lean upon those of Box and Colson, although I have tried to steer clear of the somewhat archaic parlance found in their renderings. When Philo's sentences are cumbersome because of their length, I often have cut them into two or three parts to make them more readable, and I have also avoided — if possible — the many participial constructions Philo uses, although otherwise I have striven after a rendering as literal as possible. But I can only agree with the author of volume 1 in this series when he states that "it is well-nigh impossible to render the meaning of a text both accurately and fluently, and still capture something of the style and flavour of the original."[82] The truth of the Italian proverb 'traduttore traditore' (a translator is a traitor) was constantly felt by the present translator.

The commentary does not aim to be exhaustive. The reader is offered in a concise manner what the commentator thinks is necessary for or conducive to a better understanding of Philo's text. When sometimes the reader is referred to Box or one of the other earlier commentators for more details, the essential information has never-

---

[82] Runia 2001:44.

theless been presented in the present commentary. Discussions of philological and stylistic matters and references to scholarly literature have of necessity been selective. The differences in style and format with the previous commentary in this series (Runia 2001) have for the most part been dictated by the very different nature of the treatise concerned.

A Note on 'Nachleben'

An important feature of the *Philo of Alexandria Commentary Series* (PACS) is the attention paid to the *Nachleben* of each individual treatise. In his commentary on *Opif.*, David Runia not only deals with its *Nachleben* in general in the Introduction, but also every section of the commentary closes with a paragraph on the influence that section of the treatise exercised on later ancient authors. The present commentary is different also in that respect. The simple reason for that difference is that, in contradistinction to most other treatises of Philo, *In Flaccum* had hardly any *Nachleben* in antiquity at all. Josephus' strikingly brief reference to the riots in Alexandria — in *Ant.* 18:257 he spends 11 words on these events, Philo more than 11,000 — may or may not be based on *Flacc.*, we simply do not know. Josephus generally does not show acquaintance with Philo's work (but see Runia 2002:222), and his neglect of the pogrom of 38 CE reinforces the impression that he did not know *In Flaccum*. In the section on genre I drew a parallel between Philo's treatise and Lactantius' *De mortibus persecutorum*, but again we have to conclude that, in spite of remarkable thematic agreement between the two works, there is no reason at all to assume that Lactantius knew or was influenced by Philo. As we saw in the first chapter of this Introduction, in his *Hist. Eccl.* 2.5 Eusebius briefly mentions Philo's report of the events in 38-40 (although there only the *Legatio* is mentioned by name) in his short description of the reign of Caligula, and he repeats that information in his *Chron. ad Ol. 204*, Tiberius 21 (although there he does mention the treatise by name, but cf. *Hist. Eccl.* 2.18.8). Syncellus repeats this information in his excerpts from Eusebius (*Ecl. Chron.* ed. Mosshammer p. 399, cf. p.402) as does Photius (*Bibl.* cod. 105 ed. Henry II p.72). Finally there are some unidentified quotes from *Flacc.* in John of Damascus (see Introd. ch. 7). That is all.[83]

---

[83] These texts have been conveniently assembled (and translated into Italian) in Runia-Radice 1999:378-380, 434, 436.

Nowhere else do we find a more extensive reflection on the contents of the work or any other sign of influence.[84] It is Philo's allegorical exegetical treatises that won the day, not his "historical" works.

---

[84] It is striking that the first Jewish author to devote attention to Philo since antiquity, the Italian scholar Azariah de' Rossi in his work *Me'or eynayim* of 1572, quotes numerous passages from Philo's treatises but none from *Flacc*; see Weinberg 2001:783-785.

TRANSLATION OF *IN FLACCUM*[1]

On Flaccus

I. *Flaccus' Persecution of the Jews*

§§1-7 *Flaccus' Promising Start*

(1) After Sejanus it was Avillius Flaccus who continued his policy of persecuting the Jews. Even though he was not in the same position as Sejanus to wrong the entire (Jewish) people openly in that he had less resources and occasions to do so, yet he inflicted irreparable evils upon all who came within his reach. But in addition to that, even though he seemed to attack only a part (of our people), as a matter of fact he extended his schemes, more by means of craft than of power, and tried to bring everyone everywhere within his field of fire. For those who are by nature tyrannical but do not have power at their disposal, employ cunning wiles in order to achieve their malignant designs.

(2) This Flaccus then, who was reckoned among the friends of the emperor Tiberius, was appointed as the prefect of Alexandria and the country round about it after the death of Hiberus, who had been the prefect of Egypt. Initially, this man (Flaccus) gave innumerable proofs of his excellence, as far as appearance went. For he was prudent, persevering, acute in devising and carrying out his plans, very eloquent and quick at understanding what was left unsaid better even than what was said.

(3) At any rate, in a short time he became acquainted with Egyptian affairs, and these are complex and diversified, hardly grasped even by those who have made it their task to study them from their early years. His secretaries were a superfluous crowd since everything, whether trivial or important, was within the reach of his own experience. He not only surpassed them but also, because of his accuracy, he became the master instead of the student of his former teachers.

---

[1] At only five places I adopt a reading different from Reiter's text in the standard edition by Cohn-Wendland. These places have been indicated and the text-critical problems are discussed in the commentary.

(4) All matters pertaining to financial accountancy and the administration of revenues were dealt with competently by him, but, however important and vital these matters were, they yet did not in any way give hint of the fact that he had the soul of a leader. But the qualities that did indicate (his possession of) a more illustrious and kingly nature, those he demonstrated with greater freedom. For instance, he used to walk with stateliness, for ostentation is always very useful for a ruler. He used to judge important cases in cooperation with the magistrates, he pulled down the arrogant, and he always prevented a motley crowd of people from all quarters from conspiring. He also prohibited the clubs and associations which were continually feasting together under pretext of sacrifices, whereas in fact they behaved like inebriates, and he dealt severely and vigorously with those who refused to obey him.

(5) Thereafter, when he had established law and order throughout the city and the country, he proceeded in turn to concentrate his attention on the armed forces, by setting them in array and disciplining them, and by training the infantry, the cavalry, and the light-armed soldiers. He also taught the commanders not to deprive the soldiers of their pay because by doing so they would instigate them to acts of bandritry and robbery, and (he taught) each of the soldiers not to meddle with affairs that fell outside their military service but to keep in mind that they were also appointed to be a peace-keeping force.

(6) Perhaps someone will say now, "My dear fellow, you have decided to accuse a person only to bring no charge whatsoever against him but, on the contrary, weave a long string of praises! Have you lost your mind and gone mad?" No, I have not gone mad, dear friend, neither am I a fool who is unable to see what a consistent argument is. (7) I praise Flaccus not because it is the right thing to praise an enemy but in order to enable myself to expose his wickedness even more clearly. Pardon is usually given to someone who sins through ignorance of what is better, but someone who does wrong knowingly has no excuse but is already condemned by the tribunal of his own conscience.

§§8-20 *Flaccus' Degeneration*

(8) For when he had received the prefecture for a period of six years, in the first five years — that is, when the emperor Tiberius was still alive — he not only maintained peace but also functioned as a

governor with such energy and vigour that he surpassed all his predecessors.

(9) But in his last year, after Tiberius had died and Gaius been appointed emperor, his grip began to slacken and he began to let everything slip from his hands. It may have been caused by his profound sorrow over Tiberius, for from his continuous state of dejection and the endless stream of tears that poured without interruption from him as from a fountain it was clear that he was really deeply grieved as if he had lost his closest friend. It may also have been due to the fact that he cherished animosity towards (Tiberius') successor, either because he had sided with the party of the real rather than the adopted children, or — still another possibility — because he was one of those who had conspired against Gaius' mother in the time that she was accused of matters which led to her execution. So it was also fear of being held guilty that caused his neglect of duties.

(10) For some time he still could summon the power to prevent the affairs of state from slipping entirely out of his hands. When, however, he heard that Tiberius' grandson and his partner in government had been killed at Gaius' command, he was struck by an indescribable sense of misfortune and threw himself on the ground and lay there speechless, with a mind that had been enfeebled and paralysed already long before [?]. (11) For as long as the child was still alive, he could still cherish the sparks of hope of his own survival, but now that it was dead, it seemed that his personal hope had died with it, even though a little breeze of protection might still be blowing, namely, his friendship with Macro, who initially had an all-powerful position with Gaius and whose contribution to his rise to power — and still more to his safety — is said to have been greater than anyone else's.

(12) Tiberius had often considered the possibility of getting Gaius out of the way since he regarded him as a malicious person who was not gifted by nature for the exercise of rulership, but also out of concern for his grandson, for he feared that his own death would imply that his grandson would be got rid of (by Gaius) as well. Macro had often discarded these suspicions and praised Gaius as an honest, harmless and sociable person and someone so strongly aware of his inferiority to his cousin that he would be glad to yield the supreme rulership to him alone, or at any rate the first place in everything.

(13) Deceived as he was by these words, he (Tiberius) did not notice that he left behind him an irreconcilable enemy of himself, his grandson, his family, Macro the intercessor, and the rest of humanity. (14) For when Macro saw that he went astray and let his unbridled impulses have their way, wherever and in whatever way, he would admonish and reprove him, supposing that he was still the same Gaius who during Tiberius' life had been reasonable and docile. But, to his misfortune, he paid the highest penalty for his excessive goodwill and was murdered with his whole family, wife and children, as if he were a superfluous burden and a nuisance. (15) For whenever he (Gaius) saw from afar that he (Macro) was coming to him, he used to say the following to his company: "Let us not smile, let us look downcast. There comes the censor, the strict moralist, the person who has now begun to act as a tutor of an adult man who is the emperor, and that precisely at a moment when the tutors from my early youth have been dismissed and sent away."

(16) When Flaccus realized that he (Macro) too had been put to death, he completely lost the hope that had still been left, and he was no longer able to take to hand public affairs as he used to do, for he was totally exhausted and lost control of his mind.

(17) But when a ruler begins to despair of his capacity to exercise authority, it is inevitable that his subjects immediately start a rebellion, particularly those who have a natural penchant for working themselves into a state of excitement over trivialities and ordinary occurrences. Among this kind of people the Egyptian nation holds pride of place, since it is its custom to let the tiniest spark swell into great seditions.

(18) Having come into an impossible blind-alley situation, Flaccus began to behave erratically and, in parallel with the deterioration of his reasoning capacity, he changed all of his recent policy, beginning with those who were nearest to him. Those who were well-disposed towards him and his most sincere friends, he suspected and drove away, but those who had been his declared enemies from the beginning, he reconciled himself to and made them his advisers in every matter.

(19) These, however, were rancorous people, and what seemed to be a reconciliation was a counterfeit, existing only in words; in reality they cherished in their hearts an implacable enmity against him, and although they were only feigning genuine friendship, like actors do in a theatre, they managed to carry him away completely. Thus

the ruler became a subject and the subjects became leaders. They advanced the most harmful proposals and had them immediately ratified. (20) For they became guarantors of all their own plans and, as in a theatre play, they put him (Flaccus) on stage as no more than a masked dummy with the title 'government' inscribed upon it, merely for show, they themselves being nothing but a bunch of popularity-hunters such as Dionysius, document-tamperers such as Lampo, sedition-leaders such as Isidorus, meddlers, devisers of evils, "city-troublemakers." This was the way he (Flaccus) exercised the title (of ruler).

§§21-24 *Flaccus Begins to Injure the Jews*

(21) All of them united in developing a plot that was most grievous to the Jewish community. In a private conversation with Flaccus they said: (22) "Gone are the expectations you had of the boy Tiberius Nero; gone too is your next hope, your friend Macro, and what you can expect from the emperor does not look very favorable either. For this reason, we have to find a very powerful intercessor by whom Gaius may be propitiated. (23) That intercessor is the city of Alexandria, which has been honored from the beginning by the entire imperial family, especially by the present master. Intercede it will, if it receives some present from you. And you can give it no greater bonus than by handing over and abandoning the Jews."

(24) Upon hearing these things, he should have angrily rejected the speakers as revolutionaries and public enemies, but instead he agreed with what they said. Initially, the schemes he plotted (against the Jews) were less evident, for instance, not giving an impartial and equal hearing to parties involved in conflicts and inclining more to one side than another. In other matters he did not allow equal freedom of speech to both parties, but whenever Jews approached him, he turned away from them, and it was only towards them that he showed this unpleasant behaviour. Later, however, he exhibited his ill-will openly as well.

§§25-35 *King Agrippa*

(25) His insanity, which was due to instruction from others rather than to his own nature, was further aggravated by the following incident. The emperor Gaius gave Agrippa, the grandson of king Herod, as his kingdom a third of his grandfather's inheritance, of which Philip the tetrarch, his paternal uncle, used to enjoy the usufruct.

(26) When Agrippa was about to leave, Gaius advised him not to make the voyage to Syria via Brindisium, because that made for a long and tiresome trip, but to wait for the trade winds and then take the shorter route via Alexandria. He said that the trading vessels that departed from there were very fast and had highly experienced pilots, who guided their ships like charioteers driving their race-horses, keeping them straight and on course. Agrippa complied with this advice because Gaius was his master but also because it seemed that the advice he had been given was useful.

(27) He went down to Dicaearchia and when he saw there ships from Alexandria lying at anchor and ready to sail, he embarked with his retinue. He had a prosperous voyage, and after only a few days he arrived at his destination without anybody expecting him or finding out that he was there. He commanded the pilots to furl the sails — for in the late afternoon Pharos had come into sight — and to remain offshore in the immediate neighbourhood until the late evening, and then by night to enter the harbor in order that he could disembark when everybody was asleep and get to the house of his host without anyone seeing him.

(28) The reason for such an unobtrusive arrival was that he wished, if possible, to get out of town again without anybody there having noticed. As a matter of fact, he had not come to Alexandria to sight-see as he had visited it before, when he was on his way to Rome to see Tiberius. The only reason he was there was to take a shortcut home.

(29) But envy is an inborn characteristic of the Egyptians, and they regard anyone else's good luck as their own bad luck, which is the reason why they were bursting with envy. At the same time, in their ancient and, in a sense, innate enmity towards the Jews, they were vexed by the idea that a Jew had become a king, which was to them as if each of them had been deprived of an ancestral kingdom.

(30) So, poor Flaccus was again incited by his companions, who stimulated and provoked him into the same state of envy as their own. They said, "The visit of this man here means your own downfall! He has been invested with a greater dignity of honor and prestige than you have. He is attracting the attention of all men by the sight of his spear-carrying army of bodyguards with their weapons adorned with silver and gold. (31) For was it really necessary for him to enter the territory of another ruler whereas a prosperous voyage could

have brought him safely to his own domain? For even if Gaius did permit or even command him to do so, he should have beseeched him to be excused from coming here, in order to prevent the governor of this country from being surpassed and consequently dishonored."

(32) When Flaccus heard this, his anger swelled still more than before, and although in public, out of fear of the one who had sent him, he pretended to be Agrippa's comrade and friend, in private he gave clear expression to his jealousy and hatred; he insulted him behind his back because he was too much of a coward to do so openly. (33) For he did allow the lazy and unoccupied mob of the city — that is a multitude of people practised in endless talking who spend their time with slander and calumny — to speak evil of the king, either starting the campaign of abuse himself or exhorting and inciting others to do so with the help of those who used to be his servants in such matters.

(34) They, having received the cue given them, spent their days in the gymnasium reviling the king and gibing at him non-stop. In a sense, they took the writers of mimes and farces as their teachers and thus demonstrated their natural ability in disgraceful things, slow to be trained in anything good but very quick and eager in learning the opposite.

(35) Why, then, did he not become angry?, why did he not arrest them?, why did he not punish them on account of their insolent slander? Even if Agrippa had not been a king but only one of the members of Caesar's household, did he not deserve to be treated with at least some privilege and honor? Actually, all this is clear evidence that Flaccus was guilty of and a participator in this campaign of slander. For the one who was in the position to punish them, or at the least to stop them if not prevent them, was the one who gave them permission and consented with them himself. If an undisciplined mob is given the opportunity for misconduct, it will not desist, but it will pass from one transgression to another, continually adding new forms of evil.

§§36-40 *Karabas*

(36) Now there was a lunatic named Karabas, whose madness was not of the wild and savage kind, against which neither the madmen themselves nor those in their vicinity can protect themselves, but of the more relaxed and gentler variant. He spent both day and night

naked on the streets, not discouraged by heat or cold, a plaything of the children and the youngsters who were idling about.

(37) Together they drove this poor man into the gymnasium and placed him there on a platform so that he could be seen by everyone. On his head they spread out a piece of papyrus for a diadem and clothed the rest of his body with a doormat for a robe; and someone who had seen a small piece of native papyrus lying on the street, gave it to him for a sceptre. (38) And when, as in a theatrical mime, he had been dressed up like a king and received the insignia of kingship, young men, bearing sticks on their shoulders as if they were carrying spears, stood on either side of him in imitation of bodyguards. Then others approached him, some as if to salute him, others as if to plead their cause before him, again others as if to consult him about the affairs of the state.

(39) Then there arose a strange shout from among the multitude of those standing around him: They called him 'Marin' — which is said to be the word for 'Lord' in Syriac — for they knew that Agrippa not only was by birth a Syrian but also ruled as a king over a great part of Syria.

(40) When Flaccus heard, or rather saw all this, he should not only have arrested the madman and put him in prison, in order to prevent him from giving an opportunity to the revilers to insult their superiors, but he should also have punished the ones responsible for dressing him up like that, for they had dared in both deeds and words, both openly and indirectly, to insult someone who was a king and a friend of Caesar, someone who had been honored by the Senate of Rome with the praetorian insignia. But not only did he not punish them, he did not even think fit to restrain them, but he gave license and impunity to all those who were so malevolent and malicious, and he pretended not to see what he did see and not to hear what he did hear.

§§41-44 *The Overtures to the Pogrom*

(41) The crowd perceived this — I do not refer to the peaceful and decent inhabitants but to the rabble that is always intent on creating confusion and turmoil, interfering and in pursuit of a life not worth living, habitually idle and lazy and always causing trouble. They flocked into the theatre first thing in the morning, knowing that they already had Flaccus in their pocket for less than a penny, which this man in his lust for fame, this good-for-nothing, had

accepted to the injury not only of himself but also of the public safety. They shouted, as if with one mouth, that statues should be erected in the synagogues, thus proposing an entirely novel and unprecedented violation of the law. (42) And they knew this, for they are very acute in their wickedness, and they cunningly used the name of Caesar as a smokescreen, a name to which it is unlawful to attribute any blameworthy action.

(43) What then did the governor of the country do? He knew that the city, as the rest of Egypt, has two kinds of inhabitants, us and them, and that there are no less than one million Jews living in Alexandria and the rest of the country, from the steep slope that separates us from Libya to the boundaries of Ethiopia. He also knew that the attack was directed against us all and that it would not yield anything good if they tried to disrupt our ancestral customs. Yet, in disregard of all this, he permitted them to erect the statues, even though there were innumerable considerations, all of cautionary character, which he could have put forward either as an order from the ruler or as advice from a friend.

(44) He, however, co-operated with them in each and every one of their misdeeds and therefore thought fit to use his position of superior power to kindle the sedition by adding newer forms of evil and, as far as it was in his power, one may almost say that he filled the whole world with civil wars.

§§45-52 *The Jewish Point of View*

(45) For it was more than clear that the rumor of the destruction of the synagogues that started in Alexandria would spread immediately to the districts of Egypt and speed from Egypt eastwards to the oriental nations, and from the coastal strip and Mareia, which are the borders of Libya, westwards to the nations living there. For there is not one country that can contain all the Jews, so numerous are they.

(46) It is for this reason that they settle in most of the wealthiest countries of Europe and Asia, both their islands and the mainland. However, it is the holy city where the sacred temple of the Most High God stands, that they regard as their mother city, but the regions they obtained from their fathers, grandfathers, greatgrandfathers, and even more remote ancestors, to live in, (they regard) as their fatherland where they were born and brought up. There are also some regions where they came to as immigrants at the very moment of their foundation, much to the pleasure of the founders.

(47) There was reason to fear that people all over the world would take their cue from there and treat their Jewish fellow-citizens outrageously by taking violent measures against their synagogues and their ancestral customs.

(48) The Jews, however, were not going to remain quiet at all costs — even though they are by nature a peaceful people — not only since, as is the case with all humankind, the struggle to maintain one's own traditions overrules the dangers to one's own life, but also since they were the only people under the sun who by being deprived of their synagogues would at the same time be deprived of their means of showing their piety towards their benefactors, which is something they would have regarded as worth dying for many thousands of deaths. They no longer would have sacred precincts in which they could declare their thankfulness, and they might have said to their opponents:

(49) "It apparently escaped your notice that in this way you did not pay homage to our masters but actually deprived them of it! You do not realize that for the Jews all over the world it is their synagogues that clearly form the basis for their piety towards the imperial family. If these are destroyed, what other place or method is left to us for paying this homage? (50) For if we neglect it when our ancestral customs permit us to do it, we deservedly receive the severest punishment for not giving the proper and full return for the benefits we received. But if we refuse because it is not permitted by our own laws, which Augustus himself was pleased to confirm, I do not know what kind of offence, small or great, we have committed, unless someone would want to take us to task for committing a transgression, albeit involuntarily, by not guarding against deviations from our ancestral customs, which, even if they are started by others, often end up affecting those who are <not> responsible[2] for them."

(51) But by leaving unsaid what he should have said and by saying what he should have left unsaid, Flaccus sinned against us in that way. But what motives had those whose favor he was seeking? Did they really want to honor the Emperor? Were temples scarce in the city? Have not the greatest and most important parts of the city been consecrated to gods, ready for the erection of any statues they wished?

---

[2] Here I adopt the reading τοὺς <μὴ> αἰτίους. See the note *ad locum* in the commentary.

(52) On the contrary, what we have been talking about is the aggressive deed of persons who love to make enemies and are plotters who seek to injure us so craftily that it would seem that our attackers were not acting unjustly, whereas for us, the attacked, it was not safe to oppose them. For, gentlemen, abrogating the laws and disrupting the ancestral customs of a people, outraging fellow-citizens and teaching the inhabitants of other cities to disregard unanimity, all that cannot be seen as a matter of honor(ing the Emperor)."

§§53-96 *The Pogrom at its Height*

(53) His attack on our laws by means of a seizure of our synagogues, of which he had even the names removed, seemed to be succesful to him. For that reason he proceeded to another project, namely, the destruction of our political organization. His purpose in that enterprise was that, if the only things to which our life was anchored were cut away, that is, our ancestral customs and our participation in political rights, we might be exposed to the worst misfortunes without having any rope left to which we could cling to for safety.

(54) For only a couple of days later he issued a decree in which he stigmatized us as foreigners and aliens and gave us no right to plead our cause but condemned us without trial. What could be a better promise of further tyrannical behavior than this? He himself became everything: accuser, enemy, witness, judge, and executioner. But he then added to the first two (crimes) a third one, namely, he gave permission to those who wanted to plunder the Jews, as at the sacking of a city.

(55) Well, what do people do when they get this license? The city has five districts, named after the first letters of the alphabet as we used to write it. Two of the districts are called the Jewish quarters because the majority of the inhabitants are Jews. In the other quarters there are also quite a number of Jews, although scattered about. So, what did they do then? They expelled the Jews from four of the five quarters and drove them together into a very small corner of the one left.

(56) Because of their great numbers they (the Jews) flooded the beaches, the dunghills and the tombs, deprived of all their belongings. The enemies, however, ran to the houses left empty and plundered them; they divided the booty among themselves as if it were war. Since no one hindered them, they broke into the workshops of

the Jews, even though these were closed because of the mourning for Drusilla, and they brought out all they found there, which was quite a lot. They carried it to the middle of the marketplace, handling other people's property as if it were their own.

(57) The unemployment, which was the consequence of this, was an evil that was even more unbearable than the plundering. The financers had lost their capital and no one was permitted to practice his usual business, neither farmer, nor shipper, nor merchant, nor artisan. So, poverty was brought down on them from two sides: first they were robbed, because in one day they were stripped of all their property and lost all they had, and second they were no longer able to make a living from their regular jobs.

(58) Unbearable though these things were, in comparison to later actions they were tolerable. For although poverty is grievous, especially when it is brought about by one's enemies, yet it is less grievous than even the slightest physical injury. (59) But if someone called the excessive sufferings that our people underwent '"injury" or "outrage," he would not be using these words in their proper sense. I think he would be at a loss to find adequate terms in view of the enormous scale of this unprecedented cruelty. For the treatment of prisoners of war by their victors — who are usually and naturally implacable to their prisoners — would, in comparison to what happened here, seem to be kindness itself. (60) Victors do seize property and take large numbers of people prisoner, but they run the risk of losing their own if they are defeated. And it cannot be denied that they release innumerable prisoners of war for whom relatives or friends have paid a ransom, perhaps not because they yield to mercy but because they cannot resist their love of money. So what?, one might say; the way they are saved does not matter to those who are fortunate. (61) Apart from that, it is also the case that enemies fallen in war are deemed worthy of burial. Decent and humane (victors) do that at their expense, those whose hatred extends even to corpses surrender the bodies under a truce so that they will not be denied the final gift, the customary ceremonies (of a funeral). (62) That is what enemies do in war. But let us now have a look at what is done in peace by those who were our friends a little while ago.

After the plunderings, the evictions and the violent expulsions from most quarters of the city, they (the Jews) were like a beleaguered garrison surrounded by enemies. They were oppressed by a terrible scarcity and even lack of necessary things and they saw their wives and little children dying before their eyes through a famine organized by men. (63) For in every other place all else was full of prosperity and abundance — the river had richly flooded the fields with its inundations and the wheatbearing area of the lowlands was producing grain in unstinted abundance thanks to its fertility. (64) When, finally, they could no longer endure their privation, some of them, quite contrary to what they had been used to, went to the houses of their relatives and friends to beg for the basic necessities of life, as a loan. Others, whose consciousness of their standing meant they could not endure the condition of beggars, which they saw as fitter for slaves than for the free, went to the market-place for no other reason than to buy food for their relatives and themselves, poor wretches! (65) For they were immediately seized by those who wielded the weapon of mob-rule and they were treacherously murdered; being dragged along and trampled upon through the whole city they were so completely annihilated that not even one piece was left to be buried. (66) Innumerable others, too, were overpowered and annihilated by manifold forms of maltreatment invented to gratify the atrocious cruelty of those who, maddened by bloodthirstiness, were transformed into wild animals. For they stoned any Jews they happened to catch sight of, or beat them to death with clubs, not immediately delivering blows to the vital parts in order to prevent that, by dying too soon, they might escape too soon from the awareness of their sufferings. (67) Some people became even more outrageous because of the immunity and license with which they could commit these catastrophic crimes. They discarded all blunt weapons and took up the most effective of all, fire and iron; and consequently they killed many with swords and not a few were exterminated by fire. (68) On top of all that the most merciless of all burnt even whole families, husbands with their wives, infant children with their parents, and that in the centre of the city, without any compassion for old age nor for youth nor for the innocent age of childhood. And when they were in want of timber for fire, they would collect brushwood and killed them more by suffocation than by fire, thus contriving a more pitiable and protracted death for these miserable people whose half-burnt bodies lay pell-mell, a grievous and absolutely heart-rending spectacle. (69) If the persons who were called to collect brushwood were too slow, they would burn the owners using their own furniture taken from the spoil, thus robbing them first of their most costly articles and then setting on fire anything that was not very useful to serve instead as timber. (70) Many also they bound by one foot at the ankle and dragged them around while still alive, meanwhile leaping on them and crushing them to pieces, thus devising the most cruel form of death. (71) Even when they were dead, the endless fury of their enemies did not come to an end; they inflicted still worse outrages on their dead bodies. They dragged these through — I would almost say — every lane of the city until the corpses had lost their skin, their flesh and muscles because these had been pulverised by the unevenness and toughness of the ground and were totally destroyed because all the constituent parts of the organism had been separated and dispersed in all directions.

(72) Those who committed these things acted as if they themselves were the victims, like actors in a mime. But the friends and relatives of the real victims, simply because they felt grief and compassion over the misfortunes of their relations, were led away, scourged, tortured on the wheel, and after all these outrages, which were all their bodies could endure, the final punishment that awaited them was crucifixion.

(73) After he had broken into everything as a real burglar and had let no part of the Jewish community escape his exorbitant hostility, Flaccus, this perpetrator of enormities, this inventor of ever new acts of villainy, devised a monstrous and unparallelled attack.

(74) Our council of elders had been appointed to manage Jewish affairs, after the death of the genarch, by our savior and benefactor Augustus, orders to that effect having been given to Magius Maximus just before the latter began to govern the city on Egypt's border and the country.[3] Of this council of elders, Flaccus arrested 38 members, namely those who had been discovered in their own houses, and had them immediately put in bonds. Then he organized a fine procession, in which he marched these old men through the middle of the market place, their hands bound behind their backs, some with straps, others with iron chains, and took them into the theatre. It was a most miserable spectacle that was wholly unsuited to the occasion.

(75) When they stood in front of their enemies, who were seated there, to make their disgrace even more conspicuous he ordered them all to be stripped and lacerated with scourges, an insulting form of treatment usually reserved for the worst criminals. As a result of

---

[3] This translation is based upon the reading μέλλοντα πόλιν <τὴν> ἀπ' Αἰγύπτου καὶ τὴν χώραν ἐπιτροπεύειν. See the note *ad locum* in the commentary.

the flogging some of them died the moment they were carried away, whereas others were ill for such a long time that they despaired of ever recovering.

(76) The enormity of his aggression has been fully proved by other evidence, but nonetheless it will be demonstrated even more clearly by what I am now going to tell. Three members of the council of elders, Euodus, Tryphon and Andron, were dispossessed of all their property as they were robbed at one swoop of all they had in their houses. Flaccus was well aware of what they had gone through, for he had been clearly told so when on an earlier occasion he sent for our rulers under the pretence of arranging a reconciliation between them and the rest of the city. (77) Nevertheless, even though he knew quite well that these men had been deprived of their property, he had them beaten in front of their plunderers. So, whereas they suffered the double misery of poverty and personal outrage, the others enjoyed the double pleasure of wealth that did not belong to them while sating themselves, gloating on the disgrace of those from whom they had stolen that wealth.

(78) Now I have to tell something that also took place at that time, though I hesitate to do so, since I am afraid that, in case it will be considered as trivial, it may detract from the magnitude of such enormities. But even though it is a small thing in itself, yet it is evidence of no small malignity. There are different kinds of scourges used in the city, and these differences are related to the status of the persons to be beaten. So, for instance, the practice is that Egyptians are beaten with a different kind of scourge and by different people than the Alexandrians, who are beaten with flat blades and by Alexandrian blade-bearers. (79) This custom was also observed, in the case of our people, by both Flaccus' predecessors and himself in his first years of office. For it is possible, it is really possible, to find some small element in the circumstances of degradation for persons to maintain their dignity, even in a situation of outrage, something that contributes to decorum, if one allows the nature of the case to be examined on its own merits, without the import of personal aggressive passion which removes and disperses all ingredients of a milder approach. (80) It was, therefore, unbearable that, although Alexandrian Jewish commoners had always been beaten with scourges that more befitted freemen and citizens even when they were thought to have committed things worthy of stripes, now their rulers, the members of the council of elders, whose very title implies age and

honor, were in this respect treated with a greater lack of dignity than their inferiors, as if they were Egyptians of the lowest status and guilty of the greatest crimes.

(81) I pass over the fact that, even if they had committed numerous crimes, he ought to have postponed their punishment out of respect for the occasion. For those rulers who administrate their states in the proper way and, instead of only pretending to honor, truly honor their benefactors, are accustomed not to punish any of the condemned until the [illustrious] celebrations in honor of the birthdays of the illustrious Augusti are over. (82) But he committed this violation of the law on those very days and had punishment inflicted upon those who had done nothing wrong, even though, if he had wished so, he could have punished them afterwards. But he hurried and pressed on the matter in order to please the mob that was inimical to the Jews, convinced that in this way he could more easily win them over to what he had in mind. (83) I actually know of instances of people who had been crucified and who, on the moment that such a holiday was at hand, were taken down from the cross and given back to their relatives in order to give them a burial and the customary rites of the last honors. For it was (thought to be) proper that even the dead should enjoy something good on the emperor's birthday and at the same time that the sanctity of the festival should be preserved.

(84) Flaccus, however, did not order to take down people who had died on the cross but to crucify living ones, people for whom the occasion offered amnesty, to be sure only a short-lived not a permanent one, but at least a short postponement of punishment if not entire forgiveness. And he did this after they had been maltreated with scourges in the middle of the theatre and tortured with fire and the sword. (85) The spectacle was divided into acts. The first shows, that lasted from dawn till the third or fourth hour, were as follows: Jews were scourged, hung up, tortured on the wheel, maltreated, and led away to their death through the middle of the orchestra. The shows after this fine exhibition included dancers, mimes, flute players, and all the other forms of amusement in theatrical competitions.

(86) But why dwell on these things, for he was already scheming a second round of plundering. What he also wanted was to deploy the whole army as a stronghold against us and for that reason he invented a strange calumny to the effect that the Jews had heavy suits of armour in their houses. So, he summoned a centurion in whom he

had the greatest confidence, a man called Castus, and ordered him to take the bravest soldiers of the contingent under his command and without losing time or giving previous notice to enter and search the houses of the Jews to check whether there was any store of arms laid up there.

(87) The man hastened to carry out what he had been ordered to do. But the Jews were unaware of this scheme and at first they stood dumbfounded in bewilderment, while their wives and children were clinging to them and bathed in tears for fear of being taken captive. For they were in continuous expectation of what would be only the completion of the plundering. (88) When they heard one of the investigators saying, "Where do you store your weapons?", they breathed a sigh of some relief, and they displayed everything, even what they had in their recesses. (89) They were partly pleased and partly aggrieved; pleased because the calumny would now be evidently refuted, but angry because, firstly, such serious slanders, which were concocted against them by their enemies, were believed beforehand, and secondly, because their women, who were always kept in seclusion and did not even appear at the house-door, and their unmarried daughters, who were confined to the women's quarter, women who for modesty's sake shunned the eyes of men, even their closest relatives, now became exposed to people who were not just unfamiliar men but terrifying soldiers at that.

(90) And after this careful investigation, what a great quantity of defensive weapons was found! Helmets, breastplates, shields, daggers, pikes, complete outfits of armour were brought out and piled up in heaps, and thereafter offensive weapons, javelins, slings, bows, and arrows? Of course not, absolutely nothing of this kind was found! Not even knives which the cooks use for their daily work. (91) This fact, in itself, revealed the simplicity of the kind of life led by people who do not admit extravagance and luxury, things which by their very nature engender satiety; and satiety engenders insolence, which is the source of all evil.

(92) Yet, not long ago the arms of the Egyptians throughout the countryside had been collected by a man called Bassus, to whom Flaccus had entrusted this task. And on that occasion a large fleet of ships could be seen sailing down the Nile and anchoring in the harbors of the river, loaded with all kinds of weapons, and also innumerable beasts of burden loaded with spears tied together cross-wise and hanging on either side so as to keep the animals in balance. Also

almost all the wagons from the army camp were full of armor suits, while they advanced in an orderly line in one arrangement and were visible in one view. And the total distance between the harbors and the armory in the palace, where the arms had to be deposited, was about ten stades.

(93) It was the right thing to search the houses of those who had procured all this, for after frequently having participated in revolts they were suspected again of revolutionary activities. In imitation of the religious games the authorities should have instituted a new biennial festival for the collection of arms in Egypt, so that either the people would not have time to collect them, or at least only a few instead of many, because they would get no opportunity to replace them.

(94) But we, why did we have to suffer this kind of thing? For when were we ever suspected of revolting? When were we not considered to be peaceful to all? Are not the pursuits of our everyday life irreproachable and do they not contribute to the law and order and the stability of the city? If the Jews indeed had arms in their possession, would they then have let themselves be stripped of and driven away from more than 400 houses, expelled by those who had robbed them of all their properties? Why then was no search done of the property of these people too, for they *would* have weapons, if not of their own, at any rate all the ones they had stolen from others!

(95) But, as I said, the whole affair was nothing else than a deliberate plot, due to the ruthlessness of Flaccus and of the crowds, of which even women became the victims. For they were seized like captives not only in the market place but also in the middle of the theatre, where they were dragged upon the stage on any calumnious charge whatsoever, in an intolerably and painfully insulting way. (96) When then they turned out to belong to another nation — for they arrested many women as Jewesses since they did not make any careful investigation of the truth — they were set free. But when they were found to belong to our nation, then these spectators turned into despotic tyrants and ordered swine's flesh so as to give it to these women. All who, for fear of punishment, ate from the meat were released without undergoing any further maltreatment. But the more resolute women were handed over to the torturers to suffer unbearable tortures, and this is the clearest proof that they were absolutely innocent.

II. *The Punishment and Death of Flaccus*

§§97-103 *The Declaration of Loyalty*

(97) In addition to what has already been said, Flaccus was planning and trying to harm us not only on his own accord but, from the outset, with the emperor being involved as well. For we had decreed by our votes and carried out by our actions all possible honors to Gaius as far as they were allowed by our laws, and we delivered the decree to Flaccus, begging him that it might be forwarded by him, since he would not have granted our request for an embassy.

(98) He read the decree and nodded his head many times in approval at each point. He smiled and was delighted, or at least he pretended to be pleased, and said: "I appreciate all of you for your piety and I will forward it, as you request, or else I will play the role of your ambassador myself so that Gaius may learn about your gratitude. (99) I will also give testimony myself to all the many things I know about your orderly and obedient behavior, and I need not add anything to that, for the simple truth about you is the most sufficient praise."

(100) We were delighted at these promises and gave him thanks, as if our hope had already been fulfilled that Gaius had read the decree. And this was a reasonable hope, for everything that is forwarded with urgency through the governors is usually read immediately by the ruler.[4]

(101) Flaccus, however, disregarded all our intentions and also his own words and promises, and he retained the decree in his possession, so that we alone of all people under the sun would be considered enemies (of the emperor). There can be no doubt that these were the actions of a man who had been brooding for many nights over the preparations for his attack against us, not of a man who acts upon a sudden attack of insanity, on an unseasonable fit of mental derangement.

(102) God, however, apparently takes care of human affairs for he countered his flattering words, so elegantly phrased for the sole purpose of cheating everyone, and the counsels of his lawless mind in which he devised his treacherous stratagems (against us). God took mercy on us and saw to it that not long thereafter we had good reason to think that our hopes were not lost.

---

[4] The translation is based upon the reading ἀνυπέρθετον ἔχει τὴν παρ' ἡγεμόνι δι<αν>άγνωσιν. See the discussion in the commentary.

(103) For when king Agrippa visited us, we informed him of Flaccus' intrigues, whereupon he intervened to rectify the matter. He promised us that he would forward the decree to the emperor — which, as we later heard, is what he did indeed — with apologies for the delay, showing that we were not slow at all in understanding the duty of piety towards our benefactor and his family; that, on the contrary, we had been zealous in this respect from the very beginning, but that we had been deprived of the opportunity to demonstrate this zeal in time due to the governor's maliciousness.

§§104-118 *Flaccus' Arrest*

(104) For it was at this juncture that Justice, the champion and defender of the wronged, the punisher of unholy deeds and men, began to prepare for the battle against him. To begin with, he underwent an unprecedented humiliation and a disaster such as had not befallen any of the former governors since the house of Augustus acquired the dominion over land and sea.

(105) To be true, also some of those who had held governorships during the reigns of Tiberius and his father Caesar, had perverted their office of administrator and protector into despotism and tyranny. They had done their territories irreparable damage by bribery, plunder, unjust condemnations, banishment and exile of completely innocent people, and execution of the powerful without trial. But when, after their term of office, these men returned to Rome, the emperors always demanded a rendering of their accounts and an examination of their conduct, especially when the cities that had been oppressed sent an embassy. (106) On those occasions the emperors showed themselves impartial judges. They listened equally to the accusers and the defendants, and they made it a principle not to condemn anyone in advance without a fair trial. They decided what appeared to be just, not being influenced by hostility or favor but by the objective truth. (107) But in Flaccus' case it was not after his term of office but before the regular date that he was met by Justice, who hates evil, because she was so indignant at the unimaginable excesses of his unjust and lawless activities.

(108) The way he was arrested was as follows. He supposed that, as regards the matters on which he was under suspicion, Gaius had by now been propitiated, partly by means of his letters which were full of flattery, partly by his long public speeches in which he often used obsequious language and strung together long series of insincere

laudations, partly also by the high reputation he had in the largest part of the city.

(109) What he did not realize, however, was that he was fooling himself. (The hopes of wicked people do not have any foundations: they count on what is favorable to them, but what they experience is the opposite, namely what they deserve!) For Gaius sent from Italy a centurion appointed by him, named Bassus, with the company of soldiers which stood under his command. (110) This man embarked on one of the fastest sailing ships and in only a few days he arrived at the harbor of Alexandria, off the island of Pharos, late in the afternoon. He then ordered the captain to remain offshore until after sunset. He planned to enter unnoticed so as to avoid Flaccus getting wind of his arrival beforehand and planning some violent action that could frustrate Bassus' mission.

(111) When it became evening, the ship entered and moored. Bassus disembarked with his men and went into the city neither recognizing nor being recognized by anyone. But when on the way he found a soldier who was one of the sentries in the quaternion on duty, he ordered him to point out to him the house of his commander. For to that person he did want to communicate his secret errand so that he would have someone to assist him in case he needed a strong force. (112) When he heard that both the commander and Flaccus were having a dinner party with someone, he hastened with unabated speed to the house of the host — it was a certain Stephanio, one of the freedmen of the emperor Tiberius, at whose house they were the guests. Bassus held back out of sight a little way off and sent one of his own men to reconnoitre — the man was dressed like a servant: a trick to prevent anyone from noticing what was going on. Disguised as the slave of one or other of the guests, he entered the dining room and took a close and careful look at the whole situation. Then he went back and informed Bassus.

(113) Bassus thus got to know that the entrances were unguarded and that Flaccus had only a small number of people with him, for only some ten to fifteen of his household slaves accompanied him. Then he gave the signal to his soldiers and rushed in suddenly. Some of the soldiers took position in the dining room, with swords in their girdles, and they surrounded Flaccus before he even noticed, as he was just drinking to the health of someone and toasting the company. (114) But when Bassus came forward and took his stand in the middle of the room, the moment Flaccus saw him he was speechless

from consternation. He wanted to get up, but when he saw the circle of guards around him, he knew — even before someone told him — what Gaius wanted to do with him; what orders had been given to those who had just arrived, and what he was about to undergo in the near future. For the human mind has an impressive ability to see in one glance and to hear altogether the various successive events that are going to take place over a long period.

(115) All his fellow-guests rose, shuddering and rigid with fear lest some sentence had already been fixed for the sheer fact of having been at the same party as the culprit. For it was not safe to flee, nor was it possible, because all entrances had already been blocked. Flaccus was led away by the soldiers at Bassus' command, thus returning from a party for the last time. For it had to be so that a hospitable hearth was the scene where Justice began to act against a man who had destroyed numerous hearths and homes of completely innocent people.

(116) The fact that Flaccus had to undergo this unprecedented misfortune, taken captive as he was like an enemy in the country of which he was the governor, was I think due to his treatment of the Jews, whom he had decided to exterminate completely in his craving for fame. The moment of his arrest is also a clear proof of this, for it was the national Jewish festival of the autumn equinox, in which it is the custom of the Jews to live in tents. (117) But none of the festal proceedings were carried out because our leaders were still imprisoned, after having endured irremediable and intolerable atrocities and insults. In addition, the common people regarded the misfortune of their leaders as that of the whole nation, and they were already extremely depressed by the exceptional misery that had befallen each of them individually.

(118) Grief is usually felt twice as strongly especially at festivals when people are not in a position to celebrate them, both because they are deprived of the lighthearted cheerfulness which a festival requires, and because they have their share of sorrow, which in this case broke their backs since they were unable to find any remedy for disasters of such a scale.

§§119-124 *Gratitude for Flaccus' Arrest*

(119) While they were in this extremely sad situation, oppressed by an unbearable burden and crowded in their houses as night had fallen, some people came to tell them that Flaccus had just been

arrested. They thought that this was a trap, not the truth at all, and thinking that they were being mocked and ambushed again, their grief became even greater.

(120) But when tumult arose throughout the city and the night-guards ran to and fro and horsemen rode at full speed to and from the camp in great haste, some of the Jews, aroused by the unusual events, came out of their houses to get information about what was going on. For it seemed clear that something revolutionary had taken place.

(121) When they heard that Flaccus had been arrested and was already ensnared within the hunter's nets, they stretched out their arms to heaven and began to sing hymns and songs to God who oversees all human affairs. They said, "O Lord, we are not delighted at the punishment of our enemy, for we have learned from our holy laws that we should sympathize with our fellow humans. But it is right to give thanks to you for having taken pity and compassion on us and for having relieved our constant and incessant oppression."

(122) When they had spent all night singing hymns and other songs, at daybreak they poured out through the gates and made their way to the nearby parts of the beach, for they had been deprived of their synagogues. And there, standing in the purest possible place they cried out with one accord:

(123) "O almighty King of mortals and immortals, we have come here to call on earth and sea, on air and heaven, which are the parts of the universe, and on the universe as a whole, to offer thanks to you. In these alone we can dwell, expelled as we are from all human-made buildings, deprived of the city and the public and private areas within its walls, the only people under the sun to become cityless and homeless because of the malice of their governor. (124) But you make us realize that we may be confident that what is still in need of restoration will indeed be restored, because you have already begun to answer our prayers. After all, you have suddenly brought down the common enemy of our nation, who was the instigator of our misfortunes, who thought so highly of himself and expected that these things would bring him fame. And when you did so, you did not wait until he was already far away so that those who had suffered badly under him would only have learned about it by hearsay and hence have less satisfaction, no, you did so right here, so close by that it was almost before the very eyes of those whom he had wronged. Thus you gave them a clearer picture of your swift and unexpected intervention."

§§125-145 *Lampo and Isidorus*

(125) To what I have already said I should add a third thing which I think also took place because divine providence intervened. Flaccus had set sail at the beginning of the winter, for he was destined to have his fill of the frightening dangers of the sea as well, having filled the elements of the universe with his impieties. After having endured innumerable hardships and barely having arrived safely in Italy, he was immediately confronted with the fact that two of his worst enemies, Isidorus and Lampo, took up the charges against him.

(126) These men had been his subjects only a short while ago and had hailed him as their master, benefactor, savior and the like. Now, however, they were his adversaries and as such they displayed a power that was not a mere match but in many ways vastly superior to his own. They not only had confidence in the justice of their case, but — which was of the utmost importance — they also saw that he who presides over human affairs was his implacable enemy, he who was now about to put on the cloak of justice, albeit out of calculation, namely in order to avoid the impression that he had condemned him in advance without a trial. But in fact he would behave like an enemy who, before hearing either accusation or defense, had already in his heart condemned him and sentenced him to the severest punishment. (127) And nothing is harder for those who were once superiors than to be accused by their former inferiors or for those who were once rulers by their former subjects, which is just as if masters were to be accused by slaves born in their house or purchased with their money.

(128) Yet in my opinion this was a lighter evil compared with another one which was to be still greater. For it was not just people who had been in the position of subjects who now suddenly attacked him unanimously with their accusations, having prepared themselves for the fight, but also people who had been his most bitter enemies for the greatest part of the period that he had been the governor of the country.

Lampo had been put on trial for impiety towards the emperor Tiberius and, as the trial had dragged on for two years, he was exhausted. (129) Because his judge had a grudge against him, he caused postponements and delays on various pretexts because, even if Lampo was to escape from the charge, he wanted to make his life more painful than death by keeping him in uncertainty and fear about his future for as long as possible.

(130) Later, when it seemed that he had won his case, Lampo alleged that he had been dealt with in an outrageous way as far as his property was concerned, for he had been compelled to become a gymnasiarch. It may have been so that he was stingy and thrifty and just asserted by way of excuse that he simply did not possess enough means for such great expenses; it may also have been the case that he really did not have the means. Anyway, before the trial he had pretended to be quite rich, but on closer examination he appeared not to be a very wealthy man at all, having acquired practically all he had from his illegal actions. (131) For he used to stand by the governors whenever they gave judgment and he took minutes of all that took place during the trial, because he had the rank of an introducer.[5] And then he would deliberately expunge or omit some things or insert other things which had not been said; sometimes he doctored the documents by changing, rearranging, or even totally rewriting them, the purpose of this tamperer being to charge money for every syllable, or even worse, every stroke of his pen.

(132) Often the whole people unanimously denounced him, with an accurate and well-chosen expression, as "the pen-murderer," because by the things he wrote he had caused the death of numerous people and had made the lives of as many more miserable than those of the dead: those might have won their case and enjoyed their prosperity, but what they suffered was a most undeserved defeat and poverty, because their enemies had bought both of these from this man who peddled and sold the property of others.

(133) For it was impossible that the governors, who were in charge of such a vast country, could remember all the cases in that constant stream of both private and public new affairs, especially as they had not only to administer justice but also received the calculations of the revenues and taxes, the scrutiny of which took up the greater part of the year. (134) But Lampo, who was commissioned to guard the most important archives, those of justice and the most sacred verdicts based upon it, made misuse of the forgetfulness of the judges for his own profit. He registered people who should have won their case among the defeated and those who should have lost it among the winners after first having received his accursed fee, more properly described as hire, from the victorious.

---

[5] This translation is based upon the emendation εἰσαγωγέως ἔχων τάξιν. See the notes in the commentary *ad locum*.

(135) Such was the Lampo who now appeared as one of the accusers of Flaccus. Further there was Isidorus, his equal in wickedness, a mobbish type of demagogue, always intent on creating chaos and confusion, an enemy of peace and stability, very adept at organizing riots and tumults where they did not yet exist and, once they were there, at coaching and fomenting them, always taking care to keep around him a disorderly and turbulent gang consisting of a promiscuous mob of all the refuse of the people, which he had divided up into sections as if they were a sort of squadrons.

(136) In the city there are clubs with many members whose common ideal is not something sound but only to drink liquor, be drunk, behave as a drunkard, and the offspring of these, insolence. The natives call these gatherings "synods" and "couches." (137) In all or most of these clubs Isidorus holds the first place, and for that reason he is called "symposiarch," table president, city-troublemaker. Then when he wants to perpetrate something useless, a single call suffices to bring all of them together and to have them say and do whatever they are told.

(138) On one occasion he was angry with Flaccus because, whereas at first he had the reputation of being a person with some influence on him, afterwards he no longer had that favorable position. Then he hired the scum of humanity, those who used to be vociferant and to sell their shouts as in a market to persons who are disposed to buy them, and he ordered them to assemble at the gymnasium. (139) When the building was full, they began to accuse Flaccus for no reason at all, inventing groundless charges and stringing together falsehoods spun out in anapaests, so that not only Flaccus but also the others were astonished at the unexpected event. They surmised — rightly so — that there must definitely be someone whom they were trying to please, since they themselves had not suffered anything unjust, neither had the rest of the city's inhabitants, as they knew quite well.

(140) Then, after deliberation, they decided to arrest some of them in order to try to find out the cause of this sudden outburst of blind fury and madness. The ones who were arrested confessed the truth without having to be put to torture, and they provided the proofs through facts: the payment that had been agreed upon, that is, both the part that had already been given to them and the part that would be given them later according to promises, the names of the men who had been appointed to distribute the money as the

leaders of the sedition, and the place and the time at which the bribery had taken place. (141) Of course, everyone was indignant and the inhabitants of the city found it unbearable that its reputation should be blemished by the stupidity of some individuals. For that reason Flaccus decided to summon the most respectable of the citizens and to bring before them on the next day the distributers of the payment, so as to convict Isidorus and defend his own administration by proving that he had been unjustly slandered. When they heard the summons, not only the magistrates came, but the whole city, except that part of the population that was about to be convicted of having received bribes.

(142) Those who had discharged this fine service were raised on a platform so that in this conspicuous elevation they might be recognized by all. They accused Isidorus of being behind the disturbances and the slanders against Flaccus and of having given both money and wine to no small number on his account. (143) "For where could we have got such great abundance from?" they said, "We are poor and hardly able to provide ourselves daily with the very necessaries of life. And what kind of terrible evil did we suffer from the governor so as to be forced to cherish a grudge against him? No, the originator and creator of all these things is that man, always envious of the prosperous and an enemy of law and order."

(144) When the bystanders heard this and recognized that what was being said was a clear representation and indication of the intentions of the accused, some shouted "Disfranchise him!", others "Banish him!", again others "Kill him!" These last were in the majority, and then the rest too came over and joined them, so that finally all cried out unanimously and with one voice, "Kill the common pest, the man who, ever since he came to the fore and wormed his way into state affairs, caused the whole city to become diseased!" (145) Because of his bad conscience, Isidorus ran off, fearing arrest. But Flaccus took no further steps against Isidorus, thinking that, now that he had voluntarily left, life in the city would be free from sedition and intrigue.

§§146-161 *Flaccus on Trial*

(146) I have dwelled at length on these events, not in order to keep old injuries in memory but out of admiration for Justice, who oversees human affairs. For those who had been hostile to him from the beginning and to whom he had become more hateful than

anyone else, were the ones to whom was allotted the role of accusing him so as to make his affliction as great as possible. For to be accused is already bad enough, but being accused by confessed enemies is far worse. (147) He, the ruler, was accused by his subjects, and that by men who had always been his enemies, whereas only a little before he had been the master of the life of each of the two. But that was not all, he also received a very tough verdict. He actually received a twofold blow in that his defeat went hand in hand with ridicule by his exulting enemies. To sensible people this is even worse than death.

(148) After that he reaped a rich harvest of misery. For he was immediately deprived of all his possessions, both what he had inherited from his parents and what he had acquired himself. He was a man who took special delight in beautiful things. Unlike some rich men, for him wealth was not inert matter, but everything had been scrutinized with a view to its extravagance: cups, garments, couches, utensils, and everything else that decorated his house, all of it was first class. (149) Aside from that, there was his staff of household slaves, carefully selected on the basis of their excellence, both with regard to the beauty and health condition of their bodies and to the perfect way in which they performed their services. Every one of them performed his tasks exceptionally well, so that they were looked upon as either the best among those who performed the same functions or as absolutely second to none. (150) A clear proof of all this is the fact that, while a great number of properties belonging to condemned persons were sold by public auction, that of Flaccus alone was reserved for the emperor, except a few items so as to avoid transgression of the law enacted about persons convicted on these grounds.

(151) After the confiscation of his property he was sentenced to deportation. He was banished from the whole mainland — that is, the greater and better part of the habitable world — and from every island on which people can prosper. For he would have been exiled to the most miserable of all the islands in the Aegaean Sea, called Gyara, had Lepidus not interceded. Thanks to him he could exchange Gyara for nearby Andros. (152) Then he had to travel again from Rome to Brindisium, the same journey he had also made a few years before when he had been appointed governor of Egypt and adjacent Libya. Consequently, the cities which then saw him so full of pride and making a show of the grandeur of his good fortune, would now see him again, but this time in complete dishonor. (153) Pointed at with the finger and insulted though he was, he felt

oppressed by even heavier afflictions caused by the total reversal of his fortune, for his misery was constantly being renewed and rekindled by additions of fresh evils which, as in the case of recurring diseases,[6] forcibly bring back the memories of former disasters which in the meantime seemed to have been dimmed.

(154) After he had crossed the Ionian Gulf he sailed upon the sea which extends to Corinth, a spectacle to all the Peloponnesian coastal cities when they heard of the sudden reversal of his fortune. For whenever he disembarked, the people crowded, the ill-disposed out of malice, but others, who are usually sobered by what happens to other people, out of sympathy. (155) From Lechaion he crossed the Isthmus to the opposite sea and arrived at Cenchraeae, the port of Corinth. There his guards, who did not permit him the smallest respite, forced him to embark immediately upon a small merchant vessel and put to sea. And since a strong contrary wind was rushing down, he suffered greatly and only with great difficulty did he arrive storm-tossed at the Piraeus. (156) When the storm had ceased, he coasted along Attica as far as Cape Sounion and then continued along the series of islands there, Helena, Kia, Kythnos, and all the others that lie in a row one after the other, until at last he came to his destination, the island of the Andrians.

(157) When he saw it from afar, the wretch cried so uncontrollably that his tears seemed to come from a fountain. Beating his breast and lamenting bitterly, he said: "My guards and escorts, look what a fine piece of land this Andros is, an unhappy island that I exchange for happy Italy! (158) I, Flaccus, was born and brought up and educated in imperial Rome, where I was the schoolmate and companion of the grandchildren of Augustus and chosen by Tiberius Caesar as one of his intimate friends, and entrusted for six years with the greatest of all his possessions, Egypt. (159) Why this enormous change of fortune? As if an eclipse has occurred, during the day night has overtaken my life! This little island, what shall I call it? 'My place of banishment' or 'my new fatherland,' 'a safe haven' or 'a miserable place of refuge'? No, 'tomb' would be its most appropriate name! For in a sense, wretch that I am, I am being sent to bear my own corpse as it were to a tomb. For either because of my sufferings I will make an end to my miserable life or, if I would be able to live on, I will die a drawn-out death in full consciousness."

---

[6] Reading ὑποτροπιαζούσαις. See the commentary *ad locum.*

(160) Thus he was lamenting. When the ship had moored in the harbor, he disembarked while he wholly stooped down to the ground as people do who are pressed down by a very heavy burden, his neck heavily laden with his misfortunes. He did not even have the energy to lift up his head, or he did not dare it because of the people who had come to meet him and had lined up on either side of the road in order to see him. (161) His escorts led him to the assembly of the people of Andros and showed him there to everyone, thus making them witnesses of the arrival of the exile in their island. And then, having fulfilled their service, they departed.

§§162-180a *Flaccus at Andros*

(162) But Flaccus, no longer seeing any familiar sight, felt his suffering renewed as it became more poignant by ever more vivid imaginings. Looking at the sheer desolation around him, in the middle of which he had come to a halt, it seemed to him that a violent death in his native country would have been a lesser evil, or rather a welcome solution, as compared to his present circumstances. He made such spastic movements that it was impossible to see any difference with a lunatic. He ran around, frequently jumping up and down, clapping his hands, smiting his thighs, flinging himself on the ground, while he shouted: (163) "I am Flaccus, who until recently was the governor of the great city, or rather multi-city, Alexandria, and the ruler of the most blessed land of Egypt! I am the one to whom innumerable of its inhabitants turned, the one who commanded great forces of infantry, cavalry, and navy, an army that excelled not only in numbers but also in quality. I am the one who was escorted day after day by numerous people when I went out. (164) But was all this just an illusion, not reality at all? Was it only when I slept that I saw in my dreams that former happiness, images disappearing into a void, figments of a soul which perhaps depicted non-existing things as reality? (165) Yes, I have completely deceived myself! After all these were but a shadow of realities, not the realities themselves, an imitation of clear perception, not clear perception itself which unmasks falsehood. For just as when we wake up we find nothing of the things that appear to us in our dreams — all have flown away together — so too all that brilliance which I formerly enjoyed has been extinguished in one very short moment."

(166) These kind of thoughts kept him constantly in their grip and, so to speak, broke his back. He avoided going to places where

he would meet many people because of his haunting shame, so he neither went down to the harbor nor did he dare to visit the marketplace, but he lurked in his house where he had locked up himself, for he did not even have the courage to cross the threshhold. (167) Sometimes, however, early in the morning when all the others were still in their beds, he would go outside the city wall without showing himself to anyone at all, and he would spend the day in loneliness. He would then turn aside if someone was about to meet him, so tormented and devoured was his soul by the fresh memories of his misfortunes, poor wretch. He would come back only in the middle of the night, praying in his endless and boundless sorrow that the evening would become morning again because of his fear of the darkness and the weird visions he had when he happened to fall asleep; but in the morning he prayed that it would be evening again, for the darkness that surrounded him was opposed to everything bright.

(168) A few months later he bought a small piece of land where he spent much of his time in solitude, bewailing his own fate with many tears. (169) There is a story that once about midnight he became inspired, like in the Corybantic rites, and came out of his farm-house. He then turned his eyes towards heaven and the stars and, seeing that which is really a cosmos within the cosmos, he cried out:

(170) "King of gods and men, it is now clear that you are not indifferent to the nation of the Jews, nor is what they assert about your providence false, for all who deny that the Jews have you for a champion and defender go astray from sound opinion. I am a clear proof of this, for all the mad acts that I have committed against the Jews I have now suffered myself. (171) When they were robbed of their possessions I closed my eyes and gave license to those who plundered them. For that reason I have myself been deprived of all I inherited from my father and my mother and of all that I received by way of favor and gift or that I acquired in other ways. (172) Once I cast on them the slur that they had no civic rights because they were foreigners, whereas in fact they were inhabitants possessing these rights. I did so in order to please their adversaries, a disorderly and unruly mob, by whose flattery I, miserable man that I am, was led astray. For that reason I was deprived of my civic rights, driven in exile from all the inhabited world, and shut up in this place. (173) I gave orders to bring some of them to the theatre and have them maltreated there before the eyes of their greatest enemies, unjustly so. Justly, therefore, I was marched not into only one theatre or just one city to undergo

the worst maltreatment in my wretched soul rather than in my body, but I was paraded through all Italy as far as Brindisium, through all the Peloponnese as far as Corinth, and through Attica and the islands as far as Andros, my prison. (174) And I am deeply convinced that this is not the end of my misfortunes, but that there are others still in store for me to fill up the measure of compensation for what I have perpetrated. I put some to death and when they were killed by others I did not avenge them. Some were stoned, some while still alive were burnt to death or dragged through the middle of the market place till their bodies were wholly torn to pieces. (175) Because of all that I know that the goddesses of punishment await me and that these avenging spirits are already standing as it were at the finish and press forward eager for my blood. Every day, or rather every hour, I die beforehand by suffering many deaths, not only the last one."

(176) He often was so frightened that he panicked, and then the limbs and members of his body shivered and shuddered and his soul was atremble with fear and quivering with panting and palpitation, knowing that he had lost the only thing that can naturally comfort human life, hope of something good. (177) No favorable omen ever appeared to him. Everything seemed to bode ill, presaging sounds and voices were sinister, his wakeful hours were hard to bear, his sleep full of fear, his solitude as that of a beast. Was company of other people then what pleased him most? No, time spent in a city was most unpleasant to him. His solitary life in the countryside, although disgraceful, was it safe at least? No, it was dangerous and inexorable. Anyone who approached him quietly was to be suspected. (178) "He is plotting something against me," he said, "since he is walking so fast. It does not seem that he is in a hurry for any other reason than pursuing me. The man with a smile is laying a snare for me. The frank man despises me. Food and drink are given to me as to beasts for slaughter. (179) How long can I endure so many misfortunes as if I am a man of steel? I know that I am losing courage in the face of death, due to the cruelty of a deity who does not permit me to break off abruptly my miserable life because he still has an abundance of irremediable evils in store for me, which he treasures up against me in order to do a favor to those whom I treacherously murdered."

(180a) Restlessly repeating this kind of thing he awaited his fated end and uninterrupted sorrows went on to disturb and confuse his soul.

§§180b-190 *Caligula Has Flaccus Killed*
But in the meantime Gaius, who was by nature ruthless and never satisfied with the revenge he had taken, did not — unlike others — leave alone those who had once been punished, because his hard feelings would never stop, and for that reason he continuously tried to find new and great disasters to inflict upon them. And Flaccus was a person he hated to such a degree that he even loathed his namesakes, so repulsive to him was the name of Flaccus. (181) He often regretted that he had condemned him to exile instead of death, and although he respected Lepidus, who had interceded, he also blamed him for it so that for fear of punishment the man stopped interceding. He was afraid, rightly so, that by helping to lighten the sentence of another, he himself would receive a heavier one.

(182) Since nobody any longer had the courage to say anything to make him more lenient, Gaius now gave vent to his unsoftened and unbridled fury, which should have been mitigated with time but instead had become exacerbated, as is the case with diseases which, when they recur, are more severe than at previous times. (183) So they say that once, in a sleepless night, he was thinking of his officials in exile, who in theory were supposed to live unhappy lives but in practice lived without trouble and in tranquillity and freedom. (184) He even changed the designation from "exile" to "holidays abroad." He said: "The banishment of such people is a sort of holiday abroad because all they need is there in abundance and they are able to live without trouble and in well-being. As a matter of fact it is absurd that they live in luxury and enjoy the advantages of the peaceful life of a philosopher!"

(185) Thereupon he ordered that the most distinguished and those with the highest reputation should be put to death, giving a list of names which was headed by that of Flaccus.

When the men who had been ordered to kill him arrived at Andros, Flaccus happened to arrive from the country at the city and they came from the harbor to meet him. They recognized each other from afar. (186) He then realized the purpose of their mission — for everyone's soul is highly prophetic, especially of people in misfortune — and turned from the road, running away in flight over the rugged ground. Did he perhaps forget that Andros was an island, not the mainland, so that speed is of no use since the sea surrounds it? For one of two things was to happen necessarily: either he was to go too far and end up in the sea or he was to arrive at the very edge of the island and be arrested there. (187) Now, when two evils have to be compared, death on land is preferable to death in the sea, for nature assigned to men and all other terrestrials land as their most appropriate place, not only during their lifetime but also after death: the same element should receive them not only at the moment of their birth but also at their departure from life.

(188) They pursued him without stopping to draw breath and caught him. Some of them at once started to dig a pit, the others dragged him along by force although he resisted and screamed and struggled, as a result of which he was wounded all over his body since he ran upon the blows, as wild beasts do. (189) He seized hold of his murderers and clung to them so that they were hindered to direct their swords at him directly and had to apply their blows obliquely, and so he caused himself to suffer more severely. Finally, he lay there, his hands, feet, head, breast, and sides gashed and smashed, ready as it were to be cut up like a sacrificial animal. For Justice wanted that single body to receive wounds as numerous as the number of the Jews who had been unlawfully murdered by him.

(190) The whole place was running with blood that poured forth like a fountain from the many veins, which had been gashed one after the other. When the corpse was being dragged into the pit which had been dug, most of the parts fell asunder since the ligaments by which the whole of the body was kept together had been slit.

§191 *Epilogue*
(191) Such were the sufferings of Flaccus, too, who thus became an indubitable proof that the Jewish people had not been deprived of the help of God.

COMMENTARY

The Title

On Flaccus: The title of *Flacc.* has been transmitted in a variety of forms. Our best ms., M, has Φίλωνος εἰς Φλάκκον (translated here); others have just εἰς Φλάκκον, or Φλάκκος ψεγόμενος, or the more elaborate and pious (and therefore secondary) Φίλωνος ἱστορία πάνυ ὠφέλιμος καὶ τῷ βίῳ χρήσιμος τὰ κατὰ τὸν Φλάκκον ἤτοι περὶ προνοίας. Photius (*Bibl.* cod. 105) refers to the work as Φλάκκος ἢ Φλάκκων ψεγόμενος (Φλάκκων obviously being a mistake for Φλάκκος), and Eusebius calls the treatise simply Φλάκκος (*Chron.* Tiberius 21; Jerome translates 'in libro qui "Flaccus" inscribitur'). In the quotes from *Flacc.* in John of Damascus' compilatory work (see Introd. ch. 7), the work is called τὰ κατὰ Φλάκκον or τὰ πρὸς Φλάκκον. Note that there is no tradition calling the work κατὰ Φλάκκου, *contra Flaccum*. The preposition εἰς in εἰς Φλάκκον can certainly not have the sense of κατά with genitive ("against") and neither can κατά or πρός with the accusative. So we are left with either simply Φλάκκος or εἰς Φλάκκον, both of them being rather neutral titles: "(On) Flaccus." Since our earliest witness, Eusebius, refers to the work with the simple title *Flaccus* and receives support for this from Photius, it has a good chance of being the original one, although the reading εἰς Φλάκκον in two important manuscripts cannot be ruled out entirely. *Non liquet.*

Lit.: Reiter 1915:xlvii-xlviii; Balsdon 1934:221-222; Box 1939:xxxiv-xxxviii; Leisegang 1941:48-49; Smallwood 1961:36-43; Colson 1962:xvi-xxvi; Hennig 1975:164-173; Morris in Schürer 1973/87:III 859-864; Kraus 1994:480-481; Meiser 1999:418 (on double titles of the type Φλάκκος ἢ περὶ προνοίας see the material collected by Saffrey-Segonds 2001:49 note 2).

Part I. Flaccus' Persecution of the Jews (§§1-96)

§§ 1-7: *Flaccus' promising start*

In the opening paragraphs Philo sketches Flaccus as a very capable and responsible governor (in this respect he even surpassed his predecessors, says Philo in §8). Since this sketch shows that he was able to fulfil his duties in an exemplary way, the section is primarily designed to serve as a foil against which Flaccus' later malfunctioning and malicious scheming stands out in all the sharper contrast, as Philo himself explicitly says in §7: "I praise Flaccus not because it is the right thing to praise an enemy but in order to enable myself to expose his wickedness even more clearly." The rhetorical function of this section is to drive home to the reader that Flaccus' ability to be a good governor makes him all the more responsible for the catastrophic events in the summer of 38 CE.

§1. *After Sejanus ...*: On δεύτερος see below. Lucius Aelius Sejanus was appointed *praefectus praetorio* by Tiberius in 14 CE and soon became sole commander of the praetorian guards (the *cohortes praetorianae*, which were responsible for order and safety in the imperial palaces; see Gutsfeld 2001). Sejanus' influence on the emperor was very great and his power increased over the years (Hennig 1975: *passim*; Levick 1976:148-155; Kornemann 1980:158-170; Eck 1996). In 30 CE, he was elected consul for the next year with Tiberius and he hoped for more, possibly even a partnership with the emperor. But when he was accused of planning the assassination of the future emperor Gaius (Caligula), he was arrested and executed (in 31). In *Legat.* 159-160 Philo says that Sejanus had invented false slanders against the Jews in Rome "because he wished to do away with the nation, knowing that it would take the sole or the principal part in opposing his unholy plots and actions, and would defend the emperor when in danger of becoming the victim of treachery" (see Smallwood 1961 and Pelletier 1972 *ad loc.*). There is no further evidence to support this statement, not even in Josephus who devotes much attention to Sejanus. So there may be some reason to doubt what Philo says here; his description of the affair is probably somewhat exaggerated (but see Slingerland 1997:71-72, 232-233, 240). Eusebius, however, says that Philo wrote that Sejanus wanted to eradicate the entire Jewish nation (both in *Hist. Eccl.* 2.5.7 and in *Chron.*, year 21 of Tiberius [vol. 1, p. 176 ed. Helm]), and it has been argued that he is referring not to the short opening remark of *Flacc.* but to a lost work of Philo in which the persecutions by Sejanus were dealt with on their own and to which *Flacc.* was the sequel (see Smallwood 1961:36-43; Hennig 1975:165-168; Morris 1987:860-861). Eusebius may have based his remark on *Legat.* 159-160 (quoted above), but it seems probable that Philo did write a separate work on Sejanus (see Introd., ch. 1). Philo says here (*Flacc.* 1) that Sejanus wanted to do injustice to the entire nation (συμπᾶν ἀδικῆσαι τὸ ἔθνος). It has been suggested that Sejanus was the driving force behind Tiberius' measure to expel the Jews from Rome or Italy in 19 CE (thus Box 1939: 68 and cf. Kraus 1967:39; Tacitus, *Ann.* 2.8, speaks of an expulsion from all of Italy; Suetonius, *Tib.* 36, says from Rome only), but this measure was directed not only against the Jews but also, and primarily, against the Isis-cult (see Hennig 1975:161-164, and esp. Gruen 2002:35-36). Be that as it may, Philo's tantalizingly brief remark does show that according to Philo "the Jews could no longer be confident about the emperor's attitude to their concerns, and that the influence of particular individuals in the imperial court could largely determine their fortunes" (Barclay 1996:301). And it is true that "if Philo devoted a whole book, now lost, to Sejanus' anti-Jewish policy, the threat was presumably serious" (Smallwood 1976:202 note 5). But Smallwood 1987:127 rightly remarks that Josephus' complete silence about Sejanus' supposed plans against the Jews suggests that they were actually far less serious than Philo would have us believe. All this must remain uncertain and, anyway, Philo here implies that the threat of Sejanus was hardly over when the next one (δεύτερος) made already its appearance in the person of Flaccus. For a detailed analysis and balanced discussion of this whole passage see Hennig 1975:160-179, esp. 169-173, who comes to this conclusion: "So erscheint der Verdacht durchaus berechtigt, daß Philo den Versuch unternommen hat, unter bewußter Verschleierung der Tatsachen das einmalige Vorgehen gegen die Juden unter der Regierung des Tiberius, nämlich das vom Jahre 19, das er wohl nicht gut völlig verschweigen konnte, auf das Konto Sejans zu setzen. Dazu war es vor allem notwendig, den Zeitpunkt im unklaren zu lassen und, ohne daß dies ausdrücklich gesagt wird, den Eindruck zu erwecken, daß die Attacke Sejans gegen die Juden seinem Sturz unmittelbar vorausging. Denn erst damals und nicht schon im Jahre 19 konnte ihm dann auch die volle Verantwortung zugeschoben werden" (173). It was only in this way that Philo could maintain his theory of God's terrible punishment of the enemies of the Jews (Nestle 1936:263). On Philo's portrait of Sejanus see also Lémonon 1981:224-225 and Barraclough 1984:471-472.

Avillius Flaccus: See Introd. ch. 5, Excursus.

continued his policy of persecuting the Jews: lit. "took over [from him] the attack against the Jews." Although "took over" (διαδέχεται) suggests an immediate continuation of Sejanus' policy, in actual fact seven years elapsed between Sejanus' death in 31 and the pogrom in 38. But Philo seems to imply that when, after Sejanus' death, Flaccus was appointed in 32 CE, he also immediately (as δεύτερος) took over Sejanus' heritage (thus Smallwood 1976:201; cf. Sly 1996:168), even though this is contradicted by what he himself says in §§2-5. By attributing to Flaccus an anti-Jewish frame of mind from the very beginning, Philo "avoids any suggestion of Jewish culpability for the troubles which were to follow" (Barraclough 1984:463).

he had less resources and occasions to do so: Because Flaccus had a much less central and powerful position than Sejanus.

irreparable evils: These are described in detail in §§41-96.

everyone everywhere: πανταχοῦ πάντας. Philo is fond of this kind of alliterating paronomasia; see the instances collected by Reiter 1915:li; for the rhetorical theory of *paronomasia* see Lausberg 1963:90 and Anderson 2000:93; cf. Quintilian 9.3.66. It is unclear what Philo means when he says that Flaccus "tried to bring everyone everywhere within his field of fire." It would seem that he is implying that Flaccus' anti-Jewish plans of action were quite far-reaching and aimed at more than just the Jewish population of Alexandria, but he does not tell us how he knew. This exaggerating statement is probably meant to make unambiguously clear to the reader how evil Flaccus' intents were, no better than those of the notoriously malignant Sejanus. It is a typical case of Philonic tendentious generalization.

to achieve their malignant designs: On κατορθοῦν "pour désigner le succès des malfaiteurs" see Nikiprowetzky in Winston-Dillon 1983:73.

§2. *the friends of the emperor*: friends = ἑταῖροι = *amici*. Flaccus was an *amicus Caesaris*, a somewhat formal title for a member of the informal circle of courtiers who were the emperor's main advisors. In literary evidence from the imperial period we find accounts of the emperors consulting their *amici*. They were favored members of the equestrian and senatorial *ordines* (Millar 1977:110-122, esp. 119 note 66 for references). Tiberius divided his *amici* into classes (Suetonius,

Tib. 46; Seneca, *De benef.* 6:33-34). According to the New Testament, the governor of Judaea, Pilate, too, was an *amicus* of Tiberius (John 19:12; see Barrett 1978:543).

the prefect of Alexandria and the country around it: The *praefectus Alexandreae et Aegypti* (often more briefly *praefectus Aegypti* = ἔπαρχος Αἰγύπτου) was the Roman governor of all Egypt consisting of both Alexandria proper (usually called *Alexandria ad Aegyptum*!) and the *chôra* ('country'), the rest of Egypt; cf. in §5 "throughout the city and the country" (the constitutional separation of Alexandria from Egypt probably dates back to Ptolemaic times; Huzar 1988:622 with note 8, *contra* Fraser 1972: I.107-108). This prefect usually served for a term of one to three years, but sometimes for more than four or five. Tiberius had a policy of keeping officials in provinces longer than usual; see Josephus, *Ant.* 18.168-178, and Tacitus, *Ann.* 1.80. The prefect was mostly someone of equestrian rank and, under the Julio-Claudians, his job was deemed so important that he received proconsular powers and surpassed all the other imperial prefectures (Huzar 1988:658). His position had a special weight since Egypt was the granary of the Roman Empire, especially of the city of Rome itself (cf. Acts 27:6). His most important duties were representing imperial authority, commanding the Roman legions, keeping the unruly population under control in view of the levying of taxes, and administering justice (Eck 2001:246-249). For lists of *praefecti Aegypti* see Stein 1950; Reinmuth 1954 and 1956; Schwartz 1982; Bureth 1988; Bastianini 1988; more references in Rupprecht 1994:70.

after the death of Hiberus: M. Antonius Hiberus was an imperial freedman who worked in Egypt as a high financial official in the imperial service from 26-28 CE. Hiberus was appointed (vice-) *praefectus Aegypti* by Tiberius in 32, but he died soon thereafter (Mélèze Modrzejewski 1990:VII.67 with note 48; Eck 1998:532). The reading *Hibêrou* is a widely accepted conjecture of Reiter (1915:li) for the mss.'s *Sebêrou* (G: *bêrou*) on the basis of the information given by Cassius Dio 58.19.6: "Meanwhile Vitrasius Pollio, the governor of Egypt, died, and he [Tiberius, in 32] entrusted the province for a time to a certain Hiberus, an imperial freedman" (cf. Pelletier 1967:45 note 6 and, on Cassius Dio's mistake about Vitrasius Pollio, who in fact was Flaccus' successor, see Schwartz 1982). See further Stein 1950:25-26; Bureth 1988:476.

his excellence: καλοκαγαθία, a favorite term of Philo (he uses it 77 times), often used for the superior spiritual qualities of biblical heroes such as the patriarchs and Moses. On καλοκαγαθία in Philo see Runia 1997:9-12. In the following words ("prudent, persevering, acute in devising and carrying out his plans, very eloquent and quick at understanding") Philo goes to great length in emphasizing Flaccus' highly promising start in order to serve as a foil to his behavior after Tiberius' death. In §4 he even speaks of Flaccus' "illustrious and kingly nature."

quick at understanding what was left unsaid better even than what was said: "Hyperbole qui ne trompe personne" (Pelletier 1967:46 note 1). On τὸ ἡσυχαζόμενον in the sense of 'what is left unsaid' see Box 1939:70.

§3. *complex and diversified*: The adjectives πολύτροπος and ποικίλος underscore the variety and complexity of Flaccus' tasks but, as in the previous paragraph, here again Philo goes to great lengths to stress how capable a governor Flaccus had been in the first five years of his term (32-37 CE). See Philo's own summary in §8: "In the first five years — that is, when the emperor Tiberius was still alive — he not only maintained peace but also governed with such energy and vigor that he surpassed all his predecessors." In §§9ff., however, the sudden decline sets in.

His secretaries were a superfluous crowd: On the complicated bureaucracy in Ptolemaic and Roman Egypt see Box 1939:70; Rupprecht 1994:43-93; esp. Fraser 1972: chs. 2 and 3, and Haas 1997: ch. 3. A very helpful chart showing the complex structure of the bureaucracy in Roman Egypt is to be found in Bowman 1986:67. This complex bureaucratic system is mentioned here only in order to highlight Flaccus' competence, even brilliance: he "surpassed" (ὑπερβαλεῖν) all the officials in the understanding of the system.

§4. *All matters pertaining to financial accountancy and the administration of revenues were dealt with competently by him*: Cf. §133: "For it was impossible that the governors, who were in charge of such a vast country, could remember all the cases in that constant stream of both private and public new affairs, especially as they had not only to administer justice but also received the calculations of the revenues and taxes, the scrutiny of which took up the greater part of the year." Even so, Flaccus managed to do very well, says Philo in this, undoubtedly exaggerated, report (on the fact that he does so for the purposes of contrast, see the first note *ad* §7). "Matters of financial accountancy" (λογισμοί) and "the administration of revenues" (ἡ τῶν προσοδευομένων διοίκησις) refer to the assessment and levying of the various taxes imposed by the Romans (*inter alia* the hated poll-tax, *laographia*, on which see *CPJ* 1.60). Philo praises Flaccus' competence, although 30 years later Philo's own nephew, Tiberius Julius Alexander, suggests that Flaccus may have been too mild in exaction; see his edict in *OGIS* 669:26-28 (see above in the Introduction, the Excursus on Flaccus). For the complex taxing system in Roman Egypt in general see the brief introduction with extensive bibliography in Rupprecht 1994:74-82; also Lewis 1983:159-176.

a more illustrious and kingly nature: λαμπροτέρα καὶ βασιλικὴ φύσις. This is the highest praise possible in Philo's mouth. For the idea of a "kingly nature" see *Mos.* 1.153 and 2.2 (on Moses); cf. *Post.* 101-102.

with greater freedom: μετὰ πλείονος παρρησίας. The word παρρησία here seems to be used, as Colson remarks (1941:304 note b), in a wider sense than the usual "freedom of speech;" it rather denotes self-confidence and outspokenness in behavior (see the reference to Flaccus' "stateliness" when walking, in the following line). For the large bibliography on παρρησία see *RBLG* 418; add Saffrey-Segonds 2001:101-102 note 4.

ostentation: τῦφος = delusion, affectation, humbug, nonsense (LSJ). It usually has a negative connotation, also in Philo who uses it 56 times, for instance in *Legat.* 116 for Gaius' extreme vanity. Cf. also Plato, *Phaedr.* 230a; Sextus Emp., *Adv. math.* 8.5; for other instances see Goodenough 1938:23-26, 33-36; Box 1939:71; Krauss 1934:522; and the *Philo Index* 341. Even though Philo admits that "ostentation is very useful for a ruler," also for Flaccus, he seems to anticipate already here his later criticisms of the man.

important cases: For instance, those involving capital punishment.

with the magistrates: μετὰ τῶν ἐν τέλει, i.e., with officials at a lower local level, for instance Lampo as described in §§131-134. Each year the prefect left Alexandria for a period of some four months and travelled through the country according to a fixed time schedule in order to deal with legal and civil questions, in which he needed the assistance of these local officials; "he held assizes, received petitions from grievants, and scrutinized the accounts and performances of the local administrators" (Lewis 1983:19). See further Lewis 1983:45-48, 185-195; Rupprecht 1994:69-72; esp. Delia 1991:98-107 (147-158 presents lists of Alexandrian magistrates).

a motley crowd of people from all quarters: lit. μιγάδων καὶ συγκλύδων ἀνθρώπων ὄχλον, "a mass of promiscuously and indiscriminately mixed humans." Polybius, too, calls the Alexandrians μιγάδες, a "medley" of Greeks of all sorts (34.14.5; he is not implying an admixture of Egyptian blood, see Davis 1951:69-70). In *Flacc.* Philo very often refers, in a variety of ways, to the Alexandrian "mob" (see §§4, 5, 19, 33, 35, 41, 65, 80, 82, 135-136 etc.; cf. also *Legat.* 67, 120, 132, 226, 252) for which he felt such a great contempt. That Flaccus kept the mob in their place is in Philo's eyes a proof of his capability and efficiency as a ruler. Flaccus apparently not only shut down the clubs of the city (see immediately below), but he also forbade large gatherings of Alexandrians for fear of political conspiracy; for ἐπισυνίστασθαι in the sense of "conspiring" see LSJ *s.v.* II 4.

he also prohibited the clubs and associations (ἑταιρείας καὶ συνόδους): Almost every town and city in the Roman empire had its clubs and associations (*thiasoi, synodoi, hetaireiai, eranoi; collegia, sodalitates*), Egypt was no exception (Poland 1909; San Nicolò 1913-15; Boak 1937; Danker 1992; Kloppenborg & Wilson 1996; further bibliography in Rupprecht 1994:106). They were "voluntary associations of persons more or less permanently organized for the pursuit of a common end, and so distinguishable both from the state and its component elements on the one hand, and on the other from temporary unions for ephemeral purposes" (*OCD* 351). There were religious guilds (e.g., those of the artists of Dionysus or the worshippers of Zeus Hypsistos) and secular ones (e.g., those of fellow workers in the same craft or trade, e.g. silversmiths [see Acts 19:25]), although this separation between sacred and profane is somewhat anachronistic for our period; further there were also domestic *collegia* consisting of the slaves (and freedmen) of large households. Quite often their main purpose was to foster social life among their members and to give them a sense of belonging. Philo knows various associations in Alexandria but is very critical of them; he suggests that membership of such clubs could easily lead to lascivious behaviour (Seland 1996). In §§135ff. he will make clear that he regards these clubs as the hotbeds of anti-Jewish agitation in the city and as the sally-ports of gangs of hooligans (there he uses the less common term *klinê* alongside *synodos*, on which see Seland 1996:113). There Philo emphasizes the elements of excessive drinking (cf. "like inebriates" here) and the forging of political intrigues and conspiracies (cf. *Ebr.* 20-26 and *Legat.* 312, where he contrasts these clubs with the edifying gatherings of Jewish communities, on which see Seland 1996:114-124). Other ancient authors, too, mention the notoriety of the Alexandrian clubs, e.g., Athenaeus, *Deipn.* 246C; Dio Chrysostom, *Or.* 32.70 (see further Pelletier 1967:46 note 3; Box 1939:72 for non-literary evidence; Bowman 1986:212; Barry 1993). Philo therefore praises Flaccus for his closure of the clubs, which may have been meant as a measure to prevent any recurrence of the events described in more detail in §§ 135-145 (Isidorus' agitation against Flaccus with the help of the clubs of which he was the leader), according to a not improbable suggestion of Smallwood (1976:236 note 64). Since Flaccus took these measures during the reign of Tiberius, who had a great distrust of this type of associations, his action may also have been a direct consequence of the imperial policy in general (Cotter 1996:78-88).

§5. *he had established law and order:* For "law and order" the Greek text has εὐνομία (see the literature in RBLG 289). What Philo is probably referring to is Flaccus' large-scale collecting of clandestine weapons in the year 33/34, which he describes in §§92-93 (see *ad loc.*). Apparently the catch of arms then was enormous.

throughout the city and the country: see *ad* §2.

he proceeded ... to concentrate his attention on ...: The Greek is unclear here: ἐφήδρευεν. The usual meaning of ἐφεδρεύω is "to lie in wait (for an opportunity to attack)," but it developed the sense of "to watch for ..." and even "to help" (as in *Migr.* 57). See the note in Pelletier 1967:48 note 2. What is meant here is — in view of the immediately following participles ἐκτάττων, συγκροτῶν, γυμνάζων (on which see below) — that Flaccus paid attention to putting the army in the necessary order again.

the armed forces: Egypt was garrisoned by a standing army of three legions, one of which was stationed on the borders of Alexandria, and nine auxiliary cohorts, says Strabo 17.1.12 (797), but by Tiberius' time there may have been only two legions (he reduced their number to two by 23 CE; cf. Tacitus, *Ann.* 4.5). The total number of soldiers probably never exceeded 18,000 (Pelletier 1967:48 note 3; Box 1939:73-4). Bibliography on the army in Roman Egypt in Devijver 1974 and Rupprecht 1994:85-86.

by setting them in array and disciplining them, and by training ...: Ἐκτάττειν is "to draw out in battle order" or "to keep muster-roll of," but according to Box 1939:74 here the sense could be "detailing for duties" (see, however, Pelletier 1967:49 note 4). Συγκροτεῖν is the more technical drilling of the troops; γυμνάζειν is the training in more general sense, including inculcating a morale as the following lines make clear.

not to deprive the soldiers of their pay ... acts of bandrity and robbery: Box 1939:74 remarks about the withholding of soldiers' pay: "I can find no parallel to or corroboration of this abuse." But this detail can hardly have been made up by Philo. Even though non-payment of wages cannot be confirmed from other sources, we do know that for one reason or another, often out of discontent with their wages, Roman soldiers tried to get some extra income. In Luke 3:14 John the Baptist says to some of them: "Rob no one by violence or false accusations, and be content with your wages" (referred to by De Vries 1999:261). First century CE documentary evidence for exactions by troops in Egypt is presented by Box 1939:74-75 (e.g., *OGIS* 2.665), who remarks: "The lack of any stipend for pocket-money (...) helps to explain these exactions." See on extortion by soldiers also the useful "Note complémentaire" in Pelletier 1967:157-158 and Lewis 1983:172-176.

outside their military service: ἔξω τῶν κατὰ τὴν στρατείαν. Peace-time service of the army consisted in such occupations as policing the country districts and the construction and maintenance of roads and canals. But these are not the kind of activities Philo has in mind here, he is still referring to the above mentioned undisciplined behavior. As Box 1939:75 rightly remarks, "the presence of an army of occupation in a city the inhabitants of which resented the domination of Rome required the most rigid discipline." Gerschmann *ad loc.* refers to 2 Tim. 2:4: "No soldier on service gets entangled in civilian pursuits, since his aim is to satisfy the one who enlisted him." But in the NT passage the emphasis is on total dedication to the commander, whereas here the point is to abstain from unauthorized activities.

to keep in mind: The word μεμνημένος is taken by Box 1939:5 to be correlated not to the soldier who is the subject of the verb περιεργάζηται, but to Flaccus who is the subject of ἐφήδρευεν: "he remembered that it was to maintain peace that he was appointed," which is grammatically defensible. Both Colson and Pelletier take exception to this view: "The run of the sentence is against it (...). The soldier may very properly be admonished to remember that he is a policeman as well" (Colson 1941:306-7 note a); "C'est à chacun des hommes de troupe, en effet, qu'il est recommandé (...) de se souvenir que le maintien de la tranquillité de la population fait partie, elle aussi, de son devoir de soldat" (Pelletier 1967:49 note 8). The latter interpretation is the more feasible one.

§6. *Perhaps someone will say now*: Introducing a fictive interlocutor is typically diatribe style, thus providing a degree of argument; see Stowers 1992; Schmeller 1987 in the various paragraphs on "dialogische Struktur." Here the anonymous speaker stands for the reader who is surprised to find praise for Flaccus whereas he expects the contrary. The rebuttal comes in §7.

dear fellow: For this use of οὗτος as a vocative see LSJ *s.v.* C I 5 and the literature in RBLG 407.

Have you lost your mind ...: On ἆρα expressing surprise see Denniston 1954:35-36.

No, I have not gone mad: οὐ μέμηνα. Cf. what Paul the apostle says before Festus in Acts 26:25: οὐ μαίνομαι. See Helyer 2002:314.

consistent argument: πράγματος ἀκολουθία. In *Aet.* 112 Philo uses πραγμάτων ἀκολουθία in the sense of an unbroken sequence of events. Here the meaning is rather "die Logik eines Sachverhaltes" (Gerschmann), "what is consistent with an undertaking" (Box), "the sequence of an argument" (Colson), "la suite d'un sujet" (Pelletier). The logic announced here follows in §7.

§7. *I praise Flaccus ... in order to enable myself to expose his wickedness even more clearly*: Bell 1924:16 rightly says: "Philo's remark shows a temper remote indeed from that of the historian." As a bad ruler Flaccus is all the more guilty because he had shown his obvious capacity to rule so well. Of course "this contrast was largely of Philo's making, but the lack of information from any other source on the nature of Flaccus' rule prevents us from reaching a final verdict" (Barraclough 1984:461; cf. Sevenster 1975:21). There is a striking parallel in *Legat.* 8-13 where Philo does the same with regard to the beginning of Gaius' rule: his first seven months are described as a kind of golden age, but then follows the great contrast, as here.

Pardon ... conscience: Here Philo explains what he means by Flaccus' wickedness. His sins were not committed out of ignorance (ἀγνοίᾳ) but knowingly and willingly (ἐξ ἐπιστήμης), and for that reason there is no pardon to be given. Because his evil deeds were perpetrated deliberately and on purpose, there is no defense. The distinction between sins committed on purpose and those committed unwillingly or out of inadvertence is important to Philo (see *Imm.* 128, *Ebr.* 125, *Spec.* 1.235-237); it has an Old Testament background (e.g., Num. 15:22-31); see Klauck 1994:44. The image of being condemned before the tribunal of one's own conscience "fait partie de l'imagerie judiciaire courante dans Philon" (Pelletier 1967:50); see the references in Box 1939:76 and *Philo Index* 321-322. Philo saw conscience as a faculty scrutinizing conduct and passing judgement upon it (cf. τὸ τῆς διανοίας βουλευτήριον in §102); it is both immanent in the soul and sent by God. See further Chadwick 1978; Eckstein 1983 (121-132 on Philo); and esp. Klauck 1994. For general bibliography RBLG 478.

§§ 8-20: *Flaccus' degeneration*

After these promising years, the ascension of Caligula marks the sudden and unexpected start of the decline of Flaccus' good government. Due to past events related to Caligula himself and his family, in which Flaccus had been involved, he becomes frightened. Especially the death of his powerful friend Macro, who had been influential at the court in Rome, made him desperate. Flaccus, therefore, becomes liable to pressure and lends his ear to the worst possible advisors. Dark portraits of these advisors — which later turn out to be the principal anti-Jewish agitators — are pictured by Philo. The punchline is in §19, "The ruler became a subject and the subjects became leaders." For the elitist and aristocratic thinker Philo is, this loss of control and the consequent reversal of roles is the strongest disqualification he could think of.

§8. *six years ... the first five years*: Usually the length of a prefect's term depended upon the emperor's goodwill. Flaccus' term of 6 years was no exception; his predecessor Galerius even served for 15 years (from 16-31 CE). "Five years" is not completely accurate, however, since Flaccus probably entered upon office in the first half of the year 32 (or even January 32), and even though Tiberius died in March 37, Flaccus remained in office till the middle of October of 38 (see *ad* §116), so he served more than six and a half years. See on all this, against Groag-Stein 1933:290 and Box 1939:77, now convincingly Schwartz 1982. What is called "his last year" in §9 actually lasted from March 37 till October 38, which in Philo's usual way of reckoning should actually be counted as two years.

he surpassed all his predecessors: Flaccus had 13 predecessors (from 30 BCE – 32 CE). For a list of names see the references *ad* §2 and the recent bibliography in Rupprecht 1994:70. Philo now sums up his praise for Flaccus' admirable governorship before he begins to describe his degeneration in §9.

§9. *But in his last year, after Tiberius had died and Gaius been appointed emperor*: Note the particle δέ, here strongly adversative, indicating the complete change in Flaccus' behaviour. Philo emphasizes that this turnabout had everything to do with Caligula's accession to the throne in 37. In his *Legatio ad Gaium* he will stress more heavily than in *Flacc.* the evil role of the emperor. On Gaius in general see the important monograph by Barrett 1989. For Philo's view of Tiberius see Niehoff 2001:119-128.

he began to let everything slip from his hands: The image is that of a charioteer who is losing control of his chariot and horses. Driving a chariot, like steering a ship, is a common image for rulership since Plato (e.g., *Resp.* 566d2). See the parallels in Saffrey-Segonds 2001:85 note 23 (on Marinus, *Procl.* 8 τοῖς τὰς ἡνίας ἔχουσι τῆς Αἰγύπτου). Loss of control is something Philo more often speaks of in very derogatory terms; see *ad* §7 and cf. also the following note and the chapters in which Flaccus loses control of his own emotions (§§176ff.).

the endless stream of tears ... as from a fountain: This description of Flaccus' exaggerated reaction is meant to demonstrate his lack of *enkrateia*, according to Philo the supreme Jewish *and* Roman virtue, which the Egyptians, too, are lacking. According to Niehoff 2001:134-135, this loss of his wits characterizes Flaccus as an "Egyptian" who has defected from true Roman values.

he had sided with the party of the natural rather than the adopted children: This is an important point, because Flaccus had indeed played a role in the struggle about the succession of Tiberius that was not likely to earn him the favor of Caligula. Tiberius had declared in his will that his grandson Tiberius Gemellus (a child of Tiberius' son Drusus, who died in 23 CE) would be his heir together with Gaius. Gemellus belonged to the γνήσιοι (here translated by "natural children"); see Smallwood 1961:169-172. His cousin Gaius was the son of Tiberius' nephew Germanicus (died in 19 CE), who had been adopted (θετός) into the *gens Julia*. Both had supporters in their struggle, although Gemellus' only named supporter was Flaccus (Barrett 1989:339 note 79) and we do not know whether he had (m)any more. Gaius won because he argued that Gemellus was only a child (he was 18, Gaius 25); he obtained from the Roman senate the cancellation of Tiberius' will, made Gemellus his adopted son, and later forced him to commit suicide (described in detail by Philo in *Legat.* 22-31). The personal friends of the emperor, however, to whom Flaccus belonged (see §2), were of the opinion that Gemellus had to be coequal with Gaius. So Flaccus had bet on the wrong horse, and in view of Gaius' character he had every reason to become nervous. Sherwin-White 1972, however, thinks that Philo is not well informed here since Flaccus can hardly have played a role in advocating the claims of Gemellus during the last five years of Tiberius' principate for the simple reason that he was too far away from Rome. But being away from Rome does not imply complete loss of influence there.

he was one of those who had conspired against Gaius' mother: Another important reason for Flaccus' anxiety was that Flaccus' had played an active role in the affair in which Gaius' mother, Vipsania Agrippina (14 BCE-33 CE), who had accused Tiberius of having ordered her husband's death, was finally sent into exile by the emperor in 29 CE (Suetonius, *Tib.* 53). On Agrippina see Barrett 1989:4-24; and Kienast 1996.

matters which led to her execution: According to Suetonius (*Tib.* 53) and Tacitus (*Ann.* 6.25) Agrippina starved herself to death, but there were rumors that Tiberius had her put to death, which Philo's version seems to reflect here and which Tacitus' version does not exclude ("she killed herself — unless food was denied so that her death should look like suicide"). See Sly 1996:76.

So it was also fear of being held guilty that caused the neglect of his duties: γεγονὼς καὶ διὰ φόβον ἁλώσεως ἐπιλελησμένος. The word ἐπιλελησμένος is a crux. The existing translations vary: "His fear of being held guilty on this count caused him to neglect his duties" (Colson). "Through fear of conviction he had neglected to play his part in the trial" (Box). "La crainte d'être pris l'eût rendu négligent" (Pelletier). "Aus Furcht, dessen überführt zu werden, war er gelähmt" (Gerschmann), the latter based upon Theiler's conjecture πεπεδημένος. Reiter *ad loc.* declares ἐπιλελησμένος to be corrupt but suggests no other reading. Roos 1935:241 conjectures <τῆς πρότερον ἀρετῆς> ἐπιλελησμένος. Pelletier rightly defends the mss. The sense is that it was not only grief over the death of his friend Tiberius but also (all translators overlook καί!) fear of being convicted by Gaius that caused him to forget about his regular tasks. Sherwin-White 1972 strongly doubts whether "fear of being held guilty" could be the cause of Flaccus' change of mind and behaviour (but see the previous note).

§10. *For some time he still could summon the power not to let the affairs of state slip entirely out of his hands*: In *Legat.* 14 Philo says that Gaius fell ill in the 8th month of his rule. According to Cassius Dio (59.8.1), in that time Gemellus, Tiberius' grandson, was accused of having prayed for the emperor's death. Since Gaius ordered Gemellus to commit suicide only after his own recovery (see *Legat.* 23-31, esp. 30-1), Flaccus must have been able to work in peace for at least nine months after Caligula's accession (it took some time for the news of Gemellus' death to reach Alexandria).

his partner in government: not completely correct, see the note on *he had sided* in §9 and esp. Pelletier 1967:53 note 5.

with a mind that had been enfeebled and paralysed already long before: This is hard to understand in view of what Philo has just stated in the preceding paragraphs. Colson suggests as a possible meaning for πολὺ πρότερον "a much graver matter" which would yield a translation such as "... speechless and, *much more seriously*, with his mind enfeebled and paralysed." This translation can certainly not be ruled out because, although it seems grammatically a bit contrived, it avoids an otherwise incomprehensible inconsistency in Philo's argument. Nock 1972:559 lists this suggestion among Colson's many "helpful observations."

§11. *the child*: Gemellus.

breeze: αὔρα is a cool breeze from the water; for its metaphorical uses see LSJ *s.v.* 2.

his friendship with Macro: Quintus Naevius Cordus Sutorius Macro was the head of the large fire brigade (*vigiles*) of Rome till 31 CE, when he was Tiberius' agent in the overthrow of Sejanus, whom he succeeded as commander of the praetorian guard (*praefectus praetorio*), the most predominant position in politics after the emperor. In the power struggle after Tiberius' death, Macro sided with the young Gaius and was succesful in securing his ascension. He used to play the role of tutor of the young emperor, much to the annoyance of the latter (see Philo's vivid description in *Legat.* 32-61). Gaius then appointed him prefect of Egypt (as successor to Flaccus) by the end of 37 CE, but soon thereafter, even before he could take up office, he was forced by the emperor to commit suicide with his family (Cassius Dio 59.10.6, 14). It is not impossible that Isidorus — on which see the comments *ad* §20 — had a hand in this. "Though Flaccus in consequence retained the prefecture of Egypt for the present, his recall in the near future was inevitable, and Gaius' attacks on Tiberius' supporters increased his fears for his own safety" (Smallwood 1976:236). How Flaccus came to be befriended with Macro is unknown, but it seems certain that his good contacts with this high official had given him a sense of safety that he lost after Macro's suicide. On Macro see further Pelletier 1972:50-51; Barrett 1989:28-29, 37-41, 50-55 with bibliography at 260 note 45; Eck 2000; on Philo's idealized picture of Macro in *Flacc.* and *Legat.* see Barraclough 1984:470.

who initially had an all-powerful position with Gaius ...: The data in this paragraph and §§12-13 are described in much fuller detail by Philo in *Legat.* 32-61. On Macro's power see (aside from Barrett's monograph of 1989) also Balsdon 1934:20-23.

§12. *Tiberius had often considered the possibility of getting Gaius out of the way since he regarded him as a malicious person who was not gifted by nature for the exercise of rulership*: On Tiberius' recurring plans ("often") to kill Gaius see *Legat.* 58: "Not once only but thrice Tiberius wished to kill him." Cf. *Legat.* 33: "He often looked on Gaius with disfavor." That Tiberius began to have serious doubts about Gaius' capacities as his successor is confirmed by several other ancient sources (Tacitus, *Ann.* 6.46.9; Suetonius, *Calig.* 51; Cassius Dio, *Hist.* 59.3-4; Josephus, *Ant.* 19.32-36); further references in Barrett 1989:37-41, 262 (esp. note 73).

he feared that his own death would imply that his grandson would be got rid of as well: The Greek text has παρανάλωμα γένηται, lit. "become useless waste or something expendable;" cf. what Philo says in *Legat.* 33: "He feared for his grandson that if he was left alone when young he might be made away with (παραπόληται)." Pelletier 1967:54 note 2: "Le préfixe *para-* exprime dans les 2 composés la gratuité du crime envisagé par Tibère." One can also compare it with the expression ὡς περιττὸν ἄχθος καὶ παρενόχλημα in §14 where it is said that Macro was killed with his whole family "as a superfluity and a nuisance."

§13. *Deceived as he was by these words* ...: For Macro's attempts to take away Tiberius' fears concerning Gaius see more extensively Philo's *Legat.* 35-38 and Barrett 1989:29. Philo describes Gaius here as "an irreconcilable enemy of himself, his grandson, his family, Macro the intercessor, and the rest of humanity," expressing such an utterly negative judgment that one wonders whether he could have written and published this during this emperor's lifetime.

§14. *he would admonish and reprove him*: See also *Legat.* 41. In *Legat.* 43-51 Philo gives examples of the kind of strict admonition Macro is said to have given the young emperor. Philo presents Macro as a kind of Stoic philosopher; see Kraus 1994:484 (who remarks in note 33 that "Macro the philosopher in Philo differs markedly from Macro the villain in Tacitus, *Annals* 6.48.4").

he was murdered with his whole family: In *Legat.* 61 Philo says that Macro and his wife Ennia were forced to commit suicide (even though Ennia was said to have been a mistress of Caligula). Cf. also Cassius Dio 59.10.6: "He [Gaius] was blamed likewise for compelling Macro together with Ennia to take their own lives, remembering neither the love of the latter nor the benefits of the former, who had, among other things, assisted him to win the throne for himself alone; nor did the fact that he had appointed Macro to govern Egypt have the slightest influence." On Macro's suicide see Balsdon 1934:38-40.

as if he were a superfluous burden and a nuisance: See the note on *he feared* ... in §12.

§15. *the strict moralist*: The Greek αὐθέκαστος is hard to render, and the variety in the translations of this passage is great: "the candid friend" (Box); "the stickler for straight speaking" (Colson); "der Moralprediger" (Gerschmann); "la franchise personnifiée" (Pelletier); "de vleesgeworden onfeilbaarheid [the incarnate infallibility]" (De Vries). For αὐθέκαστος LSJ list as meanings: "one who calls things by their right names, downright, blunt; inartificial, plain; self-willed; self-controlled." It is clear that it is an originally positive term that could sometimes develop negative connotations. Cleanthes lists the word among positive qualifications such as δίκαιος, καλός, αὐστηρός, αἰεὶ συμφέρων, λυσιτελής etc. (*SVF* 557); see Pelletier 1967:159-160. In *Jos.* 65 Philo uses it once more, in a clearly positive sense, in the expression "the stern, strict (αὐθέκαστος), uncompromising friend of truth." Since Gaius hates Macro's moralizing, the sense of the word seems to be here something like "strict moralist" or "moral purist."

the tutors from my early youth: See the somewhat longer version of Gaius' words in *Legat.* 54: "For from the cradle I have had a host of teachers, fathers, brothers, uncles, cousins, grandparents, ancestors, right up to the founders of the House, all my kinsmen by blood on both the paternal and maternal sides, who attained to offices of independent authority etc." It is clear that for dramatic effect Philo has put these words into Gaius' mouth. The motif of his being irritated by Macro's moral supervision may, however, definitely be historical.

§16. *Macro too had been put to death*: probably in the late winter or early spring of 38. One of the reasons why Macro was put to death (aside from Gaius' annoyance at Macro's moralism) may have been that Macro, because of his services in helping Gaius to the throne, claimed that the young emperor was now under a permanent obligation to him (see Box 1939:79 and Pelletier 1967:56 note 1).

he completely lost the hope that had still been left: As Cassius Dio (59.10.7) reports, Macro's fall entailed the death of many others, so Philo may quite well be right here, in spite of the objections by Sherwin-White 1972; for a balanced refutation of Sherwin-White's skepticism see Hennig 1974:432-433, esp. note 24.

lost control of his mind: For Philo's repeated criticism of the various forms of loss of control by Flaccus see the notes *ad* §§7 and 9. The intolerable consequences of such a loss of control are immediately spelled out by Philo in the opening line of §17: "When a ruler begins to despair of his capacity to exercise authority, it is inevitable that his subjects immediately start a rebellion."

§17. *Among this kind of people the Egyptian nation holds pride of place ... seditions*: For "the Egyptian nation" the Greek has the neuter τὸ Αἰγυπτιακόν, a form of expression that lends itself easily to abstract, stereotypical designations (it is used again in §29 and *Agr.* 62). Philo's attitude towards the Egyptians (and the Egyptian Alexandrians) is very negative. Unlike the Romans (and to a lesser degree the Greeks), they are the only people he places in direct opposition to the Jews. *Flacc.* 29: "Jealousy is an inborn characteristic of the Egytians, and they regard anyone else's good luck as their own bad luck. (...) [They have] an ancient and innate enmity towards the Jews." *Legat.* 162 and 166: "The Alexandrians are adepts at flattery and imposture and hypocrisy, ready enough with fawning words but causing universal disaster with their loose and unbridled lips. (...) [Egyptians are] a seed bed of evil in whose souls both the venom and the temper of the native crocodiles and asps were reproduced." Cf. also his remarks on the impiety and "atheism" of the Egyptians in *Mos.* 2.193 and 196, and the scathing remarks about the Egyptians having promoted to divine honors "irrational animals not only of the tame sort but also beasts of the utmost savagery" (*Vit. Cont.* 8).

Egyptians are also arrogant, inhospitable, licentious, and inhuman (*Agr.* 62; *Abr.* 107; *Mos.* 1.95); and they represent the lowest Philo can imagine for his allegories: body, pleasure, passion etc. (for references see Mendelson 1988:117; Goudriaan 1992:82; Borgen 1997:23-24; Schäfer 1997:145). Philo even adds anti-Egyptian elements to biblical accounts, e.g., in the stories of the Golden Calf and of Hagar (references in Mendelson 1988:118-119, who adds, however, that, surprisingly enough, in one passage Philo speaks in a very positive way about the Egyptians, namely in *Spec.* 1.2, where he calls the Egyptian people "pre-eminent for its populousness, its antiquity, and its attachment to philosophy;" cf. *Mos.* 1.214 and Pearce 1998:88-89). Philo usually places the Egyptians on the opposing side to civilized humanity; he even suggests that "the Egyptians have degenerated to such an extent that they can no longer be counted as normal human beings. Their character and customs are instead akin to those of animals. (...) Philo has constructed his Egyptian Other as a perversion of what is familiar and natural" (Niehoff 2001:47-48). So Philo did not scruple to treat the Egyptians with contempt and he "slips with such ease into passages which defame Egypt, its people, and its religion that one wonders how common this mode of thought was within the Jewish community. Indeed if Alexandrian Jews thought in this way about things Egyptian, perhaps we should reassess the assumption that the Jews played no part in the deterioration of relations between the two peoples" (Mendelson 1988:122). Many scholars tend to believe that, although the enemies of the Jews in 38 CE were probably primarily Greek nationalists, Philo persists in identifying them as Egyptians in order to insult them and to make them repulsive to his Roman readers; see Box 1939:79; Pelletier 1967:56 note 2, and 170-171; Barraclough 1984:463; Goudriaan 1988:113; Sly 1996:172. But the Egyptians may have played a much more active role in the riots than this interpretation allows (so rightly Gruen 2002:63-65). The best recent treatment of Philo's views on the Egyptians is the chapter "The Egyptians as Ultimate Other" in Niehoff 2001:45-74, where she stresses that the same themes were also developed in Roman literature of Philo's time, e.g., Tacitus, *Hist.* 1.11; Cicero, *Pro Rab. Post.* 34-35; Seneca, *Cons. Helv.* 19.6, *Cons. Marc.* 14.2; cf. also Pearce 1998:79-105 (85-86 for Greek texts expressing a similar contempt).

§18. *an impossible blind-alley situation*: ἐν ἀμηχάνοις δὲ καὶ ἀπόροις, a very strong expression for a hopeless situation in which one sees no way out whatsoever. Philo uses it also in *Abr.* 175; *Spec.* 4.127; *Legat.* 178.

all of his recent policy: The mss. read τὰ πρὸ μικροῦ πάντα, but it seems likely that something has dropped out here. Cohn suggested κατωρθωμένα before πάντα, but Reiter suggested, hesitantly but more plausibly, δόξαντα after πάντα. Most recent editors and translators follow Reiter here.

those who had been his declared enemies ... in every matter: Isidorus and Lampo were the most important ones among them, as will become clear in §20 and especially in §§128-145; see Pelletier 1967:31. One should bear in mind that Isidorus had probably also been instrumental in the fall of Macro, so there was reason enough for Flaccus to befriend him again (see Musurillo 1954:136 and Tcherikover-Fuks 1957/64:II.77). It is not improbable that the scene of the meeting between Flaccus and Isidorus in the *Acts of the Pagan Martyrs*, esp. *P. Oxy* 1089 = *CPJ* 154, reflects this "reconciliation" between the former enemies. See on that matter Hennig 1974:433 who remarks that it is possible that Flaccus thought he could receive some support from the leaders of the Greek nationalists since these rightly claimed to have good relationships especially with the members of Germanicus' family.

§19. ***were rancorous people:*** ἐγκότως ... εἶχον. The adverb ἐγκότως is a *hapax* in Greek literature. The verb ἐγκοτέω is used in the LXX, but the adjective ἔγκοτος is a mainly poetical word (but Philo uses it 5 times); as a noun (with the meaning of "rancor") it is common in Herodotus. Philo's language is rather unusual here. Also further on in this paragraph, the word ἐπιμορφάζειν ("was a counterfeit") is a very uncommon term, apparently used only by Philo (the *Philo Index* lists 17 instances of this *verbum Philonicum*). On its imitation by later Christian authors see the note in Pelletier 1967:57-8.

they were only feigning genuine friendship, as actors do in a theatre: καθυποκρίνεσθαι is used in combination with ἐπιμορφάζειν by Philo also in *Mut.* 170, *Abr.* 103, and *Jos.* 166. Its negative connotation of a total lack of sincerety is also clear from its use in *Flacc.* 32 and 72. On this postclassical usage see Box 1939:80 and Pelletier 1967:58 note 1 (in classical usage it usually means "to dupe or ruin someone by bad acting"). Philo often accuses the Alexandrians in general of their tendency to make a stage show of everything (see §§34, 38, 72, 84). Philo not only blames the "rancorous people" for the insincerity in their attempts to fob off Flaccus, he also blames Flaccus for not seeing through it.

They advanced the most harmful proposals and had them immediately ratified: The complot is described in §§21-24. It is not impossible that the clandestine meeting of Flaccus with Isidorus and a certain Dionysius (on which see below, *ad* §20) in the Alexandrian Serapeion as described in the *Acts of the Alexandrian Martyrs* 2 (*P. Oxy.* 1089 = *CPJ* 154), was part of these negotiations, although the Jews are not mentioned in the surviving fragment (see Smallwood 1976:237 note 67). See for text, translation and commentary of this fragment Tcherikover-Fuks 1957-1964: II.60-64; text also in Musurillo 1961:3-5.

§20. ***they put him on stage as no more than a masked dummy ... with the title 'government' inscribed upon it***: On κωφὸν προσωπεῖον ("masked dummy" [Colson], "mute stage character" [Box]) see the excursus in Pelletier 1967:182-184: "Il désigne un type précis de masque: le masque sans trou pour la bouche, réservé aux figurants" (184); it is the mask of a silent puppet (see Lucian, *Tox.* 9). By this image Philo emphasizes the fact that Flaccus had been reduced to the status of a powerless and irrelevant puppet; for Philo's use of theatre metaphors here and elsewhere see Calabi 2002. The words ἐπιγεγραμμένον ὄνομα ἀρχῆς should not be taken to mean that, in Philo's time, theatre masks were provided with letterings indicating the person represented; it is an invention by Philo designed to heap more ridicule on Flaccus.

popularity-hunters such as Dionysius: Διονύσιοι (and the following Λάμπωνες and Ἰσίδωροι) is a case of the plural of a proper name indicating a class of (such) people (Gildersleeve 1980:23, §46). Δημοκόποι (4 times in Philo) is more pejorative than δημαγωγοί. According to Plutarch (*Praec. ger. rei publ.* 5.15 [802D]), the latter try to persuade by means of words while the former try to reach this goal by means of free distributions of food and drink and by festivities. Therefore, Colson's translation "popularity-hunters" is perhaps somewhat more adequate than Box's "demagogues." See also *Jos.* 35, where Philo says about the δημοκόπος that the moment such a person mounts the platform, like a slave in the market, he becomes a bondservant instead of a free man, and, through the seeming honors which he receives, the captive of a thousand masters. Dionysius is not mentioned anywhere else by Philo (outside of *Flacc.*), but he may well be identical to the Dionysius mentioned in the *Acts of the Alexandrian*

Martyrs 1 (*P. Oxy.* 1089 = *CPJ* 154, line 28; see Tcherikover-Fuks 1957/64:II.63), where a certain Dionysius and Isidorus are having a secret meeting with Flaccus in the Serapieion of Alexandria. There is uncertainty about the question of whether or not he is also identical to the Dionysius mentioned in Claudius' famous letter to the Alexandrians as one of the Alexandrian ambassadors who pled their case against the Jews before Claudius in 41 CE (*CPJ* 153, line 17; see Tcherikover-Fuks 1957/64:II, 44). Since Dionysius was a rather common name, the identification is not certain; *pace* Bell 1924:29-30. Tcherikover-Fuks 1957/64:II, 44 rightly state: "The name Dionysius is so common that it cannot serve as an argument in favour of any theory." Of course the identification with the Dionysius of *P. Oxy.* 1089/*CPJ* 154 is much more feasible in view of the fact that there he is mentioned in combination with Isidorus and Flaccus, like here in Philo. See further the discussion in Box 1939:80; Colson 1941:532; Musurillo 1954:104; Sijpesteijn 1964:95 note 26; Pelletier 1967:30-31; Mélèze Modrzejewski 1995:161-183 *passim.*

document-tamperers such as Lampo: γραμματοκύφων is a very rare expression (Philo uses it only once more, again of Lampo, in §131; Demosthenes uses it once (*De corona* [18] 209, and Philo may have borrowed it from him) with the meaning "one who is bent over papers" (Colson 1941:315 note *a*, suggests "ledger-dredger"). Apart from caricaturizing a occupational deformity, it also implies that Lampo doctored documents when he was secretary to the prefect, as is described in more detail in §§125-134 (see the notes *ad loc.*), where we are told by Philo that Lampo's unscrupulous malversations caused the condemnation and death of many innocents (he is even called "the pen-murderer" by the Alexandrians, says Philo in §132). There we also learn that Lampo had been on trial for disloyalty (*maiestas*) to Tiberius (128) and that, against his will, he had been compelled to hold the expensive office of gymnasiarch (130), like Isidorus. Like Isidorus and Dionysius, Lampo, too, figures in the *Acts of the Alexandrian Martyrs* IV, in the fragments collected in *CPJ* 156 and labeled *Acta Isidori et Lamponis* by Tcherikover-Fuks 1957/64:66-81, and *Acta Isidori* by Musurillo 1961:11-17. This document reveals that, as leaders of the Greek nationalist parties, Isidorus and Lampo had brought charges against the Jewish king Agrippa (I) but lost their case and were sentenced to death by Claudius in 41 CE (this execution served as the starting point to the whole of this "martyr" literature). Even though these *Acta* are no official protocols of the Roman authorities but belong to the category of popular fiction or historical novels, "this does not mean that they are historically worthless; on the contrary, they provide valuable and otherwise unattested historical information which has to be examined carefully" (Schäfer 1997:153). Although the fragments attribute a much larger role to Isidorus, it is clear that in this anti-Jewish document, as in Philo, Lampo plays a prominent and active role in the Alexandrian struggle against the Jews. The combined testimony of the Jewish Philo and the pagan Alexandrian Acts leaves us in no doubt about that. See further Stein 1924.

sedition leaders such as Isidorus: στασιάρχης only here in Philo. In §4 Philo painted the Alexandrian clubs as the hotbeds of political intrigue (for which reason they were closed by Flaccus), and in §17 he said that the Alexandrians were always prone to grave seditions (στάσεις μεγάλας). In §§136-137 Philo tells us that Isidorus used these unruly clubs, in most of which he played a leading role, as bases for his seditious activities. Isidorus is castigated by Philo as one of the worst anti-Jewish agitators of Alexandria in §§135-145. He was the enemy of Flaccus when the latter "represented rigid Roman rule in Egypt" (Tcherikover-Fuks 1957/64: II.69). Afterwards, in late 38 CE, he appeared as Flaccus' prosecutor in the trial which led to the latter's banishment and execution. Isidorus, too, had been gymnasiarch, as we know from the *Acts of the Alexandrian Martyrs*, where he figures prominently; see, e.g., *CPJ* 156 *passim*. There we see Isidorus throwing rude insults in the face of the emperor Claudius ("you are the cast-off son of the Jewess Salome!", *CPJ* 156d11-12), who accuses him of having caused the death of two good friends of the emperor and of now trying to do the same with Claudius' friend Agrippa (I), whom Isidorus had called a "twopenny-halfpenny Jew" (*CPJ* 156b18), whereupon Claudius sentenced both Isidorus and Lampo to death; for a brief analysis of the document see Schäfer 1997:152-156. It is only in §130 that we are told by Philo that some of these "troublemakers" were gymnasiarchs of Alexandria. Apparently Philo fails (or does not want) to draw the logical conclusion from this fact, as Tcherikover-Fuks 1957/64: I.66 remark: Isidorus and Lampo were "men at the head of the educational institution of the Greek city, and, as such, representatives of the cultured element of the Greek community." Since the gymnasium was the access gate to Greek citizenship, it was no coincidence that it was the directors of this institution who were the leaders of the anti-Jewish Greek opposition. "Isidorus and Lampo were in a particularly good position to thwart the Jews" (Goudriaan 1992:91). Neither was it a coincidence that in 41 CE Claudius forbade the Jews of Alexandria to participate in gymnasium education (*CPJ* 153.92-94) which was a prerequisite to citizenship. In *Legat*. 355 Philo mentions Isidorus again, now as one of the members of the Greek-Alexandrian embassy to Gaius. On Isidorus see further Stein 1916; Pelletier 1967:30-32. A recently excavated inscription from late first century Alexandria honors an Alexandrian gymnasiarch named Isidorus, son of Isidorus, *i.e.*, perhaps the son of our Isidorus; see Lukaszewicz 2000 and, *contra*, Bingen 2002.

devisers of evils: κακῶν εὑρεταί, cf. §73 where Philo calls Flaccus ἀδικημάτων εὑρετής. In Rom. 1:30 Paul mentions ἐφευρεταὶ κακῶν in a long *Lasterkatalog*.

city-troublemakers: ταραξίπολις may have been coined by Philo himself; it occurs nowhere else and he uses it only once more, in §137, again of Isidorus. Pelletier 1967:59 note 8 thinks Philo has patterned it upon the satirical ταραξιππόστρατος in Aristophanes, *Eq*. 247. But it should be kept in mind here that the word ταραχή had become traditional for the anti-Ptolemaic uprisings of Egyptians (see Uebel 1962 on ταραχὴ τῶν Αἰγυπτίων and Buraselis 1995). Also Claudius uses ταραχὴ καὶ στάσις in his famous letter to the Alexandrians (*CPJ* 153.73), and in Caracalla's decree of 216 CE he expels all Egyptians from Alexandria because they have become too numerous and ταράσσουσι τὴν πόλιν (!, *P. Gissen* 40.II.20). So Philo's new word creation was built on existing terminology. If Colson's rendering of the following clause, "a name which has gained special currency," would be correct, it would imply, however, that Philo has picked up here a term that was a current designation of Isidorus in Alexandrian circles opposed to him (Jewish?, Roman?, both?); but see the next note on the problematic nature of this translation. On the phenomenon of "urban unrest" in the Roman Empire in general see MacMullen 1966:163-191.

This was the way he (Flaccus) somehow exercised the title (of ruler): Existing translations are unsatisfactory; Box has "it is this character of Authority that has carried the day," and Pelletier has "le terme est admis par l'usage" (for Colson see the previous note). Since the most natural referent of τοὔνομα is ὄνομα ἀρχῆς above, it seems inevitable to take Flaccus to be the subject of κεκράτηκε, here in the sense of "he held, he exercised." Πως expresses Philo's contempt for the way Flaccus exercised his ἀρχή. (I owe the interpretation of this line to Allen Kerkeslager.)

§§21-24 *Flaccus Begins to Injure the Jews*

After the "advisors" have pressed Flaccus into connivance by fanning his fears, he joins them in their anti-Jewish plans and activities, hoping thereby to regain favor with Gaius. Initially his actions are not too overtly inimical, but later on he exhibited his ill-will towards the Jews openly as well. Philo's main point is that Flaccus, instead of doing what he should have done as governor ("he should have angrily rejected the speakers," §24), he throws in his lot with people whom Philo considers as "public enemies."

§21. ***developing a plot***: βούλευμα βουλεύουσι, a case of *paronomasia* that Philo likes; see the note *ad* §1 (πανταχοῦ πάντας).

In a private conversation ...: One such private conversation between Flaccus and his former opponents (Isidorus c.s.), although not identical to the one Philo reports in §§22-23, is to be found in the *Acts of the Alexandrian Martyrs* 1 (*P.Oxy.* 1089 = *CPJ* 154); see Tcherikover-Fuks 1957/64: II 60-64, and also the comments by Smallwood 1961:44-45. Cf. ἐν κρυπτῷ in col. 2, line 26, of that document with ἰδίᾳ here.

§22. ***Gone ... gone***: ἔρρει μέν ... ἔρρει δέ ... αἴσια δέ. The tripartite division in Flaccus' loss of hope (Gemellus, Macro, Gaius) corresponds to the three stages of Flaccus' despair described in §§9, 11, and 16.

the boy Tiberius Nero: i.e., Gemellus; see *ad* §9.

your friend Macro: see *ad* §11.

what you can expect from the emperor does not look very favorable: Since Flaccus is now entirely dependent upon Gaius' favor, this is the best point of contact for the nationalist agitators. They will offer him a new possibility to win this favor: ***a very powerful intercessor by whom Gaius may be propitiated.***

intercessor: Παράκλητος has a wide semantic range; see the rich bibliography in BDAG 766. Its basic meaning is "one who appears in another's behalf;" here its sense is "helper, mediator, intercessor." As the following paragraph makes clear, Alexandria could act as an intercessor on behalf of Flaccus because Gaius loved the city (and hated the Jews).

§23. ***the city of Alexandria***: lit. "the city of the Alexandrians." In Philo's usage, "Alexandrian" is an elusive term; "it can signify a citizen or resident of Alexandria, or it can be unclear which of these meanings is intended" (Birnbaum 2001:50). Here it seems to denote the citizens; cf. also §78 and *Legat.* 172. When in §80 Philo speaks of "Alexandrian Jews," he indicates simply residents of Alexandria. Further discussion in Birnbaum 2001:50-54.

which has been honored from the beginning by the entire imperial family, especially by the present master: In order to convince Flaccus of the viability of their plans, the Greek nationalists make an exaggerated claim, for it was certainly not true that "the entire imperial family" (ἅπας ὁ Σεβαστὸς οἶκος = all members of the house of Augustus) had honored Alexandria. Augustus himself had deprived the city of its *boulê*, its senate, apparently as punishment for its citizens' hostile attitude towards him; this was the cause of much subsequent resentment (see *CPJ* 150 and Fraser 1972: 1:94-95; cf. Balsdon 1934:127 and Lewis 1983:27 with note 7), and Augustus never visited the city again after his first and only visit in 30 BCE. Tiberius, too, never visited Alexandria. Both emperors were probably very unpopular in Alexandria. In general it can be said that during the first six decades of the principate the relations between Alexandria and Rome were very cool (only the visit by Caligula's father, Germanicus, in 19 CE, was more or less successful according to Tacitus, *Ann.* 2.43 and 59-60, and cf. Josephus, *C. Ap.* 2.63-64, and the notes in Box 1939:81 and Pelletier 1967:160). Gaius himself, however, had, according to Philo (*Legat.* 338), an extraordinary passion for Alexandria. As Philo says (*Legat.* 250), he had planned a visit to the city and Suetonius, *Calig.* 49, even says he wished to move there; see Lindsay 1993:152 (and cf. Cassius Dio 60.27 about Nero). That predilection of the emperor is one of the trump cards of Isidorus *cum suis*.

handing over and abandoning the Jews: τοὺς Ἰουδαίους ἐκδοὺς καὶ προέμενος. The verb ἐκδίδωμι expresses the idea of surrendering persons to their enemies; προΐημι implies that these persons are done away with and left to their fate. The overall idea is that of outlawing the Jews. The only possible reason for thinking that by outlawing the Jews Flaccus would regain the favor of Caligula is that they knew that this emperor had strong anti-Jewish sentiments. It is a matter of dispute whether or not these sentiments had come to the fore already in 38, but Philo seems to imply this (see Barrett 1989:182-191; Rajak in *OCD* 620).

§24. *he should have angrily rejected the speakers as revolutionaries and public enemies:* Philo repeatedly criticizes Flaccus for not doing what he should have done in his position of governor (see, e.g., also §§35, 43). If Flaccus would have had the courage to maintain the standards of strictness that he kept up in the first 5 years of his prefecture, he would have averted a great calamity for the Jewish people. Instead, he "agreed" with "public enemies."

agreed: συνεπιγράφεται, lit. "he subscribed." Hoping, in this way, to be able to save his life, Flaccus yielded to the temptation, and declared he was willing to hand over the Jews.

not giving an impartial and equal hearing: μήτ' ἴσον παρέχων καὶ κοινὸν ἀκροατὴν ἑαυτὸν, cf. *Legat.* 183 (about Gaius) μὴ τὸν ἴσον καὶ κοινὸν ἀκροατήν. Flaccus carefully prepared the ground by beginning to show discrimination in the conduct of lawsuits to which Jews were parties. As Box 1939:xl suggests (though the text does not say so explicitly!), Flaccus began "to inquire strictly into the legal basis on which Jewish claimants were proceeding and to disallow, one by one, as they came to his notice, every usurpation of privilege by Jews which custom had sanctioned in the course of the several hundred years during which Jews and Alexandrians had lived in the same city." Philo says that Flaccus' main fault was that "he did not allow equal freedom of speech to both parties" in lawsuits, *i.e.*, he ignored the principle of *audi et alteram partem.*

his ill-will: towards the Jews.

§§ 25-35: *King Agrippa*

The unexpected visit of the Jewish king Herod Agrippa to Alexandria put the spark to the tinder. In this section there is a considerable emphasis on the fact that Agrippa visited Alexandria not of his own accord but on Gaius' advice (26), or even command (31); so it was not a deliberate visit, and certainly not intended to offend non-Jewish sensitivities, as some of the enemies of the Jews asserted. Philo seems to be on the defensive against the claim that this Jewish king had a specific aim in coming to Alexandria and at least some of the Alexandrian Jews knew about his plans to visit the city. Even so, the always jealous Egyptians with their innate hostility to the Jews reacted furiously and abused the king. Flaccus' advisors suggested to him not to swallow this visit with its ostentatious show of Agrippa's body guard since it was an eclipse of the resident governor by a Jewish visitor. So Flaccus turned a blind eye to the insults the crowds threw at a friend of the emperor, which created a dangerous precedent for the following events, again something he should not have done according to Philo. For him there is only one conclusion: "Flaccus was guilty of and a participator in this campaign of slander" (35).

§25. *due to instruction from others rather than to his own nature*: ἐκ μαθήσεως τὸ πλέον ἢ φύσεως. The opposition *c.q.* juxtaposition of μάθησις and φύσις (with ἄσκησις often added) is found at several places in Philo's work, e.g. *Ebr.* 25; *Mut.* 101 (cf. 210-211); *Somn.* 1.167-170; *Abr.* 54; *Virt.* 133; *Praem.* 65; in fact the programmatic opening line of *Jos.* 1 is: "The three factors by which we can reach our goal of excellence are: learning, nature, practice" (μάθησις, φύσις, ἄσκησις). For Philo, Abraham represents virtue as acquired by learning, Isaac by nature, and Jacob by training. These three ways of acquiring virtue correspond to the three ways of attaining happiness according to Aristotle, *Eth. Nic.* 1.9.1099b9-10. Philo uses this Aristotelian motif here in a rather unexpected way: also mental derangement (ἀπόνοια) can be a product of "instruction" and "nature" (not, of course, of 'training'). Lit. on ἀπόνοια in *RBLG* 189.

Agrippa, the grandson of king Herod: On this Agrippa (10 BCE-44CE) see the important monograph by Schwartz 1990; also Kokkinos 1998:271-304 (older lit. in Appendix N to the LCL ed. of Josephus, vol. IX, 578-9). The most informative ancient source on this Jewish king is Josephus, *Ant.* 18.133-354 and *Bell.* 2.206-220. He was born the son of Herod the Great's son Aristobulus and of Berenice in 10 BCE. His name Agrippa was probably due to his grandfather's friendship with M. Julius Agrippa who died in 12 BCE. From his early years onwards, he lived most of the time in Rome and was always in close contact with members of the imperial family there, especially Antonia, who was a friend of his mother Berenice. He was befriended by Gaius and shared his education with Claudius. Being a notorious spender he had to borrow great amounts of money from Philo's brother, the alabarch Alexander ("the Alexandrian Rothschild," Burr 1955:13), and from others. In ca. 24 CE he had to leave Rome in order to escape from his creditors. In 36 CE Tiberius imprisoned him on suspicion of treason because of a tactless remark, but when Gaius became emperor in 37 CE he released Agrippa and gave him the tetrarchies of his uncle Philip and of Lysanias for a kingdom (see Luke 3:1). In 39 CE large parts of the former kingdom of Herod Antipas were added, and in 41 CE Claudius also added Judaea and Samaria so that Agrippa's kingdom became almost as big as that of his grandfather (Barrett 1989:182-183). For other instances of Gaius' policy of granting territories to members of royal families see Box 1939:83 (esp. Cassius Dio 59.8 and 12). On the way from Rome to his new kingdom he passed through Alexandria, which marked the start of the anti-Jewish riots of 38 CE. According to Acts 12:20-23 (the chapter in which Agrippa is also said to have killed James the brother of John and imprisoned the apostle Peter), he died during (?) his appearance in the amphitheatre of Caesarea Maritima in 44 CE, but Josephus, *Ant.* 19.350, says this happened five days later (which may be implied by the author of Acts).

Philip the tetrarch: This son of Herod and Cleopatra lived from 26 BCE – 33 CE. See Josephus, *Ant.* 18:106-108 with the comments of Gabba in Horbury 1999:130, but especially Kokkinos 1998:236-240, with a discussion of the extent of Philip's territory at 280-281 (Ituraea and Abilene in Lebanon).

§26. *Gaius advised him ... to take the shorter route via Alexandria*: For preferred routes when travelling by ship in antiquity see Casson 1971:270-299 and Casson 1974:149-172; Box 1939:83-85 also has a long note on communication by sea between Italy and the Near East in imperial times. As Strabo 6.3.7 [282] indicates, the route via Brindisium and Greece and the Greek islands and vice versa was not uncommon; Philo describes it in *Flacc.* 152-156. It was a long and arduous journey which would normally take 2 to 3 months. If Agrippa had been willing to take this route, it was "no doubt in order to avoid the possible embarrassment of an encounter with his creditor, Philo's brother Alexander," says Smallwood 1976:238, but that is not compelling; see below *ad* §28. The route via Alexandria was not shorter — here Gaius, or Philo, is mistaken — but it is quicker. It was, however, also more risky because one had to cross large stretches of open sea. It would usually take 2 to 4 weeks depending upon the weather and other circumstances (cf. the story of Paul's stormy voyage to Rome with a ship from Alexandria in Acts 27). For a different view of these two routes see Kushnir-Stein 2000:232-233, who argues that the northern route was shorter, easier and less dangerous, and that the route proposed by the emperor was longer and more difficult, implying that Gaius' nonsensical advice has been wholly fabricated by Philo. Casson 1971:297-299, who (implicitly) defends Gaius' advice, is more convincing, however, since Kushnir-Stein tends to overlook the problem of the quick availability of large ships, which was no problem when travelling via Puteoli (Dicaearchia, see §27) and Alexandria whereas on the northern route it could be a real problem (even aside from the need to change ships several times). Later Christian pilgrims to the Holy Land from the West usually travelled by ship via Alexandria as well; see Hunt 1982:53, 63, 72, 74. Kushnir-Stein's point, however, that the repeated emphasis on compulsion (see also §§31 and 32) by Gaius aims to justify the very presence of Agrippa in Alexandria is very feasible. Even so this does not mean that Philo invented all this. As Gruen 2002:277 note 21 remarks, "Would it not have been far more effective for the Jews to contact Agrippa in Rome, where he could deliver the petition in person [see §103], than to summon him to Alexandria in order to present him with a document that he would later dispatch from Palestine?" The "summer winds" (ἐτησίας) mentioned here were those which blew from the north-west for 1 to 2 months in the summer; see, e.g., Pliny, *Nat. hist.* 2.47.124 (in Turkey this wind is nowadays called *meltemi*).

the trading vessels: ὁλκάδες were merchant ships used for the transport of a wide variety of goods such as glass, paper, linen, metals (see Casson 1971:169 and Pelletier 1967: 62 note 2), but between Alexandria and Rome especially for the transportation of corn, since Alexandria was Rome's most important granary. "The amount [of corn] exported to the capital about this time was 20 million bushels a year" (Box 1939:85). These ships were exploited by large companies of shipowners and their *collegia* (see Box 1939:85-86 and Casson 1971:314-316).

Agrippa complied ... because it seemed that the advice he had been given was useful: "One may doubt this, for it seems that Agrippa had things to do in Alexandria. Philo had his own apologetic reasons for covering this up" (Schwartz 1990:74). Kushnir-Stein 2000:230 points out that Philo's repeated reference to Gaius' advice (in §31 it is even said to have been a commandment) serves to drive home the point that Agrippa's presence in Alexandria was not of his own choice, which seems doubtful; she suggests that his visit may have been intended to intervene in the Jewish-Greek conflict (see §103!), which may have sparked the riots for that very reason. But in fact there is no way of knowing the actual reason for Agrippa's visit. See further below *ad* §§27 and 30.

§27. *He went down to Dicaearchia ...*: This is the harbor town of Puteoli (Pozzuoli) at the bay of Naples, where most of the Alexandrian ships landed to transfer their cargo to boats that could approach Rome up river (cf. Acts 28:13 and Strabo 17.1.7); see Josephus, *Vita* 16: "...Dicaearchia, which the Italians call Puteoli," with Mason 2001:24-25 note 108 *ad loc.* For a description of the welcome Alexandrian ships received in Puteoli see Seneca, *Ep.* 77.1-2.

he embarked with his retinue: Pelletier 1967:160-161 raises the question of how many ships Agrippa needed for all of his retinue, and he suggests that one would have sufficed if the ships mentioned here were of the size of the ship mentioned in Acts 27:37, which is said to have contained 276 persons (which is a dubious reading!), or of the one which Josephus says carried some 600 (*Vita* 15). But because the text speaks of Agrippa seeing ships and commanding pilots in the plural, Pelletier concludes that the king made the journey on several smaller ships. However, this is not a compelling argument as Agrippa may have picked just one of all the ships he saw and ships always had more than one pilot. To speak, therefore, of "les pilotes de toute la flotille," as Pelletier 1967:63 note 6 does, is unwarranted. Moreover, we have no means of knowing how large Agrippa's retinue was. If Box 1939:86 is right in suggesting that Agrippa's large bodyguard (see "army" in §30) need not belong to the *idioi* mentioned here, one ship would probably have been enough. Otherwise more would have been needed. Moreover, the large grain-freighters always travelled in a fleet, in convoy, between Alexandria and Puteoli; see Casson 1971: 297 note 2. But Kushnir-Stein 2000:236 may be right that "cargo ships were not equipped for carrying kings and their retinues."

a prosperous voyage: The word εὔπλοια is poetic (see, e.g., Homer, *Il.* 9.362) and does not occur elsewhere in prose texts, but interestingly Philo uses it 14 times in prose (see *Philo Index* 155).

only a few days later: ὀλίγαις ὕστερον ἡμέραις implies definitely a very short trip, but since we know that the absolute record for the passage from Puteoli to Alexandria was 9 days (see Pliny, *Nat. hist.* 19.1.3), the trip must in reality have taken at least one-and-a-half week but probably more.

without anybody expecting him or finding out that he was there: ἀνεπιφάτως καὶ ἀφωράτως, two *hapax legomena* in Philo which occur only extremely rarely elsewhere (although in §110 ἀνεπίφατον is the reading of most of the mss. where only one has ἀνεπίφαντον, in a very similar setting). The use of these unfamiliar words here is to emphasize the low profile kept by Agrippa; "he would have preferred to have come and gone without being seen" (Schwartz 1990:74). But later Philo himself will inadvertently present us with evidence that contradicts the supposedly "very modest arrival" (§28) of the Jewish king (see *ad* §30 on the parade of his bodyguard). Further discussion in Pelletier 1967:161. As Kushnir-Stein 2000:240 rightly argues, Philo is on the defensive against the claim that "Agrippa had a specific aim in coming to Alexandria and at least some of the Alexandrian Jews were privy to his plans to visit the city" (see further below *ad* "his host").

Pharos had come into sight: ὁ Φάρος, the lighthouse tower on the east end of the peninsula (also called Pharos, but ἡ Φάρος) around the harbor of Alexandria, guided ships to the entrance to the great harbor. It was regarded in antiquity as one of the seven wonders of the world (Ekschmitt 1984:184-197). Strabo 17.1.6 (791) describes it as a huge tower of white stone or marble with an amazing construction of many floors; cf. also Josephus, *Bell.* 4:613. Its height must have been impressive although the sources are contradictory (from ca. 80 to ca. 600 meters!); some authors say it had a statue of Zeus Soter on top. It was built around 275 BCE and destroyed only in the 14th century CE after already having been seriously damaged by many earthquakes in previous centuries. See for all the details of the ancient evidence Fraser 1972: 1.17-20, 2.43-56; for the iconography of the Pharos see Empereur 1998:82-87; cf. also Breccia 1922:105-110; Eckschmitt 1984:184-197; Sly 1996:22-27; and, for further literature, Höcker 1999:98. In Jewish tradition, the peninsula of Pharos was the place where the seventy (two) translators of the Septuagint did their sacred work: Ps.-Aristeas, *Epist.* 301; Josephus, *Ant.* 12.103-104; Philo, *Mos.* 2.34 and 41: "... the place in which the light of that version first shone out." See further Sly 1996:59-60; Pearce 1998:103-104; and Kerkeslager 1998:215.

to remain offshore ... until the late evening: This element serves to emphasize again that Agrippa did not want to interfere with the city's life in any way; he wanted to remain strictly *incognito*.

to enter the harbor: The Greek has τοῖς λιμέσι προσσχεῖν, but the plural does not refer to both harbors of Alexandria but to the great harbor (for a plan of ancient Alexandria and its harbors see Fraser 1972: I, opposite page 8; Haas 1997:2; Sly 1996:xvi). The great harbor was subdivided into various sections which were also called "harbors" (Pelletier 1967:64 on the basis of the information provided by Strabo 17.1.6 [792]; esp. Huzar 1988:623); Philo shows his familiarity with this situation.

his host: How could there be a host when Agrippa arrived "without anybody expecting him"? The presence of a host casts doubt upon the probability of the unexpectedness of Agrippa's visit (see Schwartz 1990:74). There has been speculation about who this host (ξενοδόχος) of Agrippa could have been. Some have suggested that it may have been Philo himself, being the most illustrious leader of the Jewish community; others have suggested that it was Philo's brother, Alexander the Alabarch, who had lent Agrippa so much money (Bludau 1906:68 simply suggests this is what Philo says here: Agrippa arrived "unangemeldet und unerwartet bei seinem Gastfreunde, dem Alabarchen"!). As Schwartz (1990:75 note 37) remarks, both possibilities arise "not only out of the general closeness between the two families (...) but also out of the use of the second [sic!, read: *first*] person plural in *In Flaccum* 103," where we read, "when king Agrippa visited *us*, we informed him of Flaccus' intrigues." This translation, defended by Schwartz, but not adopted in most of the other translations, is grammatically possible; see further below *ad locum* (§103). Although it is impossible to know for sure who Agrippa's host really was, in view of his connections with Philo's family — Agrippa's daughter Berenice was engaged to Alexander's son Marcus (Josephus, *Ant.* 19:277) — it is quite feasible that the host was Philo himself or his brother. Sly 1996:171 quotes in support Philo's statement in *Cher.* 99: "When we think to entertain kings we brighten and adorn our own houses." If we were to accept the speculation by Burr 1955:18 that Philo lived as an unmarried man in the house of his brother Alexander, the "we" in both *Flacc.* 103 and *Cher.* 99 becomes all the more understandable.

§28. ***The reason for this very unobtrusive arrival ...***: As we will later see (*ad* §30), Philo's claim that the king kept a very low profile "is contradicted by the logic of the matter and by the continuation of the story" (Schwartz 1990:75). Philo implies here that Agrippa was not at all responsible for sparking the ensuing hostilities. Schwartz correctly points out the apologetic function of ὁ μὲν ... οἱ δέ in §§28-9: Agrippa, on the one hand, would have preferred to remain incognito, but they, on the other hand, were full of hostility. Already Delaunay 1870:210-211 found Philo's claim "suspect."

he had not come to Alexandria for sightseeing, as he had visited it before: This is a rather poor explanation for the fact that Agrippa tried to enter and leave the city unnoticed, but apparently Philo felt that he had to come up with some motive for the king's behavior. But if Agrippa did not want to come to Alexandria as a tourist, why then did he disembark? As to the previous visit, that was not for tourism either for Josephus reveals to us that Agrippa had come to Alexandria two years before, in 36, because he had an enormous debt for which he asked Philo's brother Alexander the Alabarch a loan of 200,000 drachmas. The latter was willing to lend him the money only after Agrippa's wife, Cyprus, had pledged to pay it back (*Ant.* 18.159-160). Of course Philo felt reluctant to tell this. It might well be that Agrippa came to Alexandria to pay back part or all of the loan, or perhaps to arrange the engagement of his daughter to Alexander's son (the latter is a suggestion by Schwartz 1990:76). Mélèze Modrzejewski 1995:169 goes beyond the evidence when he writes that "Agrippa wished to pay a visit to Philo's brother, the alabarch Alexander, from whom he often borrowed money to cope with his endless financial problems."

to take a shortcut home: See §26.

In view of the abrupt and strange transition between §§ 28 and 29 it has been surmised that there is a gap in the text here (de Vries 1999:48, 87), but this impression is caused by the fact that Philo chose to mention the most important events of Agrippa's visit only later (§§30 and 103), which is indeed rather confusing. For his reasons see the notes *ad* §103.

§29. *envy is an inborn characteristic of the Egyptians ...*: See the comments on the neuter τὸ Αἰγυπτιακόν *ad* §17. In view of what follows the element of jealousy might seem to have to do here specifically with the fact that the Jews did have a king of their own ("they were vexed by the idea that a Jew had become a king," albeit in another country) whereas the Greeks — not the Egyptians! see *ad* §17 — were not even entitled to have their own city council in Alexandria. The fact that Augustus had denied them even this modicum of self-government probably made that they recollected with envy the disappearance of their own kingdom (Balsdon 1934:127-131). For the motif of envy see further §143, *Spec.* 3.3 (τὸ κακῶν ἀργαλεώτατον!) and *Mos.* 2.27 with Borgen 1997:189-190; Goudriaan 1992:82. Lit. on φθόνος and βασκανία in *RBLG* 213 and 510-511.

their ancient and, in a sense, innate enmity towards the Jews: τὴν παλαιὰν καὶ τρόπον τινὰ φύσει γεγενημένην πρὸς Ἰουδαίους ἀπέχθειαν.

Philo nowhere explains what is the source of this inveterate hostility on the part of the Egyptians, but "obviously it is not a recent development but goes back to the past, most probably to the remote past" (Schäfer 1997:145); cf. Sevenster 1975:169-170. See also *Legat.* 170; Josephus, *C. Ap.* 1.223: "The Egyptians were the first to cast slander on us." On the long history of anti-Jewish sentiments in ancient Egypt, see esp. Schäfer 1997:121-169. Instead of pointing to the Greek side, whose gymnasiarchs led the anti-Jewish riots, Philo singles out the "innate hatred" of the Egyptians as the main cause. "Their political agitation against the Jews was not seen as a response to a specific and real conflict, but as a one-sided problem of their national character" (Niehoff 2001:59). "Innate" is based on Reiter's conj. <φύσει> γεγενημένην; Cohn suggested συγγενῆ, Wendland ἐγγεγενημένην, Mangey συγγεγενημένην. The sense of all these readings is practically the same.

§30. *provoked him into the same state of envy as their own*: Cf. what Philo says about the "envy" that "plunged me in the ocean of civil cares" in *Spec.* 3.3 (see Introd., ch. 1).

The visit of this man here means your own downfall ...: On the contemptuous use of οὗτος here see LSJ *s.v.* C I 3. Unless something has been lost between §§28 and 29, Philo has not yet explained how it is possible that, if Agrippa was in town incognito, so many Alexandrians, even Flaccus' own advisers, knew about this visit. Their remark capitalizes upon Flaccus' sentiments of jealousy ("He has been invested with a greater dignity of honor and prestige than you have!"): in his own area of authority (see εἰς ἐπικράτειαν ἑτέρου in §31) a Jewish king is giving a display of power that cannot be tolerated, so he should take action. It is not impossible that, if Flaccus' advisers indeed said things of this kind to him (but how could Philo know?), the actual background is that they already knew about the Jews' request to Agrippa to tell Gaius about the fact that Flaccus had withheld their declaration of loyalty on the occasion of Gaius' accession and to send the emperor a copy of this declaration together with a covering letter of his own explaining the reason for its tardiness (Philo tells about this only later, in §97-103, apparently because to him it marked the *peripeteia* for Flaccus). If that was the case, they would have every reason to warn Flaccus, because indeed Agrippa's support of the Jews in this matter and his complaints about Flaccus' misbehaviour, about which he certainly wrote in his letter, cannot have failed to play a decisive role in Flaccus' downfall, not because Gaius liked the Jews, but because he hated everyone who did not obey him.

the sight of his spear-carrying army of bodyguards with their weapons adorned with silver and gold: This is Philo's only reference to the parade of Agrippa's ostentatiously armed bodyguards (note his "abundant" formulation). Even though he puts these words only in the mouth of the nationalists, Philo does not deny the display of arms by the bodyguards and there can be no doubt that something had happened that provoked the non-Jewish Alexandrians (Bludau 1906:69 even speaks here of "das lächerlich arrogante Auftreten dieses jüdischen Bonvivants"). The problem is how this is to be related to Agrippa's supposed wish to keep a low profile and go unnoticed. Did this show of his armed retinue take place during the nighttime disembarkation or on some other occasion? Some scholars assume the former was the case, e.g., Mélèze Modrzejewski 1995:169: "This time he took pains to erase his erstwhile image of a perpetual scrounger and threw a great party." Others take it to be the latter, e.g., Smallwood 1976:238 and 1999:182, who argues that when the Jews somehow learned of Agrippa's presence in Alexandria, they seized the opportunity of enlisting his help against Flaccus, whereupon he decided to demonstrate that he and the Jews were not to be trifled with by means of an impressive parade through the city; cf. also Colson 1941:318 note a; Barrett 1989:186. Be that as it may, it is clear anyway that the Jewish' pride of their own king and the sight of the bodyguards sparked much irritation and fury among the Alexandrian Greek nationalists, who may have looked back with nostalgia to the Ptolemies (Goudriaan 1992:91), and the native Egyptians. Characterization of the show of the bodyguards as a "Triumphzug" is, however, unwarranted (*pace* Bergmann & Hoffmann 1987:32). Later, the display of the bodyguards is copied in the Karabas incident (see §38).

§31. *For was it really necessary for him to enter the territory of another ruler...?*: Box 1939:87 rightly points out that "γάρ gives a reason for the equation of Agrippa's ἐπιδημία with Flaccus' κατάλυσις" and he speaks of "this eclipse of a resident governor by a visitor." Cf. Denniston 1954:76-81 on γάρ introducing rhetorical questions. What is suggested here by Flaccus' companions is that Agrippa violated the normal protocol by entering into another ruler's domain, but Philo rejects this suggestion by emphasizing that Agrippa acted at the emperor's own order (see the immediately following line).

a prosperous voyage: πλῷ χρησάμενος is here equivalent to εὐπλοίᾳ χρησάμενος in §27; πλοῦς is often used in the sense of "good passage" (for instances see Pelletier 1967:66 note 1), and here "sailing" would hardly make sense since it is all too obvious that Agrippa had to travel to his new domain from Rome over sea.

in order to prevent the governor of this country from being surpassed and consequently dishonored: ἵνα μὴ παρευημερηθεὶς ὁ τῆς χώρας ἡγεμὼν ἀδοξῇ. The verb παρευημερέω is a rare word that is, however, a favorite with Philo (21 occurrences; e.g. *Legat.* 150); in its passive forms it always has the connotation of being eclipsed. The word "consequently" in my translation expresses the relation between the participle and the main verb ἀδοξῇ. Loss of prestige has always been an extremely sensitive issue in countries around the Mediterranean; see *OCD* s.v. *philotimia*; Barton 2001. For the grammatical point of the use of a present subjunctive (instead of a past tense in the indicative) although the ἵνα clause is unfulfilled in past time, see the good note in Box 1939:87-88 ("ἵνα ... ἠδόξει would have been the form in a classical writer").

§32. *his anger swelled still more than before*: The Greek has ἔτι μᾶλλον ἢ πρότερον ᾤδει. Οἰδέω is "to be or become swollen" and Philo frequently uses it of persons who are filled with resentment, anger, desires, vanity, or self-conceit (*Philo Index* 238). Instead of "his anger swelled," Colson 1941:319 has "it made his temper rise;" Box 1939:13 "he was in still greater ferment;" Pelletier 1967:67 "il bouillait encore plus;" cf. Herodotus 3.127; Plutarch, *Solon* 19.

out of fear of the man who had sent him: Caligula. Flaccus was of course well informed about the friendship between the emperor and the king (see *Legat.* 323-327 *et aliter*). For a survey of the evidence see Schwartz 1990:67-89.

he pretended to be Agrippa's comrade: καθυπεκρίνετο, as in §19 "they were only feigning genuine friendship" (καθυποκρινόμενοι γνησίαν φιλίαν). See the note there.

in private he gave clear expression to his envy and hatred: How did Philo know? Maybe via his brother Alexander who in his function of Alabarch must have had regular contact with Flaccus and his circle. For the motif of envy see §29.

§33. *For ...*: Γάρ here explains the last sentence of §32, "he did not have the courage to do so openly," by telling how he gave vent to his anger by means of others, but the phrase is somewhat elliptical (as often with γάρ clauses, see LSJ *s.v.* I 3; Denniston 1954:60-68): He did not dare to do it openly, [yet he did it,] *for* he used the mob to do it for him.

he did allow the mob ... to speak evil of the king: Here Philo tries to put the guilt for the anti-Agrippa riots squarely on the shoulders of Flaccus, as if the Alexandrian mobs needed the permission or encouragement of the Roman governor to ridicule the Jewish king. Flaccus rather "had good reason to deplore the incident and fear the result" (Box 1939:88). The proofs that he let the mob run amuck or even incited them to such behavior are given by Philo in §35, but they do not carry much conviction. See further below.

the lazy ... slander and calumny: Philo's standard negative view of the Alexandrians and/or Egyptians. This manner of depicting Egyptians is something Philo has in common with Roman authors of his days, e.g., Cicero, *Pro Rabirio* 34-35; Seneca, *Cons. ad Helv.* 19.6; Tacitus, *Hist.* 1.11; see further Niehoff 2001:59 and, above, the note *ad* §17.

starting the campaign of abuse himself: This is hardly in agreement with what Philo had said in §32, "he did not have the courage to do so openly."

exhorting and inciting others to do so: Again a rather inveracious statement, because Flaccus would only further endanger his own position if it became known in Rome that he had incited the Alexandrian population against a friend of the emperor Gaius. Philo is so eager to invest Flaccus with the resposibility for the insults thrown to Agrippa that he overplays his hand here. Critical comments on the untrustworthy nature of Philo's comments here are to be found especially in Box 1939:88.

§34. *the gymnasium*: In Greek cities gymnasia were not only places for the citizens to take physical exercise but they were also intellectual centres. In the course of the centuries the element of education became more important so that gymnasia acquired the character of schools, but the element of physical exercise never completely disappeared. Gymnasia often were large buildings comprising a courtyard with adjacent lecture rooms. The one (or more?) in Alexandria was situated in the city centre, in the quarter called Bruchium, and it became "a focus for the maintenance of Greek identity in the face of non-Greek settlement and Roman political control" (*OCD* 660). It was often also a place of political decisions. Plutarch, *Ant.* 54.3-6, reports that it was in the gymnasium of Alexandria that Anthony crowned Cleopatra. Strabo describes it as "the most beautiful building [of the city] with its porticoes of more than 180 meters long" (17.1.10 [795]). It has never been excavated (it lies now probably below a Ford garage; see Empereur 1998:245). The institute was under the supervision of a gymnasiarch who was more or less the social head of the Greek citizen body, since the gymnasium was the entrance to and centre of the social life of the Greek city (see *ad* §130). For further data see Fraser 1972: Index s.v.; Haas 1997: Index s.v.

they spent their days ... reviling the king: Here the gymnasium seems to have the function that the theatre has elsewhere, but in Alexandria as well (see §§41 and 138), that of a gathering place for (large groups of) the people (cf. Acts 19:29). See also the reference to theatrical farces in the gymnasium in §38. There are good reasons to surmise that the "clubs" (see §§4 and 136) were behind the actions in the theatre; see Bergmann & Hoffmann 1987:36-41.

the writers of mimes and farces: ποιηταῖς μίμων καὶ γελοίων. A mime (lit. "imitative acting") was a theatrical genre with realistic presentations of everyday life, usually by (often solo) performers of mimetic dance with the use of dialogue. In Hellenistic times mimes were often rather vulgar performances with erotic themes in crude language (that is why Philo speaks of αἰσχρά, "disgraceful things," in this connection), which the masses loved. In Philo's time Alexandria was regarded as the centre from which the genre of the mime got strong impulses; see Cicero, *Rabir. Post.* 12.35; Dio Chrysostom's Alexandrian oration, *Or.* 32.4 and 86 (μίμους καὶ γελωτοποιούς!); and Philo's own scathing comments in *Agr.* 35 and *Mos.* 2.211. The Karabas incident described in §36-39 was in fact a kind of mime. The expression ποιηταὶ γελοίων is used again by Philo in *Contempl.* 58 in a row with "flute girls, dancers, jugglers" etc. (with an allusion to Xenophon, *Symp.* 2.1-2), that is to say, disreputable company. It is possible that "mimes and farces" is here a hendiadys: farcical mimes. Box 1939:88-89 has a good note on mimes and farces, but see now Mason 2001:25 note 111 and especially Furley-Benz 2000. Philo's point here is that the behavior of the Alexandrian masses in the gymnasium appears to have been learnt from people who aim at the basest sort of vulgar amusement, for which he has only the greatest contempt; see also Calabi 2002.

slow to be trained in anything good but very quick and eager in learning the opposite: Again one of the many generalizing negative clichés of Philo on the uneducated masses of Alexandria. He often shows this really elitist stance towards the common people. Dio Chrysostom, too, throughout his Alexandrian oration (*Or.* 32) severely rebukes the inhabitants of that city for their disgraceful behavior and lack of seriousness, especially in gymnasium or stadium or theatre settings (e.g., 32.1-5, 22-24, 41-44, 73-74, 86); Lewis 1983:196 and Barry 1993.

§35. *Why, then, did he not become angry?...*: Throughout this paragraph Philo again attempts to argue that it was fully Flaccus' responsibility that things got out of hand; he could and should have intervened. But although Flaccus certainly will not have been happy with Agrippa's presence, as Box 1939:88 rightly argued, "the charge of incitement of a mob to insult him is not proved by his incapacity or inactivity in quelling it and is all but refuted by the situation." Also Gruen 2002:58 suggests that Flaccus would hardly have encouraged the mockery of Gaius' close friend and finds this one of the least plausible paragraphs in Philo's treatise. Note the rhetorical effect of the dramatic threefold repetition in διὰ τί γὰρ οὐκ ... οὐκ ... οὐκ ...; cf. Quintilian 9.1.33, 38.

members of Caesar's household: The same expression (οἱ ἐκ τῆς Καίσαρος οἰκίας) is used by Paul in Phil. 4:22; it was a standard designation for people in the emperor's entourage. See O'Brien 1993.

all this is clear evidence that Flaccus was guilty of and participator in this campaign of slander: This is the punch line, but the evidence is much less clear than Philo would have us believe; see the previous notes.

continuously adding new forms of evil: προσεπεξεργαζόμενος ἀεί τι νεώτερον. The verb προσεπεξεργάζεσθαι is extremely rare and a *hapax* in Philo, who is fond of composita with προσεκ- and προσεπι-, here in combination; see *Philo Index* 299. Heaping of prepositions in composite verbs is typical of post-classical Greek. On the textual evidence for this reading here see Reiter 1915:lii.

§§ 36-40: *Karabas*

The enemies of the Jews staged a mocking ceremony for Agrippa in which they paraded a local lunatic, named Karabas, while hailing him as a king in the city's gymnasium. They put him on stage, and endowed him with royal honors. Again Flaccus refrained from interfering in this insult, thus in fact giving the Alexandrians immunity and free play in their actions against the Jews. Again Philo emphasizes what Flaccus should have done ("he should have punished the ones responsible," §40) but did not do, but his main point is that by neglecting his duties as the city's governor Flaccus "gave license and impunity to all who were malicious and malevolent" (40), *i.e.*, his non-interference encouraged the Jew-haters to go a step further and opened the gate to anti-Jewish violence.

§36. **Karabas**: Cohn conjectured Barab(b)as, the Aramaic name known from the passion stories in the Gospels (e.g., Matt. 27:16), but Box derived it from a supposed Aramaic word *karaba'* meaning "cabbage" which would of course be a nickname. Some, however, defend a Greek derivation: Pelletier 1967:69 note 4 suggests (following others) that it means "possessor of one or more little boats," κάραβος meaning a small ship, which he thinks a likely nickname for someone in a harbor city, but that is a rather unconvincing suggestion. Since κάραβος also means a kind of beetle or crayfish, it might as well have been a nickname based on the person's way of walking. Since it is probable that the man is Jewish (see below), an Aramaic nickname remains a possibility, although none of the existing dictionaries mentions a word of the sort.

against which ... cannot protect themselves: The Greek has here the otherwise unattested ἄσκηπτος for which LSJ *s.v.* give "that cannot be feigned" but that does not make sense here. Conjectures include ἄσκεπτος ("inconsiderate or unobserved"), ἀσκεπής ("uncovered"), ἄστεκτος ("insufferable"), σκηπτός ("hurricane"). Since the word opens a parenthesis with information about a wild and savage form of madness in relation to both the patients themselves and bystanders, what one expects is a note about its being dangerous. This may well be what ἄσκηπτος implies, but the text may be corrupt.

the more relaxed and gentler variant: In antiquity physicians often distinguished two forms of madness, a violent form and a quiet one. Usually, the wilder variety was called *mania* and the milder one *melancholia*, and the latter is probably the one Philo has in mind, although his description of the symptoms (spending days and nights naked on the streets) is rather unique; but cf. Mk. 5:1-17. See the discussion of this problem in Box 1939:89-90. For the various types of madness and melancholy in ancient medical theories see especially Roccatagliata 1986: Index s.vv. *mania* and *melancholia*.

§37. *he could be seen by everyone*: That this naked man could be seen by everyone before he was dressed up as a king may be significant in that Philo says elsewhere that many were ridiculing the practice of circumcision (*Spec.* 1.1-2). If Karabas was a Jew — in view of his possibly Aramaic name — "in the athletic context of the gymnasium the circumcision of the mock Jewish king presented a visible contrast with the uncircumsized young men that made up his bodyguard. (...) It requires little imagination to recognize the opportunity that this event provided for phallic humor" (Kerkeslager 1997:32, in a study of *CPJ* 519, 18-20, which mentions laughter about a man bearing "a Jewish burden" in an athletic context). On ridiculing circumcision see Schäfer 1997:93-105.

On his head they spread out a piece of papyrus for a diadem: βύβλον ... εὐρύναντες suggests that they took a papyrus sheet and flattened out (lit. "widened") the curling edges in order to use it as a head-covering. The diadem was a royal headband, with sceptre and purple cloak an attribute of kingship.

clothed the rest of his body with a mat for a robe: Since in *Contempl.* 69 Philo speaks about the Therapeutae using mats (χαμαίστρωτα) of papyrus, Box's suggestion that "the idiot's was presumably of the same material" (1939:91) is likely, the more so since also the third item they gave the man (the sceptre) was of papyrus. This rug served as the royal purple robe.

native papyrus ... for a sceptre: Also in *Contempl.* 69 Philo speaks of "native papyrus" (πάπυρος ἐγχώριος), which is an indication that he wrote for a non-Egyptian audience that had to be informed about the situation in Egypt. On papyrus and products made of papyrus see Rupprecht 1994: ch. 1. The sceptre is the final piece of royal insignia (παράσημα τῆς βασιλείας, §38) given to Karabas. He now could parade as a Jewish mock-king. The scene is strongly reminiscent of the story of the mocking of Jesus as a dressed-up king in the passion narratives of the Gospels, Matt. 27:27-28 and parallels; see Boring, Berger & Colpe 1995:303-304; Schwemer 2001:160-161; and, for a detailed comparison, Winter 1974:147-149. "Agrippa to the Alexandrians and Jesus to the legionaries are each equally laughable" (Box 1939:91).

§38. *as in a theatrical mime*: Box remarks about the royal mime that "what is enacted is a mime in which kingship is caricatured" (1939:91), for it is about a king "malgré lui." In his instructive note on this passage he suggests that "the Carabas affair is probably a 'king *malgré lui*' mime adapted to topical politics" (*ibid.*). Since Karabas probably was Jewish, and mentally disturbed, he was the ideal target for mockery of Agrippa in a theatrical setting (here: a gymnasium); see also Calabi 2002. For a rabbinic view of anti-Jewish theatrical mimes see the Midrash to Lamentations, *Ekha Rabbati*, Proem 17.

in imitation of bodyguards: those of Agrippa in §30.

Then others approached him ... affairs of the state: The whole scene is a ridiculing imitation of audiences at a royal court, for which see Gabelmann 1984.

§39. *'Marin' – which is said to be the word for 'Lord' in Syriac*: This is (almost) correct: *mar'in* is the Aramaic word for 'our Lord;' see Hoftijzer-Jongeling 1995:683. Dalman 1905:152 note 3 suggests *marin* is a Greek accusative form of the Aramaic *mari*, in which he is followed by Flusser 1974/76:II.1078 note 3, unnecessarily so. Cf. the form *maranatha* = *maran 'atha* ('our Lord, come') in 1 Cor. 16:23. Syriac is one of the Western Aramaic dialects and since there was no Greek (or Latin) word for "Aramaic" as a group of languages, one used terms such as "Hebrew" or "Syriac;" see, e.g., *Ep. Arist.* 11; *CPJ* 126:15 (Honigman 1993:113 note 52; Buth 2000:86-91; on γλώσση Χαλδαϊκή = Hebrew see Pelletier 1972:349-353). Philo here uses Σύροι in the sense of the Aramaic speakers of Syria-Palestine. Horbury 1994:13-14 argues that the Aramaic Jewish vernacular of Persian Egypt (in which the papyri from Elephantine were written) continued to be spoken by some Jews in Graeco-Roman Egypt (see the inscriptions in *JIGRE* nos. 3-5; further Cowey-Maresch 2001:24 note 77) and that "although Philo only says that the mob used the Syrian language because Agrippa was a Syrian, one may guess that part of the point of their insult was to mimic the use of Aramaic by some Jews, a linguistic trait which gave a handle to the widespread description of Jews as Syrians — itself by no means a polite description in Alexandria and Egypt" (14). But it might be objected that the use of the Aramaic word *marin* "does not establish the presence of Aramaic-speaking Jews in Alexandria any more than the use of *Maranatha* in 1 Cor. 16:22 proves that the Corinthians spoke Aramaic" (Sterling 2001:298-299); see also Huß 1994:12. The use of the Aramaic word may have been intended "to emphasize the allegation that the Jews' first loyalty was to the Aramaic-speaking ruler of Palestine" rather than to the Roman Emperor, says Feldman 1993:115. The prefix ἀπο- in ἀποκαλέω denotes the improper use of the designation "Marin" (see §54), which is here the title of a king (see Hoftijzer & Jongeling 1995:687) while Karabas obviously was not a king.

king over a great part of Syria: "Syria" often refers to Lebanon, Syria and Palestine; see Ruprechtsberger 2001. Agrippa's kingdom was mainly situated in the mountainous areas of Lebanon. See the note *ad* §25.

§40. *he should have ...*: By now a refrain: Flaccus completely failed to fulfill his duty as a governor. But see the note *ad* §35.

the revilers: τοῖς κατακερτομοῦσιν. The verb κατακερτομεῖν is used again in *Legat.* 122 describing the behavior of the Alexandrian plunderers towards the Jews. In *Praem.* 169 Philo uses it to characterize the attitude and action of the enemies who curse and revile the Jews before the eschatological reversal takes place; see Borgen 1997:182.

to insult their superiors: εἰς ὕβριν τῶν βελτιόνων. Although only Agrippa is meant, the generic plural is perhaps used here in order to emphasize that the revilers were the sort of people who were inclined to adopt this insulting behavior towards superiors on other occasions as well. Insult of superiors is something the aristocratic Philo utterly abhorred. He may also have implied that by deriding Agrippa, a "friend of the emperor," they indirectly offended Gaius as well. On ὕβρις see the note *ad* §136.

in both deeds and words, both openly and indirectly: Note the dramatic and emphatic repetition of καί in the phrase καὶ ἔργοις καὶ λόγοις καὶ φανερῶς καὶ πλαγίως. Cf. Quintilian 9.1.33.

a king ... praetorian insignia: On "friend of the emperor" see the note *ad* §2, although here probably it does not have the technical sense it does have there (courtiers who were the emperor's main advisors), but the more informal one of being a personal friend of Gaius; so rightly Pelletier 1967:72 note 1. The "praetorian honors" (στρατηγικαὶ τιμαί, *ornamenta praetoria*) were most probably granted to Agrippa when he was appointed king over his new kingdom.

Cassius Dio (60.8.2) mentions Agrippa's receiving consular insignia (τιμαὶ ὑπατικαί) from Claudius some years later. The praetorian rank entitled him, among other things, to wear the *toga praetexta* with its purple stripe and to be escorted by a bodyguard of *lictores* (see §30). Box 1939:93 points out that Cassius Dio (57.19.7) says that the practice of conferring praetorian honors on non-senators began with Tiberius.

he gave license and impunity ...: By failing to fulfill his duty of nipping the evil in the bud, he not only let things run out of hand but he even encouraged the rioters to go further. The words ἄδεια καὶ ἐκεχειρία imply that they knew their actions would now go unpunished (see what Philo makes Flaccus himself say in §171). They would no longer be restrained (ἐπισχεῖν) or held in check by the governor. "Mob rule" is the result (see the quote from *Legat.* 132 immediately below), and nothing could be worse in Philo's eyes.

malevolent and malicious: This translation is an attempt to render the alliteration of the Greek ἐθελοκακοῦσι καὶ ἐθελέχθρως ἔχουσι. The emphasis in these words is of course on the *wil*fulness (ἐθελ-) of their evil deeds.

he pretended not to see ...: The accusation of turning a blind eye to what happened in the city recurs in *Legat.* 132: "The prefect of the country, who single-handedly could have put an end to this mob-rule in an hour had he chosen to do so, pretended not to see and hear what he did see and hear, but allowed the Greeks to make war without restraint and so shattered the peace of the city." But in *Flacc.* 43 Philo goes further by making Flaccus directly responsible for the desecration of the synagogues (see below, *ad locum*).

§§ 41-44: *The overtures to the pogrom*

Flaccus' non-interference encouraged the enemies to go a major step further and erect statues of the emperor in the synagogues of the Jewish community, an act of utter desecration. By permitting this to happen Flaccus consciously took the risk that world-wide anti-Jewish riots would break out. Philo draws a picture of a governor that willy-nilly lets himself be drawn more and more into the quagmire of popular favor.

§41. *perceived*: συναισθόμενος in the sense of αἰσθόμενος, as usual in Philo (Box 1939:93).

THE OVERTURES TO THE POGROM 133

the rabble ... always causing trouble: a typically Philonic description of the vulgar mob for which he felt such a deep contempt.
in pursuit of a life not worth living: The Greek text has ζῆλον ἀβιώτου βίου, which is translated by Box as "a penchant for a life not to be lived," by Colson as "eager pursuit of the worthless life," and by Pelletier as "rancoeur de son existence invivable." I do not think that ζῆλος can have the meaning of "rancour" and the fact that Philo calls their lives ἀβίωτος (lit. "unlivable") does not imply that they regarded their lives as intolerable but that Philo himself thinks such lives are not worth living, although the mob pursues exactly this kind of life. The word ἀβίωτος expresses his contempt. Cf. Fraser 1972: 2.145 note 184.
They flocked into the theatre: According to Julius Caesar, *Bell. civ.* 3.112, there was a theatre not far from the main harbor of Alexandria. There was probably more than one theatre; see Fraser 1972:11, 15, 17, 23, 24, 29, 30; Haas 1997:62-64; for probable locations see the maps in Breccia 1922 opposite p.68; Green 1996:303; Haas 1997:2; Empereur 1998:22-23; Pfrommer 1999:6-7; Eichler 1999:753. This site plays an important role in *Flacc.* (41, 74, 84, 95, 173; cf. Josephus, *Bell.* 2.490, for the Alexandrian amphitheatre as the place for anti-Jewish riots in 66 CE). As a multi-purpose communal institution, the theatre held a pre-eminent position in the social life of many late antique cities, and as Haas 1997:63 remarks, it "provided a convenient forum for government officials to interact with the urban crowd." That Jews, too, visited the theatres on various occasions is clear not only from literary references (*Ebr.* 177, *Prob.* 141 *et al.*; see Sly 1996:85; Gruen 2002:125), but also from Greek inscriptions mentioning theatre seats for Jews (*CIJ* 748: Miletus; *CJZC* 71: Berenike in the Cyrenaica).
they already had Flaccus in their pocket for less than a penny: Φλάκκον ἤδη τιμῶν ἀθλίων ἐωνημένοι, lit. "bought Flaccus for a miserable price." What exactly is meant by τιμαί is, however, not wholly clear; Pelletier translates "par de misérables honneurs," Gerschmann "für einen jämmerlichen Preis" and Box combines both possibilities with "at the price of miserable honors." Box 1939:93 is probably right when he says that we should understand the passage to imply that "an agreement with the governor was reached overnight, after the mob had perceived Flaccus' connivance at the mock court," and Pelletier 1967:73 not improbably states that the τιμαί cannot have been official honors but that Flaccus "s'était laissé corrompre par leur vaines flatteries." As De Vries 1999:89 says, there is no reason to assume that

the τιμαί refer to the five talents offered to Flaccus by Isidorus and Dionysius (or exacted by him from them) according to the *Acts of the Alexandrian Martyrs* 2.57 = *CPJ* 154.57, with Tcherikover-Fuks 1957/64 *ad loc.*

this good-for-nothing: παλίμπρατος, lit. "sold again," said of a good-for-nothing slave who passes from hand to hand (LSJ *s.v.*), here with the undertone of Flaccus' easily being "bought." See the useful note in Box 1939:93 (who refers to Pollux, *Onom.* 3.125 and Dio Chrysostom, *Or.* 31.37).

that statues should be erected in the synagogues: The statues are those of the emperor Gaius, as *Legat.* 134 makes unambiguously clear, so the Greeks wanted to force the Jews against their will to participate in the emperor worship that was common in Roman Alexandria; see Pelletier 1972:26-28; Huzar 1995. Ameling ms. (forthcoming in 2003) argues that this demand on the part of the Greeks was not so much an attempt to eradicate the Jewish religion as an endeavour to create unity among the diverse groups of the population. Be that as it may, Philo regards it as nothing but a frontal attack on the Jewish religion and way of life (see the next note). For "synagogues" the Greek text has προσευχαί, "houses of prayer," which is the most common term for the synagogue in pre-70 sources (19 times in Philo, only in *Flacc.* and *Legat.*), although Philo sometimes uses the words συναγωγή and συναγώγιον; see Leonhardt 2001:74-76. Hengel 1971 argued that initially συναγωγή was primarily used in Palestine, while προσευχή was the current term in the diaspora, especially in Egypt. There is anyway no difference in meaning between the two terms; see Hüttenmeister 1993; Pucci Ben Zeev 1998:210; Kerkeslager 1998:116 note 67; Van der Horst 1999 and 2002:72-74; Levine 2000:74-123; Mason 2001:122 note 1165; but see now Runesson 2001:171-174, 429-436, 446-454. Other terms for synagogue include *hieron, sabbateion, didaskaleion, euxeion* etc.; on terminology see Levine 2000:119-120; Gruen 2002:113; Rajak 2002:27-32.

an entirely novel and unprecedented violation of the Law: Setting up statues of the emperor was of course a grave infringement of the Jewish law against graven images (Ex. 20:4; Deut. 4:16-18). As Philo says in *Legat.* 152, even in the case of Augustus the Jews "did not have to make any changes in regard to the synagogues but maintained the Law in every particular." Box 1939:93 and Pelletier 1967:73 refer to Josephus, *C. Ap.* 2.73, where he says that Apion blames the Jews for not having erected statues for the emperors, whereas he ought to have admired the magnanimity and moderation of the Romans who do not compel those who are subject to them to transgress their traditional laws. See also Tacitus, *Hist.* 5.5.4: "They hold it to be impious to make idols of perishable materials in the likeness of man (...). For this reason they erect no images in their cities, still less in their sanctuaries. Their kings are not flattered in this way, nor are the Roman emperors honored in this manner." In *Legat.* 346 Philo attributes the instigation of the whole event with the statues in the synagogues to Gaius himself, but that is much less probable than the way he presents things here. See further Box 1939:lvii-lix, Smallwood 1976:239 note 74, and Kasher 1995. On Philo's attitude towards the cult of the Roman emperors see Pelletier 1972:33-39.

§42. *they are very acute in their wickedness*: See the comments *ad* §17.

they cunningly used the name of Caesar as a smokescreen: κατασοφίζονται τὸ Καίσαρος ὄνομα προκάλυμμα ποιησάμενοι. The cunning lies in the fact that the argument that the emperor wants to be worshiped by his subjects — a worship that is associated with his statue or portrait — is used here to imply that the Jews' prerogative of being exempted from the obligation to worship the emperor, which they had had from the beginning of the Roman Empire, has to be declared null and void so that statues of the emperor could be placed in their synagogues. In *Legat.* 133-134, Philo says that the Greeks' main aim was the destruction of the synagogues, and that only where this was not practicable was desecration substituted. This is different from what he says here and contradicts the idea that the Greeks' aim was to divert Gaius' attention from their insults to Agrippa by a specious show of loyalty; so rightly Smallwood 1976:239 note 74.

§43. *two kinds of inhabitants, us and them*: By the two kinds Philo may possibly mean Jews and Greeks, thereby ignoring the native Egyptian element in the population which had been there from the beginning (see Box 1939:94), but it is much more probable that he means Jews and non-Jews (including the Egyptians). In Philo's time in Alexandria "the categorization along ethnic lines had become overriding, pushing all other categories into the background" (Goudriaan 1992:92). On the various population groups in Ptolemaic and Roman Alexandria see Fraser 1972: 1.38-92 and Delia 1988. Philo's division of Alexandria's population into ἡμᾶς τε καὶ τούτους evinces "a strong sense for the differences between his people and the peoples around him" (Mendelson 1988:131). Philo's perception of a world cleft in two "sets his peple apart and, in the process, gives expression to the Jews' sense of uniqueness" (*ibid.* 132). On Philo's basic division of humankind into "us" (Jews) and "them" (non-Jews) see Goudriaan 1992:84-86; Honigman 1997:87-88; and especially Niehoff 2001:45-74.

no less than one million Jews: These kinds of round numbers in ancient authors are always suspect, and Philo's one million is "almost certainly conjectural and too high" (Smallwood 1976:222; cf. Williams 1998:13; *pace* Juster 1914: I.209 note 9). McGing 2002:105 rightly remarks that "there is no good reason to think that Philo knew how many Jews there were in Egypt." Demographic figures provided by ancient authors are notoriously inexact and it is always extremely difficult, if not impossible, to reach any certainty in matters of population numbers, also in Egypt (see esp. Bagnall & Frier 1994). Josephus mentions in *Ant.* 12.11 the number of 120,000 Jews in Egypt for the period of Ptolemaeus II Philadelphus (282-246 BCE), and he says that 50,000 Alexandrian Jews were killed in the pogrom of 66 CE and perhaps 60,000 more in 70 CE in *Bell.* 2.497 and 7.369 (but these figures are probably very exaggerated as well). Josephus (*Bell.* 2.385) and Diodorus Siculus (1.31.8) seem to agree that the population of Egypt as a whole must have been some 7,000,000 to 7,500,000, but the number in Diodorus is very problematic: modern editors print 7,000,000 but most mss. read 3,000,000! The most thorough recent study of the matter to date comes to the conclusion that the population of Egypt as a whole numbered some 4.5 million people, and that Alexandria had no more than 500,000 inhabitants (Bagnall & Frier 1994:54 and 104). It is perhaps not impossible that some 10% of the population of Egypt were Jews, but we simply do not know. Diodorus 17.52.6 speaks of some 300,000 inhabitants of Alexandria, slaves excluded, in the first cent. BCE. Modern estimates for Alexandria range from 500,000 to 2,000,000 for all inhabitants, and, as far as the Jews are concerned, from 50,000 to 200,000, although some scholars wisely are towards the lower numbers. Possibly Jews formed approximately a quarter of Alexandria's population (they had 2 of the 5 quarters of the city, although these quarters were of course not exclusively Jewish), so they may have numbered at least some 100,000. At any rate, their number was very large, and that is what Philo's "one million" for Egypt as a whole is intended to convey. See on these numbers further Juster 1914: I.209-212; Fraser 1972: 2.164 note 315; Stern 1974/84: 2.62-63; Barraclough 1984:422; Huzar 1988:631; Delia 1988:275-292; Huß 1994:9-10; Mélèze Modrzejewski 1995:73; Sly 1996:44-46; Delling 2000:89; Sterling 2001:268; McGing 2002; Ameling 2003 (ms.).

from the steep slope that separates us from Libya to the borders of Ethiopia: Philo mentions only the westernmost and southernmost boundaries of Egypt, that is, the continental borders. The Libyan border is also mentioned by Strabo (17.1.5 [791] and 14 [799]; 17.3.22 [838]) and Pliny the Elder (*Nat. hist.* 5.38) as a valley with a very steep slope (καταβαθμός) that separates Egypt from the Cyrenaica. Some other ancient authorities (mentioned by Pelletier 1967:167-169 in the excursus "La Grande Falaise de Libye") distinguish between a greater Katabathmos near the coastal area and a lesser one more inland. As to the border with Ethiopia, it is again Strabo (17.1.3 [787] and 48 [817]) who informs us that it was formed by the town of Syene (Aswan) and the island of Elephantine. For a survey of Jewish communities in the Egyptian *chôra* see Kasher 1985:106-167; further literature in Huß 1994:10.

our ancestral customs: ἔθη πάτρια is again used in §§52-53 as well as in *Legat.* 300 (and elsewhere), every time in the context of protest against interfering with or violating the ancestral customs of the Jewish people. This was a topic of the greatest importance to Philo (see Seland 1995:168 and 174). For his view of the πάτρια ἔθη the most instructive passage is *Spec. leg.* 4.149-150: "[Ancestral] customs are unwritten laws, the decisions approved by men of old, not inscribed by monuments nor on leaves of paper which the moth destroys, but on the souls of those who are partners in the same citizenship. For children ought to inherit from their parents, besides their property, ancestral customs which they were reared in and have lived with even from the cradle, and not despise them because they have been handed down without written record. Praise cannot be duly given to one who obeys the written laws, since he acts under the admonition of restraint and the fear of punishment, but he who faithfully observes the unwritten ones deserves commendation, since the virtue which he displays is really willed" (transl. by Colson in LCL). I owe this reference to Box 1939:95 and Pelletier 1967:161-162. Πάτρια ἔθη occurs many times in the numerous Greek and Roman legal documents quoted by Josephus to the effect that the Jews' right to live according to their ancestral laws was guaranteed by the authorities; see Pucci Ben Zeev 1998:506 and 509 for references. On the closely related concept of *patrioi nomoi* see Kippenberg 1991:183-191.

Yet, in disregard of all this, he permitted them to erect the statues: Again, as in §40 and elsewhere, Philo accuses Flaccus of not having done what was his duty as a governor: intervening and taking action against those who wanted to deprive the Jews of their legitimate right to live in accordance with their ancestral customs. But, as Gruen 2002:58 rightly remarks: "He would certainly have been in an awkward position, had he attempted to block the activity. Resistance could readily have been portrayed as a challenge to the worship of the emperor — a portrayal that Flaccus could not afford to risk. The prefect found himself boxed into a corner."

§44. **He co-operated with them ... civil wars**: In *Legat.* 346 Philo presents the emperor Gaius himself as the one responsible for the troubles (although that is slightly at odds with *Legat.* 164-165), whereas in *Flacc.* the brunt of Philo's attack is to be borne by Flaccus. This difference in accent is perceptible throughout both treatises. That Flaccus "filled the whole world with civil war" is of course a gross exaggeration, as Philo himself seems to admit in his "one may almost say." In his letter to the Alexandrians, however, the emperor Claudius, too, speaks of "the disturbances and rioting, or rather, to speak the truth, the *war* against the Jews" (*CPJ* 153.73-74), albeit not a worldwide one; cf. *Legat.* 119.

§§ 45-52: *The Jewish point of view*

Philo reiterates that people all over the world could take their cue from Alexandria and treat their Jewish fellow-citizens outrageously by taking violent measures against their synagogues and their ancestral customs. This danger was real because Jews live everywhere in great numbers. And even though Jerusalem always remains their mother-city, the countries where they live are their fatherland, and for that reason the Jews are loyal to the well-being and security of their *patris*. If attacks would be done on their local synagogues, they would not remain quiet since in this way their only means of showing reverence to their benefactors, the emperors, would be taken away from them. It is this latter point that is the clincher in his fictional address to the enemies: "It apparently escaped your notice that in this way you did not pay homage to the Emperors but actually deprived them of it! You do not realize that for the Jews all over the world it is their synagogues that clearly form the basis for their piety towards the imperial family. If these are destroyed, no other place or method is left to us for paying this homage!" (49). So it is not the Jews but their enemies who deprive the emperor of his honor. It stands to reason that this argument was an important part of Philo's rhetorical strategy in his defence of the Jewish cause before the emperor.

§45. *the destruction of the synagogues*: τὴν κατάλυσιν τῶν προσευχῶν, for the terminology (προσευχή) see *ad* §41. A more elaborate description of the violence involved is to be found in *Legat.* 132: "Some they smashed, some they razed to the ground, and others they set on fire and burned, giving no thought even to the adjacent houses in their madness and frenzied insanity" (transl. Smallwood 1961:86). In the preceding paragraphs Philo had only spoken of the setting up of statues of Gaius in the synagogues, not about destruction, but, as *Legat.* 132 implies, there were gross acts of vandalism according to Philo, so κατάλυσις may imply both kinds of activity. Colson 1941:533 suggests that "Flaccus had merely ostentatiously abstained from interfering when the Alexandrians tried to install the images by force. These attacks resulted in riotous conflicts in which many synagogues were actually destroyed." It is, however, impossible to fix a chronological order of these events in the summer of 38 with any certainty according to Philo's description. That there were many synagogues in Alexandria is attested also in other sources; for references see Gruen 2002:283 note 109.

the rumor ... would spread to the districts of Egypt: As far as we know, Philo's fear that the violence would spread throughout the country was unfounded; we do not know of any incidents in this year outside of Alexandria, although that may be due to the fact that they went unmentioned in our sources. For the some 40 districts, the geographical and administrative units called 'nomes' (νομοί), in Egypt and their names see Rupprecht 1994:44-45 (with lit. at 51) and Bagnall 1993:333-335.

from the coastal strip and Mareia: ἀπὸ δὲ τῆς ὑποταινίου καὶ Μαρείας. The rare word ὑποταίνιος means "forming a long narrow strip of land (ταινία)" (LSJ); here χώρας is to be supplied. In ancient sources ταινία is sometimes used as a name for the coastal strip in the western part of the Mareotic nome (here Mareia) near the Libyan border of Egypt. Mareia is also the name of the capital city of that nome (as well as the name of the lake to the south of Alexandria). As Box 1939:96 says, Philo seems to regard the whole coastal and subcoastal strip from Katabathmos to the Alexandrian region as ὑποταίνιος χώρα.

there is not one country that can contain all the Jews, so numerous are they: What Philo implies here is that even Jewish diaspora communities outside Egypt would be endangered by the events in Alexandria, and there is a considerable diaspora, he says, because the Jews are too numerous for one country to contain. Cf. *Mos.* 2.232 "The nation has grown so populous that a single country cannot contain it and has sent out colonies in all directions;" also *Legat.* 214. Even though Philo may exaggerate somewhat here, it is certainly true that in his days more Jews lived outside Palestine than inside it. The great number of Jews — Philo uses πολυανθρωπία — is also confirmed by other (non-Jewish) sources, e.g., the geographer Strabo as quoted by Josephus, *Ant.* 14:115; Hecataeus of Abdera as quoted by Diodorus Siculus 40.3.8 (πολυάνθρωπος); Tacitus, *Hist.* 5.5.3; cf. *Or. Sib.* 3.271 "The whole world will be filled with you and every sea." For the large scale of the Jewish diaspora see the impressively long list of place names in Juster 1914: I.180-209, which is outdated now; see now especially Schürer 1973/87: 3.3-86; Levinskaya 1996. For a detailed diaspora map see the *Tübinger Atlas des Vorderen Orients,* Karte B VI 18: *Die jüdische Diaspora bis zum 7. Jahrhundert n. Chr.*, Wiesbaden: Reichert, 1992; also the small map in Noethlichs 2001:245; and the following note. See in general Barclay 1996 and Gruen 2002. On the difficult question of the numbers of Jews in the ancient world see now esp. McGing 2002.

§46. *they settle in most of the wealthiest countries of Europe and Asia*: On the slightly odd Greek (τὰς πλείστας καὶ εὐδαιμονεστάτας τῶν ...) see Colson 1941:326-7 note c *ad loc.* Philo elaborates on this topic in *Legat.* 281-282: "... the colonies which it [Jerusalem] has sent out from time to time to the neighbouring lands of Egypt, Phoenicia, and Syria (...), to the distant countries of Pamphylia, Cilicia, most of Asia as far as Bithynia and the remote corners of Pontus, and in the same way to Europe, to Thessaly, Boeotia, Macedonia, Aetolia, Attica, Argos, Corinth, and most of the best parts of the Peloponnese. It is not only the continents that are full of Jewish colonies. So are the best known of the islands, Euboia, Cyprus, and Crete. I say nothing about the regions beyond the Euphrates. With the exception of a small district, all of them, Babylon and those of the other satrapies which have fertile land around them, have Jewish settlers" (cf. *Legat.* 214). Comparable is also the famous list of diaspora countries mentioned by Luke in Acts 2:9-11. Philo's enumeration has been confirmed by the finds of inscriptions or other archaeological data; see the previous note. Cf. Seland 1995:89 note 72; Delling 2000:87-88, 123-124.

the holy city (ἱερόπολις) ... *the sacred temple* (νεὼς ἅγιος): Jerusalem and its temple, in Philo's time the (so-called 'second') temple as rebuilt by Herod the Great (see Josephus, *Ant.* 15.380-425); cf. *Somn.* 2.246 ἱερὰ πόλις ἐν ᾗ καὶ ἅγιος νεώς ἐστι; *Spec.* 1.68-69. The distinction between ἱερός and ἅγιος was originally that the former term referred to what is filled with or manifesting divine power whereas the latter meant what is devoted to the gods, ἱερός having a much wider and more general application than ἅγιος. Soon, however, this distinction became blurred and in Philo's time the two were quite often used interchangeably. Note that in Matt. 4:5 and 27:53 the holy city is called ἡ ἁγία πόλις. The LXX's alleged preference of ἅγιος to ἱερός (but see Barr 1961:282-286!) is not to be found in Philo (nor in the NT). On the concept of holiness in general see now Harrington 2001; on other Philonic texts about the Jerusalem temple see Hayward 1996:108-141. The use of ἱερόπολις for ἱερὰ πόλις is typically Philonic (9 times, of which 5 in *Legat.*: §§225, 281, 288, 299, 346). He may have coined the term to distinguish Jerusalem from other so-called "holy cities" in the ancient world; see Carlier 2002:302-303. On the attitude of Philo and other diaspora Jews towards Jerusalem and its temple see Wolfson 1947: II.396-426; Amir 1983:52-64; Schaller 1983; Klauck 1986; Wilken 1992:34-37; Kerkeslager 1998:104-109; Runia 2000:376-377; Delling 2000:54-60; Gruen 2002:239-240; Fitzpatrick 2002:70-75; Levine 2002: Index *s.v.* "Philo modelled the role of Jerusalem on the position of Rome in the empire. He hoped to render the idea of Jerusalem's centrality attractive for educated contemporary Jews. Loyalty to Jerusalem would provide them with the same kind of identity as Roman citizenship — an identity which, though ethnic in origin, transcended the narrow boundaries of a specific state and created the sense of world-wide community" (Niehoff 2001:36). In *Prov.* fragm. 2.64 Philo mentions his (only?) visit to the temple of Jerusalem.

the Most High God: ὕψιστος θεός was a current designation for the God of Israel in Judaeo-Greek literature; in the LXX it usually renders the Hebrew *'Elyon*, "Most High." But it was also used for pagan deities, almost exclusively, of course, for Zeus; see Pucci Ben Zeev 1998:241; Breytenbach 1999:439-443. Mitchell 1999:81-148 deals extensively with the pagan and Jewish components of the syncretistic cult of Theos Hypsistos, and at p. 146 nos. 283-284 he prints two inscriptions dedicated to Theos Hypsistos from Alexandria, one pagan and one Jewish (on which see also Nock 1972:414-443, esp. 421ff). In *Legat.* 290 Philo calls the temple in Jerusalem "the dwelling-place of the true (ἀληθοῦς) God." In our passage Philo implies that, like Greek colonists (see immediately below), the Jews should take the cult of their mother city as the pattern on which to model their own religion. "In this way they would maintain a distinct entity in the multi-ethnic environment of first century Egypt" (Niehoff 2001:36). But perhaps Philo too easily takes for granted that all Jews in a foreign land would maintain their allegiance to Jerusalem and its temple for many generations to come; his own nephew, Tiberius Julius Alexander, is a glaring example of the contrary. Philo's trust in Jewish steadfastness in the adherence to ancestral customs turns out to be far from absolute, however, since in several other passages "he displays an acute awareness of the dangers of assimilation that lay at the door of every diaspora Jew" (so rightly Bohak 2002:184 with reference to *Mos.* 1.31; *Virt.* 182; *Jos.* 254 *et al.*).

mother city: μητρόπολις, in the LXX only in Jer. 1:26. Jerusalem is the mother city of all of the Jews in the diaspora because being a "holy city" it creates a religious tie that binds diaspora Jewry to itself and its "sacred temple" more so than Greek colonists are tied to their mother-polis. Philo makes Jerusalem "the symbolic centre of Jewish ethnicity" (Niehoff 2001:33). See further Pelletier 1967:162-163; Kraus 1967:159-160; Van Unnik 1993:135-136; Edwards 1996:82-83; Delling 2000:59; but especially the fine chapter in Niehoff 2001:33-44; on Philo's attitude to the land of Israel in general Schaller 1983. The language is that of early Greek colonization; see Amir 1983:53 and the note on ἀποικία below. Bohak 2002:182 remarks that Philo's use of the model of Greek colonization is misleading because "Philo deliberately obscures the most important point — the communities of the Jewish diaspora were not independent colonies, but were established within existing civic units." But, as Gruen 2002:242 rightly remarks, "the expression 'colony' had a ring of pride and accomplishment, signaling the spread of the faith and its adherents, not a fall from grace."

the regions they obtained ... as their fatherland: πατρίς stands here in opposition to μητρόπολις (note μὲν ... δέ). Even though Jerusalem as a holy city always remains the Jews' mother city, it does not detract from the fact that for them the country where most of them were born and raised and where they had sometimes lived for many generations ("their fathers, grandfathers, greatgrandfathers, and even more remote ancestors"), is really their fatherland. Theirs is thus a double loyalty. But one thing should be clear, Philo says in *Conf.* 78: "When men found a colony, the land which receives them becomes their fatherland (πατρίς) instead of their mother city (μητρόπολις)." That is why the Alexandrian Jew Helenos can speak of the injury of his "being deprived of my πατρίς" (*CPJ* 151,7-8 from 5/4 BCE). As Gafni 1997:46-47 remarks, the allusion to a common past shared by Jews with the local Greek community might indeed have served some Jews as an expression of local patriotism. "The most obvious example of such an attempt would be the various claims that Alexander the Great had 'received from the Jews very active support against the Egyptians and granted them, as a reward for their assistance, permission to reside in the city on terms of equality with the Greeks' (Josephus, *War* 2.487; cf. *Ant.* 12.8 and *Apion* 2.35-6). Projecting Jews in such a manner as part of the local Greek past might certainly be considered a form of local patriotism on the part of the Jewish community, but the fact that these claims were so obviously employed for apologetic and practical motives tends to raise doubts regarding the degree of conviction that accompanied such claims. It is hard to escape the feeling that local patriotism and apologetics are frequently two sides of the same coin." He adds that even Philo's statement that Jews frequently consider their place of residence to be their *patris* requires a certain clarification. "In light of his use of the phrase in other contexts, the implication might be not so much one of patriotic implication, but merely that Jews — like others — relate to their place of residence in the proper manner, by evincing the requisite degree of loyalty and devotion to the well-being and security of the *patris*" (1997:47). In this connection Gafni refers to *Mut.* 40 and *Deus* 17, where loyalty to one's *patris* is mentioned among the standard duties (Gafni 1997:47 note 13). But Philo would rather seem to suggest here "a particular way in which Jews should define their identity" as a distinct group among others all over the world (Niehoff 2001:35; cf. Pearce 1998:100-102). It is to be noticed that in other Hellenistic Jewish authors the *patris* is more often than not Jewish

Palestine, *not* the diaspora country where one lives; see further Sterling 1998 and Gruen 2002:240-241.

were born and brought up: See the note *ad* §158.

regions where they came as immigrants at the very moment of their foundation ...: Philo here of course thinks especially of Alexandria itself. He probably agrees with Josephus, *C. Ap.* 2.39 and 62, *Ant.* 12.119, that Jews had already been part of the original population of the city of Alexandria (and of Antioch on the Orontes), doubtful though this may be. For "foundation" Philo uses ἀποικία, which is the technical term for colonization (or colony) in ancient Greek literature (cf. also the quote of *Mos.* 2.232); see Welwei 1996:850-851; Niehoff 2001:34-35; Gruen 2002:241-243. Note that the Jewish community in Hierapolis (Phrygia) is called κατοικία in *CIJ* 775. The LXX translators often use ἀποικία to render *golah* (exile), thereby "retrospectively aligning the Jewish past with the Greek past" (Mélèze-Modrzejewski 1993:70; see also his chapter "Jewish diaspora, Greek colonialism," *ibid.* 72-80); cf. Carlier 2002:308-311.

much to the pleasure of the founders: See the previous note. Philo makes here a case of special pleading. If the presence of the Jews pleased the first founders, the actions of Flaccus *cum suis* are all the more despicable.

§47. *all over the world ...*: lit. "everywhere" (πανταχοῦ). Philo's fear of a world-wide pogrom seems unfounded. We do not know of any other actions against synagogues in this period, except the one in the city of Dor in 41 CE, where pagans erected a statue of the emperor in a synagogue (Josephus, *Ant.* 19.300). Later, after Caligula's attempt to have a colossal statue of himself placed in the Jerusalem temple, Philo writes: "But by the providence and care of God (...) not a single one of the neighbouring peoples gave any provocation, so that no occasion arose for the Jews to meet a disaster from which there was no escape" (*Legat.* 336; transl. Smallwood 1961:136). It should be added, however, that the emperor Claudius seemed to have sensed a certain danger in the Alexandrian tensions that was of wider significance than just for this city. According to Josephus, *Ant.* 19:287-291, he issued an edict extending the rights given to the Alexandrian Jews to all the Jews living in the Roman Empire, apparently because he hoped that if matters in that city were settled sufficiently, it could prevent troubles from arising elsewhere; see Pucci Ben Zeev 1998:341-342.

THE JEWISH POINT OF VIEW 145

their Jewish fellow-citizens: Sly 2000:261 takes this passage to be one in which Philo "uses the term πολῖται of the Jews in the sense of fellow-citizens with the other Alexandrians," thereby implying full citizenship, but I think Philo does not imply that at all; here he uses the term in the loose sense of co-inhabitants of the city. No juridical meaning should be attached to the word, says Stern 1974/84: 1.400; see also Wolfson 1947:2.398; Applebaum 1974/76:I.450-451; Smallwood 1976:229 note 40; Barclay 1996:62; Cowey-Maresch 2001:22-23.

taking violent measures against their synagogues and their ancestral customs: εἰς τὰς προσευχὰς καὶ τὰ πάτρια νεωτερίζοντες. The verb νεωτερίζειν originally means "to make innovations" but it is often used euphemistically with the undertone of "taking violent or revolutionary actions." Philo frequently uses the term and its derivatives for attacks on the Jewish religion (cf. νεωτερισμός in §93), esp. in his *Legat.* (152, 157, 165, 190, 194, 208, 259, 292, 300, 333); for the similar τὰ πάτρια κινεῖν see Kraus 1967:160. For τὰ πάτρια, scil. ἔθη, see the note *ad* §43. Philo often uses only the substantivized adjective, as here, because this adjective had a solemn ring in the ears of his contemporaries (says Delling 2000:37). Cf. *Legat.* 306: "The High Priest enters it [the Holy of Holies] only once a year, on the so-called Fast Day to burn incense and offer prayers according to the ancestral customs (κατὰ τὰ πάτρια);" cf. *Legat.* 313. Respect for old and therefore venerable traditions was general among Greeks and Romans (think of the *mos maiorum*). Philo has Agrippa write even to Caligula, "you passionately admire your ancestral customs (τὰ πάτρια)," *Legat.* 277. Preservation of the status quo was a shared value among the ancient élites (Delling 2000:36-37).

§48. *they are by nature a peaceful people*: Cf. *Flacc.* 94 ("Were we not always considered to be peaceful?"), *Spec. leg.* 2.167 ("Some people venture to accuse of inhumanity the nation which has shown so profound a sense of fellowship and goodwill to all men everywhere"), *Legat.* 161, *Conf.* 41, 49, *Somn.* 2.166, *Spec. leg.* 4.224, *Praem.* 87 etc. See Umemoto 1994:44-45. It is noteworthy that the name Eirene occurs rather frequently among Egyptian Jews; see CPJ III.175; cf. Mayer 1987:113.

the struggle to maintain one's own traditions overrules the dangers to one's own life: Cf. *Flacc.* 52: "Abrogating the laws and interfering with the ancestral customs of a people ... cannot be regarded as a matter of honor;" *Legat.* 210: "All people are tenacious of their own customs;" *ibid.* 277: "Everyone naturally loves his homeland and the laws of his own country." On these and similar passages see Heinemann 1932:470-472. This argument was not unfamiliar to Greeks and Romans; in this connection Box 1939:97 refers to Zaleucus' dictum πάτρια τὰ κάλλιστα, quoted by Stobaeus 4.126.1, and the Stoic fragment *SVF* 327.

deprived of their means of showing their piety towards their benefactors: Being forbidden to participate in any form of the emperor cult, the Jews could honor the emperors only by dedicating synagogues to them, by official manifestations of gratitude in honorary decrees, by emblems in honor of the imperial power (such as golden crowns or shields), by donations, by prayers on behalf of the emperor etc. (see Pelletier 1967:78 note 2). By using words for "piety" (εὐσέβεια, cf. ὁσιότης in §49) in this context, Philo uses the strongest terms he could use for "proper dutiful attitude" toward powers ordained of God. As Nock 1972:564 note 23 remarks, "he is going as far as he can" without implying deification of the emperor. Box 1939:97 remarks that with the desecration of a graven image these ways of expressing gratitude disappeared because the place where these things were set up or these actions were taken ceased to be a Jewish place of worship. Colson 1941:328-329, 534 objects, however, by saying that the Jews were not unique ("the only people under the sun") in that respect since desecration or destruction of pagan temples would equally incapacitate Greeks and Romans. But the point is, of course, that the Jews' uniqueness here lies in the fact that they were literally "the only people under the sun" whose houses of worship were destroyed or desecrated, at least in the situation at Alexandria in 38. "This text is clearly apologetic in its claims that 'showing reverence to the benefactors' of the Augustan House (§49) was the central purpose of the synagogue. (...) The prayer place is portrayed as an institution not unlike a temple to the emperor in purpose." (Fine 1997:27). Cf. further Sevenster 1975:160; Pucci Ben Zeev 1998:477-478; Leonhardt 2001:76-77; and cf. *Legat.* 133 on the objects "set up in honor of the emperors: guilded shields and crowns, monuments, and inscriptions." In the temple in Jerusalem sacrifices for the well-being of the emperor were offered, but Caligula angrily reproached the Jews that these sacrifices were brought *for* him but not *to* him (*Legat.* 357).

they no longer would have sacred precincts: The Greek has οὐκ ἔχοντες ἱεροὺς περιβόλους. The words "no longer" in the translation imply that the synagogues would, before their desecration or destruction, have been "sacred precincts." Grammatically it is also possible that what is being referred to here is that — unlike other ethnic groups in Alexandria — the Jews had no temples in which to honor the emperor with sacrifices and the like, but in view of the fact that in the previous lines their "being deprived of their synagogues" is spoken of, this interpretation is less probable. The expression ἱερὸς περίβολος for a synagogue is also known from inscriptions, even from one found in Alexandria, i.e., *JIGRE* 9 (=*CIJ* 1433) where the text speaks of "the sacred precinct and the *proseuchê* and its appurtenances" (see Horbury & Noy 1992:14); further Fine 1997:27.

... in which they could declare their thankfulness, and they might have said to their opponents: οἷς ἐνδιαθήσονται τὸ εὐχάριστον, καὶ τοῖς ἐναντιουμένοις εἶπον ἄν· ... The sentence would seem to be an anacolouth, since οἱ δέ at the beginning of §48 is not followed by a main verb, "unless the καί at the end is taken = 'also,' which seems pointless" (Colson 1941:329 note b). It is also possible to take εἶπον ἄν not as a third person plural but as a first person singular ("I might have said to our opponents"), which would fit in better with οὐκ οἶδα in §50. Only De Vries 1999:52 offers this translation. Anyway, the function of what follows in §§49-50 is to demonstrate that — completely opposite to what the Jews' opponents assert — it is not the Jews but these opponents themselves who actually detract from the emperor's honor by their vandalistic actions.

§49. *our masters*: τοῖς κυρίοις. Note that Philo has no qualms in using κύριος as a designation of the emperor. Even though it is in Jewish parlance the designation of God *par excellence*, in itself it does not imply deification when used of a human being.

their synagogues ... form the basis for their piety towards the imperial family: The honorific dedications of *proseuchai* on inscriptions found in Alexandria, Schedia, Xenephyris, Nitriai, Athribis, and Arsinoe-Crocodilopolis (*JIGRE* 13, 22, 24, 25, 27, 117) demonstrate that the Jewish houses of prayer were indeed the places where at least some of the forms of "piety towards the ruling house" were realized. See also Juster 1914: I.346-348, 436-438; and especially Gruen 2002:68-69, 283 notes 110-111. Philo assumes that if only the Alexandrians realized that they were diminishing the prestige of Rome, they would call a halt to their anti-Jewish activities, but as Mendelson 1988:127 remarks, this speech strikes a modern reader as very naive: "First of all, the favored position of the Jews vis-à-vis Rome did nothing but irritate the Greeks. Then the Greeks had no reason whatsoever to promote the interests of Rome." Philo seems to forget the basic truth that "Jews could not show deference to Rome and, at the same time, expect to maintain cordial relations with Greeks whose *polis* Rome had effectively destroyed" (*ibid.*). But in reality Philo was neither naive nor forgetful of real politics: "His attempt in *Flacc.* 49-50 to create a common interest between Greeks and Jews is not a practical call to action; it is more an instance of wishful thinking, an expression of his desire for rapprochement with the one alien sector of the population whose accomplishments he respected" (*ibid.*). The whole "speech" is an expression of Philo's hope to find a middle ground on which Jews could live in peace with their Greek neighbours, based on mutual respect and continued observance of ancestral customs. One can imagine that the material of this section was also meant to play a part in Philo's defence of the Jewish cause before the emperor. See also Delling 2000:73-74; Leonhardt 2001:79. On "the imperial family" or "the house of Augustus" (ὁ Σεβαστὸς οἶκος) see the note *ad* §23.

place or method ... for paying this homage: τόπος ἢ τρόπος τιμῆς. Runesson 2001:446-454 interprets our passage as referring to Jewish temples (προσευχαί being temples within "sacred precincts") where unbloody sacrifices were brought. "Usually, animal sacrifices in the name of the emperor would be the proper way to express a good relation between ruler and subjects, as was the case in the Jerusalem temple. Such sacrifices were not performed in first century CE Egypt, apart from those at the temple of Leontopolis. Neither is it likely that any specific rituals were performed in relation to communal Torah readings on sabbaths. Instead, offerings of vegetables and incense combined with the recital of prayers on a regular basis performed in the main hall of the building by priestly representatives of the Jewish community would be the most likely method for Jews to prove their loyalty" (451). This novel and provoking thesis cannot be discussed here, but it runs counter to the present consensus (which is not to say that it is wrong).

§50. *permit*: The mss. read ἀφιέντων or ἀφεθέντων, but Wendland's conjecture ἐφιέντων has been generally accepted.

our own laws, which Augustus himself was pleased to confirm: For "laws" Philo here uses νόμιμα, in the sense of νόμοι, as often. That the Jews owed the general recognition of their ancestral laws to Augustus is repeated in *Legat.* 153 and also explicitly stated by Josephus who reports that this emperor officially decreed that "it seemed good to me and my counsellors ... that the Jews have the right to live according to their own customs as laid down in the law of their ancestors" (*Ant.* 16.163; cf. 14.188); for further evidence see Millar in Schürer 1973/87:3.116-117, and Pucci Ben Zeev 1998:419-429, esp. 423 (see also her discussion of βεβαιοῦν, the word used here by Philo, as a *terminus technicus* in connection with imperial confirmation of existing rights at pp. 308-309). In *Legat.* 140-161 Philo presents his own elaborate praise of Augustus' and Tiberius' wise policy towards the Jewish people (on which see Borgen 1997:186). See Tcherikover-Fuks 1957/64: I.56-57; Barraclough 1984:453-454; Delling 2000:340-363 ("Philons Enkomion auf Augustus"); Niehoff 2001:111-136.

I do not know: "Philo's personality breaks through the artificial form of imaginary speech" (Box 1939:98), unless εἶπον ἄν in §48 is also taken as a first person singular ("I might have said to our opponents"); see above *ad loc.* This use of a first person singular is paralleled in *Prob.* 8 and *Aet.* 119. For Philo's use of the first person singular in general see Conley 1987:7-8.

unless someone ... <not> responsible for them: πλὴν εἰ μὴ ψέγειν τις ἐθελήσειε τὸ μὴ γνώμῃ ἑκουσίῳ παρανομεῖν τὰς ἐκδιαιτήσεις τῶν ἐθῶν οὐ φυλαξαμένους, αἵ, κἂν ἀφ' ἑτέρων ἄρξωνται, τελευτῶσι πολλάκις εἰς τοὺς <μὴ> αἰτίους. The translation of this part of §50 is very uncertain because what Philo wants to say here is expressed by him in a very obscure manner ("but so is much in these sections," says Colson 1941:534; and Nock 1972:565 even speaks of "the tortuous obscurity of his language"). Firstly, πλὴν εἰ μή is pleonastic; secondly, instead of τοὺς αἰτίους one expects τοὺς ἀναιτίους, or perhaps μή has dropped out; thirdly, it is hard to know what exactly is meant by the very vague τελευτῶσι εἰς ... Colson 1941:330 note b suggests as the general meaning: "If we are to be blamed it is not because we refused to break the law by admitting images, but because we have not been strict enough in preventing defection." But what the latter refers to is also unclear (as Colson himself admits). In his long note on ἐκδιαίτησις ("deviation, departure, backsliding," in Philo always in relation to the ancestral traditions), Box 1939:98 says that its combination with φυλαξαμένους is almost absurd: "Deviations do not require guarding." Therefore φυλάξασθαι must mean here something like "taking precautions against ...." He then renders the argument of §50 as follows: "There is no τόπος or τρόπος τιμῆς left to us if our houses of prayer are desecrated, for (γάρ) while we admit liability to the gravest penalties if we fail to render adequate expression of gratitude to our benefactors in ways permitted by our customs (e.g. dedication of houses of prayer to them), yet if a particular way is not permissible to us and we take our stand on the institutions peculiar to us, which Augustus himself confirmed, how are we at fault at all in not expressing gratitude to benefactors in ways forbidden by those institutions? Unless it is to be imputed as a fault that we unwittingly transgress our institutions by not having avoided or taken precautions against deviations from our customs — deviations which, notwithstanding that they begin with the others, yet often come in the end to be practised by those who are responsible for allowing them." In this solution, too, the problem of what Philo is thinking of when he uses the phrase "... come in the end to be practised by those who are responsible for allowing them," remains riddlesome, even aside from the question of whether or not τελευτῶσι ... εἰς τοὺς αἰτίους could have this sense at all. Nock 1972:565 sees here a veiled reference to hellenizing Jews desirous of the status conferred by membership of the gymnasium: "Is not Philo alluding to this situation? And is it not probable that the leaders of the Alexandrian Greeks had made capital out of it? If Lampon and Isidorus said in effect, 'The Jewish objection on religious grounds to the presence of representations of Caligula in their synagogues is insincere: why, plenty of their own people are only too eager to come into the gymnasia and do not mind the sight of images of Hermes and the divine emperor,' Philo could not deny the fact." *Non liquet*.

§51. *by leaving unsaid what he should have said ...*: Philo here refers back to §§43-44; cf. 40. Flaccus "sinned against us" both by sins of omission and by sins of commission.

Did they really want to honor the Emperor?: A rhetorical question the answer to which is all too obvious, implies Philo. For ἆρα expressing skepticism ("really?") see Denniston 1954:46; for Philo's use of rhetorical questions Conley 1987:13. As Niehoff 2001:61 argues, Philo's interpretation, that implies that the Alexandrians pretended to honor the emperor by setting up his image in synagogues, "presupposes the prior existence of a conflict between Gaius and the Jews, who refused to pay him the expected honors." This is also the viewpoint he brings forward in the *Legatio*. But it cannot be historical, Niehoff thinks, because it is only after the Alexandrian riots that

THE JEWISH POINT OF VIEW 151

Gaius' antipathy towards the Jews becomes apparent. "He has adapted the events of *In Flaccum* to the plot of the *Legatio* which revolves around Gaius' deification" (61). Since in the *Legatio* Philo blames Gaius' hatred of the Jews on the Egyptians at his court (§§ 170, 205, 355), he implies here (*Flacc.* 51) that even the anti-Jewish measures of Gaius were of Alexandrian (Egyptian) origin. Niehoff and others base their theories on the fact that our sources mention Gaius' Jew-hatred only for the period 39-41 CE, but that is an *argumentum e silentio*. The fact that Philo asserts that Isidorus and Lampo could convince Flaccus that it was possible to regain Gaius' favor by taking anti-Jewish measures (§§22-23) implies that at least in his view the emperor's anti-Jewish sentiments were older, which would seem far from being impossible.

The greatest and most important parts of the city have been consecrated to gods: For the numerous temples and sacred areas in Alexandria see Schneider 1967/1969: I.533-535; Fraser 1972: 1.189-301 (with the notes in 2.323-461); Haas 1997:138-152. Strabo 17.1.10 [795] says that the city was full of sacred buildings and areas.

§52. *what we have been talking about...*: Philo accuses the enemies of the Jews of a reversal of roles and a total perversion of the truth: they present the Jews as the evildoers whereas the Jews are not, and themselves as attacking the Jews for a just cause (the honor of the emperor) whereas the exact opposite is the case.

for us, the attacked, it was not safe to oppose them: If they opposed their enemies, it could create the impression at the Roman court that the Jews were unwilling to honor the emperor, which could bring about a dangerous situation.

For, gentlemen, ...: γάρ explains the reason for Philo's characterization of the Alexandrians' motive as "aggression of persons who love to make enemies." The words ὦ γενναῖοι, lit. "noble men," are probably not addressed to the readers, but — ironically (see Pelletier 1967:80 note 2: "apostrophe ironique") — to the organizers of the anti-Jewish riots (for other instances of irony in *Flacc.* see §§74, 85, 93, 95, 157; cf. the ironic use of σεμνός in *Legat.* 163). De Vries 1999:91, however, suggests that it is not to be ruled out that Philo has had the opportunity, when being head of the embassy in Rome in 39/40, to read parts of the text aloud to senators so that γενναῖοι could be meant seriously; but, although this cannot be ruled out, in that case one would expect more traces of such a performance. There are several other passages in which Philo uses ὦ γενναῖοι or ὦ γενναῖε in an ironic way; see *Philo Index* 73 (e.g., *Somn*. 1.93; *Aet* . 54). If, however, Philo's use of the word is not meant in an ironical way here, it is important to observe that he addresses the social élites and that, therefore, his narrative constructs the "events" with their prejudices and expectations in mind. In §§73-77 it becomes all the more clear that a very important question for Philo was whether he could win the attention of the social élites, be they Jews or Romans or both.

abrogating the laws and disrupting the ancestral customs ...: See the comments *ad* §48.

teaching the inhabitants of other cities to disregard unanimity: again Philo expresses his (realistic or unfounded?) fear that the riots might spread elsewhere; see the note *ad* §45.

§§53-96: *The pogrom at its height*

This very long section consists mainly of a catalog of horrors. The desecration of synagogues was followed by the issuing of a decree by Flaccus to the effect that Jews were from now on to be regarded as foreigners without rights in the city. This opened the gates to massive plundering of Jewish houses and shops and rounding up the Jews in that one quarter of the city where already the majority of the Jews lived, so that an overcrowded ghetto was created. The Jews had to live there under terrible circumstances and many died of diseases that broke out because of these atrocious conditions. Synagogues and houses (probably those outside the ghetto) were sacked and set on fire. Then followed a long series of events of unchecked savagery by the Alexandrian mobs when they caught Jews who strayed outside the ghetto in search for help or food. They beat them up, or burned them to death, or bound them together and dragged them through the market square and the streets, kicking them and trampling on them until their bodies were mutilated beyond recognition. At the end of August, on Caligula's birthday, a large group of Jews was arrested, marched through the streets to the theatre where they were beaten and forced to eat pork. If they refused, they were finished off by way of birthday celebration for the emperor. In the description of these acts of cruelty and humiliation Philo displays all his rhetorical *pathos* in an attempt to evoke compassion and sympathy in his readers.

Two episodes are especially highlighted by Philo. In §§73-77 he deals at some length with the cruel treatment of the Jewish senators or elders, a treatment so insulting that Philo calls it "monstrous and unparallelled." The form of scourging used was that reserved for criminals from the lowest strata of society (the Egyptians), and that is what makes Philo extraordinarily indignant. At even greater length, in §§86-94 Philo reports the search for arms among the Jews in the city, an insult — he says — not only because the Jews were always a peaceful nation but especially since only some years before Flaccus had carried out a similar weapon search among the Egyptians and on that occasion did find innumerable caches of all sorts of arms. It is clear that the cultural distance between Jews and Egyptians as perceived by Philo plays a major role in his description of the pogrom.

§53. *His attack on our laws by means of a seizure of our synagogues ...*: ἁρπάσαντι suggest expropriation rather than destruction. Of course the effect for the Jews is the same: they lost their communal buildings and places of worship.

of which he had even the names removed: We do not know much about names of ancient synagogues, but from Jewish epitaphs in Rome we learn the names of some 10 local synagogues (the Augustesian, Agrippesian, Siburesian, Volumnesian synagogues etc.); see Van der Horst 1991:86-88. From the New Testament we learn about a "synagogue of the freedmen" in Jerusalem (Acts 6:9). How the removal of the synagogue names (lit. "not even leaving the names") was brought about is unknown; were name shields removed?

the destruction of our political organization: τὴν τῆς ἡμετέρας πολιτείας ἀναίρεσιν. The correct translation of πολιτεία is a matter of much debate. It hinges on the question of whether or not the Jews had, or claimed to have, full citizenship in Alexandria (see the Introduction). Since, as Box 1939:99 claims, most occurrences of πολιτεία in Philo are in the sense of "commonwealth" or "constitution," he translates with "the destruction of our polity;" cf. Gerschmann's "unsere Gemeinschaft," Pelletier's "notre organisation politique;" De Vries' "onze politieke organisatie;" contrast Colson's "citizenship" (cf. Carlier 2002:125 "notre cité" in the sense of "our community"). It should be borne in mind that πολιτεία can also have the sense of way of life according to the traditional laws (BDAG 845). The most recent and thorough investigation of the whole question of Alexandrian citizenship during the Roman principate (Delia 1991) comes to the conclusion that the Jewish community had not been striving for Alexandrian citizenship at all in the years leading up to and following the pogrom of 38, but only for the restoration of their former status and privileges that Flaccus had abrogated. That would imply that πολιτεία cannot mean "citizenship" here but should be taken to mean the political organization of the Jews and/or their way of life. Theirs was "a recognized, formally constituted corporation of aliens enjoying the right of domicile in a foreign city and forming a separate, semi-autonomous civic body, a city within the city; it had its own constitution and administered its internal affairs as an ethnic unit through officials distinct from and independent of those of the host city" (Smallwood 1976:225; at 229-230 she states that "*politeia* might be used of the rights of members of a *politeuma*," but that is denied by Lüderitz 1994:201; see now, however, Cowey-Maresch 2001:4-9, 22-23, 38). See also Davis 1951:101; Tcherikover 1959:315-316; Applebaum 1974:420-463; Barraclough 1984:425; Troiani 1994; Pucci Ben Zeev 1998:300. In Philo's time the Jewish community was administered by a body of elders (a *gerousia* or senate) that had a relatively wide-ranging competence (see Box 1939:xxvi-xxx). This was what Flaccus had tried to abolish, according to Philo, and that is why in the following sentence Philo expresses the fear that "if the only things to which our life was anchored are cut away, that is, our ancestral customs and our participation in political rights, we may be exposed to the worst misfortunes without having anything left to which we could cling to guarantee our safety."

the only things to which our life was anchored were cut away (ἀποκοπέντων οἷς μόνοις ἐφώρμει ὁ ἡμέτερος βίος): The image is that of a ship that threatens to get out of control because it has broken adrift from its anchors. The verb ἐφορμέω (to anchor) developed the meaning of "relying upon." For other instances of this metaphor see Stupf 1950.

participation in political rights: μετουσία πολιτικῶν δικαίων. This phrase does not necessarily imply that the Jews had equal rights with the other citizens (in the official sense) of Alexandria, it may just refer to their enjoyment of certain rights they used to have within their own civic body (since, unlike πόλις, the noun πολίτευμα does not have an adjective of its own, πολιτικός may serve for both of them; but it is uncertain whether the Jewish civic body of Alexandria was a *politeuma*; see Lüderitz 1994, but now also the new evidence in

Cowey-Maresch 2001:4-10). As Tcherikover 1959:315 remarks, "there is no reason to see in them [sc., *dikaia*] an allusion to citizen rights, since the term *dikaia* also denoted Jewish privileges."
without any rope left to which we could cling to for safety: The image is still the same as the one evoked by "anchored."

§54. *he issued a decree* (τίθησι πρόγραμμα): What exactly was the reason for this decree remains obscure, although one may surmise that the Greeks asked or rather pressed Flaccus to give his ruling on the debated issue of the right of the Jews to reside in Alexandria at all. One should keep in mind that the by now vulnerable Flaccus "had to protect his flanks, and also to stay a step ahead of the mob. A public declaration limiting Jewish prerogatives might also take some steam out of the anti-Jewish movement, and thus head off violence. For, if matters got out of hand, Flaccus' neck would be on the block for failing to keep order" (Gruen 2002:59). The reason Philo mentions the decree is that in it Flaccus states the Jews to be "foreigners and aliens" (see the next note).
he stigmatized us as foreigners and aliens (ξένους καὶ ἐπήλυδας ἡμᾶς ἀπεκάλει): The verb ἀποκαλέω implies that the designation being given is unjustified (see §39; *Mos.* 1.10, 30). In Philo's parlance, ἔπηλυς usually designates a proselyte but here he uses it without any religious connotation (Birnbaum 1996:195-199, esp. 198). Probably Flaccus had notices posted publicly in which Jews were declared to be just immigrants (maybe this only concerned those resident outside the Delta quarter; see §55). "Foreigners and aliens" does not only imply that the Jews had no Alexandrian citizenship but also that they were second rank residents. Philo often employs these terms to refer to a social status distinctly less than that of a citizen (*Cher.* 121; *Post.* 109; *Spec.* 3.168, 4.70). It reminds one of what three years later was said by the emperor Claudius in his famous letter to the Alexandrians that the Jews live there "in a city which is not their own" (*CPJ* 153.95 ἐν ἀλλοτρίᾳ πόλει). Since there can be little doubt that Jews were indeed not formal citizens of the *polis* of Alexandria, why then is Philo so indignant? We do not know, but it is not impossible that — although it is not mentioned by Philo — the Jews (or some Jews) had made a formal claim to full citizenship and that the edict was the formal refusal of their request (as it was later rejected by Claudius as well). There can be little doubt that the Alexandrian nationalists were behind this; see *CPJ* 150. "This was the first great victory of the

anti-Semites: their thesis that Jews were strangers was adopted and officially proclaimed by the Roman government" (Tcherikover-Fuks 1957/64: I.66; cf. Tcherikover 1963:18-19). In this case, as Colson 1941:535 observes, the desecration of the synagogues and the decree "have the very close connexion, that the Alexandrians strengthened their case by bringing out the disloyal refusal of the Jews to give the honors to the emperor which the true citizens give." But probably more was going on: "The Greeks turned to the achievement of their real purpose, the reduction of the Jews' present civic rights and the ending of their ambitions for advancement. They got Flaccus to undermine the *politeuma* by issuing a proclamation declaring that the Jews were "aliens and foreigners" in Alexandria. The measure degraded them from their legal status of resident aliens, on which the existence of the *politeuma* depended, to that of aliens without the right of domicile. Legally they could now all be expelled" (Smallwood 1976:240; cf. Smallwood 1987:118). Smallwood is probably right and it explains why in the following sentence Philo says that Flaccus "gave us no right to plead our cause but condemned us without a trial." In *Legat.* 119 Philo attributes the action to the emperor himself: "So we were enrolled not simply as slaves but as the lowest of slaves, when the emperor turned into a tyrant." Whether or not Caligula played an active role in all this, it may be regarded as certain that the anti-Jewish nationalists in Alexandria could count on his support. Bludau's unargued statement that Flaccus also enforced sabbath-breaking, on the basis of *Somn.* 2.123-132, has no basis whatsoever in the present text, even though his suggestion cannot be ruled out altogether since the official hinted at in *Somn.* 2.123-132 might be Flaccus, but there is no way to prove this (Bludau 1906:73, but, *contra*, Leonhardt 2001:71 and Gruen 2002:278-279; Kraft 1991 argues that the anonymous authority mentioned in *Somn.* 2 was Philo's nephew Tiberius Julius Alexander).

gave us no right to plead our cause: This clause of the edict "may have been related to the efforts by Jews to gain Alexandrian citizenship, but more likely it refers to their defence of their traditional rights" (Barraclough 1984:433). It is these rights to live according to the traditional Jewish laws and customs that are fully reconfirmed by the emperor Claudius in his letter to the Alexandrians of 41 CE, *CPJ* 153.86-88.

he then added to the first two (crimes) a third one ...: The first one was that Flaccus gave permission to erect statues of the emperor in the synagogues (§43); the second one was robbing the Jews of their political status in Alexandria in a decree (§53); the third one was "giving permission to those who wanted to plunder the Jews" (§54). Box 1939:99 rightly argues that it is important to see that the permission for plundering is here distinguished from the decree ("Flaccus' *programma* did not by itself enable the Gentiles to lay violent hands upon the persons and property of Jews"). In another interpretation, which makes the permission of plundering the contents of the decree (the first crime then being the insulting of Agrippa), it is strange that Philo says that "he then added to the first two crimes a third one" which implies a time interval between the first two and the third (note that Philo uses εἶτα here, although that might be a reference to ὀλίγαις ὕστερον ἡμέραις at the beginning of §54). The most important argument for the first interpretation is that it would be absurd for a Roman governor to publish a decree in which looting of a large part of a major city and its population would be officially permitted. Even Gaius would have been infuriated by that, his hatred of Jews notwithstanding.

§55. *The city has five districts*: The city was divided by two long and wide intersecting streets, the longitudinal Canopus street and the latitudinal Sema street (Strabo 17.1.8; for maps see the note *ad* §41). In view of that division, one would expect there to have been four quarters, but Philo mentions five and this must be regarded as reliable inside information. This division dates from the early Ptolemaic period. Cf. Ps.-Callisthenes 1.32.4 (quoted in the next note), and see Fraser 1972: 1.34-35; II.108-109 note 265; Huzar 1988:625.

named after the first letters of the alphabet: A, B, Γ, Δ, E. It has to be borne in mind that in ancient Greek letters also functioned as numbers. For other evidence on the names of the quarters see Fraser 1972: 2.108-109 notes 265-269. Ps.-Callisthenes 1.32.4 explains the letters as being the acronym of Ἀλέξανδρος βασιλεὺς γένος Διὸς ἔκτισε (sc. τὴν πόλιν), *i.e.*, "King Alexander, offspring of Zeus, founded (this city)." See Pelletier 1967:163; and on στοιχεῖον in the sense of "letter" (and in other senses) see Sterling 1998:363 with note 44; and see *ad* §125.

as we use to write it: I.e., of the Greek (not the Hebrew) alphabet.

Two of the districts are called the Jewish quarters: Strabo as quoted by Josephus, *Ant.* 14.117, says: "In Egypt the Jews have a separate dwelling-place, and a large part of Alexandria has been set aside for them." Josephus, *C. Ap.* 2.34-35, says this part of the city had been given to the Jews by Alexander the Great himself — not necessarily reliable information (cf. *Bell.* 2.487, and see Fuchs 1924:5-6) — and that it was situated near the palace on the harborless coastline in the north-eastern area of the city, which is correct; Fraser 1972: 1.35, 54-56 (but see Haas 1997:95). The main Jewish quarter was a district in the north-eastern part of the city, called Δ (Delta, according to Josephus, *Bell.* 2.495; the letter of the second Jewish quarter is unknown), but, as Philo implies in what follows in §55, the Jews lived in the other quarters of the city as well (cf. also *Legat.* 132: "They attacked synagogues of which there are many in each quarter of the city"). It is noteworthy that also in the city of Edfu (Apollinopolis Magna) the Jews lived in a quarter called Delta; see Tcherikover-Fuks 1957/64: 2.108-109; Sterling 1995:10 with note 37. Similar Jewish quarters existed also in other Egyptian cities such as Oxyrhynchus and Hermoupolis and, outside of Egypt, in Sardis, Antioch, Rome (*Legat.* 155), and elsewhere (see Juster 1914: 2.177 note 3 and Sevenster 1975:102-107). Cohen 1999:56 rightly observes that such quarters were not ghettos but ethnic neighborhoods: "Members of ethnic minorities tended (and still tend) to live in proximity to each other because they were comfortable in each other's presence and felt that their interests were better protected if they were massed as a group." Jews here simply followed the practice of other ethnic minorities in Alexandria (e.g., Lycians and Phrygians, Haas 1997:49 note 14), so it is the Jews themselves who created this demographic condition; it was not imposed upon them by others; see Juster 1914: II.177-178; Tcherikover 1959:304-305; Fraser 1972: 1.56; Mendelson 1988:115 note 1; and cf. Barclay 1996:117-118 and 331-332; Williams 1998:15.

because the majority of the inhabitants are Jews: This translation of διὰ τὸ πλείστους Ἰουδαίους ἐν ταύταις κατοικεῖν is not certain: others take it to mean, "because most of the Jews inhabit them" (so Box and Colson), while my translation implies that also gentiles lived there. In view of the fact that Philo states that in the other quarters of the city there were many Jews as well I take the situation to be that the Jews were the majority in Delta and the other "Jewish quarter" but a minority in the three remaining ones, which seems natural. Ethnic neighbourhoods seldom are inhabited exclusively by one group. See Pelletier 1967:82-83 note 4, who may be right in arguing that "l'expression πλείστους Ἰουδαίους sans article indique seulement que les Juifs sont très nombreux dans ce quartier."

They expelled the Jews ... the one left: For the phrase ἐκ τῶν τεσσάρων γραμμάτων in the sense of "from the four quarters" see Box 1939:100. "... drove them together into ... only one of them" is the first indication for compulsory Jewish ghetto formation known to us; see Sevenster 1975:105. Undoubtedly the already predominantly Jewish quarter Delta is meant here.

§56. *they (the Jews) flooded the beaches ...*: The Delta quarter bordered on the seashore. See in Breccia 1922 the map opposite page 64; Sly 1996:xvii, map 3. The Jews are also said to have spread to "the dunghills and the tombs." There were *necropoleis* located just outside the north-eastern area of the city at a short distance from the Jewish quarter (Strabo 17.1.10 [795]; Schneider 1967/1969: I.537-539). It is probable that these places were generally avoided by the Jews because of the risk of ritual impurity (which could also be incurred on a dunghill), but under the given circumstances they naturally overflowed into the area nearest to them. See Fraser 1972: 2.110 note 271.

the houses left empty: These almost certainly were the houses of the Jews who lived elsewhere in the city than in the Delta quarter.

they were closed because of the mourning for Drusilla: Julia Drusilla (16-38 CE) was a daughter of Germanicus and Agrippina and a sister of the emperor Gaius. In her very short life she married twice and also lived for some time in an allegedly incestuous relationship with her brother Gaius, whose favorite she was (Barrett 1989:85). When she died on the 10th of June 38, Gaius enforced public mourning throughout the empire. Suetonius, *Calig.* 24, writes that he decreed that during the mourning period it would be regarded as a capital crime to laugh, bathe, or dine with parents, wife, or children; cf. Cassius Dio 59.10.8, and see Lindsay 1993:109. Later he deified her as Panthea, probably on the anniversary of Augustus' birthday, September 23 of the year 38 CE. The looting of the Jewish houses and workshops took place between these two dates. See further Barrett 1989:62-63, 86-89 and Reg. *s.v.* Drusilla, and Eck 1999. The public mourning for Drusilla is mentioned here explicitly by Philo because it enables him to remark in passing that the Jews were much stricter in observing the mourning than the non-Jews. But there is a chronological problem here, as Kushnir-Stein 2000:234-235 notices: the mourning period for Drusilla was probably over by the end of June, but according to Philo the riots started only after Agrippa's arrival which it is argued can hardly have taken place before the end of July (some two weeks after the Etesian winds began to blow; see §26). It is not easy to solve this problem, unless one is willing to accuse Philo of completely inventing episodes like the present one, showing no regard for chronology. It is hard to imagine how he could make such a fool of himself in the eyes of the many readers who knew he was completely wrong. The most probable solution to this problem is, however, that Agrippa left Rome very early (sometimes the Etesian winds started as early as June, see *Mos.* 1.115!) and arrived in Alexandria before the end of June, and it is far from impossible that his stay coincided more or less with the period of mourning for Gaius' sister; see also Kokkinos 1998:281.

They carried it ... as if it were their own: Philo implies that they not only misappropriated Jewish property but also illegally sold it. For "handling" Philo has καταχρώμενοι, which has the negative connotation of misusing or improperly using.

§57. *The unemployment ... their regular jobs*: "The μέν clause expresses the results of the ἁρπαγή, the δέ clause the conditions of ἀπραξία" (Box 1939:100). As this paragraph makes clear, the Jews of Alexandria were engaged in business and commerce in the same way as the bulk of the non-Jewish population (financers, farmers, shippers, merchants, artisans etc.). See Fraser 1972: 1.84, 2.164 note 313. The broad range of occupations serves to emphasize that the pogrom led to a total paralysis of economic life for all Jews. The best and most detailed discussion of the list of occupations is to be found in Tcherikover-Fuks 1957/64: I.48-50, and the following observations are largely based on their discussion. Financers (πορισταί, translated by Tcherikover as "capitalists") were probably wealthy investors or money-lenders such as Philo's own brother Alexander (who lent a large sum to Agrippa I, according to Josephus, *Ant.* 18.159). In the letter in *CPJ* 151 an Alexandrian Greek mentions Jewish money-lenders but warns his addressee to beware of them; the letter is from August 41 CE and apparently the tensions were still high three years after the pogrom. As to the farmers (γεωργοί), one may wonder what part they could have played in Alexandria, but Philo probably had in mind peasants owning land in the environs of Alexandria who sold their corn at the city markets. Shippers and merchants (ναύκληροι, ἔμποροι) are often mentioned together, the first category being ship-owners who transported goods on board of their own ships (e.g., corn for Rome), whereas *emporoi* were merchants in the wider sense of the word. In a maritime town like Alexandria, commercial life centred around the harbor, and the *naukleroi* were far more important than mere merchants. Jewish *naukleroi* were, probably, the aristocracy among the Jewish merchants, whereas the *emporoi* formed the large majority of the Jewish middle class. The last category is the artisans (τεχνίται), here mentioned probably because they sold the products of their industry in their workshops. In the well-known Tosefta passage on the great synagogue of Alexandria (t. *Sukkah* 4:6; cf. b. *Sukkah* 51b) mention is made of goldsmiths, silversmiths, blacksmiths, weavers, and wool-dressers, every group having its own fixed place in that large basilica. Even though this late passage (mid 3rd cent. CE) cannot be used as a reliable historical source, the emphasis laid on the class of artisans may be seen as some proof of their important role in the economic life of Jewish Alexandria. Of course diaspora Jews worked in many other professions as well, and the conclusion emerging from the evidence is that the occupational structure of diaspora Jewry was not different from that of other ethnic groups. For the evidence see Juster 1914: 2.291-314; Fuchs 1924:50-69; Tcherikover-Fuks 1957/64: 1.48-55; Sevenster 1975:75, 84-85; Applebaum 1974/76:II.702-704; Huß 1994:10-11; Haas 1997:401 note 10; Williams 1998:19-26; Delling 2000:79-80.

§58. *Unbearable though these things were ...*: The ταῦτα μέν in §58 corresponds to the τοὺς δέ in §59: The poverty caused by the looting was already a terrible thing in itself, but there are no words for the unprecedented physical violence used against the Jews thereafter. In §77 Philo again emphasizes this twofold misfortune of the Jews.

poverty is grievous: Cf. Prov. 6:11; 10:4. Unlike in Christianity, in Judaism poverty was never idealized. See the chapter "The Woes of the Poor" in Cronbach 1944:125-131; also Bolkestein & Kalsbach 1950; Pleins & Hanks 1992.

§59. *I think he would be at a loss to find adequate terms*: μοι δοκεῖ προσρήσεων οἰκείων ἂν ἀπορῆσαι. The preceding lines culminate in a rhetorical statement underlining that the events were so undescribably horrible that there are no adequate terms of description to be found in human language.

the enormous scale of this unprecedented cruelty: In view of the fact that Philo time and again emphasizes the unprecedented scale of this pogrom it is all the more remarkable that Josephus, who pays much attention to Alexandrian Jewry, writes about these events in only a single phrase: "Meanwhile there was civil strife (στάσις) between the Jewish and Greek inhabitants of Alexandria" (*Ant.* 18.257), using only a *genitivus absolutus* construction at that. Philo probably exaggerates in order to heighten the dramatic effect, but we have no way of knowing the degree to which he exaggerates.

For the treatment of prisoners of war ...: Box 1939:101 suggests that in τῶν πολέμῳ μὲν κρατησάντων, ἐκ φύσεως δ' ἀσπόνδων the use of μέν ... δέ has a cumulative effect: "Under war-conditions one might expect even merciful men to be ruthless, but the Alexandrians were neither temperamentally ruthless nor at war with the Jews." Philo's point in this and the next paragraph is that the mercy one might expect from victors in a war was completely denied the Jews by their persecutors (see Pelletier 1967:86).

§60. *victors do seize property and take large numbers of people prisoner ...*: It was universally assumed in antiquity that success in war would lead to appropriation by the victor of the property and persons of the vanquished (see, e.g., Xenophon, *Cyr.* 7.5.73). The best study is to be found in the chapters "Booty," "Legal Ownership of Booty," and "Fate of Captives" in Pritchett 1971/91: 1.53-92, 5.203-311 (on ransoming esp. 5.284-289).

not ... mercy, but ... love of money: When Philo speaks about φιλαργυρία, it is always with contempt, so here he implies it to be the basest motive for releasing prisoners. That love of money or greed is the root (or source, or mother) of all evil is a current idea in antiquity; for a collection of evidence see Van der Horst 1978:142-143 (*ad* Ps.-Phocylides 42: ἡ φιλοχρημοσύνη μήτηρ κακότητος ἁπάσης).

the way they are saved: τῆς σωτηρίας ὁ τρόπος. Here τρόπος is used of the motive for releasing prisoners, whether mercy or greed. Box 1939:101 says this remark is hardly relevant to the argument and wonders whether there is a lacuna after it. But Philo's point is that, whatever the motives for behavior in wartime, there are certain rules according to which enemies deal with one another. But even that modicum of decency was denied to the Jews.

§61. *Apart from that, it is also the case that ...*: ἤδη δὲ καί "introduces the climax of a narrative proceeding by the accumulation of instances" (Box 1939:101; cf. Denniston 1954:305). Here it indicates that, in addition to what has been said before about their taking the risk of being defeated and releasing prisoners (for whatever motives), enemies often see to it that their victims receive a proper burial, again something that was denied to the Jews (see §84). Philo uses the same expression again in §68.

The decent and humane ...: This was definitely not always the case; see Pritchett 1971/91 *passim*. On the generally recognized duty of burying dead human bodies see the so-called Buzygian laws, referred to by Philo in *Hyp.* 7.7-8; see Nilsson 1967:421 and Van der Horst 1978:181.

§62. *That is what enemies do in war:* That is, in the typical war in which the warriors keep to the universally accepted rules of minimal humanity. The contrast with what the Alexandrians did to the Jews *while there was no war* ("those who only a little while ago were our friends"), is given antithetical emphasis by ἐν πολέμῳ μὲν ... ἐν εἰρήνῃ δὲ ...

they saw their wives and little children dying before their eyes through a famine organized by men: γύναια καὶ τέκνα νήπια is more dramatic than just γυναῖκες καὶ τέκνα, because γύναιον is sometimes a term of endearment but more often a word that implies weakness and helplessness (not infrequently in a contemptuous sense), as does the addition of νήπια to τέκνα. On the order — women before children — see Box 1939:101 who points out that in biblical parlance, too, women usually come before the children ("widows and orphans"). The fact that Philo speaks of famine is a clear indication that the unbearable situation lasted considerably longer than just a few days. For "organized by men" the Greek has χειροποίητος, lit. "hand-made."

§63. *For in every other place ... abundance*: Γάρ here explains why the famine Philo mentioned just before was said by him to be artificially induced (χειροποίητος): there was plenty of food everywhere else.

the river had richly flooded the fields ...: The annual floodings of the Nile had already inspired Herodotus to his famous saying that Egypt is a country that is "a gift of the river" (*Hist.* 2.5). For an elaborate description of such an inundation see Strabo 17.1.4 [789]. In the book of Genesis the proverbial fertility of the land of Egypt is mentioned as well: "Lot ... saw that the Jordan valley was well watered everywhere like the garden of the Lord, like the land of Egypt" (13:10). On the Nile see further Huddlestun-Williams 1992.

§64. *When, finally, ... poor wretches!*: The dire straits in which the Jews found themselves at last drove some of them to begging, others to the desperate act of going to the market to buy food. Box 1939:101 here deserves to be quoted in full: "Philo is in an awkward position. He wants to introduce the 'buying class' to dwell upon the atrocity of their fate, while the tone of his previous narrative has left the impression that the Jews were completely impoverished, and he is unwilling to admit the consequence of destitution-mendicancy. Hence ἔρανον modifies αἰτήσοντες, whilst the morality of buying when begging was easy is emphasized to minimize the fact that some Jews could buy." The word ἔρανος usually means a loan without interest but recoverable in instalments; see Vondeling 1961 and the lit. in *RBLG* 282. The market-place (ἀγορά) mentioned here was one of the probably two *agorai* in Alexandria; the site of both is unknown; see Fraser 1972: 1.30; 2.98 note 219.

§65. *those who wielded the weapon of mob rule*: The verb ἐπιτειχίζω meant originally building a stronghold on the enemy's frontier from which to attack him, but from there it developed the meaning of using something like a stronghold. Here ὀχλοκρατίαν ἐπιτειχίσαντες are the people who make malevolent use of the unruly Alexandrian masses in order to attack the Jews in their midst. There is little else that can inspire more disgust in the elitist Philo than ὀχλοκρατία (Barraclough 1984:520-529). In *Opif.* 171 he even calls it "the worst of evil polities" (with Runia 2001:398 *ad loc.*). The verb ἐπιτειχίζειν is one of Philo's favorites; he uses it mostly in a metaphorical way, especially for attacks by pleasures on the soul, e.g. *Opif.* 79 (24 other instances in the *Philo Index*). See further especially Pelletier 1967:88-89 note 3.

treacherously murdered: This is the first instance of actual killing mentioned by Philo. From now on this sets the tone.

not even one piece was left to be buried: Depriving a person of his or her burial was regarded in antiquity as "la suprême infortune" (Pelletier 1967:89 note 4). In Jewish circles burying the unburied dead was regarded as a divine commandment, but the importance of a proper burial is also reflected in Greek and Latin literature (see Van der Horst 1978:180-181 for evidence). It stands to reason that mutilating a body to such a degree that nothing is left for burial is the greatest offence possible for Jewish religious sensitivity. Cf. about the same events also *Legat.* 131 (quoted below *ad* §70).

§66. *were transformed into wild animals*: lit. "into the nature of wild beasts" (εἰς θηρίων φύσιν). The same expression is used in *Decal.* 110. It occurs several times in combination with ἀγριότης, like here, e.g., *Mos.* 1.43, *Spec.* 3.103, *Virt.* 87, *Praem.* 88, *Prov.* 2.69. On the basis of *Virt.* 87 Mangey conjectured that μεταβαλόντες had to be added after εἰς θηρίων φύσιν, but the idea of transformation would seem to be already sufficiently included in λελυττηκότες ὑπ' ἀγριότητος. The frenzied nature of the massacre is also brought out clearly in the passage from *Legat.* 131 quoted *ad* §70.

to prevent that, by dying too soon, they might escape too soon from the awareness of their sufferings: the repeated θᾶττον dramatically emphasizes the cruelty of the purposefully prolonged sufferings.

§67. *Some people ... these catastrophic crimes*: τῇ δὲ τῶν συμφορῶν ἀδείᾳ καὶ ἐκεχειρίᾳ τινὲς ἐπινεανιευόμενοι. The verb ἐπινεανιεύεσθαι is very rare in Greek literature but Philo uses it no less than 6 times, always in the sense of irresponsible and reprehensible audacious behaviour (like a misguided youngster), e.g., *Post.* 170. It is the element of "immunity and license" (ἀδεία καὶ ἐκεχειρία) that receives emphasis here: the fact that Flaccus did not interfere made this horrible pogrom possible.

they killed many with swords and not a few were exterminated by fire: πολλοὺς μὲν ξίφεσιν ἀνεῖλον, οὐκ ὀλίγους δὲ πυρὶ διέφθειραν. Also when he writes about large-scale massacres, Philo sees to it that his language is carefully phrased, in balanced sentences (μὲν ... δὲ) with due variation (πολλοὺς ... οὐκ ὀλίγους). Philo speaks of "many" casualties, but unfortunately we have no means of assessing how many. The 400 plundered houses mentioned in §94 cannot possibly form the basis for speculations about the number of casualties (see *ad loc.*).

§68. *On top of all that ... the innocent age of childhood*: Ὅτι ἤδη δὲ καί introducing the climax of a story see the note *ad* §61. The emphasis here lies on the fact that the mob did not even shy away from burning whole families, including innocent children. For the expression μὴ νεότητα, μὴ παίδων ἄκακον ἡλικίαν cf. *Legat.* 234. With his remark that all this happened "in the centre of the city" Philo emphasizes that these atrocities took place under the very eyes of the authorities who did nothing to prevent these crimes from taking place. The burning of Jews in general in the middle of the city is also mentioned in *Legat.* 130 but there the story apparently refers to Jews who returned to the city centre from the ghetto or from outside the city in search of food. Here, as Smallwood 1961:219 remarks, the scene, although placed after the reference to the Jews' expeditions in search of food, mentions the burning alive of whole families, and she therefore concludes that, "as the people who ventured back will hardly have included children, it looks as if the victims of the massacres described in the parallel passages of the two treatises included Jews who failed to take refuge in the ghetto in time (*Legat.* 127), as well as those who later ventured out of it." Though this argument is not compelling, this may well have been the case.

And when they were in want of timber ... heart-rending spectacle: Many people died not because they were burnt but primarily because they were slowly suffocated by lack of oxygen, as often happened when people died on the stake. Cf. *Legat.* 130: "Sometimes for lack of timber the Greeks collected brushwood, set it on fire, and threw it on top of the unfortunate Jews, who for the most part were killed by the smoke rather than by the fire while still only half-burnt, since brushwood produces a weak and smoky fire and goes out very quickly, while it is too light to be burnt to cinders."

§69. **the persons who were called:** οἱ παραληφθέντες is Mangey's acceptable conjecture for the mss.'s οἱ περιλειφθέντες (or -έντας). Roos 1935:241 ingeniously but unnecessarily suggested the reading οἱ περιπεμφθέντες ἐπὶ φρυγανισμόν. For more discussion of the textual problem here see Pelletier 1967:90-91 note 4.

they would burn ... as timber: This scene, too, is elaborated in the slightly different version in *Legat.* 129: "Another group was blockading the harbors of the river in order to seize the Jews who put in there and the goods which they were conveying for trading purposes. They boarded their ships and carried off the cargo under the eyes of its owners, and then tied their arms behind their backs and burnt them alive, using the rudders, helms, punt-poles, and the planks of the decks as fuel" (transl. Smallwood 1961:86).

§70. **Many also ... the most cruel form of death:** Cf. *Legat.* 131: "They bound many Jews, still alive, with straps and ropes, tied their ankles together, and dragged them through the middle of the market-place, jumping on them and not sparing even their dead bodies. More cruel and savage than wild animals, they tore them limb from limb, trampled on them, and destroyed their every form, so that nothing was left which could be given burial" (transl. Smallwood 1961:86). The final element is also to be found in §65.

§71. *all the constituent parts of the organism had been separated*: This element is echoed in the description of Flaccus' own death in §190. Philo's digression on the atrocities committed by the Alexandrians serves to underline the unspeakable nature of their cruelty and violation of justice. συμφυία (organism) is first found in Philo and used by him rather frequently (8 times); see Winston & Dillon 1983:294 and *Philo Index* s.v.

§72. *like actors in a mime*: On mime see the note *ad* §34. That the persecutors "acted as if they were the victims" (καθυπεκρίνοντο τοὺς πάσχοντας) implies that "they assumed the air of the injured parties, who were only inflicting a righteous punishment" (Colson 1941:341); note the contrast in τῶν δ' ὡς *ἀληθῶς* πεπονθότων.

scourged and tortured on the wheel: Flagellation was often applied as a preliminary to crucifixion; see Josephus, *Bell.* 2.308; John 19:1; Cicero, *Verr.* 5.162-3 [66]; Seneca, *De ira* 1.2.2; 3.3.6; for more references to the various forms of torture preceding crucifixion see Hengel 1977:22-32.

crucifixion: The fullest treatment of this subject is Hengel 1977; cf. O'Collins 1992. As an important form of political and military punishment, the Romans inflicted it above all on the lower classes, runaway slaves, violent criminals, deserted soldiers, and unruly elements in the provinces. Its sadistic cruelty was proverbial in antiquity. Hengel adduces evidence to the effect that "crucifixion could serve as 'popular entertainment'; according to Philo (*In Flaccum* 72.84f.) this was the case with the torture and subsequent crucifixion of Jews in Alexandria by the prefect Flaccus. It could also happen in mime [!] as in the representation of the execution of the robber thief Laureolus [Martial, *Liber de spectaculis* 7], at which a great deal of artificial blood flowed; both these instances date from the time of Caligula" (1977:35); cf. Coleman 1990:65 (on mimes involving crucifixion). The word ἔφεδρος here expresses the idea that after the body had survived all other tortures, there was finally the cross that had been waiting for it (a more extensive discussion of ἔφεδρος is to be found in Pelletier 1967:92 note 3). Philo does not say what the Jews were punished for, and his description conveys the impression of lynch-mob justice (on which see Fraser 1972 Index s.v. mob).

§73. *After he had broken into everything ... unparallelled attack*: Here Philo returns to the motif he had left at §54, Flaccus' responsibility for all the catastrophe that had befallen the Jews, and he introduces the atrocity described at length in §§74-77.

§74. *Our council of elders ...*: The γερουσία mentioned here is the central council that administered the large Jewish community of Alexandria since the time of Augustus ("our savior and benefactor"). For unknown reasons, this emperor intervened in the internal affairs of the Jewish community (in 11/12 CE) to abolish the post of ethnarch (the administrative and judicial head here called γενάρχης by Philo; see Strabo as quoted by Josephus, *Ant.* 14.117, with the comments of Stern 1974/84.I.280-281; for the synonymity of γενάρχης and ἐθνάρχης in Philo see *Heres* 279; Box 1939:102; differently but unconvincingly Solomon 1970) and put the community under the more "democratic" control of a council of elders (see Tcherikover-Fuks 1957/64: I.57; that this measure would pose a threat to the Jewish community, as Slingerland 1997:65 suggests, is unlikely). The contradiction between Philo and the text of Claudius' edict as quoted by Josephus, *Ant.* 19.283, to the effect that "when the Jewish ethnarch was dead, Augustus did *not* prohibit the creating of such ethnarchs," may be solved by supposing "that the office of ethnarch had in the later Ptolemaic period become monarchical in character, and that on the death of the ethnarch whom he had found in Alexandria when he annexed Egypt, Augustus took the opportunity, presumably in accordance with the wishes of the Alexandrine Jews, to establish a γερουσία, of which the ethnarch should be president. If no more is heard of this officer after Augustus, this is to be expected if he in fact lost any despotic powers he had before, perhaps little more than a chairman" (Box 1939:103). Another possibility is that the ethnarch who died was not replaced because he was the last of a dynasty, without any intervention of Augustus being involved. But the text of the decree in Josephus may also have been tampered with (Tcherikover-Fuks 1957/64: I.57 note 22). See further Wolfson 1947: 2.348-349; Fraser 1972: 2.141 note 160; Stern 1974/76:124 note 5; Millar in

Schürer 1973/87:3.93; Smallwood 1976:233 note 54; and now especially Pucci Ben Zeev 1998:302 and Gruen 2002:72. For elders of other Jewish communities in Egypt (attested in *P. Monac.* 49) see Mélèze-Modrzejewski 1993:78-79.

our savior and benefactor Augustus: Here as elsewhere Philo gives expression to feelings of great admiration for the first Roman emperor, Augustus, whom he regards as someone of a more than human nature; see esp. *Legat.* 143-158, 309-318. He often speaks about him in superlative terms and his lyrical language sometimes borders on the religious, like here (Slingerland 1997:32). For other passages see Delling 2001:340-363; Niehoff 2001:81, 114-119, 128-133. This is part and parcel of Philo's attempt to portray the Romans as benefactors and friends. Niehoff 2001:111-136 points out that the positive way Philo writes about the Roman Empire reflects imperial ideology. In his division of humankind in Greeks and barbarians, Philo subsumed the Romans under the Greeks since they, and especially Augustus, brought Greek culture to the barbarian countries (see esp. *Legat.* 147). For the terminology, σωτὴρ καὶ εὐεργέτης, which is typical for ruler cults, see Nock 1972:720-735 and Winiarczyk 2002:43-50. On Philo's use of σωτήρ (for God and humans) see Jung 2002:240-256, esp. 246-247.

Magius Maximus: The mss. read Μάγνον but it is certain that Μάγιον should be read; see *ILS* no. 1335. Magius Maximus was the Roman prefect of Egypt who at Augustus' command changed the interior organization of the Jewish community of Alexandria in 11/12 CE. Millar in Schürer 1973/87:3.93 notes that the πάλιν in the text is dubious "since the manuscript reading in this entire phrase is disturbed, and there is no other evidence for iteration of the Prefecture, until a single case in the fourth century" (note 12). Reiter's text runs as follows: μέλλοντα πάλιν [ἀπ'] ' Ἀλεξανδρείας καὶ τῆς χώρας ἐπιτροπεύειν, the correct translation of which is: "when the latter was about to take upon himself for the second time the office of governor of Alexandria and the country." But this cannot be right, if only because of the reason adduced by Millar (πάλιν implies an impossible earlier term of office than the one documented). Rea 1968:365-367 proposes the following solution. All mss. read ἀπ' Αἰγύπτου (the reading ἐπ' ' Ἀλεξανδρείας being Schürer's conjecture) but that yields an untranslatable sentence. In light of *CIG* 2.3142.iii.39-40, where ' Ἀλεξανδρεία ἡ ἀπ' Αἰγύπτου cannot but have the meaning of "Alexandria on the border of Egypt" (cf. *Alexandria ad Aegyptum*), he suggests the following emendation: μέλλοντα πόλιν <τὴν> ἀπ' Αἰγύπτου καὶ τὴν χώραν ἐπιτροπεύειν, "just before he began to govern the city on Egypt's border and the country." From a palaeographical point of view this is an elegant solution, that solves a series of problems, both historical and text-critical.

38 members, namely those who had been discovered in their own houses: According to rabbinic sources, this council had 71 members (Tosefta, *Sukkah* 4.6; Bavli, *Sukkah* 51b), but we have no way of knowing whether this is a reliable number or that it is patterned on the number of members of the Jerusalem Sanhedrin, again according to tradition (but see Lüderitz 1994:222 with note 105). What Philo probably means to say here is that, although Flaccus wanted to arrest the entire council, only those of the members who happened to be discovered in their homes (most probably houses located outside the ghetto), were caught.

he organized a fine procession ...: καλὴ πομπή. For this ironical use of καλός see also §157. For a description of a parade of bandits through the streets of Alexandria on their way to the place of execution see Philostratus, *Vit. Apoll.* 5.24. On official *pompai* in Greek cities see Graf 1996; on the question of how in the Roman world public processions and displays provided an opportunity to exact punishment see Coleman 1990.

wholly unsuited to the occasion: ἀλλοτριωτάτη τῷ καιρῷ. It is not wholly certain what occasion Philo is referring to here but most probably it is a reference to August 31, Caligula's birthday, as in §81 (see the comments *ad loc.*); in §83 this birthday is explicitly mentioned. On such an occasion the theatre usually did service for all kinds of festivities, among which were processions. As De Vries 1999:92 observes, August 31 of the year 38 was a sabbath, so in another sense as well the scene was "wholly unsuited to the occasion." However, if that were the case, one would expect Philo to have mentioned it more explicitly.

§75: **he ordered them all to be stripped**: Public nudity was abhorred in Jewish tradition; Gen. 9:22-23; 1 *Macc.* 1:13-15; *LAB* 18:13; cf. Rev. 3:18. Here the stripping is not only an act of public humiliation, but probably also a means of exposing their circumcision so as to identify them as Jews. Lit. in *RBLG* 228.

scourging, an insulting form of treatment usually reserved for the worst criminals: Hengel 1977:80-1 n.31 states that "from the time of the

Ptolemies onwards there were two forms of flogging as a punishment practised in Alexandria. The worse kind, scourging, was only carried out on criminals of the lower classes." He mentions no other source than *Flacc.* 75, but see below my comments *ad* §78.

§76. *by other evidence*: This translation of δι' ἑτέρων is uncertain: Box translates with "by circumstances related elsewhere," Colson with "in other ways," Pelletier with "par bien d'autres preuves," and Gerschmann with "anderweitig." The problem is partly that the genitive ἑτέρων does not specify whether it is neutral or masculine or feminine (Gerschmann 1964:144 note 2: "... läßt nicht erkennen, ob Philo damit eine andere Schrift von sich oder andere Beweise oder (...) andere Personen meint"). Box 1939:103 (and cf. xxxiii note 1) assumes that the words imply a lacuna "elsewhere" in the treatise, but that is not compelling. I think that what Philo means with ἕτερα here is what he has written in the preceding paragraphs about "the enormity of the aggression." That was in itself already sufficient proof of it, but even so, he says, "it will be demonstrated even more clearly by what I am going to tell now." For a similar ambiguity concerning the meaning of δι' ἑτέρων see *Sacr.* 77.

Euodus, Tryphon and Andron: None of these names is typically Jewish. Other Jewish men called Euodos ("successful") are to be found in the Aphrodisias inscription, side b, 14 (see Reynolds & Tannenbaum 1987:6), in Rome, *CIJ* no. 24 = *JIWE* 2.473 (cf. Euodia in *CIJ* 391 = *JIWE* 2.110), and in Jerusalem (Ilan 2002:278). The prosopography in Tcherikover-Fuks 1957/64: 3.194 lists other Jewish men in Egypt named Tryphon, mentioned in papyri (add now *P.Polit.Iud.* 12.2 in Cowey & Maresch 2001); Palestinian examples in Ilan 2002:308 (including Tarphon); for a Trypho from Hierapolis in Phrygia see Miranda 1999:123 (no.12). Perhaps Trypho was a favorite name among Egyptian Jews both because their own Bible translators had rendered *Gan Eden* in Gen. 3:23 by παράδεισος τῆς τρυφῆς and also because three Ptolemaic kings were surnamed Tryphon and various princesses Tryphaena; see Bremmer 2002:119. Also Justin's Jewish interlocutor in his *Dialogus cum Tryphone Judaeo* bore that name. Andron is probably an abridged form of Andronicus; for Jews with that name see Tcherikover-Fuks 1957/64: 3.169 (add now *P.Polit.Iud.* 1.3 and 12.8 in Cowey & Maresch 2001), *JIWE* 1.85, and Ilan 2002:263. See also the section on personal names in Hagedorn 2000:5-43.

***on an earlier occasion he sent for our rulers* ...:** Nothing else is known of this attempt to reconcile the parties, but it must have taken place after the pillaging described in §§56-57. It is debatable whether one can speak here of "a fruitless attempt to find a way out of the anarchy by negotiation with the Jewish leaders" (Smallwood 1976:240), because that would imply that Flaccus seriously tried to calm the situation, whereas Philo explicitly calls it a fake attempt (τῷ δοκεῖν!). Philo gives no reason for the failure of the negotiation apart from saying that Flaccus' intentions were not sincere (Kasher 1985:251 does not agree), although one might argue that Flaccus had good reasons to cool down tempers in Alexandria (Gruen 2002:59). As Colson 1941:344 observes, the passage "suggests the possibility that it was either the attitude there taken up by the magistrates or their failure to carry out the conditions there laid down which led to their arrest and punishment." Smallwood 1976:241 says that "it is conceivable that the *gerousia* had rejected Flaccus' attempt at conciliation and organized some kind of retaliatory attack on the Greeks which Philo has judiciously suppressed," but that is sheer speculation. The fact that in §§86ff. Flaccus orders his troops to search the Jewish houses for weapons is no proof of this hypothesis. Attempts to identify Flaccus' meeting with members of the Jewish *gerousia* mentioned here with the meeting between Flaccus and Isidorus *cum suis* described in the *Acts of the Alexandrian Martyrs* (*P.Oxy* 1089 = *CPJ* 154) because in line 31 a γεραιός is mentioned there, have now been generally abandoned; see Tcherikover-Fuks 1957/64:2.63 and Hennig 1974:429. It is more likely that this man was a member of the Alexandrian *gerousia*; see Musurillo 1954:100, 108-110. For "rulers" Philo has ἄρχοντες, on which see the note *ad* §80.

§77. *the double misery of poverty and personal outrage*: Compare what Philo says in §58.

***gloating on the disgrace of those from whom they had stolen that wealth*:** It is the ἀτιμία afflicted upon the Jewish rulers that the aristocratic Philo castigates here more than anything else, as the following passage (§§78-80) makes clear as well.

§78. *There are different kinds of scourges used in the city* ...: As Philo goes on to say, "these differences are related to the social status of the persons to be beaten: Egyptians are beaten with a different kind of scourge and by different people than the Alexandrians, who are beaten with flat blades and by Alexandrian blade-bearers." In antiquity the difference between citizens and non-citizens also expressed itself in the different ways these categories were punished; for evidence see Box 1939:103 and esp. Coleman 1990:55-57. As Coleman observes, differentiated penalties for offenders of different status (*humiliores* and *honestiores*) are a phenomenon that is characteristic of societies with a strongly differentiated class- or caste-system. "As the comparative adjectives *honestior* and *humilior* themselves suggest, the criteria for membership of either group were relative and imprecise, depending on property, power, and prestige, so that neither group was a homogeneous and identifiable sector of society" (Coleman 1990:57). Here the difference is that, unlike the Egyptian commoners in Alexandria, the real citizens in case of judicial punishment received blows with σπάθαι, which were broad blades of wood or metal which inflicted much less serious wounds than regular flogging. Philo's point is probably that Flaccus thus publicly demonstrated that he wanted to treat the Jews on a par with common Egyptians, although it is also possible that Philo's indignation is about the fact that the members of the *gerousia*, who were possibly enfranchised citizens, are here treated on a par with commoners (i.e. in the same way as the other Jews, who were not citizens). Then it is the overturning of social status that horrifies him; so Barclay 1996:69, but see Pucci Ben Zeev 1998:455-456. Both viewpoints may be right at the same time.

§79. *This custom was also observed in the case of our people*: As Tcherikover 1959:316 rightly points out, it is wrong to deduce from this passage that the Alexandrian Jews possessed equal rights with the Greeks, for the words "also in the case of our people" point to the opposite: "Philo is stressing equality of rights in the matter of corporal punishment precisely because it was not a normal thing. Had the Jews belonged among the citizens of Alexandria, he would have had no need of this emphasis, since it would have been in any case clear that what was proper for the Greeks was also proper for the Jews" (cf. also *ibid*. 512 note 64).

it is possible, it is really possible, to find ...: ἔστι γάρ, ἔστι καί ... This emphatic repetition underscores how unnecessary this humiliation was. It also makes clear how indignant Philo was because of the humiliation of upper class Jews (his own class). On this kind of repetition (ἀναφορά) see Anderson 2000:19. In this case, he says, a more humane treatment was impeded by οἴκοθεν ἐπίβουλον πάθος ("personal aggressive passion"). Πάθος, as Pelletier 1967:96 note 3 points out, is defined by Philo in a Stoic sense as follows: "Every passion is blameworthy, inasmuch as every immoderate and excessive impulse and every irrational and unnatural movement of the soul is blameable as well, for both these are nothing else than the unfolding of a long-standing passion" (*Spec.* 4.79). The passion Philo is thinking of here is, of course, hatred. The "milder approach" (ἐπιεικεστέρας ἰδέας) is the opposite of "the import of personal aggression," ἰδέα here being a mode of mental activity which does not destroy the element of rational discrimination in the apprehension of a situation or fact, as Box 1939:104 says.

§80. *Alexandrian Jewish commoners* (τῶν ἰδιωτῶν Ἀλεξανδρέων Ἰουδαίων): By "Alexandrians" Philo means Jewish inhabitants of Alexandria, formal citizenship not necessarily being implied. Philo uses a phrase that is compatible with the theory that the Jews had Greek citizenship in Alexandria but it does not compel us to accept it, since it easily allows for an alternative explanation (cf. *Legat.* 183, where Philo calls the Greeks "the other Alexandrians," with Smallwood 1961:255 and 1976:228-229 note 38; cf. also Josephus, *Ant.* 19.281, where Claudius calls the Jews of the city "Alexandrians"). "Greeks in the city had no monopoly on the term" (Gruen 2002:73). A papyrus from 5/4 BCE, *CPJ* 151, demonstrates that the Jews in Alexandria were popularly, if inaccurately, designated (or at least designated themselves) "Alexandrians," for the Jew who presented a petition there first described himself as "Alexandrian" and then altered it (had to alter it?) to "a Jew from Alexandria;" see Tcherikover 1959:312; Huß 1994:8; Mélèze Modrzejewski 1995:164; Pucci Ben Zeev 1998: 298, 315-316; Fitzpatrick 2002:83-84; on the formal and informal uses of "Alexandrian" see Davis 1951:100-101 and especially Delia 1991:23-28.

scourges that more befitted freemen and citizens (ἐλευθεριωτέραις καὶ πολιτικωτέραις μάστιξι): Box 1939:104 refers to papyrological evidence of the kind of crimes for which freemen and citizens were scourged (e.g., *P.Hal.* 1.186-213; *P. Mich.* 18). For recent literature about criminal law in Roman Egypt see Rupprecht 1994:151-152. Πολιτικώτερος refers to the civic body of the Alexandrian Greeks. Mendelson 1982:27 calls *Flacc.* 80 "the passage which reveals Philo's awareness of class distinction among Jews most clearly." In his wake

Sly 1996:174 remarks that this passage "gives the clearest hint that Philo's chief concern with the pogrom was with the indignities suffered by the elite Jews." But the prominence Philo gives to this scene also shows that "for him a central issue was whether the Jews were to be treated like Alexandrians or like 'Egyptians of the meanest rank'" (Collins 2000:119).

their rulers, the members of the council of elders: The Greek text has τοὺς ἄρχοντας, τὴν γερουσίαν, and Cohn thinks that the second term is a gloss on the first. Colson 1941:346 note 1 follows him and suggests the word was inserted in view of the words which follow (referring to "whose very title implies age and honor"). But I would rather suggest that these words imply that the term *gerousia* preceded them (or that also the words following *gerousia* should be taken as an insertion, which is very doubtful). It is better to retain the text as it stands and, in any case, the rulers (ἄρχοντες) are not distinguished from the members of the council; elsewhere in the Jewish diaspora they were sometimes called πρεσβύτεροι; for evidence see Van der Horst 1991:88-91; Millar in Schürer 1973/87:3.92-93; Cowey-Maresch 2001:10-18; Gruen 2002:114-115, who rightly emphasizes the lack of standardization in the terminology for Jewish community officals.

whose very title implies age and honor: Both *gerousia* and *archontes* (or *presbyteroi*) are designations implying that the bearers have a more or less advanced age and high positions and are, for that very reason, entitled to honor. For this motif see Van der Horst 1978:254 (*ad* Ps-Phocylides 222-224). Contempt for this basic value makes Philo very indignant. His world is here turned upside down, not so much as a Jew, but as a member of that ruling élite.

§81. *out of respect for the occasion*: Another reference to Gaius' birthday (see §§74 and 83); cf. the comments on "utterly unsuited to the occasion" in §74. This day, August 31, was only one of the many ἡμέραι Σεβασταί celebrated in Egypt, for the birthdays of both the living and the deceased and deified Augusti were celebrated not only annually but also monthly; see Price 1984:101-132, esp. 102-107 (and, e.g., *SEG* 42.810-814 for honorary inscriptions for Hadrian and his wife Sabina, probably on the occasion of the emperor's birthday). Since these days were public festivals (with parades, games, shows etc.) on which judicial business was suspended, it is all the more a serious offence that Flaccus carried out this public scourging of

Jewish dignitaries, especially as there was the practice of a certain leniency associated with the festivals for the Augusti. See Bell 1924:32; Box 1939:105; Barraclough 1984:466; and Tcherikover-Fuks 1957/64: II.45.

For those rulers ... are over: In this polemical remark Philo acutely implies that Flaccus' behaviour on Gaius' birthday is a downright show of disrespect for the emperor (but see *ad* §82). The pointless and ugly repetition of ἐπιφανεῖς ("illustrious") led Mangey to regard the first occurrence as an insertion by a careless copyist, probably rightly so.

§82. *But he committed this violation of the law on those very days.* Slingerland 1997:78 surmises that, if Flaccus felt he could inflict the most atrocious sufferings upon the Jews on Gaius' birthday with impunity, "this well-connected prefect had reason to think this sport would make a quite acceptable present for Gaius," which "suggests imperial complicity in the pogrom." Although not provable, this suggestion deserves serious consideration. After all, the same idea is also implied by Philo's *Legat.*, e.g., §§119-121 (other arguments in the rest of Slingerland's book, esp. 77-83; see 83 note 49: "Flaccus took his cue from the emperor himself").

convinced that in this way he could more easily win them over to what he had in mind: Philo here accuses Flaccus of the basest form of opportunism, even though he had no way of knowing what Flaccus thought. But Gruen 2002:59 finds this a revealing comment: "Flaccus strove urgently to conciliate the mob that opposed him, thinking that he could thereby have them adopt as their own the ends he had in view. Here the author has it right. The prefect and the Alexandrians had different objectives." Flaccus' wish to keep some control of the situation made him play to the crowd. This whole paragraph, however, serves Philo's purpose of demonstrating that the prefect acted out of sheer and calculating malevolence towards the Jewish people.

§83. *I actually know of instances ...*: ἤδη τινὰς οἶδα. On the force of ἤδη here see Box 1939:105 ("introduces a mitigation observed by other rulers, in contrast with which Flaccus' act reached a climax of cruelty"). For "crucified" Philo uses ἀνεσκολοπισμένοι, which is synonymous to ἐσταυρωμένοι; on the terminology see Hengel 1977:24.

were taken down from the cross ...: Cf. John 19:31 "Since it was the day of preparation [Friday], in order to prevent the bodies from remaining on the cross on the sabbath (for the sabbath was a high day), the Jews asked Pilate that their legs might be broken and that they might be taken away." Cf. Mark 15:43. Before the Roman period, the bodies of crucified persons were left to decay on their crosses; see Box 1939:105-6 for references (e.g., Petronius, *Sat.* 111; Lucan, *Phars.* 6.538-545; Artemidorus, *Oneir.* 2.43; Valerius Maximus 6.9). But Augustus wrote in his autobiography that he had never denied the bodies of the executed to their relatives for burial, and that this should be the rule; see Ulpian, *Digesta* 48, Tit. 24.1. For Jews, the burial of executed criminals was all the more important since it was a prescription in the Torah, Deut. 21:22-23: "If a man has committed a crime punishable by death and he is put to death, and you hang him on a tree, his body shall not remain all night upon the tree, but you shall bury him the same day, for a hanged man is accursed by God." Cf. Josephus, *Bell.* 4.317.

the sanctity of the festival: Philo seems to accredit here the same sanctity to the pagan festival of the emperor's *genethliakon* as to the Jewish sabbath (see the quote from John 19:31 in the previous note). His polemical point is again that Flaccus did *not* preserve the sanctity of the festival.

§84. *tortured with fire and the sword*: Box 1939:106 and Pelletier 1967:100 here refer to a curious work from 1594 by A. Gallonio, *De Sanctorum Martyrum cruciatibus*, where in chs. 5-7 a wide variety of torture methods with fire and sword are described (*non vidi*). See *OCD* s.v. "torture."

§85. *The spectacle was divided into acts ...*: Ironically and bitterly Philo here presents the outrageous scene of mass-torturing of Jews as an amusing and entertaining theatre show with various acts. See Pelletier 1967:100 note 2; Bowman 1986:216. For the use of theatres for this kind of purposes Harris 1976:34.

maltreated: καταικιζόμενοι is Cohn's convincing emendation of the mss.'s καταδικαζόμενοι (condemned).

led away to their death: See Colson 1941:348-349 note *a* for the Herodotean background of the expression ἀπαγόμενοι τὴν ἐπὶ θανάτῳ, sc. ὁδόν.

this fine exhibition (καλὴν ταύτην ἐπίδειξιν): Again a sample of Philonic irony. But Gruen 2002:59 remarks that these showcase executions may have been designed by Flaccus to head off further private violence.

§86. *a second round of plundering ... the Jews had heavy suits of armour in their houses*: The first round is probably the one described in §§53-57, when the Jewish residents are expelled from four of the five quarters of the city and their houses looted by the Greek mob. The search for arms in Jewish houses is the second one. Smallwood 1976:241 note 79 again speculates that "the search for arms, though related as a separate episode after the arrest and punishment of the elders, may have preceded it, and the elders may have qualified for arrest by organising unrecorded resistance." Box 1939:lix-lxii takes a similar view, supposing that the fact that in §44 Philo has said that "one may almost say that Flaccus filled the whole world with *civil wars*" implies resistance, most probably armed resistance, on the part of the Jews. He adds that the fact that Jewish houses of worship were destroyed cannot be accounted for otherwise than on the assumption that the Jews offered resistance to the attempt to introduce the emperor's portraits into them, and in the clashes that occurred the places suffered destruction. He concludes that "it appears certain that the Jews resisted the introduction of the emperor's portraits into their places of worship, and Philo omitted to mention this fact" (lx). Yet Philo writes that no arms at all were found (§90). Was there unarmed resistance then? Some have assumed that no weapons were found because the Jews had hidden them, but it is extremely improbable that all Jews had hidden all their arms so well that none of them were found. That not a single one of these caches was discovered by the Greeks is simply incredible (so rightly Box 1939:lx). If, however, weapons were found indeed, it would have been very unwise if Philo would flatly deny something that everyone knew was true and that could be checked easily. So it would seem we have to take Philo at his word: the Jews did not possess weapons, or at least not regular weapons of war, by that time.

a centurion ... called Castus: Centurions (ἑκατόνταρχοι) were the principal professional officers in the Roman army (see *OCD* s.v.). They headed *centuriae* (lit. groups of 100), which were the smallest units of a legion (a legion had 60 such units). There was a system of hierarchical ranking of the centurions. For special missions, like the one mentioned here, usually one of the highest ranking centurions was singled out; see Thompson 2000. The centurion mentioned here is called Castus in the majority of mss., and Castor in one (ms. A, a reading adopted by Mangey), but since a certain Castus is mentioned in an inscription from Egypt from the time of Tiberius (*CIL* 3 6627 on the construction of roads by Roman soldiers supervised by their centurions), Castus is the most probable reading, at least on the (not improbable) assumption that the two are identical; see also Reiter 1915:li-lii.

§87. *dumbfounded*: ἀχανεῖς can mean both "without opening the mouth" and "with wide open mouth" (see LSJ *s.v.*). Here it refers anyway to the speechlessness of the Jews being confronted with the search for arms. Cf. the use of this word in *Legat.* 189, 223.

for fear of being taken captive: The mss.'s τὸν ἐπ' αἰχμαλώτοις φόβον is very strange Greek. Mangey understandably conjectured αἰχμαλωσίᾳ, and Box 1939:107 accepts it because he doubts "if a noun can unassisted express that of which it is not yet, but will be, predicated" (see also Colson *ad loc.*). *Non liquet*, although the general sense is quite clear. The fear of being taken captive was inspired by their not-knowing the reason for the soldiers' arrival.

the completion of the plundering: The word πόρθησις means both "plundering" and "destruction." It is used in §86 for the persecution of the Jews and in *Legat.* 330 for Gaius' plan to erect a gigantic statue of himself in the Jerusalem temple. Cf. Philo's use of πορθέω in §54 and *Legat.* 114 for the ruining of the Jews.

§88. *When they heard ... in their recesses*: Philo stresses the full co-operation of the Jews with the Romans in the search for weapons; they had nothing to hide; see §90.

§89. *their women ... were always kept in seclusion ...*: γύναια κατάκλειστα. This is one of the passages that is always cited when the position of women in ancient Judaism is discussed; see Heinemann 1932:233-5; Van der Horst 1978:251-252; Archer 1990:118; Sly 1990: 206; cf. also Barclay 1996:117-8 (on the theme of seclusion of both young girls and adult women in general the most extensive treatment is Archer 1990:101-122, 239-250). In *Spec.* 3:169-171, Philo says that places where large numbers of people assemble are suitable only to men: "Women are best suited to indoor life which never strays from the house, within which the middle door is taken by the maidens as their boundary, and the outer door by those who have reached full womanhood. (...) A woman should not be a busybody, meddling with matters outside her household concerns, but should seek a life of seclusion. She should not show herself off like a vagrant in the streets before the eyes of other men." In the same vein Philo's contemporary and fellow citizen Pseudo-Phocylides states: "Guard a virgin in firmly locked rooms, and let her not be seen out of the house before her wedding day" (215-216). 2 Macc. 3:19 speaks of virgins kept in seclusion who ran to the doors or windows in an attempt to see something of the events outside. 3 Macc. 1:18 mentions the exceptional situation that young women who had been confined to their rooms rushed out with their mothers and filled the streets with cries of grief. 4 Macc. 18:7 has the mother of the seven martyrs say that as a chaste maiden she did not leave her father's house. Whether these texts justify the generalizing conclusion that Jewish women, especially unmarried ones, lived a life of seclusion within the confines of the home, is a matter of much debate. It is clear at any rate that it was Philo's ideal and also that of some other Jewish writers (including rabbis; see b. *Jeb.* 77a; *Meg.* 14b). Similar sentiments can sometimes be found in pagan literature, e.g., Seneca, *Cons. Helv.* 19.6, where he says that his aunt, who was the wife of the Roman governor of Alexandria, was never seen in public there (for other references see the literature mentioned above). But this kind of restriction of freedom of movement for women was not part and parcel of Alexandrian culture in Philo's time where women often played an active role in public life (Heinemann 1932:233-235; Gussen 1955:84; Pomeroy 1984:41-28; Niehoff 2001:102-105). Moreover, in Judaism there was a great variety of opinions about the role and position of women within the community; see Van der Horst 1995 for some counter-voices to Philo.

for modesty's sake: δι' αἰδῶ, often used of women's sense of decency and shame; see Cairns 1993 and further literature in BDAG 26 and esp. RBLG 154.

terrifying soldiers: στρατιωτικὸν δέος ἐπανατεινομένοις, lit. "men brandishing threateningly a soldier's means of inspiring terror" (Box 1939:33). The verb ἐπανατείνομαι is a technical term of the Alexandrian law of violence, as Box 1939:108 and Pelletier 1967:163-164 argue. Philo uses both the noun ἐπανάτασις (which is rather common in his writings) and the verb in *Legat.* 368 for the terrifying threats of the emperor Gaius against the Jewish community; see Smallwood 1961:323 *ad loc.* Philo's point in the present passage is that due to the behavior of these soldiers "the seclusion of the house had been breached and what had been most private became public" (Alston 1997:172).

§90. *what a great quantity of weapons*: The mss. read ὅσον but Wendland conjectured πόσον (how many, how much?). Box 1939:108 follows Wendland since this use of ὅσος is unparalleled, he says. But Colson 1941:351 rightly objects that exclamatory ὅσον is already found in Plato, *Resp.* 450a: "What a thing (οἷον) you have done ... what a huge (ὅσον) debate you have started!"

helmets, breastplates, shields, daggers, pikes, complete outfits of armour ... javelins, slings, bows, and arrows: Philo neatly divides the list into defensive (ἀμυντήρια) and offensive (ἐκηβόλα) weapons. Pelletier 1967:103 note 6 surmises that "Philon emprunte probablement à une pièce officielle sa nomenclature des armes saisissables, comme aussi leur classement en ἀμυντήρια et ἐκηβόλα." Swords are not mentioned, possibly because the bearing of swords had already been forbidden by Flaccus in an ordinance issued in 34 or 35 CE, *Pap. Boissier* = Mitteis-Wilcken 1912:22-24, no. 13. Box 1939:lxi-lxii suggests that maybe swords are not mentioned here by Philo because these weapons were indeed found among the Jews. But to this suggestion he himself rightly objects that on the basis of *Prob.* 78 — where Philo says that the Essenes do not possess darts, javelins, daggers, or persons making them — "no one would accuse Philo of concealing the manufacture of swords by Essenes on the ground that he does not mention swords specifically" (*ibid.* lxii). For some technical comments on the terms used for some of the weapons see also Box 1939:108.

not even knives which the cooks use for their daily work: Philo greatly exaggerates in order to underscore the innocence and peace-mindedness of the Jews. But all commentators wonder how, if Philo is right here, the Jews could have so many weapons less than two-and-a-half years later, when after Caligula's death in January 41 CE the Alexandrian Jews "immediately took up their arms to fight for themselves" (Josephus, *Ant.* 19.278). Maybe that had to do with the fact that in the meantime, after the pogrom of 38, they had been amassing weaponry with the help of "Jews they brought in from Syria and Egypt" (*CPJ* 153.96-97), for which they were taken to task later in that year by the new emperor Claudius in his letter to the Alexandrians; see Bell 1924:17-18. As Barraclough 1984:465 rightly remarks, "if the search for arms had been successful, Philo's duplicity could easily have been exposed" by Alexandrians familiar with the events. If there had been any armed resistance on the Jewish part at all, it must have been on a very small scale.

§91. *the simplicity of the kind of life*: εὐκολία and εὔκολος are used 12 times by Philo, usually to designate the contentment with a moderate or frugal life style; see *Prob.* 77, 84 (on the Essenes); *Contempl.* 69 (on the Therapeutae); *Legat.* 14 (on the opposite in the lifestyle of Caligula) etc.

extravagance and luxury: πολυτέλεια καὶ τὸ ἁβροδίαιτον, favorite and frequent terms in Philo to designate the opposite of the ideal of a simple and frugal lifestyle; see *Philo Index* s.vv.

... engender satiety; and satiety engenders ...: For this kind of concatenation, also called *catena, gradatio*, ἐποικοδόμησις (A is the source of B, B is the source of C etc.) see 2 Tim. 2:11-12; Rom. 8:29-30; 2 Pet. 1:5-7; Aelius Aristides 3.172; 3.559; *Rhet. ad Herenn.* 4.25.34; Demosthenes, *De corona* 179; Cicero, *Pro Milone* 61, *Pro Roscio Amerino* 75; Porphyry, *Ad Marcellam* 24; Sap. Sal. 16:17-19; more references in Dibelius-Greeven 1964:125-129 ("Die rhetorische Form der Kettenreihe"), and see the discussion of this stylistic figure in Anderson 2000:57-58. The source of Philo's words κόρου δ᾽ ὕβρις ἔκγονον is a line of Solon as quoted by Aristotle, *Ath. Pol.* 12: τίκτει γὰρ κόρος ὕβριν, ὅταν πολὺς ὄλβος ἔπηται, again alluded to by Philo in *Agric.* 32. For the history of this literary motif see Pelletier 1967:104 note 1.

insolence, which is the source of all evil: Here ὕβρις is called "the source of all evil;" elsewhere other vices are singled out for that honor: usually it is the love of money (φιλαργυρία, see the note *ad* §60), sometimes it is fornication (πορνεία); see the references in Van der Horst 1978:142-143. In §136 insolence (ὕβρις) is called the offspring of drunkenness. On *hybris* see Fisher 1992 and the rich bibliography in *RBLG* 498.

§92. *the arms of the Egyptians ... had been collected by Bassus*: This search for illegal weapons (in the *chôra*, not in Alexandria) is probably the one that took place in 34/5 CE ("not long ago," says Philo). *Pap. Boissier* (Mitteis-Wilcken 1912:22-24, no. 13) contains this ordinance of Flaccus strictly prohibiting the carrying of arms (line 9: μαχαιροφορά) and limiting the use of them to strictly circumscribed persons and groups; see the comments by Wilcken 1912:22-24. The Greek text is also printed in Box 1939:109. Cf. for the contents also the Justinian *Novella* 85 (*de armis*, from 539 CE).

on that occasion: All mss. read ἀλλ᾽ ἦν τότε here but Wendland rightly atheticized ἀλλ᾽.

THE POGROM AT ITS HEIGHT 183

anchoring in the harbors of the river: These are the harbors to the south of Alexandria which are partly located at Lake Mareotis; see the maps in Haas 1997:2-3.

visible in one view: ὑπὸ μίαν ὄψιν. Ms. A omits ὄψιν and is followed by Mangey and Wendland. The sentence then runs ὑπὸ μίαν καὶ τὴν αὐτὴν σύνταξιν ("in one and the same order"), a phrase that also occurs in *Agric.* 49: "For, having been brought under one and the same order, it [the mind] will evidently have to look only to the guidance of a single chief." But Box 1939:109 rightly remarks that "ὄψιν expresses the fact that the procession could be seen at all points *at once*, τὴν αὐτὴν σύνταξιν that it was continuous." So it is advisable to accept the reading with ὄψιν.

the palace: The palace was located on the Lochias peninsula next to the N.-E. harbor; see Schneider 1967/1969: I.532-533 and the maps in Green 1996:303; Sly 1996:xvi-xvii; Empereur 1998:22-23; Eichler 1999:753.

about ten stades: That is almost two kilometers, so — Philo implies — it was an impressively long queue of pack animals and wagons, all of them loaded with illegal weapons. The figure of 10 stades for the N.-S. measurement of the city is confirmed by Josephus, *Bell.* 2.386. See on these and other (diverging) measures of Alexandria's dimensions Fraser 1972: II.26-27 note 64.

§93. *those who had procured all this*: Even though it was the *chôra* that was disarmed, not Alexandria, Philo says that it was right that the houses of the Alexandrians (he has in mind here both the Egyptian population and the Greeks) were searched for weapons because it was they — not the Jews — who "were suspected of revolutionary activities."

In imitation of the religious games ...: Philo ironically suggests that a periodical disarmament should (ἔδει) be instituted, according to the model of sacred contests, as a kind of biennial celebration for the collection of arms (τριετηρίς means "celebrated every third year," inclusively, *i.e.*, "in alternate years;" hence "biennial"). Harris 1976:88 remarks that "it is noteworthy that Philo uses the illustration of the local biennial games, and not, as a writer merely following the ordinary literary convention would have done, the more famous quadrennial (πενταετηρίδες) Olympic or Pythian festivals."

because they would get no opportunity to replace them: καιρὸν οὐκ ἔχοντες εἰς ἀναχώρησιν. The mss.'s ἀναχώρησιν (retreat) here is "hopeless" (Colson 1941:352 note 1). Colson suggests ἀναπλήρωσιν ("refilling"), adopted by Pelletier; Reiter conjectures ἀνανέωσιν ("renewal"), adopted by Box; Theiler suggested ἀνάκτησιν ("regaining"), adopted by Gerschmann. Mangey's clever ἀναχώνευσιν ("reforging") comes closest to the mss.'s reading but is perhaps too unusual. *Non liquet*, although the general sense is clear.

§94. **But we, why did we ...**: ἡμᾶς δὲ τί ...; note the emphatic position of ἡμᾶς. The contrast (δέ) between the "we" and the Greeks/Egyptians is not sufficiently brought to expression in the translations by Box and Colson.

when were we ever suspected of revolting?: With this rhetorical question Philo wants to rebut even the slightest suggestion of a Jewish inclination to ἀπόστασις. In *Abr.* 226 Philo mentions ἀπόστασις as the hallmark of the inhabitants of Sodom: "The other nations continued to be free from sedition (ἀστασίαστα), obeying the orders of the king and paying their taxes without demur. Only the country of the Sodomites, before it was consumed by fire, began to undermine this peaceful condition by a long-standing plan of revolt (ἀπόστασιν)."

when were we not considered to be peaceful to all?: In the paragraph immediately preceding the one just quoted, *Abr.* 225, the ideal man of peace (εἰρηνικός) is contrasted with the man of revolt and sedition. In *Legat.* 161 Philo states that Tiberius issued instructions to the governors to regard the Jews as a trust committed to their care, since they were of a peaceful disposition (εἰρηνικούς) and their laws were conducive to public order (εὐστάθεια, on which see immediately below). *Ibid.* 230 he has the Jewish elders say to Petronius: "We are peace-loving by nature and by choice." Εἰρηνικός is a common word in the LXX. Box 1939:110 contrasts Philo's claim here with Claudius' letter to the Alexandrians where he prohibits the Jews to bring in other Jews from Syria or Egypt because he suspects that they were "fomenting a common plague for the whole world," where "plague" (νόσος) is equivalent to rebellion (στάσις) (see *CPJ* 153.99-100 with Tcherikover-Fuks 1957/64: II.54).

law and order and stability of the city: εὐνομίαν πόλεως καὶ εὐστάθειαν. Philo had used εὐνομία in §5 where he said about Flaccus that in his initial period he had established εὐνομία throughout the city and the country, and he will use εὐστάθεια again in §135 (where he calls Isidorus an enemy of peace and stability); cf. §184 and the passage in *Legat.* 161 quoted above. For literature on εὐνομία and εὐστάθεια see *RBLG* 289-290; add Amir 1983:202-203.

If the Jews ... all their properties?: In this translation I follow Reiter's suggestion that after ἀφῃρέθησαν the word ἄν has dropped out and should be reinserted so that the whole sentence is to be taken as a (rhetorical) question. Colson 1941:354 note *a* assumes that the apodosis is suppressed for the moment but understood from the next sentence, which seems less likely to me. His translation is not clear. The general sense seems to be: If the Jews had possessed arms, they would have defended themselves and their homes, which they did not. Philo ignores, or seems to have forgotten here, that Jews had always had prominent places in the armies of the Ptolemies (Mélèze-Modrzejewski 1995:83-87).

driven away from more than 400 houses: Ameling (2003 ms. p. 11) says that this relatively small number of plundered houses in a pogrom which Philo says affected the whole Jewish community of the city, calls into question the large numbers of Jews Philo mentions in §43. But most probably Philo refers here only to the houses of the relatively small number of Jewish families who lived outside the two Jewish quarters, not those inside the ghetto.

the ones they had stolen from others: Does Philo here admit after all that the Jews did have weapons, although they were now stolen from them? Or is his statement ironic?

§95. *of which even women became the victims*: Lit., "that even women enjoyed" (or: "had the benefit of"); ἀπολαύω is frequently used ironically. Philo does not refer back here to §89, as one might think at first sight; see the next notes.

the market place ... the theatre ... the stage: See the notes on §§41 and 64.

in an intolerably and painfully insulting way: Philo creates a problem by presenting this account of the sufferings of the Jewish women only here, whereas it clearly belongs to the description of the events in §§58-85. Colson 1941:355 suggests that possibly Philo "means that the insult to feminine modesty involved in the investigation just described did not stand alone." But that is a lame excuse. The rather rambling ordering of the events in the treatise is more the consequence of a sloppy structuring or editing of the treatise as a whole (due to haste?). Or is the reason for Philo's delay in referring to these women that they are only an afterthought to him, so that his patriarchal stance, not haste, is the real cause?

§96. *turned out to belong to another nation*: ἐγνωρίσθησαν ἑτέρου γένους. The usual translation "another race" (Box and Colson) is misleading because γένος does not have any racial connotation. What is simply meant here is that some of the arrested women were discovered to be non-Jewish. Thereupon they were released. "Obviously, Jewish women could not be easily distinguished from non-Jewish" (Cohen 1999:32). Since these women were apparently arrested in a Jewish environment, the fact that they were non-Jewish is possibly an indication of mixed marriages, for which there is also other evidence (see Juster 1914: 2.45-46; Satlow 2001:133-161; Bohak 2002). Or were they female pagan slaves?

ordered swine's flesh so as to give it to these women: As De Vries 1999:94 remarks, this is a centuries old trick to identify Jews. Best known from antiquity is the story of Eleazar in 2 Macc. 6 and of the mother and her seven martyr sons in 2 Macc. 7, all of whom were compelled by an evil king to eat pork but refused and were tortured to death (although there, of course, pork eating is not forced upon them to identify them as Jews but to test their loyalty to the Jewish faith and way of life). When after the pogrom of 38 the Jews sent an embassy to Rome to plead their case, the emperor Gaius asked the members of the delegation, "Why do you refuse to eat pork?" (*Legat.* 361). The Jews' abstention from pork amused and puzzled pagan authors who speculated about the reasons for it; see Smallwood 1961:322, and cf. Sevenster 1975:139, Mendelson 1988:69-71; and for the best survey and discussion to date of these gentile reactions Schäfer 1997:66-81.

the more resolute women were handed over to the torturers to suffer unbearable tortures: The fact that adherence to the ancestral laws — a right granted the Jews by the Roman emperors from the beginning (see Millar in Schürer 1973/87:3.107-125) — is here punished by torture until death is in Philo's view the apogee of cruel arbitrariness.

Part II: The Punishment and Death of Flaccus (§§97-191)

§§ 97-103: *The declaration of loyalty*

At the beginning of the second part of Philo's work, the tide suddenly begins to turn. On Gaius' accession to the throne the Jewish community of Alexandria had delivered a declaration of loyalty to the new emperor to Flaccus with the request to pass it on to Gaius, which he said he would do but he did not. Fortunately, when Agrippa heard of the matter, he intervened to rectify it. The fact that Philo has postponed mention of this wilful neglect on the part of Flaccus is to be explained from the structure of the treatise: it is a diptych of which the first half deals with the sufferings of the Jews and the second with Flaccus' downfall. And it is exactly the fact that Flaccus withheld the Jewish declaration that initiated this downfall, because Agrippa obviously reported this to the emperor (although Philo does not say so explicitly). It is for that reason that Philo did not yet mention this in the chapters on Agrippa's visit. So this section marks the *peripeteia* in the fate of both the Jews and Flaccus (see especially θεὸς δέ in §102).

§97. *In addition to what has already been said ...*: Philo only now adds an element that had gone unmentioned so far but that he finds of the greatest importance: Flaccus' wilful failure to forward to the emperor a resolution by the Jewish community of Alexandria in honor of Gaius on the occasion of his accession in 37 CE. Smallwood 1976: 237 note 66 suggests that Philo "may be unjust in making Flaccus act out of malice towards the Jews, for there is no other evidence of discrimination against them before the middle of 38" (but "no evidence" does not imply "no existence"). Only when in the summer of 38 Agrippa visited Alexandria, did it become obvious to the leaders of the Jewish community that the emperor had never received their congratulatory decree. The view that Flaccus' behaviour in this matter triggered his downfall is not inconsistent with the idea that the connection between Flaccus' trial and his persecution of the Jews is largely Philo's invention (see *ad* §116). Caligula did not care about persecution of Jews but he did certainly care about suppressing letters of congratulations and declarations of loyalty addressed to him.

with the emperor being involved as well: By not passing on to Gaius the Jewish declaration of loyalty Flaccus indirectly involved him in his anti-Jewish policy since it would evoke Gaius' anger towards the Jews.

For we had decreed ...: ψηφισάμενοι. This ψήφισμα, drafted most probably upon the news of Gaius' accession, "included prayers, and dedications of houses of prayers, and the setting up of inscribed metal objects therein on behalf of Gaius" (Box 1939:110). See for these objects the notes *ad* §48.

he would not have granted our request for an embassy: It was the Roman governor who had to give permission for leaving the harbor of Alexandria; see Strabo 2.3.5; *P. Oxy.* 1271; further Box 1939:110 and Pelletier 1967:108 note 2. Cf. for a similar situation *Legat.* 247; Pliny, *Ep.* 10.43-44. Philo does not explain why he thinks that Flaccus would not have given the Jews permission to send an embassy. Is he simply too suspicious or does he know that such permission would have been objected to by the Alexandrian Greeks?

§98. **or at least he pretended to be pleased:** Philo repeats his suspicion of Flaccus' evil intentions from the start of Gaius' reign; see the note on §97.

I will play the role of your ambassador myself: He will do so not by sending the complete text of the decree of the Jewish community, but by incorporating its substance in a commendatory letter or report (Box 1939:110).

your gratitude: τῆς ὑμετέρας εὐχαριστίας. Usually εὐχαριστία in Philo's works has the meaning of expression of gratitude or thanksgiving to God, only occasionally that of gratitude to a human person (§100; *Legat.* 284; *Mos.* 1.33); see Leonhardt 2001:176, 188. Instead of keeping this promise of passing on the Jews' token of gratitude to Gaius, Flaccus did the opposite (§101, "he disregarded ... his own words and promises").

§99. **all the many things I know ...:** ὅσα σύνοιδα τῷ πλήθει κτλ. Another possibility is to connect τῷ πλήθει with προστιθεὶς οὐδέν. Then the translation is "I need not add anything to the multitude ..." On σύνοιδα as almost a synonym of οἶδα see Nikiprowetzky in Winston & Dillon 1983:73.

the simple truth about you is the most sufficient praise: This literal quote of Flaccus' words suggests that Philo himself had been privy to this conversation, which is not improbable in view of Philo's leading position in the Jewish community but not necessary either. The purpose of quoting his flattering remarks here is to indicate the degree of his insincerity.

§100. *is usually read immediately by the ruler*: ἀνυπέρθετον ἔχει τὴν παρ' ἡγεμόνι δι<αν>άγνωσιν. There are some text-critical problems here. The mss. read for ἡγεμόνι either ἡμῖν or ὑμῖν. Mangey conjectured ἡγεμόνι, which is generally accepted since neither of the manuscripts' readings makes sense. For the manuscripts' reading διάγνωσιν Mangey proposed διανάγνωσιν, which is adopted by Box. The noun διάγνωσις means "distinction, discernment, decision" (LSJ), never "reading," and whether διαγιγνώσκω "is sometimes used for διαναγιγνώσκω" (Colson 1941:358 note *a*) is very doubtful; see LSJ s.v. διαγιγνώσκω III. Philo uses διαναγιγνώσκω always in the sense of "reading through," διαγιγνώσκω always in the sense of "deciding." Although Colson's translation "secures a prompt decision by the head" cannot entirely be ruled out (but a decision about what?), a term for reading is exactly what is required here. Even though διανάγνωσις is not attested elsewhere, the verb διαναγιγνώσκω is common (see in general on Greek words for "reading" Chantraine 1950). So it is almost certain that again Mangey's conjecture is correct. Cf. *Legat.* 69 where the mss. are divided between διέγνω and διανέγνω, but where a word for reading is required as well; see the discussion *ad loc.* by Smallwood 1961:191-192. On the way Roman emperors dealt with correspondence see in general Millar 1977:213-228 (216: "messengers came direct to the emperor himself, who read the letters personally").

§101. *But Flaccus disregarded all our intentions*: ὁ δὲ πολλὰ χαίρειν φράσας οἷς διενοήθημεν, lit. "telling our intentions to rejoice greatly" = dismissing them from his mind. Expressions such as πολλὰ χαίρειν εἰπεῖν or συχνὰ (μακρὰ) χαίρειν φράσαι often occur in the sense of "saying farewell to" or "putting away" something; see LSJ s.v. χαίρω III 2c.

we alone ... would be considered enemies: That Jews are actually enemies of the emperor is also strongly emphasized by the Greek nationalist leader Isidorus when, according to Philo, two years later (40 CE) he tells Gaius: "My lord, you will hate these Jews here, and the rest of their compatriots too, even more when you learn of their ill-will and disloyalty towards you" (*Legat.* 355). Even though Isidorus was one of Flaccus' worst enemies, they were united in their hatred of the Jews, implies Philo.

upon a sudden attack of insanity: κατ' ἀπόνοιαν is Mangey's widely accepted conjecture for the mss.' κατ' ἐπίνοιαν. The "sudden attack of insanity" is strongly reminiscent of Gaius' behavior as described in the *Legatio*.

§102. *God, however, apparently takes care of human affairs*: θεὸς δέ here introduces the *peripeteia*, the decisive turning point, a motif that is further elaborated in §§104ff. For God's "taking care of human affairs" = providence (πρόνοια), see the note *ad* §125.

the counsels of his lawless mind: τὸ τῆς ἐκνόμου διανοίας βουλευτήριον, lit. "the council-chamber of his lawless mind." This imagery of the inner council or council-chamber (also called συνέδριον) for the site of deliberation in the mind or for conscience is not uncommon in Philo; see *Contempl.* 27, *Det.* 40, *Conf.* 86, *Decal.* 98, *Ebr.* 165; see *Philo Index* 66 and 321; further discussion in Niehoff 2001:193.

in which he devised his treacherous stratagems (against us): ἐν ᾧ κατεστρατήγει. As Colson 1941:359 remarks, it is only here and in *Legat.* 25 that Philo uses καταστρατηγεῖν ("to overcome or outwit by a stratagem") in an absolute way; usually it governs an object in the genitive or accusative.

God took mercy ... our hopes were not lost: Both the motif of God's οἶκτος and the one of the hopes that were not lost recur in the public prayer of thanksgiving after Flaccus' downfall in §121 and 124 (see *ad loc.*). Cf. also *Legat.* 367.

§103. *when king Agrippa visited us ...*: In August 38; see §§25ff. Although chronologically misplaced, "this particular piece of information is obviously being given deliberately at precisely this point in the dramatic unfolding of Philo's story because it marks the decisive turning point: fate begins to change, justice finally will triumph" (Schäfer 1997:142). The translation "he visited *us*" is defended by Schwartz 1990:75 note 37; it is based on the grammatical possibility of connecting ἐπιδημήσας to ἡμῖν (see also the note *ad* §27) and may be taken as an indication of a meeting between Philo himself (the "host" of §27?) and Agrippa, a far from impossible scenario in view of the close connections between this king and Philo's brother, who was the monarch's money-lender. It remains uncertain, however, whether this is what Philo implied since, even though the translation offered is possible, it should be admitted that the word order is somewhat unusual (ἐπιδημήσας ὁ βασιλεὺς διηγησαμένοις ἡμῖν τὴν ...). Unfortunately we are not told by Philo how the Jews could know that Flaccus did not pass on their declaration of loyalty to the emperor.

he intervened to rectify the matter: This is what Philo refers to in *Legat*. 129 where he speaks about a copy of the petition that "we had sent shortly before [to the emperor] via king Agrippa."

which, as we later heard, is what he did indeed: Agrippa sent a copy of the congratulatory resolution to Rome, together with a letter explaining its belated arrival and probably a memorandum from the Jews dealing with their position in Alexandria and complaining of the unprecedented treatment they were receiving from Flaccus; see *Legat*. 178-179 with Smallwood 1976:251-252. Schwartz 1990:76 note 39 suggests that in *Flacc*. Philo "deliberately ignored its attack upon Flaccus, in order to leave the prefect no excuse for delaying it, and so make even clearer his anti-imperial stance."

we had been zealous in this respect from the very beginning: With ἐξ ἀρχῆς μὲν σπουδασάντων Philo refers to the fact that the Jews had drafted their congratulatory document with its declaration of loyalty immediately upon the news of Gaius' accession to the throne. He tells us this only now because it is only in connection with Agrippa's visit that its relevance becomes apparent.

§§104-118: *Flaccus' Arrest*

Justice saw to it that some weeks later suddenly a detachment of troops arrived from Rome, sent by Caligula in order to arrest Flaccus. The fact that this arrest took place during the Jewish feast of Sukkoth is a proof that it was God's punishment for his treatment of the Jews. It is in this section that Philo introduces the idea of God's (almost personified) Justice that plays a major role, alongside Providence, in the second half of this work.

§104. *Justice* (Δίκη): The personification of abstract concepts in the form of deities occurs in Greek literature from the beginning. Hesiod transforms *dikê* into a daughter of Zeus and Themis. Highly respected by the gods of the Olympus, she immediately reports to Zeus all the unrighteous deeds of humankind so that people will have to pay for their crimes (*Theog*. 901-3, *Op*. 213-285). This image of Dikê as the favorite daughter of Zeus recurs very frequently in Greek authors until the end of antiquity. In the course of the centuries, Dikê, having originally only the positive characteristics of a goddess who watches over justice, gradually assumed the more negative aspects of the

Erinyes, goddesses of punishment and revenge, as well. The original distinction between Dikê and such demonic deities became more and more blurred as Dikê progressively changed from being an accuser or complainant into a relentless deity who wielded the weapons of revenge. Thus Dikê became a goddess of the netherworld with power over life and death (for a similar development of Latin *Iustitia* see Axtell 1907:36-37). In the Jewish *Wisdom of Solomon*, a more or less personified Justice is mentioned without the implication, however, that she was a deity. When it says that Justice the accuser will not pass by anyone who celebrates injustice because a report of his words will come before the Lord (1:8-9, and cf. 11:20), it is only a metaphor. Philo too uses this metaphor: *Conf.* 118: as God's minister, Justice punishes men for their audacity (cf. 120 and 128); *Mut.* 194: the name Dinah is by interpretation Justice, the assessor of God; *Jos.* 48: even if no one denounces us, we should have fear or respect for Justice, the assessor of God, she who surveys all our doings; cf. *Jos.* 170; *Mos.* 2.162; *Decal.* 95, 177; *Spec.* 4:201; *Prob.* 89; *Migr.* 225; see Amir 1983:155; Barraclough 1984:513-514. In *Flacc.* 104 Philo sums up most of the motifs in classical literature relating to Dikê: ἡ ὑπέρμαχος μὲν καὶ παραστάτις ἀδικουμένων τιμωρὸς δ' ἀνοσίων καὶ ἔργων καὶ ἀνθρώπων δίκη. Cf. also Acts 28:4, where the pagan inhabitants of Melitê, after the shipwreck and rescue of Paul and his fellow travellers, react to Paul's being bitten by a venomous snake by saying: "No doubt this man is a murderer. Though he has escaped from the sea, Dikê has not allowed him to live." See for more references and literature Van der Horst 1999 (in *DDD* 250-252), and cf. Borgen 1999:308; extensive bibliography in *RBLG* 242. Mendelson 1997:121 suggests that, although Philo is understandably reluctant to allow *dikê* to stand outside of God, he relies on the concept because it frees God of responsibility for evil action: since Justice acts on behalf of God, God himself is not the direct agent of punishment. It may also have to do with the fact that Philo had great problems with the biblical notion of God's wrath; see Van der Horst 1993. (The 1975 diss. on Philo's use of *dikê* by S.S. Foster was unavailable to me; see the abstract in R-R 7515.) As will become clear later on in *Flacc.*, the emperor Gaius, morally corrupt though he himself may be, will ultimately act as the agent of God's *dikê.*

an unprecedented humiliation ...: Why this is such an unheard of (καινοτάτη) humiliation is spelled out in detail in §§105-115.

§105. *some of those who had held governorships ... without trial*: A good instance of this type of abuse of one's position as Roman governor in Philo's view is Pontius Pilate; see his sketch of the man in *Legat.* 299-305, with the comments of Smallwood 1961:300-307 and Lémonon 1981:205-230, and esp. Smallwood 1976:160-174 for all the sources. The classic case of abusive administration by a Roman governor is, of course, Verres, on which see Cicero's *In Verrem*.

the emperors always demanded a rendering of their accounts and an examination of their conduct: λόγον καὶ εὐθύνας διδόναι is the technical formula for the kind of account governors had to render to the emperor after their term. Λόγος (always singular) stands for the financial report and εὐθύναι (always plural) for the report about conduct; for evidence from inscriptions see Box 1939:111 and Pelletier 1967:164 (e.g., *IG* I 91.25-27), but in literary sources this expression can be found as early as Aeschines, *Ktes.* 11, 20, 24 etc. Pelletier suggests that it is fear of this kind of account that is behind Acts 24:27, where Felix, the governor of Judaea till 62, at the end of his term leaves Paul in prison "wishing to do the Jews a favor;" otherwise the Jewish authorities might have raised a complaint against him with Nero. See on charges of provincial maladministration under the early principate Brunt 1961.

§106. *the emperors showed themselves impartial judges ...*: In this idealizing picture Philo presents us with the opposite of what he wrote about Flaccus in §54: "He gave us no right of pleading our cause but condemned us without a trial. What could be a greater promise of further tyrannical behavior than this? He himself became everything: accuser, enemy, witness, judge, and executioner!" Cf. *Legat.* 349 (on Gaius): "We realized ... that we were standing not before a judge but before an accuser more hostile to us than our actual opponents." That this picture of Gaius' predecessors, especially of Tiberius, is much too flattering, if not distorted, is rightly pointed out by Niehoff 2001:125, who draws attention to the significantly different information about Tiberius in Josephus. On the procedure of bringing before the emperor criminal accusations against Roman office-holders see Millar 1977:443-444.

§107. *it was not after his term of office but before the regular date that he was met by Justice*: Here is the "unprecedented humiliation" that Philo spoke of in §104. The adjective ἐμπρόθεσμος ("before the stated time," originally an agricultural term) and the adverb ἐμπροθέσμως occur each only once in Philo (the adjective in *Mos.* 2.231); it is a very rare word that occurs further only in writers from the 2nd cent. CE and later.

Justice, who hates evil, because she was so indignant at the unimaginable excesses of his unjust and lawless activities: This is Dikê in her traditional role; see the note *ad* §104. Since in §102 and elsewhere it is God himself who takes revenge on Flaccus for his misdeeds, it is clear that in fact Dikê is nothing but God in his capacity of pursuer of justice. The adjective μισοπόνηρος (hating evil) is one of Philo's favorites (24 times); in *Spec.* 3.75 he portrays the μισοπόνηρος character.

§108. *the matters on which he was under suspicion*: These are the fact that he had sided with another rather than Gaius in the struggle for the succession of Tiberius and his stance against Gaius' mother Agrippina; see the notes *ad* §9.

his long public speeches ...: Flaccus could assume that Gaius would get acquainted with the contents of his public speeches; see *Legat.* 165: "[Gaius] paid attention to the daily reports which some people were sending to him from Alexandria, for he found these very pleasant reading, so that he regarded the compositions of other writers and poets as thoroughly unpleasant in comparison with the charm of these reports." Unfortunately Philo does not specify who these "some people" were. As Smallwood 1961:246 says, the obvious person to keep in close touch with the emperor was the prefect himself, but Philo evidently thinks of others (spies?).

the high reputation he had: This high reputation Flaccus had in the city was initially shared also by Philo himself, as he made clear in his extensive description of Flaccus' good qualities in §§2-5.

§109. *The hopes of wicked people do not have any foundation ...*: This is a biblical motif that is expressed most eloquently in Ps. 73. Note the chiastic structure in εἰκαζόντων μὲν τὰ χρηστότερα, τὰ δὲ παλίμφημα καὶ ὧν ἄξιοι τυγχάνειν εἰσὶ πασχόντων, for which Box 1939:111 compares §186 ἢ προσωτέρω χωροῦντα κατὰ τοῦ πελάγους ἐνεχθῆναι ἢ συλληφθῆναι πρὸς αὐτὸ τὸ πέρας ἥκοντα. The word παλίμφημος in the sense of δύσφημος or κακόφημος is rare elsewhere but a favorite with Philo (14 times); see §177, *Legat.* 99, 110, 322.

Bassus: This centurion who is going to arrest Flaccus is otherwise unknown. It is a common name — in §92 we already met another

FLACCUS' ARREST 195

Bassus, the man who was in charge of the collection of illegal weapons, who is definitely not the same one as this centurion.

§110. *in only a few days he arrived* ...: This is an exaggeration for the trip must have taken at least 10 days; see the notes *ad* §27. Philo hereby wants to emphasize the swiftness of the action.
the island of Pharos: See *ad* §27.
He ordered the captain to remain offshore until after sunset ...: This and other details are so similar to what Philo writes in §27 (even down to verbal details such as ἔξω θαλαττεύειν) about Agrippa's arrival in Alexandria that some scholars have speculated that one story is patterned upon the other, unnecessarily so: of course entering the harbor stealthily always followed the same pattern. See the references in Box 1939:xli-xlii note 1 and Pelletier 1967:161.
frustrate his mission: ἄπρακτον αὐτῷ τὴν ὑπηρεσίαν ἐργάσασθαι, lit. "make the expedition for him undone/unsuccessful." ὑπηρεσία, originally the body of rowers on a ship, later developed the sense of "service" (of all kinds) and "expedition, enterprise."

§111. *one of the sentries in the quaternion on duty*: τινα τῶν ἐν τοῖς τετραδίοις φυλάκων, lit. "one of the sentries arrayed in quaternions." A τετράδιον is a squad of four soldiers, one for each of the four night watches. The four detachments of four soldiers each were detailed to guard in turn during the four watches of the night (*vigiliae*, see Vegetius, *De re militari* 3.8 quia impossibilie videbatur in speculis vigilantes singulos permanere, ideo in quattuor partes ad clepsydram sunt divisae vigiliae ut non amplius quam tribus horis nocturnis necesse sit vigilare; cf. also *P.Oxy.* 2156.10 and Philostratus, *Vit. Apoll.* 7.31); cf. in the NT Acts 12:4. There were of course several of such squads in the city. Box 1939:111-112 provides more discussion.
commander: στρατάρχης is here the prefect of one of the two Roman legions in Egypt (*praefectus exercitui*) or perhaps the *praefectus castrorum* who functioned as the leader of the united camp of the two legions; see again Box 1939:112 for a technical discussion; for modern lit. see Rupprecht 1994:85.
his secret errand: τὸ ἀπόρρητον, lit. "the ineffable, the forbidden, what is not to be spoken about."

§112. *Stephanio, one of the freedmen of the emperor Tiberius* (Στεφανίων ἦν τῶν τοῦ Τιβερίου Καίσαρος ἀπελευθέρων): "The numerous subordinate officials in Egypt were largely taken from imperial freedmen and slaves. ... Stephanio no doubt enjoyed a high rank among these imperial freedmen" (Box 1939:112). Stephanio is otherwise unknown. For the role of imperial freedmen in Egypt and Alexandria see Strabo 17.1.12 [797] (for Jewish imperial freedmen see Van der Horst 1991:142).

Bassus held back ... and informed Bassus: The details in this and the following paragraphs are too specific to suspect that Philo created the whole story *ex nihilo*, but one wonders how and where he could have got this kind of information. Did he know Flaccus' host?

§113. *he was just drinking to the health of someone and toasting the company*: ἐτύγχανε γὰρ καὶ πρόποσίν τινι διδοὺς καὶ φιλοφρονούμενος τοὺς παρόντας. The expression πρόποσιν ποιεῖν or διδόναι means "to drink to someone's health," and it is clear that φιλοφρονεῖσθαι must here mean something more specific than "showing favor to or dealing kindly with somebody" (LSJ *s.v.*). Box 1939:41 translates "entertaining the company," Pelletier 1967:117 "exprimer ses bons sentiments à l'assistance," Gerschmann 1964:151 "freundliche Begrüßungsworte an die Anwesenden richten;" but I follow Colson's suggestion, albeit hesitantly, that "the context seems to need some specific action which diverted his attention" and is related to the preceding πρόποσιν διδόναι, and adopt his "toasting the company" (1941:365). Philo uses φιλοφρονεῖσθαι once more, again in a dinner setting, where he says that the three guests of Abraham (Gen. 18) "show courtesy to their host" (φιλοφρονοῦνται τὸν ξενοδόχον).

§114. *speechless*: On ἀχανής see the note *ad* §87.

He wanted to get up: Here Mangey's conjecture ἀντιστῆναι (to resist) for ἀναστῆναι is unnecessary. As Box 1939:112-113 rightly remarks, "it is not until he has had time to look at the armed guard surrounding him that he guesses the meaning of Bassus' presence. Why, then, should he wish to resist him before he knows his errand?"

For the human mind ...: This observation has no exact parellel in Philo's other works. One might compare *Leg.* 2.42-43 where he says about the *nous* that past, present, and future are within its scope because it grasps things present, remembers things past, and looks forward to things future; it is set in motion by that which is not present, if past, by way of memory, if future, by building hopes or expectations. Cf. *Det.* 89, *Spec.* 1.334; and see Kraus 1994:489. One is vaguely reminded here of the famous passage on memory in Augustine's *Conf.* 10.12-16.

§115. *For it had to be so ...*: ἔδει γὰρ ... This event had to take place in this way (at the scene of a hospitable hearth) because it was an action of *Justice* (I suggest printing Δίκη with a capital here in view of what Philo has said in §104, *pace* the current editions). The sentiment expressed here is not identical to that of the *lex talionis* (an eye for an eye, a tooth for a tooth), but rather an expression of what Box 1939:113 calls "poetic justice," *i.e.*, that the circumstances under which Flaccus is arrested are eminently suited to the nature of the crimes he has committed, namely the destroying of "numerous hearths and homes" of innocent people. "Philon sieht vielmehr in dieser etwas künstlichen ... Analogie den Beweis dafür, daß die Bestrafung nicht durch Zufall erfolgte, sondern daß Gottes Finger sie gewirkt hat" (Heinemann 1932:349). Cf. §125: "He was destined to have his fill of the frightening dangers of the sea, having filled the elements of the universe with his impieties." The principle of the *lex talionis* is expressed, however, at the end of *Flacc.*, where Philo says that "Justice wanted that single body [of Flaccus] to receive the same number of wounds as that of the Jews who had been unlawfully murdered by him" (§189).

§116. *this unprecedented misfortune*: See the note on §104.
I think: μοι δοκῶ is here not an expression of doubt (μοι δοκεῖ) but of strong conviction (LSJ *s.v.* I 3b). But "it required Jewish eyes to see a connection between Flaccus' trial and his earlier treatment of the Jews" (Niehoff 2001:41).
in his craving for fame: λιμοδοξῶν (lit., "being hungry for fame") is possibly a Philonic creation; it occurs only here and in *Spec.* 2.18; and cf. λιμοδοξία in *Deus* 115 with Winston & Dillon 1983:333 *ad loc.* Why Flaccus expected to gain fame from his extermination of the Jews, according to Philo, is left unclear.
The moment of his arrest is also a clear proof of this: Colson 1941:366 note *a*: "Philo means that providence shows itself by sending deliverance just when things are darkest. The festal season, particularly as its chief characteristic, the living in booths, could not be observed, brought their misery to a climax." But see also our next note.
the national Jewish festival of the autumn equinox ...: Sukkot, the Festival of Booths (called σκηνοπηγία in the LXX; cf. John 7:2), is the

third of the three Jewish pilgrim festivals. It is usually celebrated in September/October, on the basis of the biblical precepts in Ex. 23:16; Lev. 23:43; Deut. 16:13-17; these precepts were worked out in more detail by the rabbis; see Bornhäuser 1935 and Rubinstein 1995. In 38 CE it fell in mid October (Schwartz 1982:190 note 8). The most conspicuous characteristic of the festival (ἐν ᾗ διάγειν Ἰουδαίοις ἔθος ἐν σκηναῖς) is mentioned here by Philo for the sake of his non-Jewish readers. Philo's view of this festival (see esp. *Spec.* 2.204-213) is discussed by Heinemann 1932:134-136, Rubinstein 1995:69-73, and Leonhardt 2001:45-47. It cannot be ruled out that Philo considers Flaccus' arrest on Sukkot as a proof of divine justice because in his view the equinox (ἰσημερία) indicates that we should honor ἰσότης (equality) as the source of δικαιοσύνη (justice); see *Spec.* 2.204. This might explain why Philo calls Sukkot a festival of the autumn equinox which *stricto sensu* it is not (we have no reason to assume that Alexandrian Jews celebrated Sukkot on the basis of a calendar that differed from that of other Jews).

§117. *none of the festal proceedings were carried out ...*: This implies that "under ordinary circumstances the Jews in Alexandria celebrated the festival of Tabernacles by building tents and meeting in their *proseuchai*, and this custom was sufficiently deeply rooted for them to revert to its practice immediately after the end of the persecution" (Leonhardt 2001:46). For the celebration of the festival of booths by the Jews of Cyrene (Libya) in the same period see the inscription from Berenike in Lüderitz 1983: no. 71.1-2 (= CIG III 5361); for its celebration in Egypt a century later see *CPJ* 452a. That Flaccus' downfall coincided with the non-celebration of Sukkot is considered by Philo as God's hand at work. "God had intervened and saved the Jews at the precise moment when, because of Flaccus, their fortunes had reached their nadir" (Williams 1998:187 note 70).

the common people regarded the misfortune of their leaders as that of the whole nation: Philo stresses the unity and unanimity of the Jewish people by highlighting the solidarity of the commoners (ἰδιωτῶν) with their leaders (ἀρχόντων). His focus on the sufferings of the leaders may reflect Philo's belonging to these circles, even though he nowhere makes mention of his personal involvement in the tragic events.

§118. *because they have their share of sorrow:* μετουσίᾳ λύπης is taken in a different sense by the various translators. Colson has "because they communicate to each other their sorrow," emphasizing the element of sharing each other's grief, but Box has "through participation in grief," emphasizing the partaking in the general misery. Gerschmann and Pelletier follow Box, rightly so because it fits better the immediately following sentence about the inability "to find any remedy for such enormous disasters."

which in this case broke their backs: ὑφ' ἧς ἐξετραχηλίζοντο. In the translation the words "in this case" have been inserted in order to render the fact that Philo here makes a transition from the general, or gnomic, at the beginning (ἀνιαρὰ διπλασιάζεσθαι φιλεῖ = grief is *usually* felt twice as strongly) to the particular (note the imperfect in ἐξετραχηλίζοντο, which refers to the specific circumstances of the Jewish community in Alexandria). Ἐκτραχηλίζειν (originally said of a horse throwing the rider over its head > to overturn) is used again in §166 where Philo speaks of the very depressing thoughts of Flaccus in his exile which floored him.

§§119-124: *Gratitude for Flaccus' Arrest*

In prayers and hymns the Jews offered thanks to God for his sudden and unexpected intervention. They acknowledge that God does not abandon his people and that it is his providence that makes things turn from evil to good. The short first prayer amounts to hardly more than a disclaimer of malicious pleasure, "Schadenfreude." The longer second one states that God has made a start on the fulfilling of their prayers by causing the enemy of the Jews to fall down which gives them hope that God will go on now by also restoring other things for them that they have lost. They also express gratitude for the fact that God has immensely consoled his people by not delaying his punishment of Flaccus till after his term, which would have given them much less pleasure, but by doing it "almost before the eyes of those whom he had wronged." Both prayers are obviously Philonic creations intended to restore faith and trust in his co-religionists.

§119. *They thought that this was a trap ...:* Their initial unbelief recurs as a motif in the subsequent thanksgiving prayer when the people speak of God's "sudden and unexpected intervention" (§124: τῆς ἐν βραχεῖ καὶ παρ' ἐλπίδας ἐπεξόδου).

§120. *the nightguards ran to and fro*: In his enumeration of officials in Alexandria, Strabo 17.1.12 [797] also mentions a νυκτερινὸς στρατηγός (night commander), who was the head of the nocturnal police that patrolled the city after dark; in papyrological evidence he is usually called νυκτοστράτηγος, see Box 1939:113 and Fraser 1972: 2.180 note 34 for references. "The prominence assigned to the office by Strabo is perhaps to be explained by his acquaintance with the Roman *praefectus vigilum*, the commander of the *Vigiles*, who was probably modelled on the Alexandrian institution" (Fraser 1972: 1.99). Philo uses the term νυκτοφύλαξ only once more, in *Spec.* 1.156, where he describes the duties of the Levites, among which he mentions their task to guard the temple in Jerusalem day and night.

horsemen rode at full speed to and from the camp: One may assume that Philo reports this from his own experience, for he may have heard "their shouts and galloping horses" (Box 1939:113). The camp was possibly the united camp of the two Roman legions (see *ad* §111).

something revolutionary had taken place: This is one of the very rare instances where Philo uses νεώτερον in a non-negative sense. Usually it designates an event or form of behavior that he detests but here the "revolution" was brought about by God himself. Box 1939:43 translates by "something unusual," but that is not in accordance with the use of this same word in §§35 and 110. For the theme of the sudden reversal of the fate of God's enemies Borgen 1996:504-505 compares Apoc. 11:17-18.

§121. *ensnared within the hunter's nets*: "Nets" (which were employed by both fishermen and hunters [Schneider 1998:835]) is often used metaphorically for perils that one can get entangled in; see, e.g., Aeschylus, *Agam.* 1115 (nets of Hades), *Prom.* 1078; Euripides, *Med.* 1278; Aristenaetus, *Ep.* 2.23; *Test. Abr.* (long rec.) 8.10; cf. the "nets of Belial" in the Dead Sea Scrolls (e.g., *CD* 4.15) and the metaphorical "fisher of men" in Mark 1:17 par.; note that the parallel text in Luke 5:10 has "hunter" (ζωγρῶν); further 2 Tim. 2:26; see BDAG 44 and 429-430.

they stretched out their arms to heaven: Philo introduces this dramatic scene by saying that the Jews "stretched out their arms to heaven" when they began to praise God. The raising of hands is also mentioned in the description of the Egyptian Jews in *3 Macc.* 5:25, where they beseech God to save them from the king's plan to execute all Jews. In Josephus, too, we find several references to this prayer gesture, e.g. in the case of the long prayer of Moses in *Ant.* 4:40. And one is also reminded of the raised hands carved above the Jewish imprecation incised on the famous tombstone from Rheneia (*CIJ* 725; Horbury 1998:307). But the raising of hands is, of course, a widespread prayer posture in antiquity in general; see Gross 1985:14-24; Pulleyn 1997:189. For an Alexandrian inscription mentioning the raising of hands by Jews in prayer see Mitchell 1999:146 no. 284.

began to sing hymns and songs: ὕμνουν καὶ παιᾶνας ἐξῆρχον. In §122 Philo says that they spent the night ἐν ὕμνοις καὶ ᾠδαῖς (a combination that occurs also elsewhere, e.g. *Leg.* 3.62, *Agr.* 80-82; cf. Eph. 5:19 and Col. 3:16). "Hymns" in Philo may also include Psalms; see Leonhardt 2001:142-174, esp. 156-158. Παιᾶνες were originally ritual exclamations addressed to healing gods, but later it denoted — like ὕμνοι — religious songs on a variety of occasions (see *OCD* s.v.; Schröder 1999; Furley & Bremer 2001: 1.84-91). Philo uses the word only once more, *Legat.* 96. As Leonhardt 2001:171 remarks, this passage is Philo's only reference to the singing of a non-sectarian community of his time (*i.e.*, apart from what he says about the Therapeutae and the Essenes).

God who oversees all human affairs: In §125 Philo makes clear that he sees God's providence (πρόνοια) at work in Flaccus' arrest. This is echoed again in Flaccus' own prayer in §170 where he confesses that "you are not indifferent to the nation of the Jews, nor is what they assert about your providence false, for all who say that the Jews do not have you for a champion and defender go astray from sound opinion." Moreover, in the very last line of the whole treatise Philo remarks that the fate of Flaccus proved beyond doubt that "the Jewish people had not been deprived of the help of God" (191). Even though not frequently made explicit, the motif of God's *pronoia* is a *Leitmotif* in *Flacc.* In the opening paragraphs of *Legat.*, the immediate sequel of *Flacc.*, we find Philo speaking about people who "have come to disbelieve that the deity exercises his providence for men, and particularly for the suppliant nation which the Father and King of the universe and the source of all things has taken for his portion" (*Legat.* 3), namely the people of Israel. It is clear that Philo addresses here a real and urgent pastoral need that had arisen in the wake of the persecution. That providence was an important concept in Philo's thought is also apparent from the fact that he wrote a separate treatise about the subject, *De providentia*, and that in the closing paragraphs of *Opif.* (170-172), one of the five vital lessons taught by

Moses is that "God takes thought for the cosmos" (προνοεῖ τοῦ κόσμου ὁ θεός); see Runia 2001:400-401. On providence in Philo see Frick 1999 (Frick is unsatisfactory on *Flacc.* on which he devotes less than one page [188-9]; "yet it is the guiding thought in the entire work, to such a degree that one of the manuscripts actually gives it the alternative title Περὶ προνοίας," says Runia in his review in *JSJ* 32 [2001] 301); cf. Runia 2001:118 *et al.* (see Index *s.v.*); Winston 2002:127-130. On providence in the ancient world in general see the short but excellent article by Gordon 1999:664-667; in later Greek philosophy see Dragona-Monachou 1994; in early rabbinic thought see Urbach 1975:255-285.

we are not delighted at the punishment of our enemy: These are pious, perhaps all too pious words from the pen of Philo, for the whole second part of the book would seem to be nothing else than a glaring demonstration of "Schadenfreude" on his part. Colson 1941:301 wryly remarks: "This is easily said but not so easily done, and if Philo believed that he himself had learned the lesson, I think he deceived himself." And it would seem to be true that Philo gloats upon the series of misfortunes that come over Flaccus, which he describes with obvious pleasure. But this disclaimer of malicious pleasure, "Schadenfreude," inspired the French Philonic scholar Nikiprowetzky to his study of this prayer bearing the title "*Schadenfreude* chez Philon d'Alexandrie?" (Nikiprowetzky 1996:96-109), in which he comes to a different conclusion. He argues that, although at first sight the whole second part of the treatise seems to be nothing other than a demonstration of "Schadenfreude" on Philo's part, the emphasis is clearly on the fact that seeing the downfall of their enemy right before their own eyes convinces the Jews that God can and will intervene quickly and effectively (see §124!). So the "Schadenfreude" is not a goal in itself, it stands in the service of the creation of hope and faith among God's people. Their joy is not about the misery of an individual person, it is about the meaning and implication of this, namely the merciful intervention of God. "Même dans ses écrits historiques, Philon ne cesse pas d'être un théologien" (Nikiprowetzky 1996:102). What he aims at in this treatise is not to demonstrate a triumph of revenge but of divine justice. See Van der Horst 2003:24-26.

we have learned from our holy laws that we should sympathize with our fellowhumans: Cf. the long section on φιλανθρωπία in *Virt.* 51-124. It has been suggested that Philo may be thinking here of the passage in Ex. 23:4-5 about bringing back the domestic animals of one's enemy when one sees them going astray or helping them when they collapse under a burden. Much more likely, however, he does not allude to a passage from the Torah at all, but to Prov. 24:17-18: "Do not rejoice when your enemy falls and let not your heart be glad when he stumbles, lest the Lord see it and be displeased and turn away his anger from him." Heinemann 1932:526-7 explains this misattribution of a passage from the Writings to the Torah as due to Philo's defective knowledge of biblical books other than those of the Pentateuch, for which see also Amir 1983:181 (Leisegang's [1934:132] objection is lame). Or does Philo use "law(s)" here as a *pars pro toto* for the whole Bible (as Torah is sometimes used for Tanakh)? That is also quite possible; see for this use of νόμος see BDAG *s.v.* 3b.

thanks to you for having taken pity and compassion on us: οἶκτος καὶ ἔλεος is also the expression Philo uses in *Spec.* 4.180, where, in his exposition of Deut. 10:17-18, he says that "Moses tells us that the orphan-like desolate state of his people is always an object of pity and compassion to the Ruler of the universe whose portion it is" (see the remarks in Borgen 2000:49).

§122. *singing hymns and other songs*: See the notes *ad* §121. Note that καί here has the meaning of "and other" or "and generally."

made their way to the nearby parts of the beach: For the location of the Jewish quarter (Delta) near the waterfront see the note *ad* §55. It is notable that Josephus mentions a decree from Halicarnassus permitting the Jews "to offer prayers near the sea according to their custom" (*Ant.* 14.258), and there is also archaeological evidence for synagogues near water, e.g. at Delos, Ostia and at the Lake of Tiberias. The water was undoubtedly needed for purificatory purposes. It would seem that "the Jews regarded the shore as the nearest equivalent as place of worship" (Leonhardt 2001:79); see further Tcherikover 1959:508-9 note 33; Pucci Ben Zeev 1998: 210-211; and Levine 2000:97, 100, 106, 109, 120, 281, 283, 291, 293, 311. Cf. Acts 16:12-13.

for they had been deprived of their synagogues: This implies that they would have gone to their houses of prayer (προσευχαί) in a situation like this, if these had not been desecrated (Leonhardt 2001:79; Gruen 2002:117). For the multipurpose character of the ancient synagogue see Levine 2000: *passim* and Gruen 2002:115-119. That the Jews sing and pray here implies that this kind of worship was also what they would commonly do in a synagogue service; see Van der Horst 1999:18-43.

standing in the purest possible place: ἐν τῷ καθαρωτάτῳ. Box and Colson translate "in the most open space," Gerschmann "wo am meisten Platz war," and Pelletier "à l'endroit le plus dégagé," adding in a note that this refers back to §56 where it is said that the Jews "poured out to the beaches, the *dunghills* and the tombs," and the "purity" of the place referred to here is no more than that the place where the Jews were praying was clear of rubbish heaps. In view of the fact that for the sense of "in the open air" the usual Greek would be ἐν τῷ καθαρῷ, not ἐν τῷ καθαρωτάτῳ, Pelletier is probably right. This is confirmed by the fact that in *Mos.* 2.34 "the most pure place (τὸ καθαρώτατον) outside the city" is chosen by the Septuagint translators for their sacred work, and *Mos.* 2.72 uses the same word for the site of the Jerusalem temple. Runesson 2002:121 also refers to Josephus, *Ant.* 4.79-81 for τὸ καθαρώτατον as a designation of a place of ritual purity. "In all cases, the idea of the purity of the place makes good sense as that required for the dwelling place of God or communication with God in a quasi-temple setting" (Pearce 1998:104 note 138). Cf. also Celsus in Origen, *CC* 5.4. This explanation would also accord with the later rabbinic prohibition against praying in dirty or stinking places (e.g., Babylonian Talmud, *Berakhot* 24b). For a detailed treatment of the matter see Runesson 2002:115-129.

they cried out with one accord: Since the text of the now following prayer is obviously a creation of Philo, this statement should be taken *cum grano salis*.

§123. ***King of mortals and immortals***: That God is the king of humans is a current idea, but his being king of immortals is strange at first sight because it sounds polytheistic. If "immortals" means "gods," it would imply that God is not the only but the highest god in a pantheon. It is then a variant of the well-known formula "father of humans and gods" in pagan literature (parallels in Meiser 1999:425 note 37). And indeed, elsewhere Philo speaks of "Him, whom all Greeks and barbarians unanimously acknowledge, the supreme Father of gods and humans and the maker of the whole universe" (*Spec.* 2.165). It would almost seem here as if Philo tries to blur the distinction between monotheists and polytheists (see Niehoff 2001: 78). This need not be implied, however, if we take into account that Philo here draws upon traditional prayer formulae as we come across them in Jewish prayers such as the one by Esther (addition C 23 in the LXX) and the synagogal prayer incorporated in the *Apostolic*

Constitutions (7.33.2). In both of these texts we see God invoked as "king of the gods." This formula is evidently patterned upon the originally polytheistic formulations we find in Ps. 95:3 and 82:1, where God is called "the great king above all gods" and the like. This is no more than a verbal relic of an earlier (polytheistic) stage in the history of Israelite religion. However, as used by the authors of these later prayers they certainly do not imply a polytheistic stance. Philo even has Moses use this formula in a prayer in which the great Lawgiver adresses God as "Lord, King of the gods" (*Conf.* 173, in an inaccurate quote from Deut. 10:17). Aside from that, we should keep in mind that Philo often calls the heavenly bodies "gods" (e.g. *Opif.* 27), so he may be simply referring to the stars and sun and moon here. In addition to that, in view of the fact that Philo had not only a Jewish but also a non-Jewish readership in mind, we need not be surprised by his choice of apparently "pagan" vocabulary here.

to call on earth and sea, on air and heaven, which are the parts of the universe: There has been some debate over whether or not Philo refers here to the four elements earth, water, air, and fire, which does not seem an unreasonable supposition at first sight. But there is now a growing consensus (see Box 1939:113-114; Colson 1941:368-369; Pelletier 1967:121 note 4) that Philo here uses a popular classification to express the four regions of the visible world (for "elements" he certainly would have used στοιχεῖα, as in §125). He mentions the same four in the same way as he does here also in *Mos.* 1.113 and 2.37, as "parts [=regions] of the universe" and not as elements. As a matter of fact Philo nowhere explicitly identifies heaven with fire and he never mentions heaven as the fourth element, even though he did know the theory of the four elements. So what is meant here is that the whole universe is called upon to join the Israelites in thanking God for his deliverance. This is done, so the author says, because the Jews have been robbed of their homes and other private and public buildings so that only the regions of the universe are left to them as places to dwell. One should not use this, of course, to argue that Philo considered the sea and the air as places for humans to live in. The emphasis is on the homeless state of the Jews after the pogrom. Of course, calling heaven and earth to witness is a well-known biblical theme; see Deut. 4:26; 30:19; 31:28 etc.

homeless: ἀνέστιοι, lit. "without hearth," see *ad* §116.

§124. *But you make us realize ... answer our prayers*: The train of thought in §124 is not easy to follow (which is partly due to uncertainties in the translation, see below), but it seems to be as follows: God has made a start on the fulfilling of their prayers by causing their enemy to fall down and that gives them hope that he will continue by also restoring other things to them that they have lost. As is often the case in Philo, it is possible for thanksgiving to function in fact as a petition (Larson 1946:190). Although it is clear that Philo makes the Jews urge God not to leave it at that, what exactly Philo has in mind when he speaks of the amendment of things that are still in need of restoration is uncertain. It is certainly not (only) the demolished houses and synagogues that he has in mind; there must be more, but we can only guess. Does he express here the hope for God's support in the Jewish striving for full citizenship of Alexandria, which according to some had been one of the main points of friction between Jews and non-Jews in the period preceding the pogrom? Or is it — more probably — about the restoration of the former rights of the Jewish community that Flaccus had abolished? We do not know but, anyway, Philo does not stress the point and seems to make only a vague reference. Part of the vagueness lies in the fact that it is unclear what Philo means by τὰ λειπόμενα, here tentatively translated as "what is still in need (of restoration);" lit. "the things which are in need of, or deficient in, or lacking something."

the common enemy of our nation: Flaccus was the enemy not only of the Alexandrian Jews but of Jews all over the world for, as Philo said in §45, "the rumor of the destruction of the synagogues that started in Alexandria would spread immediately to the districts of Egypt and speed from Egypt eastwards to the oriental nations, and from the coastal strip and Mareia, which are the borders of Libya, westwards to the nations living there." See Gruen 2002:250-251.

who thought so highly of himself: On this use of πνέειν to express moods and emotions see the collection of parallels in Van der Horst 1970. The expression μέγα πνέοντα occurs also in §152; in *Virt.* 171 Philo uses it of the person who provokes God (with reference to Num. 15:30; see Borgen 2000:48-49).

you did not wait ... your swift and unexpected intervention: God has immensely consoled his people by not delaying his punishment of Flaccus till after his term, which would have given them much less satisfaction (but not "Schadenfreude"!), but by doing it "almost before the eyes of those whom he had wronged." That was very important because by doing so God gave them a clearer picture and therefore a stronger conviction of how swiftly he could and would intervene, which is of course a source of great encouragement to the Jews. Philo's message for his fellow-Jews is that God's providence (see §125) was, is, and will always be active in their favor. As Leonhardt 2001:172 remarks, the theme of God humbling the proud and saving the distraught is common in the Bible: 1 Sam. 2:4-7 and Luke 1:46-55 are only the two best known examples (but cf. also Judith 16). More important, however, is that "although Philo does not refer to Ex. 15 explicitly in his description, there are three points of similarity: the occasion (the salvation from danger to the Jews by Gentiles [in Egypt! PWvdH]), the place (at the seashore or beach), and the purpose (praise of God's saving action). It is possible, therefore, that Philo models his account of the praise after Flaccus' defeat along the lines of Ex. 15" (Leonhardt 2001:172).

a clearer picture: τρανοτέρα φαντασία, a more distinct image. Φαντασία in Philo is the mental result of a sense-datum or the effect of realities not falling within the field of sense-data (Box 1939:114-115). On φαντασία in general see now Brachtendorf in Horn & Rapp 2002:336-337. In §162 φαντασία has the more dramatic sense of "imagining, hallucination."

§§125-145 *Lampo and Isidorus*

The men who were mentioned earlier as leaders of the faction and had urged him to secure his position wiith the emperor by persecuting the Jews, now appear as his accusers, namely the archcriminals Isidorus and Lampo. An elaborate sketch of their malicious practices in the past is given. Philo does not mention what Flaccus was charged with by them, probably because these charges had little or nothing to do with his treatment of the Jews while Philo wants to present Flaccus' condemnation as God's punishment for his anti-Jewish measures. The fact that Philo gives such a detailed account of the wicked deeds of Isidorus and Lampo is to be seen in the light of his wish to demonstrate how deeply Flaccus was humiliated: Not only "is nothing harder for those who were once superiors than to be accused by their former inferiors or for those who were once rulers by their former subjects, which is just as if masters were to be accused by slaves born in their house or purchased with their money" (127), which was only the lighter evil, but on top of that "it was not just people who had been in the position of subjects who now suddenly attacked him unanimously with their accusations (...), but people who had been his most bitter enemies for the greatest part of the period that he had been the governor of the country" (128). God begins to punish Flaccus by utterly humiliating him.

§125. *To what I have already said I should add a third thing which I think also took place because divine providence intervened*: The first two aspects of Flaccus' downfall that were due to the intervention of θεία πρόνοια were the manner of Flaccus' arrest (in a home setting) and the time that he was arrested (at the Feast of Booths); see §§115-116 with the notes.

Flaccus had set sail ... with his impieties: The third sign of divine providence (ἔδει) is that Flaccus, who had tainted the elements of the universe with his transgressions, is now being harassed by these elements himself, namely here by water (θαλάττη = ὕδωρ, land being implied by καί), a rather far-fetched imagery. Flaccus had set sail "at the beginning of the winter," while the seafaring season had already ended by the beginning of November because thereafter storms and poor visibility began to make navigation hazardous (see §26). Cf. Acts 27:9-12. On "elements" (στοιχεῖα) see Sterling 1998:363 (with note 45).

two of his worst enemies, Isidorus and Lampo: These persons were already introduced in §20; see the notes *ad locum*. Box 1939:115 acutely remarks: "The addition δύο τῶν ἐχθίστων is artistically out of place. The fact that they were ἔχθιστοι is regarded as the next misfortune in the ascending scale of disasters, described from 116 to 148. It is their character as ὑπήκοοι that is in place here. Their character as ἔχθιστοι is regarded as a still worse evil in §128." From Philo's point of view, this reversal of the roles of ruler and subject is the most disgraceful experience an aristocrat can have. Isidorus and Lampo must have gone to Gaius already before Flaccus' arrest, "probably though not certainly as ambassadors of the city" (Millar 1977:444).

§126. *These men had been his subjects only a short while ago*: See the remark by Box quoted immediately above (*ad* §125). Note the *peripeteia* motif in οἱ πρὸ μικροῦ μέν ... νυνὶ δέ ... Hennig 1974:434 suggests that the words "only a short while ago" refer back to the attempt at reconciliation between Flaccus and Isidorus *c.s.* as described in §18 and possibly also in *Acts of the Pagan Martyrs* 1 (*P.Oxy.* 1089 = *CPJ* 154), which probably took place in the spring of 38 CE.

hailed him as their master, benefactor, savior and the like: δεσπότην καὶ εὐεργέτην καὶ σωτῆρα καὶ τὰ τοιαῦτα ἀνακαλοῦντες. Even though this kind of terminology may sound exaggerated to modern sensitivities, in antiquity they were part and parcel in certain forms of address in the hierarchy of ranks, as noted by De Vries 1999:96. See further *ad* §74 and Jung 2002:246 (on "savior").

a power ... vastly superior to his own: δυνατωτέραν ἰσχὺν ἐκ πολλοῦ τοῦ περιόντος. The expression ἐκ πολλοῦ τοῦ περιόντος is used by Philo several times to indicate exceptional superiority; see e.g. *Prob.* 149, *Agric.* 112, *Contempl.* 63, *Mos.* 1.93, 2.75; and cf. *Post.* 161 and *Aet.* 80. Pelletier 1967:123 suggests on the basis of *Agric.* 112 that it is "un terme du vocabulaire des concours," but without giving further proof.

he who presides over human affairs: τὸν πρύτανιν τῶν ἀνθρωπίνων πραγμάτων, not God, as in §121 (τὸν ἔφορον θεὸν τῶν ἀνθρωπίνων πραγμάτων), but the emperor Gaius, as the following phrase makes clear.

But in fact he would behave as an enemy ...: This description of Gaius' attitude shows a strong resemblance to that of Flaccus himself in §24. Again Philo implies that divine justice sees to it that Flaccus meets the same fate that he himself had meted out to others.

sentenced him to the severest punishment: With τὰς ἀνωτάτω τιμωρίας the death penalty is meant; see for further instances of this usage Hengel 1977:33-34 note 2.

§127. *And nothing is harder ... purchased with their money*: For Philo, who was himself a member of the ruling elite, this kind of dishonor would be the ultimate humiliation. He rightly assumes that the same sentiment would be harbored by Flaccus (see Barton 2001). Yet it was "a lighter evil" (§128) as compared to what is said in the following passage: they had also been his bitterest enemies. See the same notion also in §§146-147.

§128. *but people who had also been his most bitter enemies*: This transitional phrase introduces the lengthy section on the malicious activities of Lampo and Isidorus. The unusual expression μάλιστ' αὐτῷ δι' ἀπεχθείας ἐγεγένηντο has a parallel in Aristophanes, *Ran.* 1412: "I will not be on hostile terms (δι' ἔχθρας γενήσομαι) with either one."

Lampo had been put on trial for impiety towards the emperor. Lampo, described in §20 as a "document-noser," was for two long years accused on suspicion of *maiestas* (disloyalty), "which, under Tiberius, was not a trifling affair" (Tcherikover-Fuks 1957/64: 2.69), but he seems somehow to have won the lawsuit. It is unknown which form of disloyalty he was accused of but it was a charge that could be easily incurred under Tiberius according to Cassius Dio 57.9.2.

§129. ***Because his judge ... as long as possible:*** The dragging on of lawsuits and extended incarceration were not uncommon in the ancient Roman judicial system; see Rapske 1994:315-323. "As long as possible" is the translation of πρὸς μήκιστον χρόνον, but it is also possible to take it to mean "for a very long time." It is uncertain whether or not there was a statute of limitations on prosecutions to two years (see §128, and cf. Acts 28:30); for a discussion of the problems see Rapske 1994:322.

§130. ***he had been compelled to become a gymnasiarch:*** ἠναγκάσθη γὰρ γυμνασιαρχεῖν, probably by Flaccus (see Bowman & Rathbone 1992: 116). A gymnasiarch in a Hellenistic and Roman *polis* had general supervision over the physical and intellectual training provided in the gymnasium (or gymnasia; see the note *ad* §34) and was responsible (helped by a staff of assistants and specialists) "for its practical administration and the moral supervision of its youthful users, for whom he was a fearsome authority-figure empowered to fine and flog" (*OCD* 659). The office entailed heavy expenses (mainly oil for athletics and fuel for hot baths) and burdensome responsibilities, which is the main reason why rich citizens often were inclined to escape it, even though it ensured the gymnasiarch local prominence. Heavy pressure to fulfil this task was sometimes exerted by the authorities on the wealthier citizens. See Jones 1940:220-226, esp. 221-223; Delia 1991:106-107; for Philonic evidence Harris 1976:75-76. "Lampon's endeavours to escape the office were quite usual and must not be regarded as a calumny on Philo's part" (Tcherikover-Fuks 1956/ 64: 2.70). In cities with several gymnasia several gymnasiarchs could be employed at the same time (Delia 1991:107). An important duty of their office was to control the civic rights of their *alumni*, and for that reason they were "the natural champions of the Alexandrian nationalists, and so we may easily understand why persons known as fanatical demagogues were regarded as suited for the office" (*ibid.*).

In the *Acts of the Alexandrian Martyrs* Lampo's companion Isidorus is also mentioned repeatedly as an Alexandrian gymnasiarch (*CPJ* 156a 2.3, 156b 2.34, 156d 3.11). On the question of whether or not their term was limited see Box 1939:115-116. For a list of gymnasiarchs in Roman Egypt see Sijpestijn 1986.

It may have been ... his illegal actions: Philo implies here that Lampo's attempt to avoid the office was discreditable on either supposition: Either he was rich and mean or, if he was not rich, he had pretended to be rich; so rightly Colson 1941:375 note *a*. Roos 1935:241 wants to read ὅσα <δ'> ἐκτήσατο: "he appeared not to be a very wealthy man, but whatever he did possess he had acquired practically all from his criminal actions."

§131. *For he used to stand by the governors ... the rank of an introducer*: The mss. have δικάζοιντο but Cohn's conjecture δικάζοιεν has been generally accepted (in view of δικάζοντας in §133). For "he took minutes" the Greek has ὑπεμνηματίζετο, so Lampo was ὑπομνηματογράφος (or εἰσαγωγεύς; see below). Ὑπομνηματισμοί ("memoranda, minutes") were the official reports of proceedings taken by clerks attached to the officials in charge. Box 1939:116-117 quotes at length from a papyrus copy of such a memorandum (*BGU* V.114, from the year 117 CE). The difficult phrase εἰσάγων ὡς ἔχων τάξιν has given rise to understandable doubts about its correctness. Mangey suggested εἰσάγων ὡς ἔχοιεν τάξιν ("introducing them as they came in order"), but Box's paleographically ingenious εἰσαγωγέως ἔχων τάξιν ("having the rank of an introducer") has more to say for it, εἰσαγωγεύς being the technical term (as attested in papyri and inscriptions) for the official who brought cases into court, wrote the reports, and saw to it that these were put into an archive (on these archives in Graeco-Roman Egypt see Rupprecht 1994:139-140). Lucian, *Apol.* 12, describes this function as follows: "the introduction of court-cases (τὰς δίκας εἰσάγειν) and their arrangement (τάξιν), the recording (ὑπομνήματα γράφεσθαι) of all that is done and said, guiding counsel in their speeches, keeping the clearest and most accurate copy of the president's decisions in all faithfulness, and putting them on public record to be preserved for all time" (see Whitehorne 1987 and Thür 1997). So the reading proposed by Box 1939:117 and supported by Colson 1941:536 and Pelletier 1967:164-165 has a very good chance of being original, although the mss.' reading is not entirely impossible.

***he would deliberately expunge* ...**: Of course what was written during the session in court was only a draft. Thereafter the official had to work out his stenographic notes so as to make a readable copy for deposition in the archive. It was at this stage that Lampo began to doctor the documents.

documents: All mss. read here πράγματα, only the excerpt in John of Damascus' *Sacra Parallella* has retained the original γράμματα. For other instances of the confusion between γράμματα and πράγματα in the manuscript tradition of Philo see Reiter 1915:xlii.

this tamperer: For γραμματοκύφων see the note *ad* §20 (*init.*).

to charge money: The suggestion is, of course, that Lampo was so thoroughly corrupt that he would change documents at will if he was being paid enough in bribes; see also the end of §132.

every stroke of his pen: κεραίαν ἑκάστην. A κεραία, lit. "horn," is a hook as part of a letter, a serif; it is often used in the sense of something quite insignificant or trivial (BDAG *s.v.*); e.g., Dio Chrysostom 31.86; Matt. 5:18; Lk. 16:17.

§132. ***the pen-murderer***: καλαμοσφάκτης is a *hapax* in Greek literature. Philo says that this "accurate and well-chosen expression" was coined by "the whole people unanimously," a hyperbole for the many Alexandrians who were duped by Lampo's malversations. For εὐθυβόλως ("accurately"), as adverb first attested in Philo, see Winston & Dillon 1983:314.

by the things he wrote ... property of others: Philo uses all his rhetorical skill to make clear to his readers that Lampo was an absolutely unscrupulous personality whose only real interest was self-enrichment. The verb ἐπευωνίζειν originally meant "to make cheaper, to lower the price of something." Philo uses it several times but often there is no special emphasis on the element of cheapness (e.g., *Cher.* 123; *Prob.* 37). Here, too, Philo does not want to stress that Lampo sold other people's property for a low price, for the point is precisely his great greed. Hence the translation "peddled."

§133. ***it was impossible* ...**: Hence the "crowd of secretaries" that §3 speaks of in this connection.

received the calculations of the revenues and taxes: See the notes on "matters pertaining to financial accountancy and the administration of revenues" in §4, and Rupprecht 1994:74-82.

§134. *to guard the most important archives* ...: Lit. "the most essential deposit" (ἀναγκαιοτάτη παρακαταθήκη). Of course these were the judicial archives since the sentences contained therein often were matters of life and death. These sentences are called here "the most sacred verdicts" since being supposedly based upon a strict administration of justice they were on principle unalterable. And this is exactly the area where Lampo badly went astray by "making misuse of the forgetfulness of the judges for his own profit." For "he made misuse" the Greek text has ἐνεπορεύετο, which can have the neutral sense of "carrying on business, being engaged in buying and selling" (e.g., *Contempl.* 89, *Congr.* 112), but is sometimes used, as here, in the more pejorative meaning of "exploiting" (e.g., in 2 Pet. 2:3).

his accursed fee, more properly described as hire: The difference between μισθός and μίσθωμα is probably that, although both are in themselves *voces mediae*, the latter was more easily used in pejorative contexts (for instance, what was paid to a prostitute). Kraus 1994:491 says: "Philo is distinguishing between an arbitrary, spontaneous award (μισθός) and a contractual 'rent' (μίσθωμα) which highlights the conspirational and habitual character of Lampo's immorality."

§135. *Such was the Lampo who now appeared as an accuser*: τοιοῦτος ὢν ἐφειστήκει κατήγορος. The contrast between "such" (τοιοῦτος) a despicable person and someone with the moral right to act as an "accuser" (κατήγορος) is brought to the fore here.

Isidorus: On Isidorus see the notes *ad* §20.

his equal in wickedness ... a sort of squadrons: In this extremely negative portrait of Isidorus, Philo attempts to picture him as the arch-rioter of Alexandria; cf. his use of "city-troublemaker" (ταραξίπολις) for Isidorus in §20. Even though as a gymnasiarch of the city Isidorus was certainly a highly respected person among the Alexandrian Greeks, Philo suggests that this man was intent on stimulating constant rioting in the city (στάσεις καὶ θορύβους κατασκευάσαι) for which purpose he mobilized and even organized the worst rabble of the city (ὄχλον ἀσύντακτον καὶ πεφορημένον ἐκ μιγάδων καὶ συγκλύδων ἡρμοσμένον); cf. Sevenster 1975:23; Feldman 1993:115. The word συμμορίαι here is apparently a technical term for committees or another sort of official body (note the formulation καθάπερ τινὰς συμμορίας) the nature of which remains vague, although the context suggests something like "squadrons" (see MacMullen 1964:181); for papyrological evidence see Box 1939:118 (e.g., *P.Tebt.* 316); for epigraphical evidence Graf 1985:407 note 20. On the organizational function of these bodies in riot settings see especially Bergmann & Hoffmann 1987:34-35. Undoubtedly, Isidorus functioned as the patron of many members of "his" clubs; see Seland 1995:87.

§136. *clubs* (θίασοι): See on the various clubs in Alexandria the notes *ad* §4 and the bibliography given there; on this passage esp. Seland 1996:112-3; Gager 1983:48. For literature on θίασοι see *RBLG* 304.

not something sound: οὐδὲν ὑγιές. Here ὑγιής does not have a medical sense — Philo is not worried by the bad effects of alcohol on one's health — but, as often in Philo, an ethical one; it is about correct and responsible thinking and behaving; see BDAG 1023 for references to other ancient authors. Cf., e.g., δόξα ὑγιής for "right-mindedness" in §170, and λόγος ὑγιής in Tit. 2:8.

to drink liquor, be drunk, behave as a drunkard: Philo's great abhorrence of anything that has to do with drunken behavior is spelled out in detail in his *De plantatione* and *De ebrietate*. It is certainly true that meals and drinking-bouts played a significant role in the life of the many clubs and associations, even if their primary purpose was of a religious nature (Borgen 1997:170-171). "The religious side was often left very much in the background" (Colson 1941:537).

the offspring of these, insolence: ἡ τούτων ἔκγονος ὕβρις. On *hybris* see Fisher 1992 and the rich bibliography in *RBLG* 498. Nowhere else does Philo use the word *hybris* as frequently as in *Flacc*.: this is the 10th occurrence (it also occurs in §§40, 58, 59, 77, 79, 91, 95, 104, 117, 173). For the traditional connection between *hybris* and drinking see Fisher 1992 Index s.v. "drink and *hybris*."

'synods' and 'couches': σύνοδοι καὶ κλῖναι. Associations with these names are attested in papyri and inscriptions from Egypt (Hagedorn 2000:91 and 119). Well-known is the invitation to attend the dinner party at the table (κλίνη) of Sarapis in *P.Oxy*. 110 (2nd cent. CE). Also attested are πρωτοκλίναρχοι of associations of worshipers of Isis etc. (Bell 1939:118); cf. συμποσίαρχος and κλινάρχης in §137. Colson 1941:537 suggests that originally κλίνη referred to the couch on which the divine statue was laid, but that remains uncertain.

§137. *'symposiarch,' table president, city-troublemaker*: ὁ συμποσίαρχος, ὁ κλινάρχης, ὁ ταραξίπολις. For ταραξίπολις see the note *ad* §20 (the only other occurrence of the word). Συμποσίαρχος means "leader of the symposium" (here in the original sense of "drinking party;" contrast the metaphorical use in *Somn.* 2.249); κλινάρχης is more or less synonymous. Note that elsewhere the Alexandrian clubs are called συσσίτια (e.g., Cassius Dio 78.23.3), another term in which the original notion of "eating together" had faded into the background (see Buraselis 1995:173-180). That Philo places these three designations asyndetically next to each other is because he wants to suggest that being a symposiarch or klinarch is tantamount to being a city-rioter.

§138. *afterwards he no longer had that favorable position*: This vague remark most probably refers to Flaccus' closure of the political clubs of Alexandria (see §4) in which Isidorus had played such a leading role (§137); see Hennig 1974:432.

the scum of humanity: τοὺς ἀλειφοβίους. The rare word ἀλειφόβιος is of uncertain meaning. LSJ *s.v.* gives "one that lives by anointing" and (generally) "poor". There are only two other occurrences, one in an unclear fragment of Aristophanes (fr. 766), the other in the late lexicographer Hesychius who explains it as "poor." Colson 1941:537 and De Vries 1999:97-98 regard it as a derogatory term for unemployed people hanging around all day in or near the gymnasium and and trying to make a living by offering their services to the wrestlers who had to be anointed.

those who used to be vociferant ...: For φωνασκεῖν (lit. "exercising the voice") see Colson 1941:378 note *b*. Philo here probably refers to the supporting shouts and yellings by the ἀλειφόβιοι during the athletic contests in the gymnasium. That they "sell their shouts as in a market" probably means that they receive some money from the sporting combatants for their vocal support (after having helped with their anointing?).

he ordered them to assemble at the gymnasium: Cf. Acts 19:28-40, where Demetrius the silversmith assembles his supporters in the theatre of Ephesus (on the comparable functions of gymnasia and theatres see the notes *ad* §34).

§139. *they began to accuse Flaccus for no reason at all*: One is reminded here of what Seneca says about Egypt, "a province that is clever at insulting its rulers" (*Ad Helv. matr.* 19). Huzar 1988:637 remarks that in Roman Alexandria "verbal abuse, especially of Roman officials, was frequent and developed to a high level of insults" (with further references in note 87).

stringing together falsehoods spun out in anapaests: ψευδεῖς ῥήσεις δι' ἀναπαίστων καὶ μακρὰς συνείροντες. This is at first sight a somewhat enigmatic statement. Anapaest is the designation of a metrical verse form consisting of series of two short syllables and a long one (a reversed dactylus). But in later authors it is also used for "ribald or satirical songs," see LSJ *s.v.* II 2, who refer to Cassius Dio 65.8 (again about Alexandrians!) and Plutarch, *Pericles* 33 for this meaning; see also Box 1939:118, Colson 1941:537 and Pelletier 1967:130-131 note 2 for some further evidence; for more literature see *RBLG* 173. This "ribald doggerel" (Colson's translation) need not have been anapaestic in the strict sense. "The Greek ear could find in certain metres and rhythms, as in music, something undignified and suited to burlesque, and these are called anapaestic, presumably because anapaests often predominated in them" (Colson 1941:537). The whole scene is reminiscent of §34. For "stringing together falsehoods" cf. Dio Chrysostom 32.9: "stringing together (συνείροντες) rough jokes and much tittle-tattle" (in an Alexandrian setting!).

neither had the rest of the city's inhabitants, as they knew quite well: As Box 1939:118 rightly remarks, the Greek phrase μήτε τὴν ἄλλην πόλιν εὖ εἰδότες πλημμεληθεῖσαν is somewhat odd, for one expects τήν τε ἄλλην πόλιν εὖ εἰδότες μὴ πλημμεληθεῖσαν, but it is the first μήτε that suggested a second one by association; see also Colson 1941:379 note *d*.

§140. *Then, after deliberation, ... had taken place*: Whatever the historicity of Philo's report here may be, this whole paragraph has the rhetorical function of demonstrating that proof of the bribery and other machinations of Isidorus *cum suis* was not at all hard to find — the arrested persons even "confessed the truth without having to be put to torture!"

§141. *the inhabitants of the city found it unbearable that its reputation should be blemished by the stupidity of some individuals*: τῆς πόλεως χαλεπῶς φερούσης ἐπὶ τῷ τὴν ἐνίων ἀγνωμοσύνην προσαναμάττεσθαι τοὔνομ' αὐτῆς, lit. "the city bore with pain the fact that its name received the impression [= smirch] of the stupidity of some." But the text is as uncertain as is its interpretation. The mss. are in disorder here, as the *app. crit.* in the Cohn-Wendland edition (vol. VI 146) clearly shows, and Mangey conjectured ἔτι τῆς τῶν ἐνίων ἀγνωμοσύνης προσαναμάττεσθαι τοὔνομ' αὐτῇ. But Box 1939:119 objected that ἔτι hardly makes sense, that changing the cases of two words is too drastic, and that the use of τοὔνομα with a double genitive (the reputation of someone for something) is dubious, the latter being an unjust objection because Mangey's conjecture does not imply that. With the other editors Box adopts the text as printed above and translates, "the city grievously resented her name incurring in addition the want of sense of a few" (cf. Pelletier 1967:131: "la cité supportait mal que pour la sottise de quelques-uns sa réputation fût éclaboussée"). The sense of the *hapax* προσαναμάττεσθαι (which occurs further only in *Aet.* 59, where Colson translates it by "to reflect") has to be derived from the middle voice of ἀναμάσσω, "to receive an impression," the prefix προσ- probably indicating that "the loss of reputation was an addition to the actual inconvenience caused by the uproar" (Colson 1941:379 note *e*). The question of whether τὴν ἐνίων ἀγνωμοσύνην or τοὔνομα αὐτῆς is the grammatical subject of προσαναμάττεσθαι depends not only upon the meaning of the verb but also upon whether one takes it to be medial or passive. LSJ takes it to be medial and translates by "to besmirch in addition" clearly implying that ἀγνωμοσύνην is the subject. In an Appendix *ad locum*, Colson 1941:537 too argues on the basis of occurrences of other compounds of -μάττομαι in Philo that usually these are in the middle voice but with the meaning of "receiving an impression of," implying that τοὔνομα is the subject. In spite of these philological uncertainties the general sense of the phrase is clear.

decided to summon: μεταπεμψαμένῳ is the generally accepted conjecture for the mss.'s μεταπεμψάμενον.

the most respectable of the citizens: τὸ καθαρώτατον τοῦ δήμου, lit. "the purest section of the population," a very snobbish expression. Philo identifies this group with "the magistrates" (see next note) and again appeals to the interests of the social élites of the city.

the magistrates: οἱ ἐν τέλει, local municipal officials. See the note *ad* §4. Box 1939:119 refers to the list of officials in *P.Oxy.* 1412, but that document is from the year 284 CE.

the whole city, except ...: De Vries 1999:73 translates "the whole city, even the group ..." I do not think ἔξω has that sense here. Even though it can occasionally mean "besides," here it would not make sense.

§142. *this fine service*: Another instance of the ironic use of καλός; see *ad* §74.

on his account: δι' αὐτόν probably refers to Flaccus: it was in order to get rid of him that Isidorus distributed money and wine to the rioters. But Colson 1941:378 note 1 follows the only manuscript that reads δι' αὐτῶν and translates by "... and had employed them to supply both money and wine ...," taking the αὐτῶν to be the people hired by Isidorus, which sounds a bit lame.

§143. *always envious of the prosperous and an enemy of law and order*: ἀεὶ τοῖς εὖ πράττουσι βασκαίνων καὶ εὐνόμῳ καταστάσει πολέμιος. The point is here that even the people who had been bribed by Isidorus accuse him of the basest of motives, not only the seditiousness so much stressed by Philo in the preceding paragraphs (e.g., §135), but now also envy of the more well-to-do; for the motif of the envy of "the Egyptians" see §29. For εὐνόμῳ καταστάσει πολέμιος see also Philo's comments in *Conf*. 109.

§144. *the bystanders*: In §141 Philo has said that "the whole city" was present. Box 1939:119 finds οἱ παρατυγχάνοντες "a feeble word" for the whole city, which is true, but probably Philo had in the meantime forgotten this exaggeration.

what was being said ... of the accused: Instead of waiting for an examination of the accusations, the citizens have the impression that these are correct and ask for punishment. Τύποι ἀρίδηλοι τῆς τοῦ κατηγορουμένου προαιρέσεως implies that the accusations gave a reliable enough image (for this use of τύπος cf. *Legat*. 178) of Isidorus' hidden intentions to condemn him straightaway.

'Disfranchise him!' ... 'Banish him!' ... 'Kill him!': ἀτιμοῦν, φυγαδεύειν, αἴρειν. The verb ἀτιμοῦν (lit. "to dishonor") here has the meaning of "to deprive of the privilege of citizenship" (see the lit. mentioned in *RBLG* 203). Αἴρειν in the sense of ἀναιρεῖν (not from the same verb!), "to kill, to destroy," is also found in Josephus, *Ant*. 19.17 (note the variation with ἀναιρεῖν in 19.20); Matt. 24:39; John 19:15; more references in BDAG 28-29.

wormed his way into state affairs: διέκυψεν ἐπὶ τὰ κοινά. It is difficult to determine the precise significance of the verb here, as Box 1939: 119 says. Διακύπτειν originally meant "to stoop through something," and develops the sense of "to stoop so as to peep in." Hence Pelletier's translation "a jeté un regard par sa fenêtre sur les affaires publiques" (1967:133). In the 20 other instances of this word in Philo (see *Index* s.v.) it always means "to have a closer look at," but that would yield too weak a sentence here. Hence I follow Colson 1941: 380-381 note *a*, in his suggestion that it must convey here the stronger sense of "worming one's way into something" or "put one's nose into something," which seems "a fairly natural development from the original meaning." See further *RBLG* 236 (lit. on διακύπτειν).

he caused the whole city to become diseased: Literally, "he left no part of the city in a healthy condition" (μηδὲν μέρος τῆς πόλεως ἄνοσον ἐάσαντα).

§145. *Because of his bad conscience*: Lit., "because of his conscience," but in later literature τὸ συνειδός often has the sense of "bad conscience," e.g., Josephus, *Ant.* 16.102; see BDAG *s.v.* σύνοιδα 2. The sense of "bad conscience" is in most cases evident from the context; see Klauck 1994:50. Literature on conscience is mentioned *ad* §7.

Flaccus took ... sedition and intrigue: It is hard to say how Philo knew what exactly motivated (νομίσας) Flaccus' decision to leave the matter at that, but his point is that the decision was mistaken in the sense that Flaccus mistakenly thought he was safe now: Isidorus would later reveal himself to be his worst and most fatal enemy. Therein Philo sees the hand of Justice; see §146.

§§146-161: *Flaccus on Trial*

God's Justice saw to it that Flaccus stood trial and was condemned. His property was confiscated and he himself sentenced for deportation to the miserable island of Andros in the Aegean Sea. His journey to Andros was an unbearable humiliation because the people who had seen him on his way to assume the honored office of governor of Egypt now saw him back as an dishonored deportee. Philo sketches Flaccus' journey in detail and stretches out the whole trip as a rhetorical device enabling him to highlight time and again the effectiveness of the retribution by God's Justice. Again the emphasis is on humiliation, which "to sensible people is even worse than death" (147).

§146. *Justice, who oversees human affairs*: On personified Δίκη see the note *ad* §104. The motif that Justice watches over human affairs is found also in *Jos.* 170, *Dec.* 95, 177, *Spec.* 3.19, 129; see Borgen 1999:308. Note that in §121 it is said of God that he is the one "who oversees all human affairs." So "Justice" is here, as elsewhere in Philo, nothing but a personified function of God; see Van der Horst 1999: 250-252; extensive bibliography in *RBLG* 242.

For those ... far worse: It is divine Justice who saw to it that the one who had brought the worst possible afflictions upon the Jewish people is now undergoing the worst possible afflictions himself as well.

§147. *He, the ruler, was accused by his subjects*: Philo unfortunately does not tell us of what Flaccus was accused. In his interior monologue in §173 Flaccus himself says that he was accused and condemned because of his crimes against the Jews, but that is, of course, Philo's theological interpretation of the events and does not inform us about the real charges, which certainly "differed significantly from Philo's own interpretation" (Niehoff 2001:41). Philo's silence about the charges might be due to the fact that they had nothing to do with the Jews. But see also the following note.

he also received a very tough verdict: As Box 1939:119 points out, we may get an idea of the situation from what we are told by Cassius Dio 59.4.3: "[Gaius] put an end to the charges of *maiestas*, but nevertheless he made these the cause of a great many persons' downfall. Again, though, according to his own account, he had given up his anger against those who had conspired against his father and mother and brothers, and even burned their letters, he yet put to death great numbers of them on the strength of those letters." But, as Philo himself indicates in §9, in Flaccus' case it was probably the combination of his pro-Gemellus position and his stance against Gaius' mother that ruined him. There can be little doubt that Flaccus was condemned by Caligula on charges which were wholly unrelated to his persecution of the Jews; his accusers, Jew-haters themselves, no doubt realized that such a charge could have grave repercussions on their own group (Delaunay 1870:254-255 note 1; Balsdon 1934:134). Failure to keep peace and order probably formed part of the charges brought against Flaccus as well (probably by his erstwhile "friends" Isidorus and Lampo; see Gruen 2002:61). This, however, certainly does not exclude the possibility that Flaccus was sentenced partly also as a result of the memorandum sent by Agrippa I to Gaius about the fact that Flaccus withheld the Jewish declaration of loyalty (see my note on §97; Sijpesteijn 1964:94 note 24; Yavetz 1997:107 says the charge was "Verrat am römischen Reich," which is wholly unfounded). The fact that Philo does not tell us what took place at the trial is probably to be explained from his conviction of the divine character of Flaccus' punishment (Kraus 1994:483). Even if Gaius condemned Flaccus on account of his role in the prosecution of his mother and in the succession of Tiberius, in Philo's view it is still true that at a deeper level God punishes him for his misdeeds against the Jews.

ridicule by his exulting enemies: Being ridiculed, especially by one's enemies, was felt by the ancients as a defamation of one's honor to a far greater degree than in modern times; see Malina 1981:25-50; Cairns 1993 (on the origins of the Greek honor and shame culture); Barton 2001. In their turn, Lampo and Isidorus were condemned to death in 41 by the emperor Claudius (see the notes *ad* §20).

To sensible people this is even worse than death: With οἱ εὖ φρονοῦντες Philo means (aristocratic) persons with a highly developed sense of honor and dignity (see the previous note).

§148. *a rich harvest of misery*, εὐφορία κακοπραγιῶν. The noun εὐφορία means "fertility, abundant produce," so the image is one of a very rich crop that is harvested by the one who had sown the seeds of his own misery.

he was immediately deprived of all his possessions: Loss of all property is mentioned repeatedly in ancient sources as the punishment for persons convicted of *maiestas* in the early Roman Empire; see e.g. Tacitus, *Ann.* 3.50.6; 3.68.2; 4.21.5. It often went hand in hand with the *aquae et ignis interdictio*, the legal prohibition of access to drinking water and fire which was tantamount to banishment or capital punishment. See *OCD* s.v. "Punishment, Greek and Roman practice." But apparently, "Flaccus retained enough to buy an estate in Andros (§168)" (Box 1939:120).

He was a man who took special delight in beautiful things ...: Is this remark the comment of an eye-witness? The description of the exquisite nature of Flaccus' possessions may be compared to what Philo says, in a more critical vein, about "Italian luxury" in *Contempl.* 48-49: "Sets of three or more couches made of tortoiseshell or ivory or even more valuable material, most of them inlaid with precious stones; coverlets purple-dyed with gold interwoven, others brocaded with flower patterns in all sorts of colours to allure the eye; a host of drinking cups set out in their several kinds, beakers, stoops, tankards, other goblets of many shapes, very artistically and elaborately chased by scientific craftsmen." Cf. also Juvenal, *Sat.* 10.27.

§149. *Aside from that, there was his staff of household slaves... absolutely second to none*: Cf. *Contempl.* 50 (still a part of the description of "Italian luxury"): "For waiting there are slaves of the utmost comliness and beauty, giving the idea that they have come not so much to render service as to give pleasure to the eyes of the beholders by their appearance on the scene. Some of them who are still boys pour the wine, while the water is carried by full-grown lads fresh from the bath and smooth shaven, with their faces smeared with cosmetics and paint under the eyelids and the hair of the head prettily plaited and tightly bound. Etc." Here the emphasis lies more on the outer beauty whereas in the passage under discussion it is more "the perfect way in which they perform their services" which is stressed.

§150. *a great number of properties belonging to condemned persons were sold by public auction*: δημόπρατος is a hapax legomenon in Greek literature, but apparently with the same meaning as the more common δημιόπρατος (put for sale at a public auction). What Philo describes here was the official procedure in the Roman Empire; see Millar 1977:163-174.

that of Flaccus alone was reserved for the emperor: ταμιεύεσθαι ("to store up") is also used in the famous letter of Claudius to the Alexandrians (41 CE), where he says that "I have within me a store (ταμιευόμενος) of immutable indignation against those who renewed the conflict" (*CPJ* 153, 77-78). The emphatic position of μόνην here underlines the exceptional nature of this procedure.

except a few items so as to avoid transgression of the law ...: τὸν ἐπὶ τοῖς οὕτως ἑαλωκόσι τεθέντα νόμον refers probably to the *Lex Julia* of 46 BCE which provided the penalty of *aquae et ignis interdictio* in case of *maiestas*. "Seizure and sale on behalf of the *aerarium* of the property was a logical corollary if not an actual judicial sentence" (Box 1939: 121). Actually all of Flaccus' possessions had to be sold at a public auction, but apparently because of the precious nature of his property most of it went directly to the emperor except for a few pieces in order to retain a semblance of justice (on this practice of reserving especially valuable items of *bona damnatorum* for the emperor see Millar 1977:163-174, esp. 167-168). Some sources mention the fact that Gaius, who was always in need of money, purposely sentenced many people to banishment or death in order to confiscate their possessions; see Cassius Dio 59.10.6-11.5; 59.15.6; 59.21.4; and cf. *Legat.* 341. Millar 1977:168, however, also suggests that the few articles excepted may have been kept by the condemned persons themselves (note that later on Flaccus is able to buy a small house on Andros, §168). See further Box 1939:121 and De Vries 1999:98.

§151. *he was sentenced to deportation*: κατέγνωστο αὐτοῦ φυγή. Φυγή is the equivalent of the Latin *deportatio*, banishment. To the penalty of *aquae et ignis interdictio* sometimes a specific place of confinement was added, as is attested, e.g., by Tacitus, *Ann.* 3.68.2, "He [Piso, under Tiberius] declared that Silanus ought to be outlawed from water and fire and to be banished to the island of Gyarus" (aqua atque igni Silano interdicendum censuit ipsumque in insulam Gyarum relegandum). Note that Flaccus, too, was first banished to Gyarus/Gyara (see further below in this paragraph). *OLD*, s.v. "*aqua*" 5h, lists many passages where forbidding the use of water and fire as one of the necessities of life is the judicial means of excluding a person from human society, of outlawing him or her.

He was banished from the whole mainland ... in which people can prosper: After the description of Flaccus' prosperity and exquisite possessions in the previous paragraph, his banishment to a place as far as possible from where people prosper is a glaring contrast, in which Philo sees the hand of God's Justice.

the most miserable of all the islands ... Gyara: Gyara (or Gyaros) is a small rock-island in the Aegaean that served as a kind of Roman St. Helena (just like Amorgos and Andros). It lies between Keos and Andros, off the coast of Attica. It was a poor and barren island that was inhabited only by a handful of fishermen. It became proverbial as the spot to which criminals or suspected persons were banished by the Roman emperors; see the references in Kalcyk 1998. The modern name of the island is Yioura.

had Lepidus not interceded: This is M. Aemilius Lepidus, husband of Drusilla (Gaius' sister who died earlier that year; see the note *ad* §56), who was put to death by Gaius in 39 CE in connection with the conspiracy of Lentulus Gaetulicus; see Suetonius, *Claud.* 9; Cassius Dio 59.22.7; Barrett 1989:106-111, and cf. Sherwin-White 1972:827.

Thanks to him he could exchange Gyara for nearby Andros: There are more known instances of an exchange of the place of banishment. Note, e.g., that the above quoted passage from Tacitus, *Ann.* 3.68, continues with the remark that Tiberius said that "Gyarus was a dreary and uninhabited island, and that, as a concession to the Junian family and to a man of the same order as themselves, they might let him retire by preference to Cythnus" (3.69). For Andros as a place for banished persons see Box 1939:121 and Pelletier 1967:137 note 6 (Tacitus, *Ann.* 15.71 in combination with the inscriptions in *Syll.* 811-812); further Kalcyk 1996 and Saffrey-Segonds 2001:121 note 5. In spite of the bad reputation Andros had in antiquity, today it is a pleasant place to live or spend one's holidays.

§152. *Then he had to travel again ... but this time in complete dishonor.* Here μεστὸν ἀτιμίας stands in sharp contrast to μέγα πνέοντα καὶ τὸν ὄγκον τῆς εὐτυχίας ἐπιδεικνύμενον (see on the rhetorical device of *antiphrasis* Anderson 2000:23 and cf. Quintilian 9.2.47). For the use of πνέειν to express moods and emotions see the note *ad* §124. In the fact that Flaccus is now watched by the same people who had boosted his pride when he was on his way to Egypt, whichs adds greatly to his ἀτιμία, Philo sees divine providence at work. On the great role of the notions of honor and dishonor in the ancient Mediterranean world see the note *ad* §147 (on "ridicule...").

§153. *Pointed at with the finger.* δακτυλοδεικτούμενος, a gesture implying loss of honor and dignity; see *RBLG* 230.

insulted though he was, he felt oppressed by even heavier afflictions caused by the total reversal of his fortune: ὀνειδιζόμενος τῆς ἀθρόας μεταβολῆς πιέζεται βαρυτέραις ἀνίαις. The problem here is that some translators take τῆς ἀθρόας μεταβολῆς as the complement to ὀνειδιζόμενος and render, "reproached for his complete change of fortune" (Box 1939:55), but as Colson 1941:384 note *b* remarks, ὀνειδίζομαι is usually followed not by a genitive but by an *accusativus rei*, and complete change of fortune is hardly a matter for reproach. In my translation I follow Colson's interpretation, but yet another possibility is taking the genitive τῆς ἀθρόας μεταβολῆς as a *genitivus comparativus*: "He was oppressed by afflictions which were even heavier than the total reversal of his fortune," namely the fact that "his misery was constantly being renewed and rekindled by additions of fresh evils." The latter solution is proposed in the translation by Gerschmann 1964:159. I prefer Colson's view since it implies that the finger-pointing and insults "affected him comparatively little, because the sense of ruin occupied his mind" (1941:385), which seems quite logical.

for his misery was constantly being renewed: καινουμένης is Mangey's convincing conjecture for the mss.'s corrupt κινουμένης.

evils which ... seemed to have been dimmed: For "(evils) which, as in the case of recurring diseases, forcibly bring back also the memories of former disasters" Cohn-Wendland's edition has, with the mss., ἃ καθάπερ ἐν ταῖς νόσοις ὑποτροπιάζειν ἀναγκάζει καὶ τὰς τῶν ἀρχαίων κακοπραγιῶν ὑπομνήσεις. Mangey objected to ὑποτροπιάζειν ἀναγκάζει and conjectured ὑποτροπιαζούσαις ἀνάγει, which is adopted by both Box and Pelletier but rejected by Colson and Gerschmann. As in §182, ὑποτροπιάζειν is a medical term for the recurrence of diseases and this favors Mangey's ὑποτροπιαζούσαις. What Philo seems to say here is that the constant renewal of evils which befell Flaccus did not leave time for the former evils to fade out because they perforce evoked memories of the old ones. It is, he says, as with recurring diseases which also constantly evoke (ἀνάγει) the memories of the previous phases of the disease. Since this comparison only makes sense if he speaks of recurring diseases (not of just diseases in general), it would seem that νόσοις needs a qualification such as Mangey's ὑποτροπιαζούσαις. The position of καί before τὰς τῶν ἀρχαίων κακοπραγιῶν ὑπομνήσεις instead of before ὑποτροπιαζούσαις ἀνάγει (or ἀναγκάζει, although ἀνάγει seems more appropriate) is a "slight difficulty" (Colson 1941:387; not "absurd" as Box 1939:121 has it); it is surely not Philo's best. On Philo's medical knowledge see Hogan 1992:191-207 and Sly 1996:154-166. Philo's exposure to medical notions "was certainly facilitated by the environment of Alexandria which had become the capital of medicine under Herophilus" (Niehoff 2001:18 note 5).

§154. *the Ionian Gulf*: ὁ Ἰόνιος κόλπος is the designation of the waters between Italy and the Balkan peninsula. The expression is often used as an alternative to "Adriatic Sea" and sometimes extended to include all of the sea east of Sicily.

the sea which extends to Corinth: ἡ ἄχρι Κορίνθου θάλαττα designates the strait which is now called the Gulf of Corinth.

the Peloponnesian coastal cities: Here the cities on the northern coast of the Peloponnesus are meant, such as Dyme, Patrae, Aegium, Aegeira; see Strabo 8.7.4 [386-7].

the sudden reversal of his fortune: Cf. *Praem.* 169: "The reversal of everything will be sudden, God will turn the curses against the enemies of these penitents, the enemies who rejoiced in the misfortunes of the nation and mocked and railed at them."

For whenever he disembarked ... out of sympathy: Note the elitist antithesis between the common people who are here called the μοχθηροί τὰς φύσεις ἐθελοκακοῦντες and the more noble natures οἷς ἔθος ταῖς ἑτέρων τύχαις σωφρονίζεσθαι, where the verb σωφρονίζεσθαι can mean both "to be sobered," "to be chastened" and "to draw a wise lesson from something." It is a favorite word of Philo; the *Philo Index* lists 34 instances.

§155. *From Lechaion he crossed the Isthmus to the opposite sea*: Lechaion is the north-western harbor town of Corinth. Flaccus disembarked there to cross the land over the isthmus between the Corinthian and the Saronic Gulf, which forms the connection between the Peloponnesian peninsula and the mainland of Greece.

arrived at Cenchraeae, the port of Corinth: Cenchraeae is the eastern harbor town of Corinth, situated at the Saronic Gulf.

did not permit him the smallest respite: For this use of ἀναχώρησις cf. *Spec.* 1.58: "Some labour under a madness carried to such an extravagant extent that they do not leave themselves any means of escape (ἀναχώρησις) to repentance."

a small merchant vessel: On ὁλκάς see the note on §26.

only with great difficulty did he arrive storm-tossed at the Piraeus: μόλις ἄχρι τοῦ Πειραιῶς κατασύρεται. Piraeus is the harbor town of Athens in the eastern part of the Saronic Gulf. Κατασύρεσθαι ("to be dragged along, swept away"), often used by Philo (19 x), "would naturally suggest a rapid passage, the reverse of μόλις" (Colson 1941:387 note *b*), but here the verb explains μόλις in the sense that Flaccus reached the Piraeus only with great difficulty for the simple reason that he kept being swept or tossed around by the storm, almost adrift, all of the time.

§156. *as far as Cape Sounion*: Sounion or Sunium is the southernmost part of Attica including the promontory with its famous temples of Poseidon and Athena.

continued along the series of islands there: τὰς ἑξῆς λοιπὸν ἐπεραιοῦτο νήσους. Box 1939:122 says it is impossible that ἐπεραιοῦτο means "crossed" (which is the usual meaning, as in §154 περαιωσάμενος δὲ τὸν Ἰόνιον κόλπον, and elsewhere in Philo) because that would not make sense here, while the sense required ("to sail along, to pass by") would be unparallelled. Pelletier 1967:165 devotes an excursus to this problem and argues that what is implied here is that "tout le trajet depuis l'entrée dans le golfe de Corinthe jusqu'à Andros lui apparait comme un défilé où il avançait entre deux rangés de terres hostiles" (with reference to §§160 and 174). This seems a bit far-fetched. It would seem more likely that Philo uses the verb rather carelessly here (or does it mean that he sailed *in between* the islands?).

Helena, Kia, Kythnos: Helena is modern Makronisi. Kia is Keos, modern Kea; on the different spellings of this name in antiquity see Reiter 1915:lviii. Kythnos still bears that name. All three islands are situated to the south-east of Cape Sounion.

all the others that lie in a row one after the other: That row could consist of Syros, Rheneia, Mykonos and Tenos. Box 1939:122 also suggests Seriphos, Siphnos, Paros, Naxos, Mykonos and Tenos, but that would seem an unnecessary detour. But in a sense the same objection could be raised against the first "row," and Box plausibly suggests "that the journey is prolonged in Philo's imagination in order to exhibit Flaccus to as many places as possible" (1939:xlviii note 5). In view of the inconsistencies with what is said in §174 (see the comments *ad locum*) one might surmise that "the journey is staged as a gauntlet for Flaccus to run, the divine recompense for the gauntlet of spectators which the condemned Jews ran to the theatre of Alexandria" (*ibid.*).

the island of the Andrians: Andros, some 100 kilometers east of Athens.

§157. *his tears seemed to come from a fountain*: The metaphor of a πηγή as the source of a stream of tears is especially frequent in the Greek tragedians; see LSJ *s.v.* I 2.

Beating his breast: A traditional sign of great grief, see Lk. 18:13, 23:48 etc.

My guards and escorts, ...: Philo here uses the rhetorical device of προσωποποιΐα (or ἠθοποιΐα), introducing a specific character and letting him or her speak. Ancient orators found this device especially suiting to the portrayal of characters and emotions; see, e.g., Quintilian 3.8.49-54; 9.2.29-37. For a discussion see Anderson 2000:106-107 (and 61).

look what a fine piece of land this Andros is: καλήν γε χώραν Ἄνδρον. For this ironic use of καλός see §74 on the καλὴ πομπή of the arrested Jewish elders.

§158. *I, Flaccus, was born and brought up and educated* ...: γεννηθεὶς μὲν καὶ τραφεὶς καὶ παιδευθείς. This is a traditional triad, on which see van Unnik 1973:259-327, esp. 274-296, where he presents a large collection of parallels to Acts 22:3: the apostle Paul says that he is γεγεννημένος ἐν Ταρσῷ τῆς Κιλικίας, ἀνατεθραμμένος δὲ ἐν τῇ πόλει ταύτῃ (sc. Jerusalem), παρὰ τοὺς πόδας Γαμαλιὴλ πεπαιδευμένος κατὰ ἀκρίβειαν τοῦ πατρῴου νόμου, "born at Tarsus in Cilicia, but brought up in this city, (and) educated at the feet of Gamaliel according to the strict manner of the Law of our fathers" (a similar triadic formulation is used about Moses in Acts 7:20-22). This triad may also occur in the form not of the verbs used here but of the nouns γένεσις, τροφή, παιδεία. See e.g. Plato, *Leg.* 643c, 783b, 842e, *Crito* 50d-e; Plutarch, *Conv. disp.* 8.7 (727B), *Quom. adul.* 25 (65F); Jamblichus, *De vita Pyth.* 213; see further Saffrey-Segonds 2001:80 note 16. Philo himself uses it also in *Spec.* 2.229 and *Leg.* 1.99; cf. *Mos.* 1.2, *Somn.* 2.147 and *Flacc.* 46. The difference between τρέφεσθαι and παιδεύεσθαι is often that the former takes place in the parental home and embraces both the physical and intellectual upbringing by the parents, whereas the latter refers mainly to study (Saffrey-Segonds 2001:lxii). But τροφή can also be used in a broader sense, running parallel to παιδεία or overlapping with it. In such cases τρέφεσθαι "covers a significantly wider field than the first six years of a child's lifespan" (Du Toit 2000:380). Du Toit refers, *i.a.*, to Plato, *Theaet.* 172C; Isocrates, *Areop.* 41; Plutarch, *Vit. Cic.* 48; Josephus, *Ant.* 4.261. In Philo, *Mos.* 2.1 and especially *Spec.* 1.314 are good instances of this overlap.

I was the schoolmate and companion of the grandchildren of Augustus: τῶν θυγατριδῶν τοῦ Σεβαστοῦ means the children of Augustus' daughter(s), i.c. of Julia from her marriage with M. Vipsanius Agrippa: C. Caesar (20 BCE-4CE), L. Caesar (17 BCE-2CE), and Agrippa Postumus (12 BCE-14CE); all of them died before Augustus' death (maybe Agrippa Postumus was killed shortly after Augustus' death; but cf. Cassius Dio 57.3.6). We may infer from this that Flaccus himself, too, was probably born about 15 BCE.

chosen by Tiberius Caesar as one of his intimate friends: κριθεὶς δὲ τῶν πρώτων φίλων, cf. the expression ἐν τοῖς ἑταίροις κριθείς in §2 and the note *ad loc.*, although here Philo does not use the technical terminology.

entrusted for six years with the greatest of all his possessions, Egypt: He was *praefectus* there from 32-38 CE.

§159. *during the day night has overtaken my life!*: Flaccus realizes that a complete reversal of roles in his life has taken place; later he will show awareness of God's hand in his fate; see §§170-175 and cf. Kraus 1994:493.

place of banishmment: φυγαδευτήριον is used elsewhere by Philo only once, in *Fuga* 100, where he borrows the term from the LXX for the "cities of refuge" in Num. 35. Here it must have the sense of "place of exile."

my new fatherland: The mss's κενήν is an obvious mistake for καινήν, unless one takes "empty fatherland" to refer to the fact that Andros was not densely populated, which seems less likely.

'tomb' would be its most appropriate name: This metaphorical use of the word "tomb" for a life not worth living reminds one of Plutarch's κενοταφεῖν τὸν βίον (*Lat. viv.* 6, 1130C); see Hirsch-Luipold 2001:112-114.

For in a sense ... a drawn-out death in full consciousness: Cf. *Abr.* 64: "In my opinion, it [banishment] is not second to death (...) but rather a far heavier punishment, since death ends our troubles but banishment is not the end but the beginning of other new misfortunes and entails in place of the one death which puts an end to pains a thousand deaths in which we do not lose sensation." *Praem.* 70: "What is his punishment? That he should live for ever in a state of dying and so to speak suffer a death which is deathless and unending." See also *Conf.* 120-121, and Gruen 2002:233.

§160. *had lined up*: The mss. read προεστήκεσαν, but Wendland conjectured παρειστήκεσαν, unnecessarily so, in spite of Box 1939: 122 ("seems necessary"): προΐσταμαι here has the sense of "coming forward" or "standing so as to face another" (LSJ s.v. B.I,3). People were standing on both sides of the street in order to see Flaccus (ἐπὶ θέαν ἥκοντας).

§161. *His escorts led him to the assembly ... their island*: Philo emphasizes that the delivery of the banished prefect has been officially ascertained by the plenary assembly of the Andrians. This adds to the dishonor of Flaccus.

§§162-180a: *Flaccus at Andros*

Flaccus' plight after his arrival at Andros is great. He holds dramatic soliloquies and even says prayers in which he acknowledges that his punishment by the God of Israel is just. By having Flaccus himself portray the high status and prestige he once had, Philo highlights the depth of the abyss into which God has thrown him now. The central passage in this section is undoubtedly the phrase in Flaccus' prayer where he says, "I am a clear proof of this [sc., that the Jews have you for a champion and defender], for all the mad acts that I have committed against the Jews I have now suffered myself" (170). Here Philo again underlines the fact that God's *justitia retributiva* is unfailing. The motif that God is the defender of the Jews anticipates the final line of the work (§191). Flaccus' prayer in §§170-175 is a fine example of how Philo combines rhetoric and creed.

§162. *by ever more vivid imaginings*: φαντασίαις ἐναργεστέραις, see the note *ad* §124. Φαντασία here almost has the sense of "hallucinations." "Flaccus' αἴσθησις was no better in Andros than in Rome, but to see nothing familiar makes one more distinctly aware of ruin than one is when seeing familiar sights" (Box 1939:122).

spastic movements: σφαδᾴζειν is "to toss the body about, to have convulsions, to be strongly agitated" (LSJ *s.v.*). Philo uses the word 15 times (also in §§18 and 180), and it usually suggests strong emotions, so I agree with Colson 1941:390 that in itself a translation such as "so violent were his emotions" is possible, but what Philo writes in the immediately following phrases militates against this view ("He ran around, frequently jumping up and down, clapping his hands, smiting his thighs, flinging himself on the ground"). Colson's conclusion that "only in *Praem.* 140 is bodily struggling necessarily implied" (see his note at p. 538) is therefore incorrect, *pace* Pelletier 1967:142-143 note 3.

He ran around ... the ground: This description of a desperate or psychotic state of mind and its physical expressions is rather unique in ancient literature. Some ancient descriptions of demon possession come close to it (e.g., Mark 9:20), but Philo does not give the slightest hint of a demonological explanation of the phenomena.

§163. *I am Flaccus ...*: Stählin 1940:12 is of course right when he says that "die Selbstgespräche des Flaccus während seiner Verbannung von Philon frei erfunden worden sind." On the rhetorical function of this kind of *prosôpopoiia* see Quintilian 9.2.29-37. Kraus 1994:490 suggests that the style ἐγὼ Φλάκκος εἰμί has been influenced by the language of the aretalogies of Egyptian deities ("I am Isis"), but it is hard to see what would be the function of such an association in this context, certainly not that Philo wants to say that "Flaccus is one of God's 'forces'" (*ibid.*).

of the great city, or rather multi-city, Alexandria: τῆς μεγαλοπόλεως ἢ πολυπόλεως Ἀλεξανδρείας. In view of the fact that elsewhere Philo always uses μεγαλόπολις for the universe, "it is revealing that the one time Philo does call an earthly city a megalopolis, he is referring to Alexandria" (Runia 1989:405). But, as Pearce 1998:103 remarks, one may wonder to what extent such praise of the city reflects Philo's own view, for elsewhere he "expresses a more negative attitude towards the city ... as a place unsuitable for the contemplation of higher realities." The wise man avoids busy and noisy cities (*Contempl.* 20; *Decal.* 2-9). The unusual word πολύπολις (multi-city) occurs only here in Philo; elsewhere it is very rare, e.g., Callimachus, *Hymn to Diana* 225. It can be explained "as referring to the diverse ethnic πολιτεύματα (including the Jewish community) embraced within the πολιτεία of Alexandria as a whole" (Runia 1989:405; cf. Runia 2000). So πολύπολις conveys the idea of a metropolis in the modern sense (not in Philo's sense of that word; see *ad* §46).

the one who commanded great forces of infantry, cavalry, and navy: See the notes *ad* §5. For the expression δυνάμεις πολλὰς πεζὰς καὶ ἱππικὰς καὶ ναυτικάς Pelletier 1967:143 note 5 refers to a papyrus of about 118 BCE from Philae (*SB* 3448) where the same expression is used.

I am the one who was escorted day after day: Cf. Nero's similar complaint just before his death according to Cassius Dio 63.28 (I owe this reference to the kindness of G.H. de Vries).

§164. *But was all this just an illusion*: For this use of φάσμα see *Jos.* 140 and 143 (quoted immediately below). See on this and other elements in §§164-165 also Niehoff 2001:134-135, 253.

Was it only when I slept that I saw in my dreams ... as reality?: Cf. *Jos.* 140 "We flounder as though in deep sleep, unable to compass anything by accurate reasoning or to grasp it vigorously and firmly, for all are like shadows and phantoms (σκιαῖς γὰρ ἔοικε καὶ φάσμασι)." *Jos.* 143 "Since, then, human life is full of this vast confusion and disorder and uncertainty also, the statesman must come forward and, like some wise expounder of dreams, interpret the day-time visions and illusions (φάσματα) of those who think themselves awake, and with suggestions commended by reason and probability show them the truth about each of these visions."

depicted: Mss. ἀναγραφούσης, Mangey conj. ἀναζωγραφούσης, but ἀναγράφω can have the meaning of "to depict" as well (Box 1939:122; LSJ *s.v.* II 3).

§165. *Yes, I have completely deceived myself!*: The Greek has only one word, διηπάτημαι, the shortest sentence of *In Flaccum*. Other commentators take the verb to have a passive sense ("I have been deceived"), but I prefer the middle sense since Philo does not portray Flaccus here as the victim of deception by others (as in *Hyp.* 11.15 *et al.*). Philo uses διαπατάω (3x) and ἀπατάω (69x) indiscriminately.

After all, these were but a shadow of realities, not the realities themselves: For ἄρα expressing a sense of disillusionment after the fact see Denniston 1954:46 ("as it subsequently transpired"). Σκιά in the sense of that which is in contrast to reality occurs often in Philo: *Jos.* 140 (quoted *ad* §164); *Somn.* 1.206; *Plant.* 27; *Leg.* 3.102; *Post.* 112. He is, of course, strongly inspired by the famous imagery of shadows in the cave of Plato's *Resp.* 514a-517c. Other parallels in pagan and Christian Greek literature (e.g., Achilles Tatius 1.15.6; Hebr. 8:5; 10:1) are given in *BDAG* 929-930; cf. Van der Horst 1992 and Sterling in Lévy 1998:357. "Flaccus' growing awareness of the quixotic character of political life, his sense of the illusionary nature of partisan achievement, and his experience of betrayal by 'the family' he tried to serve, all torment him" (Sills 1997:185).

For just as when we wake up ... short moment: Cf. the passages from *Jos.* 140 and 143 quoted *ad* §164. Colson 1941:392 suggests "by a momentary change in what time brings," i.e. in fortune, as a more exact translation for βραχυτάτῃ καιροῦ ῥοπῇ, but that fits the context far less. Philo has Flaccus emphasize the fleeting nature of all λαμπρά, as he himself does often as well.

§166. *These kind of thoughts ... broke his back*: On ἐκτραχηλίζειν see the note *ad* §118.

He avoided ... the threshhold: Wilcken 1909:3 note 1 and Box 1939:122 say that this passage and §167 are reminiscent of the description of king Nebuchadnezar in Dan. 4:33, but the echoes are somewhat weak (see, however, also *ad* §§169 and 177). Philo paints a grim picture of Flaccus' paralyzing fear of meeting other people out of shame.

§167. *he would spend the day in loneliness*: This stands in stark contrast to what Flaccus said in §163: "I am the one to whom innumerable of [Alexandria's] inhabitants turned."

by the fresh memories of his misfortunes: ταῖς ἐναύλοις μνήμαις τῶν κακοπραγιῶν. For this use of ἔναυλος ("fresh") in relation to memory see *Leg. all.* 3.91. The original sense of the word (of a sound "still ringing in the ears") is still present in passages such as *Ebr.* 177, *Congr.* 67, perhaps also *Post.* 155.

He would come back ... everything bright: All commentators here refer to Deut. 28:66-67: "Your life shall hang in doubt before you; night and day you shall be in dread and have no assurance of your life. In the morning you shall say, 'Would it were evening!' and at evening you shall say, 'Would it were morning!' because of the dread which your heart shall fear, and the sights which your eyes shall see." In *Praem.* 151 this biblical passage is at the background as well: "Life will be made unstable and suspended as it were to a halter by one terror succeeding another, day and night, hustling the soul up and down, so that in the morning they will pray for evening and in the evening for morning through the palpable miseries of their waking hours and the horrible dreams which appear to them in sleep." See further Box 1939:xlviii note 1; Borgen 1997:191; Leonhardt 2001:104.

§168. *he bought a small piece of land*: See the note *ad* §148.

bewailing his fate with many tears: τὸν οἰκεῖον ἐπιστένων καὶ κατακλαίων δαίμονα, lit. "bewailing and lamenting his peculiar fate." Δαίμων (originally "god") here has the meaning of "fate" or "destiny," as often in classical authors (see LSJ *s.v.*, Horn & Rapp 2002:96-97, and the rich bibliography in *RBLG* 229). For the wide semantic range of δαίμων in Philo see Nikiprowetzky 1996:240. The word οἰκεῖον seems superfluous here, "but expresses, perhaps, the feeling of one who asks 'Why should I in particular have this fate?'" (Colson 1941:394 note *a*). Cf. Pelletier 1967:145 note 4.

§169. *There is a story*: λέγεται, implying that Philo here relies — or claims to rely — on oral tradition or other sources, although quite probably much of what he tells us here and in the following paragraphs is a product of his own imagination. For classical parallels and the effect of "scheinbare Distanzierung" see Meiser 1999:422.

he became inspired: ἔνθους γενόμενος. Originally meaning "inspired or possessed by a god," ἔνθους became the term for various kinds of frenzied state; see Pfister 1959 (esp. 959 on Philo); Graf 1997; Horn & Rapp 2002:136-137. Here, however, the implication is also that it is due to God's inspiration that in the following prayer Flaccus gives clear testimony to God's greatness and his providence on behalf of the Jewish people. Similarly, in his retelling of the story of the pagan prophet Balaam (Num. 23), Philo uses the same term ἔνθους to characterize that prophet's inspiration, with the clarifying addition προφητικοῦ πνεύματος ἐπιφοιτήσαντος (*Mos.* 1.277). For literature on Philo's concept of ecstasy see R-R Index *s.v.*

like in the Corybantic rites: In Greek mythology and cult the Corybantes were the ecstatic and orgiastic dancers or priests in the cults of Cybele, Zeus and Dionysus (they are often confused with the Curetes), who worked themselves into a state of frenzy (μανία) or trance; see Graf 1985:319-324. In Philo's parlance the corybantic metaphor is utilized to describe the mystical ascent of the intellect; see *Opif.* 71; *Ebr.* 146; *Fug.* 32, 166; *Contempl.* 11-12, 89 etc. See Kraus 1994:489

farm-house: ἔπαυλις, "une maisonnette rustique" (Pelletier 1967: 145), a kind of "dacha."

He then turned his eyes towards heaven: Cf. John 17:1, and note that according to Dan. 4:34 Nebuchadnezzar, too, lifted up his eyes to heaven and praised the Most High God; see Borgen 1999:303.

seeing that which is really a cosmos within the cosmos: τὸν ἐν κόσμῳ κόσμον ὄντως ἰδών. Box 1939:123 (followed by others) observes that ὄντως does not belong to the participle but to the noun, but it may be said that ὄντως usually modifies a verb, and the idea that Flaccus "really sees" (*i.e.*, has true knowledge of) the order within the order makes good sense here as well; see Kraus 1994:489. Κόσμος here still very much retains the original sense of "order." Philo uses the same imagery also in *Praem.* 41: "They have seen too the air and breezes so happily tempered, the yearly seasons changing in harmonious order, and over all the sun and moon, planets and fixed stars, the whole heaven and heaven's host, line upon line, a true cosmos in itself revolving within the cosmos." Cf. *Abr.* 159: "... above all heaven, which has been created as a cosmos within a cosmos." Philo here expresses a sentiment that was rather universal among the ancients. The orderly movements of the heavenly bodies was an important element in much theological speculation (cf. *Spec.* 1.35). The motif serves here to explain why Flaccus comes to a real awareness of God's righteousness. But, as Philo makes clear, it is too late for that, a motif that is also stressed in 2 Macc. 9 (on the death of Antiochus IV) and in other Jewish and Christian stories about the death of God's enemies; see Gauger 2002 (esp. 46 note 12).

§170. *King of gods and men*: See the note on §123 ("King of mortals and immortals"). Cf. *Conf.* 173.

it is now clear to me that ...: The Greek only has ἄρα, which here denotes the apprehension of an idea not before envisaged but realized only at the moment of speaking; see for full discussion and many instances of this usage Denniston 1954:36, 38.

you are not indifferent to the nation of the Jews: Here Philo clearly adresses a pastoral problem that had been caused by the pogrom. Apparently some or several of his coreligionists had lost their faith that God would take care of them. This is also visible in *Legat.* 3: "Some people have come to disbelieve that God exercises providence for humanity, and particularly for the nation of suppliants (i.e. Israel)."

nor is what they assert about your providence false: οὐδ᾽ ἐπιψεύδονται τὴν ἐκ σοῦ πρόνοιαν. The indefinite plural ("they") refers especially to Philo himself: "They do not lie" is a rhetorical understatement for "what I say is nothing but the truth." It is the purpose of his whole treatise to prove God's providence; see esp. §121 and the commentary *ad locum*; also *Spec.* 4.179-182; Birnbaum 1996:174-178; Frick 1999:188-189. Flaccus ultimately comes to a real knowledge of God, but it is too late.

the Jews ... have you for a champion and defender: The combination προαγωνιστὴς καὶ ὑπέρμαχος occurs also in *Abr.* 232 ("God is the champion and defender of the just"); in other passages it does not refer to God, e.g., *Opif.* 160, *Spec.* 3.75, 132. The same theme recurs in the originally Jewish prayer in the *Apostolic Constitutions* 7.33 where God is called "defender of the offspring of Abraham" with an unmistakable reference to Gen. 15:1: "Do not be afraid, Abraham, I am your shield." Cf. 2 Macc. 8:36.

sound opinion: See the note on "sound" *ad* §136. One is reminded here of the λόγος ὑγιής and the ὑγιαίνουσα διδασκαλία in the Pastoral Epistles: 1 Tim. 1:10; 6:3; 2 Tim. 1:13; 4:3; Tit. 1:9; 2:1; 2:8.

I am a clear proof of this, for all the insane acts that I have committed against the Jews I have now suffered myself: σαφὴς δ᾽ ἐγὼ πίστις implies that, if even Flaccus himself admits that his fate is a proof of divine intervention, the Jews should not have any doubts about God's providence. The motif that his sufferings match those of the Jews is part of Philo's concept of divine Justice; see the note *ad* §104, and cf. Borgen 1997:190; 1999:304. One is reminded of what Josephus writes about another notorious Jew-hater, Apion: After having mentioned in *C. Ap.* 2.137 Apion's derision of circumcision, he says in 2.143 that this man was punished for that in a very just way, for he had to be circumcised himself because of an ulcer on his private parts from which he finally died amidst terrible suffering.

§171. *When they were robbed ... plundered them*: The events alluded to here are those described in §§56-57.

For that reason ... in other ways: It is in the words διὰ τοῦτο, repeated in §172 and in a modified form (τοιγαροῦν) in §173, that Philo again emphasizes the motif of divine justice, for which see the note on Δίκη *ad* §104. Borgen 1999:305 draws attention to a close parallel in Rev. 18:6-8, where also the punishment for the crime is introduced with διὰ τοῦτο.

§172. *Once I cast on them the slur that they had no civic rights because they were foreigners, whereas in fact they were inhabitants possessing these rights*: ὠνείδισά ποτε ἀτιμίαν καὶ ξενιτείαν αὐτοῖς ἐπιτίμοις οὖσι κατοίκοις. This is a much debated statement. Of course Flaccus never said a thing like this, it is Philo who, by putting these words into his mouth, tries to convince his audience that what Flaccus said in the decree "in which he stigmatized us as foreigners and aliens" (§54) was totally untrue: the Jews did have full rights as citizens of Alexandria. In fact, "the Jews of Alexandria, like other foreign groups constituted as *politeumata* in Greek cities, were 'citizens' only in relation to each other as members of the *politeuma*. Their status vis-à-vis the Greeks was that of metics, aliens with the right of domicile. They occupied an intermediate position between the Greek citizens of Alexandria and the wholly unprivileged Egyptians, who lacked any sort of franchise. They enjoyed the rights of residence and organized civic life, but they were not an integral part of the Greek body politic" (Smallwood 1976:230; for criticism of her use of the term *politeuma* here see Lüderitz 1994, but also the criticism of Lüderitz by Cowey-Maresch 2001:4-9, 22-23, 38). The existence of a Jewish semi-autonomous civic body might have been the reason for making claims of equality, or even of citizenship although much remains uncertain here; see also Nock 1972:960-962; Delia 1991:3; Huß 1994:8; Barclay 1996:64; Pucci Ben Zeev 1998:299-300; Sly 2000:259-261; Gruen

2002:73-83; and the note *ad* §47. It must be observed that, unlike Josephus (*Bell.* 2.487; *Ant.* 12.8; 12.121; 14.188; 19.281-2; *Ag. Ap.* 2.35), Philo's statements about the Alexandrian civic status of the Jews can be taken as deliberately vague, "an indication perhaps that he did not consider the fine points of Alexandrian citizenship worth arguing about" (Sly 2000:261). Here Philo alludes to the Alexandrian Jews as *epitimoi katoikoi*, though it remains uncertain whether we should take these words here in the technical sense of "inhabitants with full rights" or as just "privileged settlers" (see Stern 1973/83: I.401; Barclay 1996:66; Gruen 2002:73).

I did so in order to please their adversaries ...: In these lines Philo has Flaccus confess that he (Philo!) is right in his assessment of Flaccus' deepest motives.

For that reason ...: See the note *ad* §171.

§173. *I gave orders ... their greatest enemies*: See §74.

Justly, therefore ...: See the remarks *ad* §171, and note that the motif of divine justice is given here extra emphasis by δικαίως.

in my wretched soul rather than in my body: πρὸ τοῦ σώματος τὴν ἀθλίαν ψυχήν. Box 1939:123 compares *Legat*. 324, where king Agrippa says to Gaius: "You set me free when I was fettered in iron chains; everyone knows that. Do not fetter me now with more painful chains, Emperor, for the chains which you loosed encircled a part of my body, whereas those which I now foresee are chains for the soul, which will crush my whole soul utterly" (transl. Smallwood 1961:134, slightly modified).

I was paraded through all Italy as far as Brindisium, through all the Peloponnese as far as Corinth, and through Attica and the islands as far as Andros: The problem here is that this description of Flaccus' journey from Rome to Andros is incompatible with what Philo writes in §§154-156; especially the phrase "through all the Peloponnese" does not concord with the words "after he had crossed the Ionian Gulf he sailed upon the sea which extends to Corinth, a spectacle to all the Peloponnesian coastal cities" in §154, and "through Attica" does not fit "he coasted along Attica as far as Cape Sounion" in §156. Other translators (Colson, De Vries) try to solve this problem by translating διά as "past, along," but in view of the obvious meaning of this preposition in the immediately preceding διὰ πάσης Ἰταλίας, this seems impossible. Pelletier 1967:148 note 2 suggests that Philo presents Flaccus here as exaggerating the number of his humiliations due to the impact of his grief, but it is rather Philo himself again who is guilty of rhetorical exaggeration.

§174. *the measure of compensation for what I have perpetrated*: Again the idea of Dikê's acting according to a principle of *talio*. As Borgen 1999:307 says, the retribution is carried out "with mathematical precision," as is made also very clear in §189: "It was the will of Dikê that the butcheries which she wrought on his single body should be as numerous as the number of Jews whom he had unlawfully put to death."

I put some to death ... avenge them: Note the explicative asyndeton (Lausberg 1963:107) in ἀνεῖλόν τινας. Here the reference is to (a) the Jewish elders who died after having been scourged (§75), and (b) the Jews who after torture in the theatre were led to execution (§85).

Some were stoned ... torn to pieces: Here the reference is to the Jews who showed themselves again in the quarters from which they had been driven and who were killed by stoning (§66), burning (§67), and dragging (§70-71).

§175. *the goddesses of punishment await me*: ἀναμένουσί με αἱ Ποιναί. Philo has Flaccus phrase his complaint in typically pagan language. The *Poenae* were goddesses or spirits of vengeance. Philo mentions them once more, in *Prob.* 7.

avenging spirits: ἀλάστορες are here identical to the Ποιναί. The fact that Flaccus speaks of spirits taking revenge upon him after death makes clear that in Philo's view he was aware that he had committed unforgivable crimes.

standing ... at the finish: ἐπὶ βαλβῖσιν, lit. the ropes which formed the starting-point or finish. The image of life as a racing competition with a finish is rather common in later ancient sources, e.g., 1 Cor. 9:24-26; Hebr. 12:1; 2 Tim. 4:7. For other references and literature see BDAG *s.vv.* ἀγών and τρέχω.

Every day, or rather every hour, I die ...: Cf. 1 Cor. 15:31 καθ' ἡμέραν ἀποθνῄσκω, and see Helyer 2002:316.

I die beforehand by suffering many deaths, not only the last one: Cf. §159 and *Praem.* 70.

§176. *He often was so frightened ... hope of something good*: One is reminded here of the description of the anxiety and panic of the Egyptians at the time of the exodus in *Wisdom* 17 (a book written in

FLACCUS AT ANDROS 239

Alexandria probably just before or during the time of Philo). See Cheon 1997:125-149 for a comparison of that chapter with Philo.

with panting and palpitation: This would seem to be a reference to the phenomenon known as hyperventilation, which Philo here rightly regards as a symptom of psychological disturbance.

§177. *No favorable omen*: ὄρνις αἴσιος οὐδείς, lit. "no favorable bird." Since birds were often regarded as conveying messages from the gods, the word "bird" became almost synonymous with "omen," so much so that in Aristophanes' comedy, *Aves* 719-721, the chorus of birds sings: "You even use the word bird for anything that brings good luck or bad luck, whether it's a chance remark, a sneeze, an unexpected meeting, a noise, a servant or a donkey, you call it a bird!" See Van der Horst 1998:18.

presaging sounds and voices were sinister: κληδόνες παλίμφημοι. This is a reference to the so-called cledonomancy, i.e., the interpretation of auditive omens, e.g. sneezing and casual remarks, which were interpreted as signs from the gods. For κληδόνες (or φῆμαι) see Flacelière 1965:9-11 and Graf 1985:203-204.

his solitude as that of a beast: Like Nebuchadnezzar in Dan. 4:32. See Borgen 1999:302-3 and Box 1939:xlviii note 1, who adds that this biblical parallel does not justify a rejection of the whole story of Flaccus' life on a lonely plot as a purely literary invention. Henze 1999 does not mention our passage (neither §166) at all in his study of the reception history of the Nebuchadnezzar story in Daniel 4. It should be added that, if Philo alludes to Daniel 4 here, it would probably be the only place in all his works in which he uses this book.

Was company ... to be suspected: Note the staccato asyndeta in these final lines, meant to convey Flaccus' restless nervousness.

§178. *He is plotting something against me ... beasts for slaughter*: This paragraph and the following picture Flaccus' anxiety in a very graphic way that is reminiscent of what is said about the end of the unrighteous in *Wisdom* 4:19-20: "They will suffer anguish (...), they will come with dread when their sins are reckoned up, and their lawless deeds will convict them to their face." Again the description of the fear and trembling of the unrighteous Egyptians in *Wisdom* 17 comes to mind. The words ὁ θᾶττον βαδίζων could also be connected to what follows so as to make it the grammatical subject of σπεύδων ἔοικεν instead of βουλεύεται.

§179. *I know that I am losing courage in the face of death*: οἶδ' ὅτι μαλακίζομαι πρὸς θάνατον. Box 1939:123 compares Xenophon, *Apol.* 33 (on Socrates), ἐπεδείξατο δὲ τῆς ψυχῆς τὴν ῥώμην ... οὐδὲ πρὸς τὸν θάνατον ἐμαλακίζετο, "... and he did not meet death like a coward."

due to the cruelty of a deity: Or, "of my destiny." Δαίμων can have either meaning; see on this Nikiprowetzky 1996:240, who interprets δαίμων here to mean the God of the Jews who punishes Flaccus, as he himself had already conceded in §170.

which he treasures up against me: For this use of θησαυρίζειν cf. Rom. 2:5 θησαυρίζεις σεαυτῷ ὀργὴν ἐν ἡμέρᾳ ὀργῆς. More parallels in BDAG *s.v.* 2b.

to do a favor to those whom I treacherously murdered: A reference to post-mortem gratification, more or less reminiscent of the reference to the satisfaction of the survivors who heard of Flaccus' arrest in §124.

§180a. *Restlessly repeating ...*: ἀναπολῶν καὶ σφαδᾴζων. Ἀναπολέω ("to go over again") is used 9 times by Philo, mostly in the sense of rehearsing or repeating, e.g., *Legat.* 17, 310. The nervous restlessness of this repetition is expressed forcefully by σφαδᾴζων, on which see the note *ad* §162.

§§180b-190: *Gaius Has Flaccus Killed*

In the meantime in Rome, the emperor Caligula takes the decision that, since the fate of his many deportees is too mild a punishment, they have to be executed, and Flaccus is at the top of the list. Soldiers are sent out, land on Andros and chase Flaccus. He immediately realizes what is going to happen to him and fights back with the only result that "his body received the same number of wounds as that of the Jews who had been unlawfully murdered by him," again a refernce to the dominating theme of the *justitia retributiva Dei*.

§180b. *Gaius, who was by nature ruthless*: All ancient biographers of this emperor or historians who write about his reign make mention of his excessive cruelty. References can easily be found in Barrett 1989: Reg. *s.v.* "cruelty." I disagree with Goodenough 1938:10 that the past tenses used here prove that Gaius was already dead when Philo wrote this treatise, although in fact it may be true that Philo did the final editing and publication after January 41 CE.

GAIUS HAS FLACCUS KILLED   241

he even loathed his namesakes: A detail so curious but at the same time so fitting to Gaius' character that it must be more than a figment of Philo's imagination.

§181. *he respected Lepidus*: See for Lepidus the note *ad* §151. Cf. Barrett 1989:106-111.
so that ... stopped doing so: The mss. read ὡς but Reiter conjectured ὥστε which has been adopted by all later editors. The verb ἀπηγόρευσε is translated by Colson 1941:399 by "was prostrate," which is not impossible, but "he gave up doing so" is more natural in this context (even though it is then usually followed by a participle, which has to be supplied here *e mente*).
by helping to lighten the sentence of another: This is what Lepidus had already done "thanks to which he (Flaccus) could exchange Gyara for nearby Andros" (§151).

§182. *diseases which, when they recur ...*: See the note *ad* ὑποτροπιάζουσαι in §153.

§183. *So they say that once, in a sleepless night, ...*: See the note on λέγεται in §169. *Ad* νύκτωρ ποτὲ διαγρυπνῶν Box 1939:123 quotes Suetonius, *Calig.* 50.3: incitabatur insomnio maxime neque enim plus quam tribus nocturnis horis quiescebat ac ne iis quidem placida quiete ("He was especially tormented with sleeplessness, for he never rested more than three hours at night, and even for that length of time he did not sleep quietly"); see Lindsay 1993:156: "In antiquity this was thought to be a common symptom of insanity;" cf. Roccatagliata 1986:240-241.
he was thinking ... tranquillity and freedom: Here Philo already adumbrates what in §184 Caligula will call a βίος φιλόσοφος.

§184. *He even changed the designation from 'exile' to 'holidays abroad'*: ἀποδημία, lit. "being away from home, going abroad." In *Legat.* 338 it is used of Gaius' planned visit to Egypt. Pelletier 1967:153 adequately translates by "villégiature."
to live without trouble and in well-being: σὺν ἀπραγμοσύνῃ καὶ εὐσταθείᾳ ζῆν. The noun ἀπραγμοσύνη denotes *otium*, "freedom from politics, love of a quiet life" (LSJ *s.v.*). For εὐσταθεία see *ad* §§94 and 135. Living a life in ἀπραγμοσύνη and εὐσταθεία was a philosophical ideal; see the last note to this paragraph.

it is absurd: Mss. ἄτοπον εἶναι, Mangey conj. ἄτοπον ἐφεῖναι, adopted by Pelletier 1967:153 ("il est absurde de laisser ces gens-là ..."), unnecessarily so, although the conjecture by Roos 1935:242 οὓς ἄτοπον ἐᾶν τρυφᾶν is very attractive.

the peaceful life of a philosopher: "The implication of a βίος φιλόσοφος is a financial margin (cf. τρυφᾶν in this passage), even if modest" (Box 1939:123). That is why De Vries 1999:83 translates by "a life at the expense of the state [op kosten van de staat]," implying a careless existence with a state pension, as was the case with philosophers who worked in the Alexandrian Mouseion. But perhaps the issue rather is the freedom that rural life offers away from the headaches of the often heavy political and civic responsibilities of upper-class citizens in urban centers (as Allen Kerkeslager suggested to me).

§185. *Thereupon ... put to death*: Both Suetonius, *Calig.* 28 (with Lindsay 1993:120), and Cassius Dio 59.18.3 make mention of the fact that those who had been sentenced to exile were not safe at all; many of them were killed by Caligula in their places of banishment. Cf. *Legat.* 341-342: "Another time he (Gaius) imposed a sentence of banishment on some people who expected to be put to death, not because they were aware of having committed any offence deserving death or indeed any milder punishment, but because the judge's excessive ferocity robbed them of any hope of being let off. To them exile was a boon, and as good as a return from exile, when they considered that they had escaped from the supreme danger which was threatening their lives. But only a short time afterwards, although nothing new had happened, he sent some of his troops and put to death in a body those fine, noble exiles who were already making homes of the islands in which they were living and were bearing their misfortunes most cheerfully. Thus he brought poignant and unexpected grief to the families of Rome's leading citizens" (transl. Smallwood 1961:138). For further historical background information see Sherwin-White 1972:825-828, who suggests that this change of attitude on Caligula's part took place only after the death of his sister Drusilla in the summer of 38 which had an enormous impact on his already deranged psyche. His aggressive activities against high officials continued on an even larger scale in 39 CE.

a list of names which was headed by that of Flaccus: "This placing could be Philo's invention to underscore the moral of his work that God brought full retribution upon the ruler who persecuted the Jews" (Barraclough 1984:461).

GAIUS HAS FLACCUS KILLED 243

When the men ...: From here onwards the story takes on more and more the character of a "passion story of the justly cursed and punished governor" (Borgen 1999:302).

§186. *everyone's soul is highly prophetic, especially of people in misfortune*: For the theme that everyone is a potential prophet see especially Plutarch, *Def. orac.* 39,431E-432C, *Gen. Socr.* 20,588D-589C; Cicero, *Div.* 1.34-71 (on "natural divination") with Pease 1963:150-216. See also *Div.* 1.81 where it is said that Aristotle believed *melancholici* to have special divinatory capacities, with Pease 1963:242-243 *ad locum*; also Aune 1983:349 note 13. For a similar remark by Philo about the mind (*nous*) see §114 *in fine*.
Did he forget ... arrested there: This whole scene illustrates the state of utter panic that had taken hold of Flaccus.

§187. *to men and all other terrestrials*: ἀνθρώποις καὶ πᾶσι χερσαίοις. Note that καί here has the meaning of "and other," cf. Acts 5:29 Πέτρος καὶ οἱ ἀπόστολοι. On Philo's use of χερσαῖος and its Platonic background (*Tim.* 40a) see Runia 2001:215.
the same element ... from life: See Gen. 3:19 γῆ εἶ καὶ εἰς γῆν ἀπελεύσῃ. From Jewish sources Sir. 17:1; Sap. 15:8; Ps-Phocylides 107-108; from pagan sources Xenophanes, fr. 27; *Epigr. graeca* (ed. Kaibel) 75; more instances of the ἐκ γῆς — εἰς γῆν motif in Van der Horst 1978:191. Philo could better have left out this lame §187.

§188. *They pursued him ... as wild beasts do*: The grisly details in this paragraph and the following ones serve to underline that divine Justice saw to it that Flaccus' fate would be just as cruel and horrible as that of his Jewish victims.

§189. *gashed and smashed*: διατμηθεὶς δὲ καὶ διακοπείς. Severance of his bodily parts occurs only when he is dragged to the pit (§190).
like a sacrificial animal: By the term ἱερεῖον Philo often designates the animal sacrifices in the temple cult; see *Spec.* 1.161-298 *passim*. Here, however, he uses it in the regular sense of to slaughter cattle; see Meiser 1999:424 note 34.
Justice wanted that single body to receive wounds as numerous as the number of the Jews who had been unlawfully murdered by him: σφαγὰς ἰσαρίθμους raises the question of the number of Jewish casualties in the pogrom. Philo does not present us with any pertinent data. In

Legat. 124 he says that "many myriads" were driven from their homes, which is possibly an exaggeration (see Smallwood 1961:215); and in §94 he says they were driven away from more than 400 houses. But that does not give us a clue as to the numbers of people that were actually killed in the persecution. It may have been several hundreds, it may even have been some thousands, but we do not know. Philo's message is again that of *justitia retributiva*. "It is the precise reciprocity of the punishment which irrefutably proves God's providential care for the Jewish *ethnos*" (Kraus 1994:494).

§190. *poured forth*: The mss. have ἐκχεομένων, sc. φλεβῶν, but Mangey rightly conjectured ἐκχεομένῳ, sc. αἵματι.

most of the parts ... had been slit: Box 1939:124 objects that this is an inaccurate phrase since a κοινωνία cannot be "united" or "bound together," but Pelletier 1967:154-155 rightly says that ἡ κοινωνία συνεδεῖτο πᾶσα τοῦ σώματος "n'est pas une tautologie: κοινωνία est simplement employé par prolepse." This element echoes Philo's description of the death of Flaccus' Jewish victims in §71 ("they were totally destroyed because all the constituent parts of their organism had separated and dispersed in all directions"). All the horrible details in §§188-190 are meant to make it seem as though Philo himself witnessed Flaccus' cruel execution. "Yet this same dramatic intensity, which increases in force precisely because of the example that the narrative intends to make of Flaccus, is precisely what should remind us that the text is primarily a work of historical fiction" (Sills 1987: 186).

§ 191: *Epilogue*

The final sentence of the work is very significant in that it summarizes succinctly but clearly Philo's main concern when writing this book: to encourage his fellow Jews not to give up their trust in God's help, and to warn his non-Jewish readers not to stretch out their hands to the Jewish people with evil intent because God will never abandon the Jews.

§191. *Such were the sufferings of Flaccus, too*: The καί here probably refers back to the opening sentence of the book, where Philo has said that "after Sejanus it was Flaccus Avillius who continued his policy of persecuting the Jews" (§1). Sejanus, too, underwent fatal punishment, as does Flaccus now. See the notes on §1 and also ch. 1 of the Introduction.

an indubitable proof that the Jewish people had not been deprived of the help of God: By the negative formulation μὴ ἀπεστερῆσθαι Philo no doubt responds to what he had heard fellow Jews saying during the pogrom, namely, that they were deprived of God's help. His significant denial once again clearly and emphatically expresses what was Philo's deepest motive for writing this exceptional work.

BIBLIOGRAPHY

Alexandre Jr., M. 1999. *Rhetorical Argumentation in Philo of Alexandria*, Atlanta: Scholars Press.
Alston, R. 1997. "Philo's In Flaccum: Ethnicity and Social Space in Roman Alexandria," *Greece and Rome* 44:165-175
Alston, R. ed. 2001. *The City in Roman and Byzantine Egypt*, London: Routledge.
Ameling, W. Manuscript, to be published in 2003. "'Market-place' und Gewalt: Die Juden in Alexandrien 38 n.Chr."
Amir, Y. 1983. *Die hellenistische Gestalt des Judentums bei Philon von Alexandrien*, Neukirchen: Neukirchener Verlag.
Anderson, H. 1983/85. "3 Maccabees," in Charlesworth II.509-530
Anderson, R.D. 2000. *Glossary of Greek Rhetorical Terms Connected to Methods of Argumentation, Figures and Tropes, from Anaximenes to Quintilian*, Leuven: Peeters.
Applebaum, Sh. 1974/76. "The Legal Status of the Jewish Communities in the Diaspora," in Safrai & Stern 1.420-463
———. 1974/76. "The Organization of the Jewish Communities in the Diaspora," in Safrai & Stern 1.464-503
———. 1974/76. "The Social and Economic Status of the Jews in the Diaspora," in Safrai & Stern 2.701-727
Archer, L.J. 1990. *Her Price is Beyond Rubies. The Jewish Woman in Graeco-Roman Palestine*, Sheffield: Sheffield Academic Press.
Aune, D.E. 1983. *Prophecy in Early Christianity and the Ancient Mediterranean World*, Grand Rapids: Eerdmans.
Axtell, H.L. 1907. *The Deification of Abstract Ideas in Roman Literature and Inscriptions*, Chicago: University of Chicago Press (reprint New Rochelle: Caratzas Publishing, 1987)
Aziza, C. 1987. "L'utilisation polémique du récit de l'Exode chez les écrivains alexandrins (IVme siècle av. J.-C. – Ier siècle ap. J.-C.," *ANRW* II 20, 1, Berlin – New York: W. de Gruyter, 41-65
Bagnall, R.S. 1993. *Egypt in Late Antiquity*, Princeton: Princeton University Press.
———. 2001. "Archaeological Work on Hellenistic and Roman Egypt, 1995-2000," *American Journal of Archaeology* 105:227-243
Bagnall, R.S., & Frier, B. 1994. *The Demography of Roman Egypt*, Cambridge: Cambridge University Press.
Balsdon, J.P.V.D. 1934. *The Emperor Gaius (Caligula)*, Oxford: Clarendon Press (repr. New York: AMS Press, 1976)
Baltrusch, E. 2002. *Die Juden und das Römische Reich. Geschichte einer konfliktreichen Beziehung*, Darmstadt: Wissenschaftliche Buchgesellschaft.
Barclay, J.M.G. 1996. *Jews in the Mediterranean Diaspora*, Edinburgh: Clark.
———. 2002. "Apologetics in the Jewish Diaspora," in Bartlett 129-149
Barr, J. 1961. *The Semantics of Biblical Language*, Oxford: Oxford University Press.
Barraclough, R. 1984. "Philo's Politics: Roman Rule and Hellenistic Judaism," *ANRW* II 21.1, 417-553
Barrett, A.A. 1989. *Caligula. The Corruption of Power*, London: Batsford.
Barrett, C.K. 1978. *The Gospel According To John*, London: SPCK.
Bartlett, J.R. (ed.) 2002. *Jews in the Hellenistic and Roman Cities*, London & New York: Routledge
Bergmann, W., & Ch. Hoffmann. 1987. "Kalkül oder 'Massenwahn'? Eine soziologische Interpretation der antijüdischen Unruhen in Alexandria 38 n. Chr.,"

in R. Erb & M. Schmidt (hrsg.), *Antisemitismus und jüdische Geschichte. Studien zu Ehren von H.A. Strauss*, Berlin: Wissenschaftlicher Autorenverlag, 15-46.
Bernand, A. 1992. *La prose sur pierre dans l'Egypte hellénistique et romaine*, 2 vols., Paris: Centre national de la recherche scientifique.
Bilde, P. *et al.* (eds.). 1992. *Ethnicity in Hellenistic Egypt*, Aarhus: Aarhus University Press.
Bingen, J. 2002. "Un nouvel épistratège et arabarque alexandrin," *ZPE* 138:119-120
Birnbaum, E. 1996. *The Place of Judaism in Philo's Thought: Israel, Jews, and Proselytes*, Atlanta: Scholars Press.
———. 2001."Philo on the Greeks: A Jewish Perspective on Culture and Society in First-Century Alexandria," *SPhA* 13:37-58.
———. 2002. Review of Niehoff 2001, *SPhA* 14:186-193.
Blasius, A., & Schipper, B.U. (eds). 2002. *Apokalyptik und Ägypten. Eine kritische Analyse der relevanten Texte aus dem griechisch-römischen Ägypten*, Leuven: Peeters.
Bloch, R.S. 2002. *Antike Vorstellungen vom Judentum. Der Judenexkurs des Tacitus im Rahmen der griechisch-römischen Ethnographie*, Stuttgart: Franz Steiner.
Bludau, A. 1906. *Juden und Judenverfolgungen im alten Alexandria*, Münster: Aschendorff.
Boak, A.E.R. 1937. "The Organization of Gilds in Graeco-Roman Egypt," *TAPA* 68:212-220.
Bohak, G. 1997. "Good Jews, Bad Jews, and Non-Jews in Greek Papyri and Inscriptions," in B. Kramer e.a. (eds.), *Akten des 21. internationalen Papyrologenkongresses*, Stuttgart-Leipzig: Teubner, vol. 1:105-112.
———. 2002. "Ethnic Continuity in the Jewish Diaspora in Antiquity," in Bartlett 175-192.
———. 2003. "The Ibis and the Jewish Question: Ancient 'Anti-Semitism' in Historical Perspective," in M. Mor & A. Oppenheimer (Eds.), *Jewish-Gentile Relations in the Periods of the Second Temple, the Mishna and the Talmud*, Jerusalem: Yad Yizhak Ben Zvi (forthcoming).
Bolkestein, H. & A. Kalsbach. 1950."Armut I: Beurteilung der Armut," *RAC* 1:698-705.
Borgen, P. 1992. "Philo of Alexandria," *ABD* 5:333-342.
———. 1992. "Philo and the Jews in Alexandria," in Bilde 122-138.
———. 1996. "Emperor Worship and Persecution in Philo's In Flaccum and De Legatione ad Gaium," in H. Cancik, H. Lichtenberger & P. Schäfer (eds.), *Geschichte – Tradition – Reflexion. FS für M. Hengel zum 70. Geburtstag*, 3 vols., Tübingen: Mohr Siebeck, vol. 3, 493-509.
———. 1997. *Philo of Alexandria, an Exegete for his Time*, Leiden: Brill.
———. 1999. "Two Philonic Prayers and Their Contexts," *NTS* 45:291-309.
———. 2000. "Philo's *Against Flaccus* as Interpreted History," in K.J. Illman e.a. (eds.), *A Bouquet of Wisdom: Essays in Honour of Karl-Gustav Sandelin*, Abo: Abo Akademi, 41-57.
Borgen, P. e.a. 2000. *Philo Index. A Complete Word Index to the Writings of Philo of Alexandria*, Leiden: Brill – Grand Rapids: Eerdmans.
Boring, M.E., Berger, K., & Colpe, C. 1995. *Hellenistic Commentary to the New Testament*, Nashville: Abingdon Press.
Bornhäuser, H. 1935. *Sukka (Laubhüttenfest)* [Die Mischna II 6], Berlin: Töpelmann.
Bowman, A.K. 1986. *Egypt After the Pharaohs 332 BC-AD 642*, London: British Museum Publications.
Bowman, A.K. & Rathbone, D. 1992. "Cities and Administration in Roman Egypt," *JRS* 82:107-127.
Box, H. 1939. *Philonis Alexandrini In Flaccum*, London: Oxford University Press.
Breccia, E. 1922. *Alexandria ad Aegyptum: A Guide to the Ancient and Modern Town and to Its Graeco-Roman Museum*, Bergamo: Istituto Italiano d'arti grafiche.
Bremmer, J.N. 2002. *The Rise and Fall of the Afterlife*, London-New York: Routledge.

Breytenbach, C. 1999. "Hypsistos," *DDD* 439-443.
Brunt, P.A. 1961. "Charges of Provincial Maladministration Under the Early Principate," *Historia* 10:189-223.
Buraselis, K. 1995. "Zu Caracallas Strafmaßnahmen in Alexandrien (215/6)" *ZPE* 108:166-188.
Bureth, P. 1988. "Le préfet d'Egypte (30 av. J.-C. – 297 ap. J.-C.): État présent de la documentation en 1973," *ANRW* II 10.1:472-502.
Burr, V. 1955. *Tiberius Julius Alexander*, Bonn: Habelt.
Buth, R. 2000. "Aramaic Language," in C.A. Evans & S.E. Porter (eds.), *Dictionary of New Testament Background*, Downers Grove: Intervarsity Press, 86-91.
Cairns, D.L. 1993. *Aidos. The Psychology and Ethics of Honour and Shame in Ancient Greek Literature*, Oxford: Clarendon Press.
Calabi, F. 1998. *The Language and the Law of God. Interpretation and Politics in Philo of Alexandria*, Atlanta: Scholars Press.
——. 2002. "Il governante sulla scena. Politica e rappresentazione nell' "In Flaccum" di Filone alessandrino," in F. Calabi (ed.), *Immagine e rappresentazione: Contributi su Filone di Alessandria*, Binghamton: Global Publications, 45-57.
Carlier, C. 2002 (unpublished). *La cité de Moïse. La réprésentation du peuple juif chez Philon d'Alexandrie*, diss. Paris.
Casson, L. 1971. *Ships and Seamanship in the Ancient World*, Princeton: Princeton University Press (repr. 1986)
——. 1974. *Travel in the Ancient World*, Baltimore: Johns Hopkins University Press.
Chadwick, H. 1978. "Gewissen," *RAC* 10:1025-1107.
Chantraine, P. 1950. "Les verbes grecs signifiant 'lire'," *AIPHOS* 10:115-126.
Charlesworth, J.H. (ed.). 1983-1985. *The Old Testament Pseudepigrapha*, 2 vols, Garden City: Doubleday.
Cheon, S. 1997. *The Exodus Story in the Wisdom of Solomon*, Sheffield: Sheffield Academic Press.
Christ, W. von, Schmidt, W., & Stählin, O. 1920-1924. *Geschichte der griechischen Litteratur*, 2 vols., München: Beck.
Clarke, A.D. 2000. "Alexandria," *DNTB* 23-25.
Cohen, N.G. 1995. *Philo Judaeus. His Universe of Discourse*, Frankfurt etc.: Peter Lang.
Cohen, S.J.D. & E.S. Frerichs (eds.). 1993. *Diasporas in Antiquity*, Atlanta: Scholars Press.
——. 1999. *The Beginnings of Jewishness. Boundaries, Varieties, Uncertainties*, Berkeley etc.: University of California Press.
Cohn, L. 1896/1915. "Prolegomena," in Cohn-Wendland 1 [1896] i-lxxxiv.
——. 1896/1915. "Prolegomena," in Cohn-Wendland 4 [1902] i-xxxii.
——. 1899. "Einleitung und Chronologie der Schriften Philos," *Philologus* Supplementband 7:385-437.
Cohn, L., & Wendland, P. (edd.). 1896-1915. *Philonis Alexandrini opera quae supersunt*, 6 vols., Berlin: Reimer.
Cohn, L., Heinemann, I., Adler, M., Theiler, W. (eds.). 1909-1964. *Philo von Alexandria. Die Werke in deutscher Übersetzung*, 7 Bände, Berlin: W. de Bruyter.
Coleman, K.M. 1990. "Fatal Charades: Roman Executions Staged as Mythological Enactments," *JRS* 80:44-73.
Collins, J.J. 2000 (2nd ed.). *Between Athens and Jerusalem. Jewish Identity in the Hellenistic Diaspora*, Grand Rapids: Eerdmans.
Collins, J.J., & Sterling, G.E. (eds.). 2001. *Hellenism in the Land of Israel*, Notre Dame: University of Notre Dame Press.
Colson, F.H. 1941. *Philo*, vol. 9, Cambridge MA: Harvard University Press – London: William Heinemann (with *Flacc.*).
——. 1962. *Philo*, vol. 10, Cambridge MA: Harvard University Press – London: William Heinemann (with *Legat.*).

Conley, Th.M. 1987. *Philo's Rhetoric: Studies in Style, Composition and Exegesis*, Berkeley: Center for Hermeneutical Studies.
Conzelmann, H. 1981. *Heiden-Juden-Christen. Auseinandersetzungen in der Literatur der hellenistisch-römischen Zeit*, Tübingen: Mohr.
Cotter, W. 1996. "The Collegia and Roman Law: State Restrictions on Voluntary Associations 64 BCE-200 CE," in Kloppenborg-Wilson 74-89.
Courcelle, P. 1967. Review of Pelletier 1967, *Revue des études anciennes* 69:452-454.
Cowey, J.M.S., & Maresch, K. 2001. *Urkunden des Politeuma der Juden von Herakleopolis (144/3-133/2 v.Chr.) (P. Polit. Iud.)*, Wiesbaden: Westdeutscher Verlag.
Creed, J.L. (ed. and transl.). 1984. *Lactantius: De mortibus persecutorum*, Oxford: Clarendon Press.
Cronbach, A. 1944. "The Social Ideals of the Apocrypha and Pseudepigrapha," *HUCA* 18:119-156.
Dalman, G. 1905. *Grammatik des jüdisch-palästinischen Aramäisch*, Leipzig: Hinrich'sche Buchhandlung.
Daniel-Nataf, S. (ed.). 1986. *Philo of Alexandria: Writings I: Historical and Apologetical Writings*, Jerusalem [in Hebrew; contains A. Kasher's translation of *In Flaccum* with annotations].
Danker, F.W. 1992. "Associations, Clubs, Thiasoi," *ABD* 1:501-503.
Davis, S. 1951. *Race-Relations in Ancient Egypt: Greek, Egyptian, Hebrew, Roman*, London: Methuen.
Delaunay, F. 1867. *Philon d'Alexandrie. Écrits historiques: influence, luttes et persécutions des Juifs dans le monde romain*, Paris: Didier (2nd ed. 1870).
Delia, D. 1988. "The Population of Roman Alexandria," *TAPA* 118:275-292.
———. 1991. *Alexandrian Citizenship During the Roman Principate*, Atlanta: Scholars Press.
———. 1996. "'All Army Boots and Uniforms?': Ethnicity in Ptolemaic Egypt," in Green 41-53.
Delling, G. 1987. *Die Bewältigung der Diasporasituation durch das hellenistische Judentum*, Göttingen: Vandenhoeck & Ruprecht (repr. in Delling 2000:23-121).
———. 2000. *Studien zum Frühjudentum*, Göttingen: Vandenhoeck & Ruprecht.
Denniston, J.D. 1954. *The Greek Particles*, Oxford: Clarendon Press (2nd ed.; orig. 1934).
Devijver, H. 1974. "The Roman Army in Egypt," *ANRW* II.1:452-492.
Dibelius, M. & Greeven, M. 1964. *Der Brief des Jakobus*, Göttingen: Vandenhoeck & Ruprecht.
DiTomasso, L. 2001. *A Bibliography of Pseudepigrapha Research 1850-1999*, Sheffield: Sheffield Academic Press.
Dragona-Monachou, M. 1994. "Divine Providence in the Philosophy of the Empire," *ANRW* II.36.7, 4417-4490.
Du Toit, A.B. 2000. "A Tale of Two Cities: 'Tarsus or Jerusalem' Revisited," *NTS* 46:375-402.
Dyck, J. 2002. "Philo, Alexandria and Empire. The Polititcs of Allegorical Interpretation," in Bartlett 149-174.
Eck, W. 1996. "Aelius Seianus," *NP* 1:174.
———. 1998. "Hiberus," *NP* 5:532.
———. 1999. "Iulia Drusilla," *NP* 6:5.
———. 2000. "Naevius Cordus Sutorius Macro," *NP* 8:690.
———. 2001. "Praefectus Aegypti," *NP* 10:246-249.
Eckstein, H.J. 1983. *Der Begriff Syneidesis bei Paulus*, Tübingen: Mohr Siebeck.
Edwards, D.R. 1996. *Religion and Power. Pagans, Jews, and Christians in the Greek East*, New York – Oxford: Oxford University Press.
Eichler, S. 1999. "Alexandreia," in K. Brodersen (ed.), *Antike Stätten am Mittelmeer*, Darmstadt: Wissenschaftliche Buchgesellschaft 751-754.

Ekschmitt, W. 1984. *Die Sieben Weltwunder. Ihre Erbauung, Zerstörung und Wiederentdeckung*, Mainz: Philipp von Zabern.
Empereur, J.Y. 1998. *Alexandria Rediscovered*, London: British Museum Press.
Engers, M. 1923. "Die staatsrechtliche Stellung der alexandrinischen Juden," *Klio* 18:79-90.
Evans, C.A., & S.E. Porter (eds.). 2000. *Dictionary of New Testament Background*, Downers Grove: Intervarsity Press.
Feldman, L.H. 1993. *Jew and Gentile in the Ancient World*, Princeton: Princeton University Press.
Ferguson, E. 1993. *Backgrounds of Early Christianity*, Grand Rapids: Eerdmans.
Fikhman, I.F. 1998. "Liste des Rééditions et Traductions des Textes Publiés dans le *Corpus Papyrorum Judaicarum*, Vols. I-III," *SCI* 17:183-205.
Fine, S. 1996. "From Meeting House to Sacred Realm: Holiness and the Ancient Synagogue," in *idem* (ed.), *Sacred Realm. The Emergence of the Synagogue in the Ancient World*, New York – Oxford: Oxford University Press, 21-47.
———. 1997. *This Holy Place. On the Sanctity of the Synagogue during the Greco-Roman Period*, Notre Dame: University of Notre Dame Press.
———. (ed.). 1999. *Jews, Christians, and Polytheists in the Ancient Synagogue. Cultural Interaction during the Graeco-Roman Period*, London-New York: Routledge.
Fisher, N.R.E. 1992. *Hybris: A Study in the Values of Honour and Shame in Ancient Greece*, Warminster: Aris & Phillips.
Fitzpatrick-McKinley, A. 2002. "Synagogue Communities in the Graeco-Roman Cities," in Bartlett 55-87.
Flacelière, R., 1965. *Greek Oracles*, London: Elek Books.
Flusser, D. 1974/76. "Paganism in Palestine," in Safrai & Stern 2.1065-1100.
Frankfurter, D. 1998. *Religion in Roman Egypt*, Princeton: Princeton University Press.
Fraser, P.M. 1972. *Ptolemaic Alexandria*, 3 vols., Oxford: Clarendon Press.
Freund, R.A. 1982. *Principia Politica: The Political Dimensions of Jewish and Christian Self-Definition in the Greco-Roman Period*, diss. JTSA, Ann Arbor: University Microfilms International.
Frey, J.-B. 1936-1952. *Corpus Inscriptionum Judaicarum*, 2 vols., Rome: Pontificio Istituto di Archeologia Cristiana.
Frick, P. 1999. *Divine Providence in Philo of Alexandria*, Tübingen: Mohr.
Fuchs, L. 1924. *Die Juden Ägyptens in ptolemäischer und römischer Zeit*, Wien: Rath Verlag,
Furley, W.D., & L. Benz. 2000. "Mimos," *NP* 8:201-207.
Furley, W.D., & J.M. Bremer. 2001. *Greek Hymns. Selected Cult Songs from the Archaic to the Hellenistic Period*, 2 vols., Tübingen: Mohr Siebeck.
Gabba, E. 1989. "The Growth of Anti-Judaism or the Greek Attitude Towards the Jews," in W.D. Davies & L. Finkelstein, *The Cambridge History of Judaism*, vol. 2, Cambridge: Cambridge University Press, 614-656.
Gabelmann, H. 1984. *Antike Audienz- und Tribunalszenen*, Darmstadt: Wissenschaftliche Buchgesellschaft.
Gafni, I.M. 1997. *Land, Center and Diaspora. Jewish Constructs in Late Antiquity*, Sheffield: Sheffield Academic Press.
Gager, J. 1983. *The Origins of Anti-Semitism*, New York & Oxford: Oxford University Press.
Gauger, J.-D. 2002. "'Der Tod des Verfolgers.' Überlegungen zur Historizität eines Topos," *JSJ* 33:42-64.
Gelzer, M. 1918. "Iulius (133)" [=Caligula], *PW* 10.1:381-423.
Gerschmann, K.H. 1964. "Gegen Flaccus," in *Philo von Alexandria, Die Werke in deutscher Übersetzung*, vol. 7, ed. W. Theiler, Berlin: W. de Gruyter.
Gildersleeve, B.L. 1980. *Syntax of Classical Greek*, repr. Groningen: Bouma's Boekhuis.

Goddio, F. et al. (eds.). 1998. *Alexandria: The Submerged Royal Quarters*, London: Periplus.
Goodenough, E.R. 1926. "Philo and Public Life," *Journal of Egyptian Archaeology* 12:77-79.
——. 1938. *The Politics of Philo Judaeus: Practice and Theory*, New Haven: Yale University Press (repr. Hildesheim: Olms, 1967).
——. 1962. *An Introduction to Philo Judaeus*, Oxford: Blackwell, (2nd ed.).
Goodman, M. (ed.). 1998. *Jews in a Graeco-Roman World*, Oxford: Clarendon Press.
Gordon, R.L. 1999. "Pronoia," *DDD* 664-667.
Goudriaan, K. 1988. *Ethnicity in Ptolemaic Egypt*, Amsterdam: Gieben.
——. 1992. "Ethnical Strategies in Graeco-Roman Egypt," in P. Bilde e.a. (eds.), *Ethnicity in Hellenistic Egypt*, Aarhus: Aarhus University Press, 79-99.
Grabbe, L.L. 1992. *Judaism from Cyrus to Hadrian*, 2 vols., Minneapolis: Fortress Press.
Graf, F. 1985. *Nordionische Kulte. Religionsgeschichtliche und epigraphische Untersuchungen zu den Kulten von Chios, Erythrai, Klazomenai und Phokaia*, Rome: Schweizerisches Institut.
——. 1996. "*Pompai* in Greece. Some Considerations About Space and Ritual in the Greek Polis," in R. Hägg (ed.), *The Role of Religion in the Early Greek Polis*, Stockholm: Paul Åströms Förlag, 55-65.
——. 1997. "Ekstase," *NP* 3 951-952.
Green, P. (ed.). 1996. *Alexandria and Alexandrianism*, Malibu: The J. Paul Getty Museum,
Grimm, G. 1998. *Alexandria, die erste Königsstadt der hellenistischen Welt*, Mainz: Ph. von Zabern.
Groag, E. & A. Stein (edd.). 1933. *Prosopographia Imperii Romani saec. I. II. III.*, vol. 1, Berlin: W. de Gruyter.
Gross, K. 1985. *Menschenhand und Gotteshand in Antike und Christentum*, Stuttgart: Hiersemann.
Gruen, E.S. 1998. *Heritage and Hellenism. The Reinvention of Jewish Tradition*, Berkeley: University of California Press.
——. 2002. *Diaspora: Jews Amidst Greeks and Romans*, Cambridge MA – London: Harvard University Press.
Guignard, V. 1998. "Le rapport de Philon d'Alexandrie à la philosophie grecque dans le portrait des empereurs," in C. Lévy (ed.), *Philon d'Alexandrie et le langage de la philosophie*, Turnhout: Brepols, 459–469.
Gussen, P.J.G. 1955. *Het leven in Alexandrië volgens de cultuurhistorische gegevens in de Paedagogus (boek II en III) van Clemens Alexandrinus*, Assen: Van Gorcum.
Gutsfeld, A. 2001. "Praefectus praetorio," *NP* 10:249-253.
Haas, Ch. 1997. *Alexandria in Late Antiquity: Topography and Social Conflict*, Baltimore – London: Johns Hopkins University Press.
Hadas-Lebel, M. 1987. "L'évolution de l'image de Rome auprés des Juifs en deux siècles de rélations judéo-romaines -164 à +70," *ANRW* II.20.2:784-812.
Hagendorn, D. (ed.). 2000. *Wörterlisten aus den Registern von Publikationen griechischer und lateinischer dokumentarischer Papyri und Ostraka* (on internet).
Hanson, A.E. 1992. "Egyptians, Greeks, Romans, *Arabes*, and *Ioudaioi* in the First Century A.D.," in J.H. Johnson (ed.), *Life in a Multicultural Society: Egypt from Cambyses to Constantine and Beyond*, Chicago, 133-145.
Harrington, H.K. 2001. *Holiness. Rabbinic Judaism and the Graeco-Roman World*, London-New York: Routledge.
Harris, H.A. 1976. *Greek Athletics and the Jews*, Cardiff: University of Wales Press.
Hata, G.. 2000. *Filon Furakusu he no Hanron + Gaiusu he no Shisetsub* (Japanese: *Philo Against Flaccus and Embassy to Gaius*) (Kyoto) [non vidi].
Hay, D.M. 1979. "What is Proof? Rhetorical Verification in Philo, Josephus and Quintilian," *SBLSP* 17:2:87-100.

———. 1991. "Philo's View of Himself as an Exegete," *SPhA* 3:40-52.
Hayward, C.T.R. 1996. *The Jewish Temple. A Non-Biblical Sourcebook*, London-New York: Routledge.
Heinemann, I. 1931. "Antisemitismus," *PW* Suppl. 5:3-43.
Heinemann, I. 1932. *Philons griechische und jüdische Bildung*, Breslau: Marcus (repr. Hildesheim-New York: Georg Olms, 1973).
Helyer, L.R. 2002. *Exploring Jewish Literature of the Second Temple Period*, Downers Grove: InterVarsity Press.
Hengel, M. 1971. "Proseuche und Synagoge. Jüdische Gemeinde, Gotteshaus und Gottesdienst in der jüdischen Diaspora und in Palästina," in *Tradition und Glaube (FS K.G. Kuhn)*, eds. G. Jeremias *et al.*, Göttingen: Vandenhoeck & Ruprecht, 157-184.
———. 1974. *Judaism and Hellenism*, London: SCM Press.
———. 1977. *Crucifixion in the Ancient World and the Folly of the Message of the Cross*, London: SCM Press.
Hennig, D. 1974. "Zu der alexandrinischen Märtyrerakte P. Oxy. 1089," *Chiron* 4:425-440.
———. 1975. *L. Aelius Seianus. Untersuchungen zur Regierung des Tiberius*, München: Beck'sche Verlagsbuchhandlung.
Henze, M. 1999. *The Madness of King Nebuchadnezzar: The Ancient Near Eastern Origins and Early History of Interpretation of Daniel 4*, Leiden: Brill.
Hilgert, E. 1995. "Philo Judaeus et Alexandrinus: The State of the Problem," in J.P. Kenney (ed.), *The School of Moses: Studies in Philo and Hellenistic Religion in Memory of Horst R. Moehring*, Atlanta: Scholars Press, 1-15.
Hirsch-Luipold, R. 2001. "Gedeihen im Licht – Verderben im Dunkel: Bilder für die existentielle Bedeutung einer Ethik des Politischen," in R. Feldmeier u.a. (edd.), *Plutarch: ΕΙ ΚΑΛΩΣ ΕΙΡΗΤΑΙ ΤΟ ΛΑΘΕ ΒΙΩΣΑΣ. Ist "Lebe im Verborgenen" eine gute Lebensregel?*, Darmstadt: Wissenschaftliche Buchgesellschaft.
Höcker, Chr. 1999. "Leuchtturm," *NP* 7:98.
Hölbl, G. 1994. *Geschichte des Ptolemäerreiches. Politik, Ideologie und religiöse Kultur von Alexander dem Großen bis zur römischen Eroberung*, Darmstadt: Wissenschaftliche Buchgesellschaft.
Hoftijzer, J., and K. Jongeling. 1995. *Dictionary of the North-West Semitic Inscriptions*, 2 vols., Leiden: Brill.
Hogan, L.P. 1992. *Healing in the Second Temple Period*, Fribourg: Universitätsverlag – Göttingen: Vandenhoeck & Ruprecht.
Holladay, C.R. 1992. "Jewish Responses to Hellenistic Culture in Early Ptolemaic Egypt," in Bilde 139-163.
Honigman, S. 1993. "The Birth of a Diaspora: The Emergence of a Jewish Self-Definition in Ptolemaic Egypt in the Light of Onomastics," in Cohen & Frerichs 93-127.
———. 1997. "Philon, Flavius Josèphe et la citoyenneté alexandrine: vers une utopie politique," *JJS* 48:62-90.
Horbury, W. 1994. "Jewish Inscriptions and Jewish Literature in Egypt with Special Reference to Ecclesiasticus," In J.W. van Henten & P.W. van der Horst (eds.), *Studies in Early Jewish Epigraphy*, Leiden: Brill, 9-43.
———. 1998. "Early Christians on Synagogue Prayer and Imprecation," in Stanton & Stroumsa 296-317.
Horbury, W., e.a. (eds.). 1999. *The Cambridge History of Judaism III: The Early Roman Period*, Cambridge: Cambridge University Press.
Horbury, W. & D. Noy. 1992. *Jewish Inscriptions of Graeco-Roman Egypt*, Cambridge: Cambridge University Press.
Horn, Chr., & Rapp., Chr. (eds.). 2002. *Wörterbuch der antiken Philosophie*, München: Beck.

Horst, P.W. van der. 1970. "Drohung und Mord schnaubend (Acta IX 1)," *NT* 12:256-269.
———. 1978. *The Sentences of Pseudo-Phocylides*, Leiden: Brill.
———. 1990. "Hellenistic Parallels to the Acts of the Apostles, I:1-26," *ZNW* 74 (1983) 17-26, repr. in Van der Horst & Mussies 121-130.
———. 1984. *Chaeremon: Egyptian Priest and Stoic Philosopher. The Fragments* (EPRO 100), Leiden: Brill (2nd ed. 1987).
———. 1990. *Essays on the Jewish World of Early Christianity*, Fribourg: Universitätsverlag – Göttingen: Vandenhoeck & Ruprecht.
———. 1991. *Ancient Jewish Epitaphs. An Introductory Survey of a Millennium of Jewish Funerary Epigraphy (300 BCE – 700 CE)*, Kampen: Pharos.
———. 1992. "Shadow," *ABD* 5:1148-1150.
———. 1993. "Thou Shalt Not Revile the Gods: The LXX Translation of Ex. 22:28 (27), its Background and Influence," *SPhA* 5:1-8.
———. 1993. "Philo Alexandrinus over de toorn Gods," in A. de Jong & A. de Jong (edd.), *Kleine encyclopedie van de toorn*, Utrecht: Universitaire Pers, 77-82.
———. 1995. "Images of Women in Ancient Judaism," in R. Kloppenborg & W. J. Hanegraaff (edd.), *Female Stereotypes in Religious Traditions* (Studies in the History of Religions 66), Leiden: Brill, 43-60.
———. 1998. *Hellenism – Judaism – Christianity: Essays on Their Interaction*, Leuven: Peeters (2nd ed.).
———. 1999. "Dike," *DDD* 250-252.
———. 1999. "Was the Synagogue a Place of Sabbath Worship Before 70 CE?," in S. Fine (ed.), *Jews, Christians, and Polytheists in the Ancient Synagogue. Cultural Interaction during the Graeco-Roman Period*, London-New York: Routledge, 18-43.
———. 2002. *Japheth in the Tents of Shem. Studies on Jewish Hellenism in Antiquity*, Leuven: Peeters.
———. 2002. "Who Was Apion?," in van der Horst 207-221.
———. 2003. "Common Prayer in Philo's *In Flaccum* 121-124," *Kenishta* 2:21-27.
———. 2003b. "Jews and Blues in Late Antiquity" (forthcoming).
Horst, P.W. van der, & Mussies, G. 1990. *Studies on the Hellenistic Background of the New Testament*, Utrecht: Rijksuniversiteit Utrecht.
Huddlestun, J.R., & B.B. Williams. 1992. "Nile," *ABD* 4:1108-1116.
Hunt, E.D. 1982. *Holy Land Pilgrimage in the Later Roman Empire, AD 312-460*, Oxford: Clarendon Press.
Huß, W. 1994. "Die Juden im ptolemaiischen Ägypten. Ein Beitrag zur Geschichte einer multikulturellen Gesellschaft," in S. Füssel, G. Hübner & J. Knape (eds.), *Artibus. Kulturwissenschaft und deutsche Philologie des Mittelalters und der frühen Neuzeit* (FS D. Wuttke), Wiesbaden: Harassowitz, 1-31.
———. 2001. *Ägypten in hellenistischer Zeit 332-30 v.Chr.*, München: Beck.
Hüttenmeister, F. 1993. "'Synagoge' und 'Proseuche' bei Josephus und in anderen antiken Quellen," in D. A. Koch & H. Lichtenberger (eds.), *Begegnungen zwischen Christentum und Judentum in Antike und Mittelalter* (FS H. Schreckenberg), Göttingen: Vandenhoeck, 163-181.
Huzar, E.G. 1988. "Alexandria ad Aegyptum in the Julio-Claudian Age," *ANRW* II.10.1:619-668.
———. 1995. "Emperor Worship in Julio-Claudian Egypt," *ANRW* II.18.5:3092-3143
Ilan, T. 2002. *Lexicon of Jewish Names in Late Antiquity, Part 1: Palestine 330 BCE – 200 CE*, Tübingen: Mohr Siebeck.
Jansen-Winkeln, K. 1996. "Alexandreia," *NP* 1:463-466.
Jones, A.H.M. 1940. *The Greek City from Alexander to Justinian*, Oxford: Clarendon Press.
Jung, F. 2002. ΣΩΤΗΡ. *Studien zur Rezeption eines hellenistischen Ehrentitels im Neuen Testament*, Münster: Aschendorff Verlag.

Juster, J. 1914. *Les juifs dans l'empire romain: leur condition juridique, économique et sociale*, 2 vols, Paris: Geuthner.
Kahn, J.G. 1998. "La valeur et la légitimité des activités politiques d'après Philon d'Alexandrie," *Méditerranées* 16:117-127.
Kalcyk, H. 1996. "Andros," *NP* 1: 695.
———. 1998. "Gyaros," *NP* 5:15.
Kasher, A. 1985. *The Jews in Hellenistic and Roman Egypt*, Tübingen: Mohr.
———. 1992. "The Civic Status of the Jews in Ptolemaic Egypt," in Bilde 100-121.
———. 1995. "Synagogues as 'Houses of Prayer' and 'Holy Places' in the Jewish Communities of Hellenistic and Roman Egypt," in D. Urman & P.V.M. Flesher (eds.), *Ancient Synagogues*, vol. 1, Leiden: Brill, 205-220.
Kerkeslager, A. 1997. "Maintaining Jewish Identity in the Greek Gymnasium," *JSJ* 28:12-33.
———. 1998. "Jewish Pilgrimage and Jewish Identity in Hellenistic and Early Roman Egypt," in D. Frankfurter (ed.), *Pilgrimage and Holy Space in Late Antique Egypt*, Leiden: Brill, 99-225.
Kienast, D. 1996. "Agrippina (2)," *NP* 1:297-298.
———. 1997. "Avillius Flaccus," *NP* 2:371.
Kippenberg, H.G. 1991. *Die vorderasiatischen Erlösungsreligionen in ihrem Zusammenhang mit der antiken Stadtherrschaft*, Frankfurt: Suhrkamp.
Klauck, H.J. 1986. "Die heilige Stadt: Jerusalem bei Philo und Lukas," *Kairos* 28:129-151.
———. 1994. "Ein Richter im eigenen Innern. Das Gewissen bei Philo von Alexandrien," in his *Alte Welt und neuer Glaube. Beiträge zur Religionsgeschichte, Forschungsgeschichte und Theologie des Neuen Testaments*, Göttingen: Vandenhoeck & Ruprecht – Freiburg i/d Schweiz: Universitätsverlag, 33-58.
Kloppenborg, J.S., & Wilson, S.G. (eds.). 1996. *Voluntary Associations in the Graeco-Roman World*, London: Routledge.
Kokkinos, N., 1998. *The Herodian Dynasty*, Sheffield: Sheffield Academic Press.
Kornemann, E. 1980. *Tiberius*, Frankfurt: Societäts-Verlag.
Kraft, R.A. 1991. "Philo and the Sabbath Crisis: Alexandrian Jewish Politics and the Dating of Philo's Works," in B. A. Pearson *et al.* (eds.), *The Future of Early Christianity. Essays in Honor of Helmut Koester*, Minneapolis: Fortress Press, 131-141.
Kraus, C. 1967. *Filone Alessandrino e un' ora tragica della storia ebraica*, Naples: Morano.
Kraus Reggiani, C. 1984. "I rapporti tra l'impero romano e il mondo ebraico al tempo di Caligola secondo la 'Legatio ad Gaium' di Filone Alessandrino," *ANRW* II.21.1:554-586.
Kraus, M. A. 1994. "Philosophical History in Philo's In Flaccum," *SBLSP* 33:477-494.
Krauss, S. 1934. Review of Heinemann 1932, *Orientalistische Literaturzeitung* 37:519-523.
Kugel, J.L. 1998. *Traditions of the Bible.A Guide to the Bible As It Was at the Start of the Common Era*, Cambridge MA – London: Harvard University Press.
———. (ed.). 2002. *Shem in the Tents of Japhet. Essays on the Encounter of Judaism and Hellenism*, Leiden: Brill.
Kushnir-Stein, A. 2000. "On the Visit of Agrippa I to Alexandria in AD 38," *JJS* 51:227-242.
Larson, C.W. 1946. "Prayer of Petition in Philo," *JBL* 65:185-203.
Lausberg, H. 1963. *Elemente der literarischen Rhetorik*, München: Max Hüber.
Leisegang, H. 1934. Review of Heinemann 1932, *Göttingische gelehrte Anzeigen* 196:130-141.
———. 1938. "Philons Schrift über die Gesandtschaft der alexandrinischen Juden an den Kaiser Gaius Caligula," *JBL* 57:377-405.
———. 1941. "Philon," *RE* XX.1:1-50.

Lémonon, J.-P. 1981. *Pilate et le gouvernement de la Judée. Textes et monuments*, Paris: Lecoffre.
Leonhardt, J. 2001. *Jewish Worship in Philo of Alexandria*, Tübingen: Mohr.
Levick, B. 1976. *Tiberius the Politician*, London: Thames & Hudson.
Levine, L.I. 2000. *The Ancient Synagogue. The First Thousand Years*, New Haven: Yale University Press.
———. 2002. *Jerusalem: Portrait of the City in the Second Temple Period (586 B.C.E. – 70 C.E.)*, Philadelphia: Jewish Publication Society.
Levinskaya, I. 1996. *The Book of Acts in its First Century Setting, vol. 5: Diaspora Setting*, Grand Rapids: Eerdmans.
Lévy, C. (ed.). 1998. *Philon d'Alexandrie et le language de la philosophie*, Turnhout: Brepols.
Lewis, N. 1983. *Life in Egypt Under Roman Rule*, Oxford: Clarendon.
Lewy, H. 1935. *Philon von Alexandrien: Von den Machterweisen Gottes. Eine zeitgenössische Darstellung der Judenverfolgungen unter dem Kaiser Caligula*, Berlin: Schocken Verlag.
Lichtenberger, H., & Oegema, G.S. (eds.). 2002. *Jüdische Schriften in ihrem antikjüdischen und urchristlichen Kontext*, Gütersloh: Gütersloher Verlagshaus.
Lindsay, H. 1993. *Suetonius: Caligula, edited with Introduction and Commentary*, Bristol: Bristol Classical Press.
Lüderitz, G. 1983. *Corpus jüdischer Zeugnisse aus der Cyrenaika*, Wiesbaden: Reichert.
———. 1994. "What is the Politeuma?," in J.W. van Henten & P.W. van der Horst (eds.), *Studies in Early Jewish Epigraphy*, Leiden: Brill, 183-225.
Lukaszewicz, A. 2000. "Some Remarks on the Trial of Isidorus and on Isidorus Junior", *Journal of Juristic Papyrology* 30:59-65.
Lust, J., Eynikel, E., & Hauspie, K. 1992-1996. *A Greek-English Lexicon of the Septuagint*, 2 vols., Stuttgart: Deutsche Bibelgesellschaft.
McGing, B. 2002. "Population and Proselytism: How Many Jews Were There in the Ancient World?," in Bartlett 88-106.
MacMullen, R. 1964. "Nationalism in Roman Egypt," *Aegyptus* 44:179-199.
———. 1966. *Enemies of the Roman Order. Treason, Unrest, and Alienation in the Empire*, Cambridge MA: Harvard University Press.
Malina, B.J. 1981. *The New Testament World. Insights from Cultural Anthropology*, London: SCM Press.
Mangey, T.. 1742. Φίλωνος τοῦ Ἰουδαίου τὰ εὑρισκόμενα ἅπαντα. *Philonis Iudaei opera quae reperiri potuerunt omnia*, 2 vols., London: William Humphrey.
Martin, L.H. 1987. *Hellenistic Religions: An Introduction*, Oxford: Oxford Univeristy Press.
Martinet, J.F. 1787. *Alle de werken van Flavius Josephus, met aanmerkingen uitgegeven*, vol. 8, Amsterdam: Allart & Holtrop, 293-467 (Dutch translation of *Flacc.* and *Legat.*).
Mason, S. 2001. *Life of Josephus. Translation and Commentary* (vol. 9 in *Flavius Josephus: Translation and Commentary*), Leiden: Brill.
Mayer, G. 1987. *Die jüdische Frau in der hellenistisch-römischen Antike*, Stuttgart: Kohlhammer.
Meiser, M. 1999. "Gattung, Adressaten und Intention von Philos In Flaccum," *JSJ* 30:418-430.
Mélèze Modrzejewski, J. 1981. "Sur l'antisémitisme païen," in M. Olender e.a. (eds.), *Le racisme: Mythes et sciences. Pour Léon Poliakov*, Brussel: Editions Complexe, 411-439.
———. 1990. *Droit impérial et traditions locales dans l'Égypte romaine*, Aldershot: Variorum Reprints.
———. 1993. "How to Be a Jew in Hellenistic Egypt?," in Cohen & Frerichs:65-92.
———. 1995. *The Jews of Egypt*, Philadelphia-Jerusalem: Jewish Publication Society.

Mendelson, A. 1982. *Secular Education in Philo of Alexandria*, Cicinnati: Hebrew Union College Press.
———. 1988. *Philo's Jewish Identity*, Atlanta: Scholars Press.
———. 1997. "Philo's Dialectic of Reward and Punishment," *SPhA* 9:104-125.
Meyer, B.F., A.I. Baumgarten & E.P. Sanders (eds). 1980-1982. *Jewish and Christian Self–Definition in the Graeco-Roman World*, 3 vols., London: SCM Press.
Millar, F.G.B. 1977. *The Emperor in the Roman World 31 BC – AD 337*, London: Duckworth (2nd ed. 1992).
Miranda, E. 1999. "La comunità giudaica di Hierapolis di Frigia," *Epigraphica Anatolica* 31:109-155.
Mitchell, S. 1999. "The Cult of Theos Hypsistos Between Pagans, Jews and Christians," in P. Athanassiadi & M. Frede (eds.), *Pagan Monotheism in Late Antiquity*, Oxford: Oxford University Press, 81-148.
Mitteis, L. & U. Wilcken. 1912. *Grundzüge und Chrestomathie der Papyruskunde*, 4 vols., Leipzig – Berlin: Teubner.
Mondésert, C., e.a. 1966. "Philon d'Alexandrie ou Philon le juif," *DBS* 7:1288-1348.
Mondésert, C. 1999. "Philo of Alexandria," in Horbury 877-900.
Montevecchi, O. 1988. "L'amministrazione dell' Egitto sotto i Giulio-Claudi," *ANRW* II.10.1:412-471.
Morris, J. 1973/87. "The Jewish Philosopher Philo," in Schürer 3.809-889.
Musurillo, H. (ed.). 1954. *The Acts of the Pagan Martyrs*, Oxford: Clarendon Press.
———. (ed.). 1961. *Acta Alexandrinorum*, Leipzig: Teubner.
Néher-Bernheim, R. 1986. "L'assimilation linguistique des Juifs d'Alexandrie: une des sources de l'antisémitisme antique," in A. Caquot, M. Hadas-Lebel & J. Riaud (eds.), *Hellenica et Judaica. Hommage à Valentin Nikiprowetzky*, Louvain-Paris: Peeters, 313-319.
Nestle, W. 1936. "Legenden vom Tod der Gottesverächter," *ARW* 33:246-269.
Nicole, J. 1898. "Avillius Flaccus, préfet d'Egypte et Philon d'Alexandrie d'après un papyrus inédit," *Revue de Philologie* 22:18-27.
Niehoff, M.R. 1998. "Philo's Views on Paganism," in Stanton & Stroumsa 135-158.
———. 2001. *Philo on Jewish Identity and Culture*, Tübingen: Mohr Siebeck.
Nikiprowetzky, V. 1983. "L'Exégèse de Philon d'Alexandrie dans le *De gigantibus* et le *Quod deus sit immutabilis*," in Winston & Dillon 5-75.
———. 1996. *Etudes philoniennes*, Paris: Ed. du Cerf.
Nilsson, M.P., *Geschichte der griechischen Religion*, 2 vols., München: Beck, 1967-1974
Nock, A.D. 1972. "The Gild of Zeus Hypsostos" in Nock 414-443.
———. 1972. "Philo and Hellenistic Philosophy" in Nock 559-565.
———. 1972. "*Soter* and *Euergetes*" in Nock 720-735.
———. 1972. "Isopoliteia and the Jews" in Nock 960-962.
———. 1972. *Essays on Religion and the Ancient World*, 2 vols., Oxford: Clarendon Press.
Noethlichs, K.L. 1996. *Das Judentum und der römische Staat*, Darmstadt: Wissenschaftliche Buchgesellschaft.
———. 2001. *Die Juden im christlichen Imperium Romanum (4.-6. Jahrhundert)*, Berlin: Akademie Verlag.
Norris, F.W. 1998. "Alexandria," in E. Ferguson (ed.), *Encyclopedia of Early Christianity*, New York & London: Garland Publishing, 30-34.
O'Brien, P. 1993. "Caesar's Household," in G.F. Hawthorne et al. (eds.), *A Dictionary of Paul and His Letters*, Downers Grove: Intervarsity Press, 83-85.
O'Collins, G.G., 1992. "Crucifixion," *ABD* 1:1207-1210.
Oppenheimer, A. (ed.). 1999. *Jüdische Geschichte in hellenistisch-römischer Zeit. Wege der Forschung: Vom alten zum neuen Schürer*, München: Oldenbourg Verlag.
Parker, H.N. 2000. "Flaccus," *Classical Quarterly* 50:455-462.
Pearce, S. 1998. "Belonging and Not Belonging: Local Perspectives in Philo of Alexandria," in S. Jones & S. Pearce (eds.), *Jewish Local Patriotism and Self-*

Identification in the Graeco-Roman Period, Sheffield: Sheffield Academic Press, 79-105.
Pearson, B.A. 1992. "Alexandria," *ABD* 1:152-157.
Pearson, B.A., & Goehring, J.E. (eds.). 1986. *The Roots of Egyptian Christianity*, Philadelphia: Fortress Press.
Pease, A.S. 1963. *M. Tulli Ciceronis de divinatione libri duo*, Darmstadt: Wissenschaftliche Buchgesellschaft.
Pelletier, A. 1967. *Contre Flaccus* (Les Oeuvres de Philon d'Alexandrie, vol. 31), Paris: Cerf.
———. 1972. *Legatio ad Gaium* (Les Oeuvres de Philon d'Alexandrie, vol. 32), Paris: Cerf.
Pfister, F. 1959. "Ekstase," *RAC* 4:944-987.
Pfrommer, M. 1999. *Alexandria: Im Schatten der Pyramiden*, Mainz: Ph. von Zabern.
Pleins, J.D., & Hanks, T.D. 1992. "Poor, Poverty," *ABD* 5:402-424.
Poland, F. 1909. *Geschichte des griechischen Vereinswesens*, Leipzig: Teubner (repr. Leipzig: Zentral-Antiquariat der DDR, 1967).
Pomeroy, S.B. 1984. *Women in Hellenistic Egypt*, New York: Schocken Books.
Porten, B. 1992. "Elephantine Papyri," *ABD* 2:445-455.
Porten, B., et al. 1996. *The Elephantine Papyri in English: Three Millennia of Crosscultural Continuity and Change*, Leiden: Brill.
Price, S.R. 1984. *Rituals and Power. The Roman Imperial Cult in Asia Minor*, Cambridge: Cambridge University Press.
Pritchett, W.K. 1971-1991. *The Greek State at War*, 5 vols., Berkeley etc.: University of California Press.
Pucci Ben Zeev, M. 1990. "New Perspectives on the Jewish-Greek Hostilities in Alexandria During the Reign of Emperor Caligula," *JSJ* 21:226-235.
———. 1998. *Jewish Rights in the Roman World. The Greek and Roman Documents Quoted by Josephus Flavius*, Tübingen: Mohr Siebeck.
Pulleyn, S. 1997. *Prayer in Greek Religion*, Oxford: Clarendon Press.
Radice, R., & D.T. Runia. 1988. *Philo of Alexandria: An Annotated Bibliography 1937-1986*, Leiden: Brill (2nd ed. 1992).
Rajak, T. 2000. *The Jewish Dialogue with Greece and Rome. Studies in Cultural and Social Interaction*, Leiden: Brill.
———. 2002. "Synagogue and Community in the Graeco-Roman Diaspora," in Bartlett 22-38.
Rapske, B. 1994. *The Book of Acts in its First Century Setting, vol. 3: Paul in Roman Custody*, Grand Rapids: Eerdmans.
Rea, J., 1968. "Five Papyrological Notes on Imperial Prosopography," *Chronique d'Égypte* 43 [86]:365-374.
Reinmuth, O.W. 1954. "Praefectus Aegypti," *PW* 22/2:2353-2377.
———. 1956. "Praefectus Aegypti," *PWSuppl.* 8:525-539.
Reiter, S. 1915. "Prolegomena II," in L. Cohn & P. Wendland (eds.), *Philonis Alexandrini opera quae supersunt*, vol. VI, Berlin: Reimer, xxxviii-lxxxvii.
———. 1915. ΦΙΛΩΝΟΣ ΕΙΣ ΦΛΑΚΚΟΝ, in L. Cohn & P. Wendland (edd.), *Philonis Alexandrini opera quae supersunt*, vol. VI, Berlin: Reimer, 120-154.
———. 1927. "'Αρετή und der Titel von Philos Legatio," in *ΕΠΙΤΥΜΒΙΟΝ Heinrich Swoboda dargebracht*, Reichenberg: Stiepel, 228-237.
Roccatagliata, G. 1986. *A History of Ancient Psychiatry*, New York – London: Greenwood Press.
Rohden, P. von. 1896. "Avillius (3)," *RE* II.2:2392.
Roos, A.G. 1935. "Lesefrüchte," *Mnemosyne* 3rd series 2:233-244.
Rubinstein, L. 1995. *The History of Sukkot in the Second Temple and Rabbinic Periods*, Atlanta: Scholars Press.
Runesson, A. 2001. *The Origins of the Synagogue. A Socio-Historical Study*, Stockholm: Almqvist and Wiksell.

———. 2001. "Water and Worship: Ostia and the Ritual Bath in the Diaspora Synagogue," in B. Olsson *et al.* (eds.), *The Synagogue of Ancient Ostia and the Jews of Rome*, Stockholm: Paul Åström [published 2002], 115-129.
Runia, D.T. 1989. "Polis and Megalopolis: Philo and the Founding of Alexandria," *Mnemosyne* 42:398-412.
———. 1993. *Philo in Early Christian Literature*, Assen: Van Gorcum – Minneapolis: Fortress Press.
———. 1997. "The Reward for Goodness: *De vita contemplativa* 90," *SPhA* 9:3-18.
———. 1999. (transl. R. Radice), *Filone di Alessandria nella letteratura christiana*, Milano: Vita e Pensiero.
———. 2000. "The Idea and the Reality of the City in the Thought of Philo of Alexandria," *Journal of the History of Ideas* 61:361-379.
———. 2000. *Philo of Alexandria. An Annotated Bibliography 1987-96*, Leiden: Brill.
———. 2001. review of Frick 1999, *JSJ* 32:299-302.
———. 2001. *Philo of Alexandria, On the Creation of the Cosmos according to Moses, Introduction, Translation and Commentary*, Leiden: Brill.
Rupprecht, H.-A. 1994. *Kleine Einführung in die Papyruskunde*, Darmstadt: Wissenschaftliche Buchgesellschaft.
Ruprechtsberger, E.M. 2001. "Syrien," *NP* 11:1173-1181.
Saffrey, H.D., & Segonds, A.-Ph. (eds.). 2001. *Marinus: Proclus ou sur le bonheur*, Paris: Les Belles Lettres.
Safrai, S., & M. Stern (eds). 1974-1976. *The Jewish People in the First Century*, 2 vols., Assen: Van Gorcum.
Samuel, A.E. 1972. *Greek and Roman Chronology: Calendars and Years in Classical Antiquity*, München: Beck.
———. 1983. *From Athens to Alexandria: Hellenism and Social Goals in Ptolemaic Egypt*, Louvain: Katholieke Universiteit Leuven.
San Nicolò, M. 1913-15. *Ägyptisches Vereinswesen zur Zeit der Ptolemäer und Römer*, 2 vols., München: Beck, repr. 1972.
Sandmel, S. 1979. *Philo of Alexandria. An Introduction*, New York: Oxford University Press.
Sartorius, J. 2001. *Alexandria, Fata Morgana*, Darmstadt: Wissenschaftliche Buchgesellschaft.
Satlow, M.L. 2001. *Jewish Marriage in Antiquity*, Princeton: Princeton University Press.
Schäfer, P. 1997. *Judaeophobia. Attitudes Toward the Jews in the Ancient World*, Cambridge (MA)-London: Harvard University Press.
Schäfer, P., & B. Schaller. 1998. "Antisemitismus/Antijudaismus," *RGG* 1:557-565.
Schaller, B. 1983. "Philon von Alexandreia und das 'Heilige Land'," in G. Strecker (ed.), *Das Land Israel in biblischer Zeit*, Göttingen: Vandenhoeck & Ruprecht, 172-187.
Schmeller, Th. 1987. *Paulus und die Diatribe. Eine vergleichende Stilinterpretation*, Münster: Aschendorff.
Schneider, C., 1967-1969. *Kulturgeschichte des Hellenismus*, 2 vols., München: Beck.
Schneider, H. 1998. "Jagd," *NP* 5:834-836.
Schröder, S. 1999. *Geschichte und Theorie der Gattung Paian*, Stuttgart-Leipzig: Teubner.
Schubart, W. 1950. "Alexandria," *RAC* 1:271-283.
Schubert, P. (ed.). 2000. *Vivre en Égyote gréco-romaine. Une sélection de papyrus*, Vevey: Éditions de l'Aire.
Schürer, E., 1973-1987. *History of the Jewish People in the Age of Jesus Christ*, rev. ed. by G. Vermes, M. Goodman & F. Millar, 3 vols., Edinburgh: Clark.
Schwartz, D. 1989/90. "On Drama and Authenticity in Philo and Josephus," *SCI* 10:113-120.
———. 1990. *Agrippa I: The Last King of Judaea*, Tübingen: Mohr Siebeck.

———. 2000. "How at Home Were the Jews of the Hellenistic Diaspora?," *Classical Philology* 95:349-357.
Schwartz, J. 1982. "Préfets d'Égypte sous Tibère et Caligula," *ZPE* 48:189-192.
Schwartz, M.B. 2000. "Greek and Jew: Philo and the Alexandrian Riots of 38-41 CE," *Judaism* 49:206-216.
Schwemer, A.M. 2001. "Die Passion des Messias nach Markus und der Vorwurf des Antijudaismus," in M. Hengel & A.M. Schwemer, *Der messianische Anspruch Jesu und die Anfänge der Christologie*, Tübingen: Mohr Siebeck, 133-163.
Segré, A. 1944. "The Status of the Jews in Ptolemaic and Roman Egypt," *Jewish Social Studies* 6:275-282.
———. 1946. "Antisemitism in Hellenistic Alexandria," *Jewish Social Studies* 8:127-136.
Seland, T. 1995. *Establishment Violence in Philo and Luke. A Study of Non-Conformity to the Torah and Jewish Vigilante Reactions*, Leiden: Brill.
———. 1996. "Philo and the Clubs and Associations of Alexandria," in Kloppenborg & Wilson 110-127.
Sevenster, J.N. 1975. *The Roots of Pagan Anti-Semitism in the Ancient World*, Leiden: Brill.
Sherwin White, A.N. 1967. *Racial Prejudice in Imperial Rome*, Cambridge: Cambridge University Press.
———. 1972. "Philo and Avillius Flaccus: A Conundrum," *Latomus* 31:820-828.
Sijpesteijn, P.J. 1964. "The Legationes ad Gaium," *JJS* 15:87-96.
———. 1986. *Nouvelle liste des gymnasiarques des métropoles de l'Egypte romaine*, Zutphen: Terra.
Sills, D. 1997. "Strange Bedfellows: Politics and Narrative in Philo," in S.D. Breslauer (ed.), *The Seductiveness of Jewish Myth: Challenge or Response?*, Albany: State University of New York Press, 171-190.
Slingerland, H.D. 1997. *Claudian Policymaking and the Early Imperial Repression of Judaism at Rome*, Atlanta: Scholars Press.
Sly, D. 1990. *Philo's Perception of Women*, Atlanta: Scholars Press.
———. 1996. *Philo's Alexandria*, London & New York: Routledge.
———. 2000. "The Conflict over *Isopoliteia*: An Alexandrian Perspective," in T.L. Donaldson (ed.), *Religious Rivalries and the Struggle for Success in Caesarea Maritima*, Waterloo: Wilfrid Laurier University Press, 249-265.
Smallwood, M. 1961. *Philonis Alexandrini Legatio ad Gaium*, Leiden: Brill.
———. 1967. *Documents Illustrating the Principates of Gaius, Claudius and Nero*, Cambridge: Cambridge University Press.
———. 1968. Review of Pelletier 1967, *JTS* n.s. 19:258-259.
———. 1976. *The Jews Under Roman Rule*, Leiden: Brill.
———. 1987. "Philo and Josephus as Historians of the Same Events," in L.H. Feldman & G. Hata (eds.), *Josephus, Judaism, and Christianity*, Detroit: Wayne State University Press, 114-129.
———. "The Diaspora in the Roman Period Before CE 70," in Horbury 1999:168-191
Smith, R.W., 1974. *The Art of Rhetoric in Alexandria: Its Theory and Practice in the Ancient World*, Den Haag: Nijhoff.
Solomon, D. 1970. "Philo's Use of γενάρχης in 'In Flaccum'," *JQR* 61:119-131.
Speyer, W.1981. "Gottesfeind," *RAC* 11:996-1043.
Stählin, O. 1940. Review of Box 1939, *Berliner Philologische Wochenschrift* 60:10-13.
Stanton, G.N., and G.G. Stroumsa (eds.). 1998. *Tolerance and Intolerance in Early Judaism and Christianity*, Cambridge: Cambridge University Press.
Starobinski-Safran, E. 1987. "La communauté juive à Alexandrie à l'époque de Philon," *Alexandrina (Mélanges C. Mondésert)*, Paris: Ed. du Cerf, 45-75.
———. 2000. "Philon von Alexandrien über Krieg und Frieden," in W. Stegmaier (ed), *Die philosophische Aktualität der jüdischen Tradition*, Frankfurt: Suhrkamp, 133-149.
Stein, A. 1903. "A. Avillius Flaccus," *PWSuppl.* 1:228-229.

———. 1916. "Isidorus (8)," *PW* 9.2:2061-2062.
———. 1924. "Lampo (4)," *PW* 12.1:581.
———. *Die Präfekten von Ägypten in der römischen Kaiserzeit*, Bern: Francke, 1950
Stein, M., *Philo of Alexandria: Historical Writings*, Tel Aviv 1937 (in Hebrew; non vidi)
Sterling, G.E. 1995. "'Thus Are Israel': Jewish Self-Definition in Alexandria," *SPhA* 7:1-18.
———. 1998. "A Philosophy According to the Elements of the Cosmos: Colossian Christianity and Philo of Alexandria," in Lévy 349-373.
———. 1998. "'Opening the Scriptures': The Legitimation of the Jewish Diaspora and the Early Christian Mission," in D.P. Moesner (ed.), *Jesus and the Heritage of Israel*, Harrisburg: Trinity Press, 199-225.
———. 2001. "Judaism Between Jerusalem and Alexandria," in J.J. Collins & G.E. Sterling (eds.), *Hellenism in the Land of Israel*, Notre Dame: University of Notre Dame Press, 263-301.
Stern, M. 1974/76. "The Jewish Diaspora," in Safrai-Stern 17-183.
———. 1974-1984. *Greek and Latin Authors on Jews and Judaism*, 3 vols., Jerusalem: The Israel Academy of Sciences and Humanities.
Stern, S. 1998. "Dissonance and Misunderstanding in Jewish-Roman Relations," in Goodman 241-250.
Stowers, S.K. 1992. "Diatribe," *ABD* 2:190-193.
Stuart Jones, H. 1926. "Claudius and the Jewish Question at Alexandria," *JRS* 16:17-35.
Stumpf, P. 1950. "Anker," *RAC* 1:440-443.
Taylor, L.R. 1931. *The Divinity of the Roman Emperor*, Middletown: The American Philological Association.
Taylor, N.H. 2001. "Popular Opposition to Caligula in Jewish Palestine," *JSJ* 32:54-70.
Tcherikover, V.A. 1959. *Hellenistic Civilization and the Jews*, Philadelphia: Jewish Publication Society.
———. 1963. "The Decline of the Jewish Diaspora in Egypt in the Roman Period," *JJS* 14:1-32.
Tcherikover, V.A., & A. Fuks (eds.). 1957-1964. *Corpus Papyrorum Judaicarum*, 3 vols., Cambridge (MA): Harvard University Press.
Theiler, W. 1964. "Sachweiser zu Philo," in L. Cohn e.a. (eds.), *Philo von Alexandria. Die Werke in deutscher Übersetzung*, Band 7, Berlin: W. de Gruyter, 386-411.
Thompson, G.L. 2000. "Roman Military," *DNTB* 991-995.
Thür, G., 1997."Eisagogeus," *NP* 3:923.
Toorn, K. van der, B. Becking & P.W. van der Horst (eds.). 1999. *Dictionary of Deities and Demons in the Bible*, 2nd ed., Leiden-Grand Rapids: Brill-Eerdmans.
Trebilco, P. 1991. *Jewish Communities in Asia Minor*, Cambridge: Cambridge University Press.
Triviño, J.M. 1976. *Obras completas de Filón de Alejandría*, vol. 5, Buenos Aires (*non vidi*).
Troiani, L. 1994. "The ΠΟΛΙΤΕΙΑ of Israel in the Greco-Roman Age," in F. Parente & J. Sievers (eds.), *Josephus and the History of the Greco-Roman Period. Essays in Memory of Morton Smith*, Leiden: Brill, 11-22.
Uebel, F. 1962. "Ταραχὴ τῶν Αἰγυπτίων," *Archiv für Papyrusforschung* 17:147-162.
Umemoto, N. 1994. "Juden, 'Heiden' und das Menschengeschlecht in der Sicht Philons von Alexandria," in R. Feldmeier & U. Heckel (eds.), *Die Heiden. Juden, Christen und das Problem des Fremden*, Tübingen: Mohr Siebeck, 22-51.
Unnik, W.C. van. 1973. "Tarsus or Jerusalem? The City of Paul's Youth," in his *Sparsa collecta*, vol. I, Leiden: Brill, 259-32.7.
———. 1993. *Das Selbstverständnis der jüdischen Diaspora in der hellenistisch-römischen Zeit*, aus dem Nachlaß herausgegeben und bearbeitet von Pieter W. van der Horst, Leiden: Brill.

Urbach, E.E. 1975. *The Sages. Their Concepts and Beliefs*, 2 vols., Jerusalem: Magnes Press.
Vondeling, J. 1961. *Eranos*, Groningen: Wolters.
Vries, G.H. de. 1999. *Philo Judaeus: Pogrom in Alexandrië, Gezantschap naar Caligula*, Amsterdam: Ambo.
Wander, B. 1998. *Gottesfürchtige und Sympathisanten: Studien zum heidnischen Umfeld von Diasporasynagogen*, Tübingen: Mohr Siebeck.
Weinberg, J. 2001. *Azariah de' Rossi: The Light of the Eyes*, New Haven – London: Yale University Press.
Weinreich, O. 1909. *Antike Heilungswunder. Untersuchungen zum Wunderglauben der Griechen und Römer*, Gießen: Töpelmann.
Welwei, K.W. 1996. "Apoikia," *NP* 1:850-851.
Whitehorne, J.E.G. 1987. "The *hypomnematographus* in the Roman Period," *Aegyptus* 67:101-125.
Wilcken, U. 1899. *Griechische Ostraka aus Ägypten und Nubien*, 2 vols., Leipzig: Gieseke & Devrient (repr. Amsterdam: Hakkert, 1970).
———. 1909. *Zum alexandrinischen Antisemitismus*, Leipzig: Teubner.
Wilken, R.L. 1992. *The Land Called Holy. Palestine in Christian History and Thought*, New Haven & London: Yale University Press.
Williams, M. 1998. *Jews Among Greeks and Romans*, Baltimore: The Johns Hopkins University Press.
Williamson, R. 1989. *Jews in the Hellenistic World: Philo*, Cambridge: Cambridge University Press.
Winiarczyk, M. 2002. *Euhemeros von Messene. Leben, Werk und Nachwirkung*, München-Leipzig: Saur.
Winston, D. 1979. *The Wisdom of Solomon*, Garden City: Doubleday.
———. 1984. "Philo's Ethical Theory," *ANRW* II.21.1:372-416.
———. 1987. "Philo Judaeus," *ER* 11:287-290.
———. 2002. "Philo and the Wisdom of Solomon on Creation, Revelation, and Providence: The High-Water Mark of Jewish Hellenistic Fusion," in Kugel 109-130.
Winston, D. & J. Dillon (eds.). 1983. *Two Treatises of Philo of Alexandria*, Chico: Scholars Press.
Winter, P. 1974. *On the Trial of Jesus*, Berlin: W. de Gruyter.
Wire, A. 2002. *Holy Lives, Holy Deaths. A Close Hearing of Early Jewish Storytellers*, Atlanta: Society of Biblical Literature.
Wolfson, H.A.. 1947. *Philo: Foundations of Religious Philosophy in Judaism, Christianity, and Islam*, Cambridge MA: Harvard University Press (repr. 1968).
Yavetz, Z. 1993. "Judeophobia in Classical Antiquity: A Different Approach," *JJS* 44:1-22.
———. 1997. *Judenfeindschaft in der Antike*, München: Beck.
Yonge, C.D. (transl.). 1993. *The Works of Philo, Complete and Unabridged*, Peabody: Hendrickson (= reprint of the edition London: Bohn, 1854).
Yoyotte, J. 1962. "L'Égypte ancienne et les origines de l'antijudaïsme," *Revue de l'histoire des religions* n.s. 11:133-143.
Zuckerman, C. 1985/88. "Hellenistic Politeumata and the Jews: A Reconsideration," *SCI* 8-9:171-185.

INDICES

1. Index of passages from ancient authors

Philonic texts

Abr.		Congr.	
54	115	67	233
64	229	112	213
103	107		
107	106	Contempl.	
159	234	8	105
175	107	11-12	234
225	184	20	231
226	184	27	190
232	235	48-49	221
		50	222
Aet.		63	209
54	152	69	129, 182
59	217	89	213, 234
80	209		
112	98	Decal.	
119	149	2-9	231
		95	192, 219
Agr.		98	190
32	182	110	165
35	126	177	192, 219
62	105, 106		
80-82	201	Det.	
112	209	40	190
		89	196
Cher.			
99	120	Deus	
121	155	17	143
123	212	115	197
Conf.		Ebr.	
41	145	20-26	95
49	145	25	115
78	142	146	234
86	190	165	190
109	218	177	133, 233
118	192		
120	192, 229	Flacc.	
128	192	1	245
173	205, 235	2-5	194
		2	34, 228
		4	47, 95

INDEX OF PASSAGES FROM ANCIENT AUTHORS 263

5	95, 184	76	50
7	219	77	161, 214
8	93	78	113
9	35, 112, 220	79	214
11	34, 112	80	95, 113
14	103	81	170
16	112	82	95
17	121	83	170
18	208, 230	84	133
19	95, 124	85	238
20	36, 210	86	179
21-24	108	89	185
24	209	90	178
25	15	91	214
26	208	92-93	96
27	190, 195	92	36, 194
28	119	93	145
29	2, 17, 18, 105, 124, 218	94	145, 165, 241
		95	133, 214
30	2	97-103	122
31	117	100	188
32	107	101	188
33	95	102	16, 99, 187, 194
34	210, 215, 216	103	117, 120
35	95, 114, 115, 200	104	16, 17, 214
40	214	105-115	192
41	95, 126, 133, 185	107	16, 17
43-44	150	110	118, 200
43	114, 157	111	200
44	178	114	243
45	206	115-116	208
46	228	115	16, 17
48	17	116	15, 187, 205
49	146	117	42, 214
52-53	137	121	16, 190, 209, 219, 235
52	145		
53-57	178	123	235
53	157	124	190, 199, 202, 224, 230, 240
54	157, 168, 179, 193		
55	15, 155	125	16, 190, 197, 201, 205
56-57	172, 236		
56	204, 223	126	16
58-85	185	128-145	107
58	172, 214	133	93
59	214	135-145	47, 95-96, 110
64	185	135-136	95, 110
65	95, 167	135	184, 218, 241
66	238	136	126
67	238	137	111
70-71	238	138	126
71	244	143	121
72	107	146-147	209
73	111	146	16, 17
74	133, 175, 217, 237	147	224
75	238	151	35, 241

152-156	116	14	102, 182
152	206	17	240
154	226	25	190
157	170	28-31	102
158	34	32-61	103
160	227	33	103
162	207	35-38	103
163	233	41	104
168	223	43-51	104
169	232, 241	54	104
170-174	47, 229	58	103
170	2, 16, 201, 214, 240	61	104
171	132, 237	67	95
173	133, 214, 236	69	189
174	227	96	201
177	194, 232	99	194
180	4, 230	110	194
182	225	114	179
184	241	116	94
186	194	119-121	176
189	13, 17, 197, 238	119	138
190	167	120	95
191	1, 15, 16, 201	122	131
		124	244
Fuga		129	191
32	234	131	166-167
100	229	132	95, 132, 139, 158
166	234	133-134	135
		134	134
Her.		140-161	149
279	168	143-158	169
		147	169
Hyp.		152	134, 145
7.14	30	157	145
11.15	232	159-160	89
		161	145, 184
Jos.		162	105
35	108	163	151
48	192	164-165	138
65	104	165	145, 194
140	231, 232	166	105
143	231, 232	170	151
166	107	172	113
170	192, 219	178	107, 218
254	142	183	114, 174
		189	179
Leg.		190	145
1.99	228	194	145
2.42-43	196	205	151
3.62	201	208	145
3.91	233	210	145
3.102	232	214	140, 141
		223	179
Legat.		225	141
3	1, 201, 235	226	95
8-13	98		

INDEX OF PASSAGES FROM ANCIENT AUTHORS

230	184	2.27	121
234	165	2.34	119, 204
247	188	2.37	205
250	113	2.41	119
252	95	2.75	209
259	145	2.162	192
277	145, 146	2.193	105
281	141	2.196	105
281-282	140	2.211	126
284	188	2.231	194
288	141	2.232	140, 144
290	142		
292	145	*Mut.*	
299-305	193	40	143
299	141	101	115
300	137, 145	170	107
306	145	194	192
309-318	169		
310	240	*Opif.*	
312	95	27	205
313	145	71	234
322	194	79	164
323-327	124	160	235
324	237	170-172	201
330	179	171	164
333	145		
338	113, 241	*Plant.*	
341-342	242	27	232
346	135, 138, 141	*Post.*	
349	193	101-102	94
355	151, 189	109	155
357	146	112	232
361	186	155	233
367	190	161	209
368	180	170	165
Migr.		*Praem.*	
57	96	41	234
225	192	65	115
		70	229, 238
Mos.		87	145
1.2	228	88	165
1.10	155	151	233
1.30	155	169	131, 225
1.31	142		
1.33	188	*Prob.*	
1.43	165	7	238
1.93	209	8	149
1.95	106	37	212
1.113	205	77	182
1.115	160	78	181
1.153	94	84	182
1.214	106	89	192
1.277	234	141	133
2.2	94	149	209

Prov.		2.165	204
2.69	165	2.167	145
		2.204	198
Quaest. in Gen.		2.229	228
3.47-48	30	3.1-6	2
		3.3	121, 122
Sacr.		3.19	219
77	171	3.75	194, 235
		3.103	165
Somn.		3.129	219
1.93	152	3.132	235
1.167-170	115	3.168	155
1.206	232	3.169-171	179
2.123-132	156	4.70	155
2.166	145	4.79	174
2.246	141	4.127	107
2.249	215	4.149-150	137
		4.179-182	235
Spec.		4.180	203
1.1-2	30, 129	4.201	192
1.2	106	4.224	145
1.35	234		
1.58	226	*Virt.*	
1.68-69	141	51-124	202
1.156	200	87	165
1.161-298	243	133	115
1.334	196	171	206
2.18	197	182	142
2.60	30		

Biblical passages

Genesis		10.17-18	203, 205
3.19	243	16.13-17	198
9.22-23	170	21.22-23	177
13.10	163-164	28.66-67	233
15.1	235	30.19	205
18	13, 196	31.28	205
Exodus		1 Samuel	
15	207	2.4-7	207
20.4	134		
23.4-5	202	Esther	
23.16	198	7	13
Leviticus		Psalms	
23.43	198	73	194
		82.1	205
Numbers		95.3	205
15.22-31	98		
23	234	Proverbs	
35	229	6.11	161
		10.4	161
Deuteronomy		24.17-18	203
4.16-18	134		
4.26	205		

Jeremiah		26.25	98
1.26	142	27	116
43	19	27.9-12	208
		27.37	118
Daniel		28.4	192
4.32	239	28.13	118
4.33	232	28.30	210
4.34	234		
		Romans	
Matthew		1.30	111
4.5	141	2.5	240
5.18	212	8.29-30	182
24.39	218		
27.5	13	1 Corinthians	
27.16	128	9.24-26	238
27.27-8	129	15.31	238
27.53	141	16.23	130, 131
Mark		Ephesians	
1.17	200	5.19	201
5.1-17	129		
9.20	230	Philippians	
15.43	177	4.22	127
Luke		Colossians	
1.46-55	207	3.16	201
3.1	115		
3.14	97	1 Timothy	
5.10	200	1.10	235
16.17	212	6.3	235
18.13	227		
23.48	227	2 Timothy	
		1.13	235
John		2.11-12	182
7.2	197	2.26	200
17.1	234	4.3	235
19.1	167	4.7	238
19.12	92		
19.15	218	Titus	
19.31	176	1.9	235
		2.1	235
Acts		2.8	214, 235
1.18	14		
2.9-11	141	Hebrews	
5.29	243	8.5	232
6.9	153	10.1	232
7.20-22	228	12.1	238
12.4	195		
12.20-23	14, 116	2 Peter	
12.23	13	1.5-7	182
19.25	95	2.3	213
19.28-40	215		
19.29	126	Revelation	
22.3	228	3.18	170

Jewish Documents

CIJ		12.8	143, 237
24	171	12.11	136
391	171	12.103-104	119
725	201	12.119	144
748	133	12.121	237
775	144	14.115	140
1433	147	14.117	22, 157, 168
		14.127-136	21
CJZC		14.188	21, 149, 237
71	133, 198	15.380-425	141
		16.102	219
CPJ		16.163	149
126	130	18.106-108	116
141	20	18.133-354	115
150	23, 155	18.159-160	121
151	143, 160, 174	18.159	160
153	10, 24, 40, 109, 111, 138, 155, 156, 181, 184, 222	18.168-178	92
		18.257	52, 162
		19.17	218
154-156	10	19.32-36	103
154	36, 107, 108, 109, 112, 134, 172, 212	19.276	4
		19.277	120
		19.278	181
156	22, 109, 110	19.281	174, 237
452	198	19.283	168
519	129	19.287-291	144
		19.300	144
Ep. Arist.		*Bell. Jud.*	
11	130	1.187-192	21
301	119	2.206-220	115
310	40	2.308	167
		2.385	136
JIGRE		2.487	143, 158, 237
3-5	130	2.490	133
9	147	2.492-498	40
13	147	2.495	158
22	147	2.497	136
24	147	4.613	119
25	147	7.369	136
27	147	*C. Ap.*	
117	147	1.223	122
		1.237	31
JIWE		2.34-35	158
2.110	171	2.35	237
2.473	171	2.35-36	143
		2.39	144
Josephus		2.60	21
Ant.		2.61	21
4.40	201	2.62	144
4.79-81	204	2.63	113
4.261	228	2.65	23

INDEX OF PASSAGES FROM ANCIENT AUTHORS 269

2.73	134	Pseudo-Philo	
2.80	31	*LAB*	
2.81-88	31	18.13	170
2.135	29		
2.137	236	Pseudo-Phocylides	
2.143	13, 236	42	162
Vita		107-108	243
15	118	215-216	180
16	118	222-224	175

Judith		Rabbinic sources	
13	13	Midrashim	
		Bereshith Rabba 10.7	13
1 Maccabees		*Ekhah Rabbati*, Proem 17	130
1.13-15	170	*Pirqe de R. Eliezer* 49	13
		Vayyikra Rabba 22.3	13
2 Maccabees		Talmud	
2	13	b. *Berakhoth* 24b	204
3.19	180	b. *Gittin* 56b	13
6-7	186	b. *Jebamoth* 77a	180
8.36	235	b. *Megillah* 14b	180
9	13, 234	b. *Sukkah* 51b	161, 170
		Tosephta	
3 Maccabees		*Sukkah* 4.6	161, 170
1.18	180		
2.28-30	22	*Sapientia Salomonis*	
		1.8-9	192
4 Maccabees		4.19-20	239
18.7	180	11.20	192
		15.8	243
		16.17-19	182
Oracula Sibyllina		17	238, 239
3.271	140		
		Sirach	
Pap. Polit. Iud.		17.1	243
1.3	171		
12.2	171	*Test. Abr. (A)*	
12.8	171	8.10	200

Christian Documents

Apostolic Constitutions		2.5	52
7.33.2	205	2.5.1	5
7.33.6	235	2.5.7	5, 89
		2.7	14
Augustine		2.18.8	52
Conf.			
10.12-16	197	Justinian	
		Novella 85	182
Eusebius			
Chron.		Lactantius	
Tiberius 21	52, 88, 89	*De mort. pers.*	
Hist. Eccl.		50.1	12-13

270 INDICES

Origen
CC
5.4   204
5.41   31

Photius
Bibl.
cod. 105   52

Tertullian
Scap.
3   14

Pagan Documents

Achilles Tatius
1.15.6   232

Acts of the Alexandrian Martyrs
(see also *CPJ* 154-156 and *P. Oxy.*
1089)
2.57   134
4C25   18

Aelius Aristides
3.172   182
3.559   182

Aeschines
Ktes.
11   193
20   193
24   193

Aeschylus
Agam.
1115   200
Prom.
1078   200

Aristaenetus
Epist.
2.23   200

Aristophanes
Aves
719-721   239
Equ.
247   111
Ran.
1412   209

Aristotle
Ath. Pol.
12   182
Eth. Nic.
1.9.1099b9-10 115

Artemidorus
Oneir.
2.43   177

Athenaeus
Deipn.
246C   96

BGU
V.114   211

Caesar
Bell. civ.
3.112   133

Cassius Dio
Hist. Rom.
37.17.1   31
57.9.2   210
57.3.6   228
57.19.7   132
58.19.6   92
59.3-4   103
59.4.3   220
59.8.1   102
59.8.12   116
59.10.6-11.5 222
59.10.6   102, 104
59.10.7   105
59.10.8   159
59.10.14   102
59.15.6   222
59.18.3   242
59.21.4   222
59.22.7   223
60.8.2   132
60.27   113
63.28   231
65.8   216
78.23.3   215

INDEX OF PASSAGES FROM ANCIENT AUTHORS

Cicero		3.127	124
De Div.			
1.34-71	243	Hesiod	
1.81	243	*Erg.*	
Pro Mil.		213-285	191
61	182	*Theog.*	
Pro Rab. Post.		901-903	191
34-35	106, 125, 126		
Pro Rosc. Amer.		Homer	
75	182	*Il.*	
In Verr.	193	9.362	118
5.162	167		
		IGRR	
CIG		1.1164	35
3142	169	1.1263	35
4716	35		
4957	35	*ILS*	
		1335	169
CIL			
3.6627	178	Isocrates	
		Areop.	
Cleanthes		41	228
SVF 557	104		
Demosthenes		Jamblichus	
De corona		*Vit. Pyth.*	
179	182	213	228
209	109		
		Juvenal	
Dio Chrysostom		*Sat.*	
31.37	134	10.27	221
31.86	212		
32.1-5	127	Lucan	
32.4	126	*Phars.*	
32.9	216	6.538-545	177
32.22-24	127		
32.41-44	127	Lucian	
32.70	96	*Apol.*	
32.73-74	127	12	211
32.86	126, 127	*Tox.*	
		9	108
Diodorus Siculus			
Bibl. hist.		Marinus	
1.31.8	136	*Procl.*	
17.52.6	136	8	100
24.1.1-5	28		
40.3.8	140	Martialis	
		Lib. de spect.	
Euripides		7	167
Med.			
1278	200	*OGIS*	
		661	35
Herodotus		665	97
2.5	163	669	35, 94
3.64	13		

Papyri
P. Boissier 1   36
P. Gissen 40   111
P. Hal. 1   174
P. Mich. 18   174
P. Monac. 49   169
P. Oxy. 110   214
P. Oxy. 1089   36, 107, 108, 109, 112
P. Oxy. 1412   217
P. Oxy. 1271   188
P. Oxy. 2156   195
P. Tebt. 316   213

Petronius
Satyr.
111   177

Philostratus
Vit. Apoll.
5.24   170
7.31   195

Plato
Crito
50d-e   228
Leg.
643c   228
783b   228
842e   228
Phaedr.
230a   94
Resp.
450a   181
514a-517c   232
566d   100
Theaet.
172c   228
Tim.
40a   243

Pliny the Elder
Nat. hist.
2.47.124   117
5.38   137
19.1.3   118

Pliny the Younger
Ep.
10.43   188

Plutarch
Conv. disp.
8.7   228

Def. orac.
49   243
Gen. Socr.
20   243
Lat. viv.
6   229
Praec. ger. rei publ.
5.15   108
Quom. adul.
25   228
Anton.
54.3-6   126
Cic.
48   228
Pericl.
33   216
Solon
19   124

Pollux
Onom.
3.125   134

Polybius
34.14.5   95

Porphyry
Ad Marc.
24   182

Pseudo-Callisthenes
Vita Alex.
1.32.4   157

Quintilian
Inst. Orat.
3.8.49-54   227
9.1.33   131
9.2.29-37   227, 231
9.2.47   224
9.3.66   91

Sammelbuch
3448   231
8329   35
8444   35

SEG
42.810-814   175

Seneca
Benef.
6.33-34   92
Cons. ad Helv.
19.6   106, 125, 180, 215

INDEX OF PASSAGES FROM ANCIENT AUTHORS

Cons. ad Marc.		Tacitus	
14.2	106	*Ann.*	
De ira		1.80	92
1.2.2	167	2.8	90
3.3.6	167	2.43	113
Epist.		2.59-60	113
77.1-2	118	3.50.6	221
		3.68.2	221, 223
Sextus Empiricus		3.69	224
Adv. Math.		4.5	96
8.5	94	4.21.5	221
		6.25	101
Stobaeus		6.46.9	103
4.126.1	146	6.48.4	104
		15.71	224
Strabo		*Hist.*	
Geogr.		1.11	106, 125
2.3.5	188	5.3-5	25-26
6.3.7	116	5.5.1	30
8.7.4	225	5.5.3	140
17.1.3	137	5.5.4	135
17.1.4	163		
17.1.5	137	Ulpian	
17.1.6	119	*Digesta*	
17.1.7	118	48 Tit. 24.1	177
17.1.8	157		
17.1.10	126, 151, 159	Valerius Maximus	
17.1.12	96, 196, 200	6.9	177
17.1.48	137		
17.3.22	137	Vegetius	
		De re mil.	
Suetonius		3.8	195
Tib.			
36	90		
46	92	Xenophanes	
53	101	*fr.* 27	243
Calig.			
24	159	Xenophon	
49	113	*Apol.*	
50	241	33	240
51	103	*Cyrop.*	
		7.5.73	162
SVF		*Symp.*	
327	146	2.1-2	126
557	104		

2. Index of subjects and names (including Greek and Latin terms)

Acts of the Alexandrian Martyrs 10, 18, 21, 36, 108, 109-110, 172, 211
Agrippa I 10, 14, 114-127, 145, 190-191
Agrippa Postumus 228
Agrippina 35, 101, 194
Aigyptiakon, to 105, 121
aleiphobios 215
Alexander (Philo's brother) 23, 115, 120, 121, 124, 160, 190
Alexander the Great 20, 143, 158
Alexandrian 112-113, 174
amicus Caesaris 91-92
anapaest 216
anaphora 173
ancestral customs 137, 145
anchor 154
Andron 171
Andronicus 171
Andros 224, 227
anti-Jewish propaganda 25-31
Antiochus IV 13, 42, 47
Antipater 21
Apion 2, 9, 13, 18, 28-29, 31, 134, 236
Apis 13
apoikia 144
aquae et ignis interdictio 221, 222, 223
Aramaic 130
archives 213
arms, search for 36, 178-179, 182-183
army 96-97
artisans 161
askêptos 128
ass 31
atheism 28, 31
audience (of *Flacc.*) 15-16
Augustus 21, 113, 134, 148-149, 168, 169, 177
authekastos 104
Avaris 26, 31
Azariah de' Rossi 53

banishment 223
Bassus (1) 182
Bassus (2) 194-195
beaches 159, 203
bebaioô 149
begging 164
bird (= omen) 239
birthday, Caligula's 170, 175-176

bodyguards 123, 132
bona damnatorum 222
Booths, festival of 197-198
burial, duty of 163, 164, 177
burning (of Jews) 165-166
Buzygian laws 163

Caesar 127, 135
Caligula 4, 100, 102-105, 112, 113, 115, 116, 156, 159, 187-188, 192, 194, 242
Cambyses 13
cannibalism 29
Castus 178
catena 182
centurion 178
Chaeremon 29
circumcision 30, 129
citizenship (of Alexandria) 21-24, 40, 41, 145, 153-154, 155-156, 174, 236
Claudius 9, 10, 23, 24, 111, 144, 168
cledonomancy 239
Cleopatra 21
clubs 95-96, 214, 215
colony 144
commerce 160-161
compassion 203
concatenation 182
conscience 98-99, 219
control, loss of 100, 105
Corybantes 234
cosmos 234
council of elders 168, 170, 175
crucifixion 167-168, 176-177

daimôn 233, 240
date of composition 4
declaration of loyalty 122, 187-191
decree, Flaccus's 155-156
Delta (Jewish quarter) 158-159, 203
demagogues 108
demography 136
deportation 223
dia 237
diadem 129
diagnôsis 189
Diagoras 13
diakyptein 218-219
dianagignôskô 189

INDEX OF SUBJECTS AND NAMES 275

diaspora 140
diatribe style 98
Dicaearchia 117-118
Dikê, see Justice
Dionysius 108
diptych 1, 6
districts (of Alexandria) 157
dramatic historiography 11-12
drunkenness 214
Drusilla 159-160

ecstasy 233-234
Edfu 158
Egyptians 17-18, 48, 105-106, 121, 172-173
eisagôgeus 211
ektrachêlizô 199
elements 205, 208
Elephantine 19-20
emperor cult 146
emperors 193
enaulos 233
enkrateia 100
envy 3, 121, 124, 218
epanateinomai 180
epimorphazô 107
epiteichizô 164
eranos 164
Etesian winds 117, 160
Ethiopia 137
ethnarch 168
ethnicity 18, 135
eucharistia 188
Euodus 171
Eusebius 52

famine 163
farmers 160
fatherland 143
Flaccus *passim* (esp. 34-38)
flagellation 167, 170-171, 172-173, 174
foreigners and aliens 155-156
freedmen 195-196
friend of the Emperor 91-92

Gaius, see Caligula
Galerius 99
Gemellus 35, 100-101, 102, 112
genarch 168
gennaioi 151-152
genre 11-16
Germanicus 113
gerousia 168, 170, 172, 175
ghetto 152, 159

girls 179-180
godfearers 32
governors 193
gradatio 182
Gyara 223
gymnasiarch 210-211
gymnasium 125-126, 210, 215

Hadrian 175
Haman 13, 42
harbors of Alexandria 119
Hermoupolis 158
hetaireia 95
Hiberus 92
hieropolis 141
historiography (ancient) 11
Hitler 39
Holophernes 13
holy city 141
honor, loss of 123, 175, 209, 218, 221, 224, 229
hybris 131, 182, 214
hygiês 214, 235
Hyksos 27
hymns 201
hypomnêmatismos 211
hypotropiazô 225
hypsistos 141-142

immortals 204
impartiality 114
imperial family 113, 148
impiety 27-29
impurity, ritual 159, 204
insolence 214
inspiration 234
insult 131
irony 151-152, 170, 177, 183, 227
Isidorus 10, 21, 107, 108, 110-111, 133, 189, 207-219

Jerusalem 141
Jew-hatred 25-31, 32-33, 45, 121-122
Jewish quarter(s) 157-158
John of Damascus 49-50
Judaeophobia 45
Judas 13
Julia 228
Julius Caesar 21
Justice (*Dikê*) 16-17, 191-192, 194, 197, 198, 219, 236, 238, 244

Karabas 128-131
katabathmos 137
katharôtaton 204, 217

kathypokrinomai 107
keraia 212
Khnum 20
klinê 214

Lactantius 12-13, 14, 52
Lampo 10, 107, 109-110, 207-219
laographia 21, 23, 94
laziness 29-30
leipomena 206
Lepidus 35, 223, 241
Levites 200
Lex Julia 222
Libya 137
Lysimachus 27-28

Macro 34-35, 102-105
madness 128-129
Magius Maximus 169
maiestas 109, 210
malicious pleasure, see *Schadenfreude*
Manetho 26-27
mania 128
manuscripts 49-51
Mareia 139-140
marin 130
mask 108
megalopolis 231
melancholia 129
merchants 160-161
mêtropolis 142
mimes 126, 130, 167
misanthrôpia 27
mixed marriages 186
mob, Alexandrian 94-95, 125, 132, 133, 153-186 (*passim*), 213
mock-king 129
modesty 180
money-lenders 160
monotheism 31, 40
Most High God 141-142
mother city 142
mutilation 165

names of synagogues 153
namesakes 241
nauklêroi 161
Nebuchadnezar 232, 234, 239
necropolis 159
nets 200
night watch 195
nightguard 200
Nile, inundation of the 163
nomos 203
novels (Greek) 11

nudity 170
numbers (of Jews) 136, 140

occupations (of Jews) 160-161
Osarsiph 26
otium 241
Oxyrhynchus 158

paean 201
paideia 228
palinôdia 5-6, 43-44
papyrus 129
paranalôma 103
paronomasia 91
parrhêsia 94
pathos 174
patria ethê 22, 137-138, 145
patris 143
pen-murderer 212
peripeteia 190
persecution 12-15, 89-91
personal names 171
Petronius 9
phantasia 207
Pharos 119
philargyria 162
Philip (the tetrarch) 116
philophroneomai 196
philosopher's life 242
Photius 52
Pilate 5-6, 92, 193
plundering 157
Plutarch 30
Poenae 238
pogroms 19
politeia 153
politeuma 154-156, 236
polypolis 231
polytheism 204-205
pork 30, 186
porthêsis 179
poverty 161
praefectus Aegypti 35, 92, 169
praefectus praetorio 102
praetorian insignia 131
prayer 204-207, 235
prestige, loss of 123
prisoners of war 162-163
procession 170
professions (of Jews) 160-161
pronoia, see providence
prophetic soul 243
prosanamattomai 217
proseuchê 134
prosôpopoiia 227, 231

INDEX OF SUBJECTS AND NAMES   277

Protagoras 13
Protocols of the Elders of Zion 33
providence (*pronoia*) 1, 16-17, 190, 201-202, 235
puppet 108
purity, ritual 159, 204
Puteoli 117-118

quaternion 195

raising of hands (prayer gesture) 200-201
reading 189
religious games 183
resistance, Jewish 178, 181
rhetorical historiography 11-12
ruler cult 169
rulers 172, 175

sabbath 29-30
Sacra parallella 49-50
Samaritans 34
savior and benefactor 169
sceptre 129
Schadenfreude 202
scourging 167, 170-171, 172-173, 174
seafaring 116-117
seclusion (of women) 179-180
secretaries 93
Sejanus 5-6, 89-90
self-government, Jewish 22
Seneca 30
Seth 31
shadow 232
shipowners 117, 160
ships 117, 118
sins 98
skôlêkobrôtos 13
sleeplessness 241
songs 201, 203
sôphronizomai 226
sôtêr 169
sphadaizô 230
statues (of Caligula) 9, 134, 144

Stephanio 195-196
suffocation 166
Sukkot 197-198
symmoria 213
symposiarch 214
synagogue 134, 139, 144, 145, 146-147, 203
Syncellus 52
synodos 95, 214
Syria 131
Syriac 130

Tacitus 25-26, 30
taraxipolis 111, 214
taxes 93-94
temple (in Jerusalem) 9, 31, 141, 146
theatre 126, 133, 185
Themis 191
theodicy 2, 11
theomachos 13
Tiberius 89-90, 92, 96, 100, 102, 113, 193, 228
Tiberius Julius Alexander 23, 35-36, 156
title (of *Flacc.*) 88
Titus 13
Torah 203
torture 177 *et passim*
trading vessels 117
Tryphaena 171
Tryphon 171
Typhon 31
typhos 94

Verres 193
Vipsanius Agrippa 228
Vitrasius Pollio 9

water 203
weapons 181, 182, 183
women 179-180, 185-186
worms, eaten by 13

Zeus 191

www.ingramcontent.com/pod-product-compliance
Lightning Source LLC
Chambersburg PA
CBHW021804220426
43662CB00006B/178